*"Why should not the New Englander
be in search of new adventures?"*
THOREAU: *Walden*

THE BERKSHIRE TRAVELLER PRESS
Stockbridge, Massachusetts

Country Inns and Back Roads

VOLUME XVIII

New England, West Coast, Canada,
Middle Atlantic, South, Midwest, Rocky Mountains

BY THE BERKSHIRE TRAVELLER
Norman T. Simpson

TRAVEL BOOKS FROM THE BERKSHIRE TRAVELLER PRESS

Country Inns and Back Roads, North America
Country Inns and Back Roads, Britain and Ireland
Country Inns and Back Roads, Continental Europe
Bed and Breakfast, American Style
How to Open a Country Inn
Farm, Ranch, and Country Vacations
Adventure Travel
Where to Eat in Canada
Historic Inns of Ontario
Switzerland . . . The Inn Way
Caribbean . . . The Inn Way
Austria . . . The Inn Way
Music Festivals in America
Music Festivals in Europe and Britain
Romantik Hotels and Restaurants
Europe on 84¢ a Day

COVER PAINTING: Nanci Sam de Matties

If this cover looks familiar to some of our Constant Readers it is because it was first used in 1976. It depicts activities at a country inn on the Fourth of July about 1840. The accompanying music might be Charles Ives' *Variations on America.*

BOOK DESIGN AND DRAWINGS: Janice Lindstrom

Library of Congress 70-615644
ISBN 0-912-94475-7

Printed in the United States of America by The Studley Press Inc., Dalton, Massachusetts
Published by Berkshire Traveller Press, Stockbridge, Massachusetts 01262, (413) 298-3636

PREFACE

Before this book went to press I was browsing through some of the earlier editions, particularly those in the late 1960s and the early 1970s. I enjoyed rereading the accounts of my first visits to many inns that are still included in the book. In those days it was necessary to define what a country inn was. The great value of the book lay in the fact that it told everyone *where* they were. Country inns were just not well known in those days.

Today that is all turned around. There has been a significant proliferation of inns, whether they are full-service, offering both lodgings and all meals, or bed-and-breakfast inns. As a result the governing standards of this book have naturally become highly selective, and only inns of mature experience and proven capabilities have been included.

As I suspected it might, this book has finally reached its optimum dimensions. Even though the scope of the book is North America, the number of inns included will not increase. Inns from a waiting list take the place of inns that are not being continued. This happens most frequently when there is a change in ownership and we must regretfully omit the inn from the following edition. It is reentered only after I pay a visit to the new innkeepers at least a year later.

Almost from the very beginning in 1966 each inn in this book has become a member of an informal innkeeping association through which each is vigorously encouraged to maintain the highest standards. These principles are strengthened by yearly regional innkeeper's meetings throughout North America and a three-day general meeting annually. The association provides a continual interchange of ideas and information among the inns.

In my evaluation of the important qualities that I am delighted to find in an inn, I look for a distinct personal involvement with guests on the part of the innkeepers and their staff; the rudiments of good innkeeping that include clean, comfortable lodging rooms furnished with individuality; an imaginative menu with good, well-prepared food; and an atmosphere that encourages guests to become acquainted with each other. In the decision as to which of the many applicants to include, one of the determining factors is their enthusiasm for holding to the high ideals and standards which the inns themselves have set for the past eighteen years.

Eighteen, or even one-hundred-and-eighteen, years has not seen any changes in the basic fundamentals of good innkeeping, although most of today's innkeepers are families who have sought out innkeeping as a second career. In many cases they have moved their own family heirlooms and personal furniture into the inn and are sharing them with their guests. Each inn is a highly individual enterprise reflecting the philosophies, tastes, and enthusiasms of the innkeeper and his family. That's one of the great reasons why inns continue to grow in popularity each year.

In much the same way that staying at inns is a different experience from staying at commercial, impersonal hotels or motels, so is the attitude of the inn guest different from that of the motel traveler. The ideal inn guest is someone who values the qualities offered by a country inn, and who contributes to that ambience with his or her own consideration and friendliness. When visiting an inn, think of yourself as a guest in the home of a good friend—in the smaller, more intimate inns becoming friends with the innkeeper and his family is a distinct possibility. And there is always the opportunity to make friends with other inn guests.

Here are some basic guidelines for reservations and cancellations in most of the inns listed in this book:

A deposit is required for a confirmed reservation. Guests are requested to please note arrival and departure dates carefully. The deposit will be forfeited if the guest arrives after date specified or departs before final date of reservation. Refund will be made only if cancelled from 7 to 14 days (depending on the policy of the individual inn) in advance of arrival date and a service charge will be deducted from the deposit.

It must be understood that a deposit insures that your accommodations will be available as confirmed, and also assures the inn that the accommodations are sold as confirmed. Therefore, when situations arise necessitating your cancellation less than the allowed number of days in advance, your deposit will not be refunded.

WHERE ARE THE BACK ROADS?

In 1966 when the first edition of this book appeared, it was quite possible to travel between many country inns using back roads. I think the happiest moments of my life for the last twenty years have been spent on untraveled ways trying to find a longer, more intriguing and rewarding route, be it for two days or just an afternoon drive. In early editions I took great delight in sharing with my readers some of the remaining dirt roads in many states. Today, there are only a handful of inns that can boast of being on a real back road.

What is a back road? To me, it is a road that might gently wind through the meadows, plunge into the mountains, be bordered by placid farms, and meander through many forests. It's a better way of getting from point A to point B, and a better way is not necessarily the fastest or straightest. It certainly will take a great deal longer than the federal or state highways, and even though paved, there might be an errant frost heave or crumbling shoulder to remind the traveler that roads are subject to the vicissitudes of the weather.

For this edition, I have persuaded quite a few of the *CIBR* innkeepers to share some of their own favorite back roads. These accounts, in their own words, are interspersed throughout the book. Not only are they wonderful backroading suggestions but many of them include quite a bit of history, sociology, and geography as well.

If you have a favorite back road you would like to share with us tell us about it and we'll try to include it in a future edition.

Contents

UNITED STATES

Arizona
LODGE ON THE DESERT, Tucson 340
RANCHO DE LOS CABALLEROS, Wickenburg 342
TANQUE VERDE, Tucson 346

California
BED AND BREAKFAST INN, San Francisco 288
BENBOW INN, Garberville 296
BRITT HOUSE, San Diego 298
CASA MADRONA INN, Sausalito 302
EILER'S INN, Laguna Beach 284
GREY WHALE INN, Fort Bragg 306
HARBOR HOUSE, Elk 292
HERITAGE HOUSE, Little River 294
INN, THE, Rancho Santa Fe 318
OJAI VALLEY INN, Ojai 300
OLD MILANO HOTEL, Gualala 304
OLD SEAL BEACH INN, Seal Beach 308
THE PELICAN INN, Muir Beach 312
RED CASTLE INN, Nevada City 310
SANDPIPER INN, Carmel-by-the-Sea 316
SUTTER CREEK INN, Sutter Creek 314
UNION STEET INN, San Francisco 286
VAGABOND HOUSE INN, Carmel 322
WINE COUNTRY INN, St. Helena 324

Colorado
ASPEN LODGE, Estes Park 350
BRIAR ROSE, Boulder 348
HEARTHSTONE INN, Colorado Springs 352
OUTLOOK LODGE, Green Mountain Falls 354

Connecticut
BOULDERS INN, New Preston 108
CURTIS HOUSE, Woodbury 106
GRISWOLD INN, Essex 114
HOMESTEAD INN, Greenwich 118
SILVERMINE TAVERN, Norwalk 112

TOWN FARMS INN, Middletown 120
WEST LANE INN, Ridgefield 116

Florida
ALBEMARLE HOTEL, St. Petersburg 490
BRAZILIAN COURT HOTEL, Palm Beach 494
CHALET SUZANNE, Lake Wales 492

Georgia
GREYFIELD INN, Cumberland Island 488

Indiana
PATCHWORK QUILT, Middlebury 446

Iowa
INN AT STONE CITY, Anamosa 448

Kentucky
BEAUMONT INN, Harrodsburg 392
BOONE TAVERN HOTEL, Berea 388
DOE RUN INN, Brandenburg 390
INN AT PLEASANT HILL, Shakertown 394

Maine
BLACK POINT INN, Prouts Neck 248
BRADLEY INN, New Harbor 246
CAPTAIN LORD MANSION, Kennebunkport 242
CHARMWOODS INN, Naples 254
CLAREMONT HOTEL, Southwest Harbor 250
COUNTRY CLUB INN, Rangeley 258
DOCKSIDE GUEST QUARTERS, York 256
GOOSE COVE LODGE, Deer Isle 260
GREY ROCK INN, Northeast Harbor 264
HARTWELL HOUSE, Ogunquit 262
HOMEWOOD INN, Yarmouth 266
OLD FORT INN, Kennebunkport 244
PENTAGOET INN, Castine 270
PILGRIM'S INN, Deer Isle 272
SQUIRE TARBOX HOUSE, Westport Island 276
WATERFORD INNE, E. Waterford 278
WHISTLING OYSTER, Ogunquit 274
WHITEHALL INN, Camden 280

Maryland
MARYLAND INN, Annapolis 360
ROBERT MORRIS INN, Oxford 358

Massachusetts
BRAMBLE INN, Brewster, Cape Cod 126
CHARLOTTE INN, Edgartown, Martha's Vineyard Island 124
COBB'S COVE, Barnstable, Cape Cod 122
COLONEL EBENEZER CRAFTS INN, Sturbridge 128
COUNTRY INN AT PRINCETON, Princeton 132
HAWTHORNE INN, Concord 138
JARED COFFIN HOUSE, Nantucket Island 142
LONGFELLOW'S WAYSIDE INN, South Sudbury 130
MORRILL PLACE, Newburyport 134
NORTHFIELD COUNTRY HOUSE, Northfield 146
PEIRSON PLACE, Richmond 140
QUEEN ANNE INN, Chatham, Cape Cod 144
RALPH WALDO EMERSON, Rockport 148
RED INN, Provincetown, Cape Cod 150
RED LION INN, Stockbridge 154
STAGECOACH HILL INN, Sheffield 152
VICTORIAN, Whitinsville 156
VILLAGE INN, Lenox 160
WINDSOR HOUSE, Newburyport 162
YANKEE CLIPPER, Rockport 164

Michigan
BOTSFORD INN, Farmington Hills 458
MICHILLINDA BEACH LODGE, Whitehall 462
NATIONAL HOUSE, Marshall 460
STAFFORD'S BAY VIEW INN, Petoskey 464

Minnesota
LOWELL INN, Stillwater 468
ST. JAMES HOTEL, Red Wing 470
SCHUMACHER'S NEW PRAGUE HOTEL, New Prague 472

Missouri
ST. GEMME BEAUVAIS INN, Ste. Genevieve 474

New Hampshire
COLBY HILL INN, Henniker 216
DANA PLACE, Jackson 218

DARBY FIELD INN, Conway 222
DEXTER'S INN, Sunapee 226
HICKORY STICK FARM, Laconia 230
THE INN AT CROTCHED MT., Francestown 220
JOHN HANCOCK INN, Hancock 210
LOVETT'S, Franconia 232
LYME INN, Lyme 228
PHILBROOK FARM, Shelburne 236
ROCKHOUSE MOUNTAIN FARM, Eaton Center 240
SPALDING INN CLUB, Whitefield 234
STAFFORD'S IN THE FIELD, Chocorua 238
WOODBOUND INN, Jaffrey 212

New Jersey
COLLIGAN'S STOCKTON INN, Stockton 62
MAINSTAY INN, Cape May 64
WOOLVERTON INN, Stockton 66

New York
ALGONQUIN HOTEL, New York 22
ASA RANSOM HOUSE, Clarence 20
BEEKMAN ARMS, Rhinebeck 24
BENN CONGER INN, Groton 26
BIRD AND BOTTLE INN, Garrison 28
CLARKSON HOUSE, Lewiston 32
GARNET HILL LODGE, North River 36
GLEN IRIS INN, Castile 34
GREENVILLE ARMS, Greenville 40
HOLLOWAY HOUSE, East Bloomfield 38
LINCKLAEN HOUSE, Cazenovia 42
MILLHOF INN, Stephentown 44
OLD DROVERS INN, Dover Plains 46
REDCOAT'S RETURN, Tannersville 48
1770 HOUSE, East Hampton 54
SHERWOOD INN, Skaneateles 52
SPRINGSIDE INN, Auburn 56
SWISS HUTTE, Hillsdale 60
THREE VILLAGE INN, Stony Brook 58

North Carolina
HEMLOCK INN, Bryson City 398
HOUND EARS LODGE, Blowing Rock 396
NU-WRAY INN, Burnsville 402
PINE CREST INN, Tryon 404
SNOWBIRD MOUNTAIN LODGE, Robbinsville 406

Ohio

BUXTON INN, Granville 454
GOLDEN LAMB, Lebanon 452
WELSHFIELD INN, Burton 456

Oregon

PARADISE GUEST RANCH, Grants Pass 326

Pennsylvania

BARLEY SHEAF FARM, Holicong 74
CAMERON ESTATE INN, Mount Joy 70
CENTURY INN, Scenery Hill 72
EAGLES MERE INN, Eagles Mere 76
EVERMAY-ON-THE-DELAWARE, Erwinna 78
FAIRFIELD INN, Fairfield 82
GATEWAY LODGE, Cooksburg 80
HICKORY BRIDGE FARM, Orrtanna 86
INN AT STARLIGHT LAKE, Starlight 90
OVERLOOK INN, Canadensis 96
PINE BARN INN, Danville 100
PUMP HOUSE INN, Canadensis 88
1740 HOUSE, Lumberville 84
SIGN OF THE SORREL HORSE, Quakertown 94
STERLING INN, South Sterling 98
THE TAVERN, New Wilmington 102

Rhode Island

INN AT CASTLE HILL, Newport 166
INNTOWNE, THE, Newport 170
LARCHWOOD INN, Wakefield 168
1661 INN, Block Island 172

Vermont

BARROWS HOUSE, Dorset 176
BIRCH HILL INN, Manchester 180
BLUEBERRY HILL, Goshen 182
CHESTER INN, Chester 184
INN AT SAWMILL FARM, West Dover 186
INN AT WEATHERSFIELD, Weathersfield 192
INN ON THE COMMON, Craftsbury Common 196
KEDRON VALLEY INN, South Woodstock 178
MIDDLETOWN SPRINGS INN, Middletown Springs 188
NORTH HERO HOUSE, North Hero 198
OLD NEWFANE INN, Newfane 200

QUECHEE INN AT MARSHLAND FARM, Quechee 204
RABBIT HILL INN, Lower Waterford 194
THREE MOUNTAIN INN, Jamaica 208
VILLAGE INN, Landgrove 206

Virginia
ALEXANDER-WITHROW HOUSE, Lexington 374
GRAVES MOUNTAIN LODGE, Syria 386
GRISTMILL SQUARE, Warm Springs 378
MEADOW LANE LODGE, Warm Springs 384
OLD CLUB RESTAURANT, Alexandria 370
PROSPECT HILL, Trevilians 382
RED FOX TAVERN, Middleburg 372
WAYSIDE INN, Middletown 380

Washington
CAPTAIN WHIDBEY INN, Coupeville 328
CONWAY'S FARMHOUSE, Port Townsend 332
INN OF THE WHITE SALMON, White Salmon 336
LAKE QUINAULT LODGE, Quinault 330
PARTRIDGE INN, Underwood 334

West Virginia
THE COUNTRY INN, Berkeley Springs 364
GENERAL LEWIS INN, Lewisburg 366
RIVERSIDE INN, Pence Springs 362

Wisconsin
JAMIESON HOUSE, Poynette 480
OLD RITTENHOUSE INN, Bayfield 476
SEVEN PINES LODGE, Lewis 484
WHITE GULL, Fish Creek 478

CANADA

British Columbia
OAK BAY BEACH HOTEL, Victoria 338

New Brunswick
MARATHON HOTEL, Grand Manan Island 424
MARSHLANDS INN, Sackville 422

Nova Scotia
    BLOMIDON INN, Wolfville   412
    INVERARY INN, Baddeck   410
    KILMUIR PLACE, Northeast Margaree   414
    MILFORD HOUSE, South Milford   416

Ontario
    THE BRIARS, Jackson's Point   440
    GRANDVIEW FARM INN, Huntsville   434
    OBAN INN, Niagara-on-the-Lake   436
    OPINICON, THE, Elgin   438
    RATHFON INN, Port Colborne   442

Prince Edward Island
    SHAW'S HOTEL, Brackley Beach   420

Quebec
    AUBERGE HANDFIELD, St-Marc-Sur-Le-Richelieu   426
    CUTTLE'S TREMBLANT CLUB, Mont Tremblant   432
    HOVEY MANOR, North Hatley   428

To our readers in Great Britain and other countries in Europe:

Welcome to North America! Many of you are making your first visit and we're delighted that you'll be experiencing some of the *real* United States and Canada by visiting these country inns. Incidentally, all of them will be very happy to help you make arrangements and reservations at other inns in the book.

For your further convenience, automobile rental reservations for the United States can be made before your departure through a world-wide rental corporation: AutoEurope.

Here are some AutoEurope telephone numbers in major European cities to make easy contact before departing: Brussels: 649-9524; Copenhagen: 153636; Paris: 2733520; Munich: 223333; Athens: 9225718; Amsterdam: 178505; Rome: 484-810; Luxemburg: 441938; Lisbon: 884257; Madrid: 2479117; Stockholm: 231070; Zurich: 3632164; London: 7270123; Ireland, Shannon: 61819; Ireland, Dublin: 371156.

Once in North America, the toll-free number for AutoEurope is 1-800-223-5555.

Although the basic theme of this book is traveling by automobile from inn to inn, whether it be by back road or interstate highway, I find that I can make the best use of my available time by flying from the Berkshires to all points south of Washington, D.C., and west of Pittsburgh. I've probably logged as many air miles as I have land miles. Until relatively recently, one of the biggest problems was the necessity of changing air lines frequently in order to land as close as possible to country inns in the South, the Midwest and the Far West before renting an automobile.

That's why I'm a big fan of Republic Airlines. It flies close to just about every inn that I visit. Furthermore, I don't have to walk from one end of a major airport to another if a change of planes is necessary. This should draw a nod of approval from those of you who have walked from one end to the other of the Detroit, Atlanta, or Denver airports.

There's one other most favorable aspect to flying Republic— for a quite reasonable additional fare, it's possible to enjoy the really convenient comfort of traveling in the first-class section.

A TYPICAL DAY IN THE LIFE OF AN INNKEEPER

0630   Up / turn on grill—coffee machine / check entries on bills for check-outs / count cash from last night / check daily report / walk dogs / check pool and terrace

0700   Set tables (one waitress short—29 people)

0730
to
1000   Cook breakfast / make up sausage patties for week / call from renter Unit I (garbage disposal not working)—arranged for pick-up of new part

1045   Talked front-office girl out of quitting in Sept.—she agreed to stay thru Oct.

1115   Complaint about bed in room #12 (bed uncomfortable—found two bed boards on bed)

1130   Put bed boards in #16 (guest arriving has bad back) / separated mail / returned a call concerning Oct. reservation

1200   Talked to maintenance man about schedule / worked on dishwasher with him

1230
to
1530   Worked on books / interviewed chambermaid to replace summer help / made reservations for a rental car for guests arriving from England via Boston / ordered parts for dishwasher / worked on service charge distribution to employees / wrote checks / checked on Harvard football game advance reservations (Harvard class '30)

1530
to
1730   Took afternoon mail to post office / got gas / picked up eggs and melons (to tide us over till wholesalers deliver on Thursday) / made up order for liquor store / changed clothes

1745   Couple came to desk to inquire about inn (as I relieved the day girl, showed them around)

1800   Checked with dining room on seatings / sliced sauerbraten for cook

1830   Took over bar / helped in dining room / wrote a letter to Norman Simpson

2000	Ate 1/2 a pot pie in kitchen
2030	Was asked to be fourth at bridge, but was able to beg off
2130	Checked dining room and kitchen / closed out bar tickets / made out dinner chart for Thursday (tomorrow)
2200	Was asked to fill in for guest leaving bridge game for bed — played one rubber
2245	Saw wife for a few minutes while we discussed menu / relaxed

True record, August 4, 1982. Made up by Frank H. Simpson of Dexter's Inn for guests who wanted to know what the daily life of an innkeeper was like.

SO YOU WANT TO OPEN A COUNTRY INN!

Every year we get many telephone calls, letters, and visits from readers of *CIBR* who find the idea of leaving the corporate or business world and becoming innkeepers very attractive. As you can see, Innkeeper Frank Simpson from Dexter's Inn in New Hampshire spends a very busy day and has had to master many skills, including not trumping his partner's ace.

If you have an urge to learn more about innkeeping, may we suggest that you ask your local bookshop for a copy of *How To Open A Country Inn* by Karen Etsell and Elaine Brennan of the Bramble Inn on Cape Cod. It is also published by the Berkshire Traveller Press and will provide you with a good insight into some of the practical problems and solutions of innkeeping.

Written in a lively style with quite a few humorous touches, this book may well answer some of the principal questions that you have about innkeeping today.

Mid-Atlantic

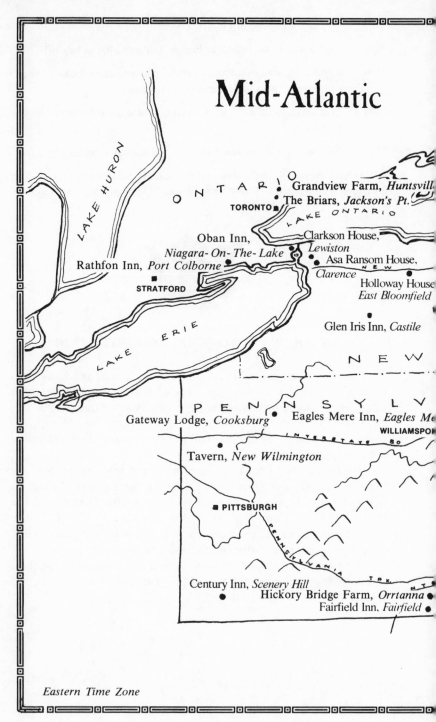

LAKE HURON

O N T A R I O

Grandview Farm, *Huntsvill*
The Briars, *Jackson's Pt.*
TORONTO

LAKE ONTARIO

Oban Inn,
Niagara-On-The-Lake
Rathfon Inn, *Port Colborne*

Clarkson House,
Lewiston
Asa Ransom House,
Clarence
NEW
Holloway House
East Bloomfield

STRATFORD

LAKE   ERIE

Glen Iris Inn, *Castile*

N   E   W

P   E   N   N   S   Y   L   V

Gateway Lodge, *Cooksburg*   Eagles Mere Inn, *Eagles Me*

INTERSTATE 80
WILLIAMSPO

Tavern, *New Wilmington*

■ PITTSBURGH

PENNSYLVANIA   TPE.

Century Inn, *Scenery Hill*
Hickory Bridge Farm, *Orrtanna*
Fairfield Inn, *Fairfield*

Eastern Time Zone

18

MONTREAL

Opinicon, *Chaffey's Locks*

Garnet Hill Lodge, *13th Lake*

Springside Inn, *Auburn*
Sherwood Inn, *Skaneateles*
Lincklaen House.
Cazenovia
Benn Conger Inn, *Groton*

Millhof Inn, *Stephentown*

ALBANY

Greenville Arms, *Greenville*
Swiss Hutte, *Hillsdale*

Redcoat's Return, *Tannersville*

Y O R K
Inn at Starlight Lake,
Starlight

Beekman Arms, *Rhinebeck*

Old Drovers Inn, *Dover Plains*

Sterling Inn,
South Sterling

A L N I
Overlook Inn,
Pump House. *Canadensis*

Bird & Bottle, *Garrison*

Evermay,
Pine Barn Inn, *Erwinna*
Danville

The Algonquin Hotel,
New York City

Three Village Inn,
Stony Brook

Sign of the Sorrel Horse,
Quakertown
Stockton

NEW YORK CITY

The Woolverton Inn,
Colligan's Stockton Inn

1770 House,
East Hampton

1740 House, *Lumberville*

Barley Sheaf Farm, *Holicong*

Cameron Estate Inn,
Mount Joy

PHILADELPHIA

GETTYSBURG

N E W
J E R S E Y

The Mainstay, *Cape May*

19

ASA RANSOM HOUSE
Clarence, New York

I was looking at a copy of the "Home Living" section of the *Buffalo News* and there, occupying nearly the entire front page, was a wonderful four-color photograph of the library of the Asa Ransom House furnished in period antiques and very good reproductions with Bob and Judy Lenz posing in typical Victorian fashion. Another four-color photograph showed the Asa Ransom House guest room Number Two, "The Blue Room." The caption mentioned the dreamy canopy bed that makes it so very popular with honeymoon couples.

It pleases me to find feature articles in either local newspapers or national magazines about the inns in this book, and I must say that the writer of this article, Barbara Snyder, did right by the Asa Ransom House, which is just a few miles east of the city line of Buffalo.

In addition to the library and the two distinctly different dining rooms, there are four totally different bedrooms, and each has a name to suit its own particular personality. An 1825 Cannonball double bed proudly presides in the Red Room. The larger Gold Room is outfitted with twin iron and brass beds. This room has originally designed stenciling on the upper walls with coordinated patchwork coverlets whose theme is old-fashioned American hospitality. The Green Room has two double beds, a sitting area with a love seat, a bookcase, and a view of the herb garden.

The two dining rooms each has its own decorative theme. The Ransom Room which has been set aside for non-smokers has green table cloths, ball-fringe curtains, many growing flowers, and two matching antique lamps hanging from the ceiling.

The other dining area, the Clarence Hollow Room, has blue placemats and ladder-back chairs. There are framed maps of western New York State, a plate rail with plates and teapots interspersed with a lantern or two that Bob and Judy Lenz have collected over the years. The curtains are blue, and there's a big fireplace at one end.

The Asa Ransom House menu reflects the Lenzes' innovative flair as well as some deep convictions about their life. For example, their religious persuasion prohibits serving pork and shellfish. As a pork substitute, "One of our favorite dishes," asserts Bob, "is smoked corned beef with apple-raisin sauce." There are also "country pies," including "salmon pond" which is a house specialty, chicken pot pie, and steak and kidney pie. In the kitchen of the inn they whip their own cream, use honey and natural raw-milk cheese from a local cheese factory, and never any MSG. Three different types of butter are served.

Breakfast for houseguests consists of fresh fruit, muffins and a beverage, as well as Judy's special breakfast egg pie.

Overnight guests at the inn are frequently assisted by either Bob or the sparkly-eyed Judy with suggestions and brochures about attractions they might encounter, among which is an antiques tour of Clarence and vicinity. They will also exchange your old copy of *Country Inns and Back Roads* for a new one.

The Asa Ransom House is closed on Fridays and Saturdays because of the religious beliefs of Bob and Judy who are members of the World Wide Church of God. Friday provides them with the opportunity to spend time with their families or to set off with their two daughters, Abby and Jennie, for some point in western New York or southern Ontario to enjoy many scenic attractions. As Bob says, "We frequently end the day with a fine dinner at an old favorite or sometimes discover some new place."

ASA RANSOM HOUSE, Rte. 5, Clarence, N.Y. 14031; 716-759-2315. A 4-room village inn approximately 15 mi. from Buffalo near the Albright Knox Art Gallery, the Studio Arena Theatre, the Art Park, and Niagara Falls. European plan. Dinner served Monday through Thursdays 4:30 to 9 p.m.; Sundays, 12:30 to 8 p.m. Lunch is available on Wednesday only. Closed Friday and Saturday. No pets. No credit cards. Tennis, golf, fishing, swimming nearby. Limited amusement for children under 12. Bob and Judy Lenz, Innkeepers.

Directions: From the New York Thruway traveling west, use Exit 48A-Pembrook. Turn right to Rte. 5 and proceed 11 mi. to Clarence. Traveling east on the N.Y. Thruway, use Exit 49; turn left on Rte. 78, go 1 mi. to Rte. 5 and continue 5¼ mi. Coming from the east via Rte. 20, just east of Lancaster, N.Y., turn right on Ransom Rd., go to end and turn left.

ALGONQUIN HOTEL
New York, New York

I have always had a great deal of fun writing about my experiences at the Hotel Algonquin in New York City.

The first time I mentioned it was in the 1971 edition when I explained how it really came to my attention when so many people following *Country Inns and Back Roads* felt the need of a place to stay in New York City. One recommended the Algonquin and after a long visit, I agreed that it was the closest thing to a country inn I'd found yet in New York.

In the 1972 edition I spoke about seeing a well-known French movie actor having tea in the lobby, and about riding up in the elevator with a famous stage actress who announced in the glorious tones of a French horn, "Fifth floor, please."

Andy Anspach, the innkeeper, explained that people like actresses, diplomats, and internationally famous people deserved a private life, and the Algonquin attempts to provide it while they are in New York. As he said, "We are terribly conservative by inclination. We've tried not to change too many things around here since the early 1920s, when it was famous as a meeting place for the Algonquin Round Table wits. People seem to enjoy our accommodations which include oversized bathtubs and meticulous room service."

In 1974 I spoke at length about the friendliness of the staff and how guests are quite likely to be remembered even though the Algonquin is, in truth, a very busy place.

In 1975 I did a long piece on the late evening supper buffet where guests come in after the theater, the opera, or basketball or hockey games to enjoy Welsh rarebit, lobster Newburg, salad, fluffy cakes, apple pie, and ice cream.

(It is now possible to enjoy a delightful repast every evening of the week, including Sunday. Steve Ross, a most entertaining man, is at the piano several evenings a week.)

In 1976 I luxuriated with breakfast in bed at the Algonquin, and described the browned corned beef hash with a poached egg, warm Dutch coffee cake, and above all, the superb Algonquin hot chocolate.

In recent years I am not the only one who has discovered that the Algonquin Hotel, in addition to having a literary past, also has a very plump reputation as a quiet, conservative, and interesting place to lodge and dine while in New York. *Travel and Leisure* in a full-length article refers to it as "the Unicorn of Big-City Hotels." Eight books have been written on the subject of the hotel and it has been featured in dozens of others. Writers have pointed out that the redecorated bedrooms and suites resemble those of an English country house, with the emphasis on chintz.

Chintz! I wonder what Dorothy Parker and the other Algonquin Wits would say to that?

ALGONQUIN HOTEL, 59 W. 44th St., New York, N.Y. 10036; 212-840-6800. A quiet, conservative 200-room country inn in the heart of Manhattan. Convenient to business, theaters, and shopping. Breakfast, lunch served every day. Dinner is served Monday through Saturday, and a Sunday supper is served on Sundays from 5:30 p.m. The late supper buffet is offered Monday through Saturday at 9:30 p.m. Open year-round. Very near bus, rail, and air transportation. Garage directly opposite entrance, with complimentary parking for weekend visitors arriving after 5 p.m., Fri., for minimum 2-night visit. No pets. Andrew Anspach, Innkeeper.

Directions: 44th St. is one-way from west to east; 43rd St., from east to west. Garage is accessible from either street.

BEEKMAN ARMS
Rhinebeck, New York

Chuck LaForge, innkeeper at the Beekman Arms, claims that this is the "oldest hotel in America." Since Francis Koppeis of Longfellow's Wayside Inn in South Sudbury, Massachusetts, makes the same claim for his establishment, this has created a great deal of friendly rivalry between the two inns.

By 1769 the Beekman Arms, which started from rather humble beginnings in 1700, had increased in size to two full stories with a roomy attic that later became a ballroom. When trouble arose with the Indians in the area, the entire community would take refuge within the inn's walls.

During the Revolution, George Washington and his staff enjoyed the fare of the inn, and the window from which he watched for his couriers is still in place. There were anxious days also, when Lafayette, Schuyler, Arnold, and Hamilton spent many hours at the inn. In fact, over the years hundreds of men who have helped fashion the destiny of our nation partook of the inn's hospitality. These included Aaron Burr, Horace Greeley, William Jennings Bryan, Martin Van Buren, Theodore Roosevelt, and Franklin Delano Roosevelt.

Recently on an early December evening I enjoyed dinner in the low-ceilinged Tap Room. The light from the flickering candles was reflected in the varnished tabletops, and Christmas wreaths with bright red ribbons and other decorations added a festive air. The walls were hung with ancient documents and prints, many of them dating back to the era of the Revolution.

The first thing brought to the table was a loaf of freshly baked bread. The waitress, dressed in a red uniform and little colonial cap, suggested that I might enjoy the rack of lamb which was the special that day. It was delicious.

While the colonial Beekman Arms menu probably included such items as roast beef, venison, bear steak, pheasant, quail, and turkey, this evening's menu had many varieties of beef dishes as well as lamb chops, pork chops, duck l'orange, lobster Newburg, and shrimp.

Since my most recent visit, a new greenhouse-dining area on the front of the building has gained considerably in popularity. The curving glass extends up the front of the building providing ample amounts of sunshine, and louvered windows permit fresh air when needed. The interior, indeed, has a most pleasant aspect for breakfast and lunch, and is a welcome addition to the other dining areas.

Guests at the Beekman Arms also have the option of staying overnight just a few steps down the street at the Delameter House, one of the architectural jewels of the Hudson Valley. It was designed and built by Alexander Jackson Davis in 1844. The batten-and-board residence provides seven additional lodging rooms for the guests at the Beekman Arms, and a rapidly-growing number of travelers finds the peaceful atmosphere much to its liking.

So we see that the Beekman Arms today is more than a historic inn where thousands of guests enjoy its fascinating and authentic colonial decor and menu; like many other country and village inns, it is still the community meeting place. Decisions great and small have been made within its walls for almost three hundred years.

It is a living link to America's past.

BEEKMAN ARMS, Rhinebeck, N.Y. 12572; 914-876-7077. A 13-room village inn with an adjacent 4-room guest house, 1 mi. from Amtrak Station at Rhinecliff. Short drive to F.D.R. Library and Home in Hyde Park. European plan. Lunch and dinner served to travelers daily. Closed Christmas. Open year-round. Golf, tennis, swimming nearby. No amusements for young children. Charles LaForge, Innkeeper.

Directions: From N.Y. Thruway, take Exit 19, cross Rhinecliff Bridge and pick up Rte. 199 south to Rte. 9. Proceed south on Rte. 9 to middle of village. From Taconic Pkwy. exit at Rhinebeck and follow Rte. 199 west 11 mi. to Rte. 308 into village.

BENN CONGER INN
Groton, New York

Margaret Oaksford and her son Robert, who is also the chef, had joined me for breakfast in the Morning Room of the Benn Conger Inn. The view through the large Palladian windows was of the woods and grounds that border this inn on the north side.

Margaret was filling me in on the details about the inn. "For many years this building was the Benn Conger mansion and the house is rich in local history. Benn Conger was the first president of the Corona Corporation and gave Groton an ongoing industry that is still in operation today—the SCM Corporation. He was a New York State senator."

Our breakfast was generous to say the least, including bacon and eggs, homemade breads out of which marvelous toast was made, and a bowl of fresh fruit. When I remarked about this, Robert pointed out that he and Margaret do not believe in so-called continental breakfasts. "We like to send our guests into the new day with a good, firm country breakfast."

The Benn Conger is a mansion in every sense of the word and it has a splendid two-story, four-column portico topped by a classic Greek pediment. It was the type of house that a successful business-man living in New York State a number of years ago would find much to his liking, and the interior, floors, woodwork, and sweeping staircase reflect the opulence of bygone days.

The Oaksfords have redecorated the inn with gold-trimmed wallpaper panels, keyhole moldings, corner cupboards, and crystal chandeliers.

Besides the Morning Room, there are other dining rooms called the Blue Room, the Cantwell Room (which was the original living room of the mansion), and the Conservatory.

There are what Margaret calls "six-and-a-half" lodging rooms and three bathrooms with showers and heat lamps. All of them are most attractively and appropriately decorated and I found many antiques.

The newest accommodation is the North Suite, a set of rooms that includes a private bath, dressing room, bedroom, and sitting room with fireplace.

One of the double rooms is called the "Dutch Schultz" suite. Noticing my wrinkled forehead, Margaret explained that for some period of time during the 1920s the infamous New York gangster of the same name lived in this house.

Robert, who is a trained chef, explained that the cuisine at Benn Conger could best be described as "American Nouvelle."

"This is really a new movement of American chefs towards

dishes that, through the use of fresh domestic produce and ingredients, are more genuine culinary expressions of our country and our heritage. We have such things as Pennsylvania-grown mushrooms, liver paté from fresh chickens raised in Maryland, and fresh baby asparagus spears from California and Arizona whenever they are available."

Margaret is the librarian at the Cornell School of Hotel Administration in nearby Ithaca. The inn is already a gathering place for groups of Cornell alumni.

Groton is within a very short driving distance of the entire Finger Lakes region of southern New York State and the area abounds in ample recreational opportunities both summer and winter. There's good cross-country skiing nearby and both Greek Peak and Song Mountain ski areas are a short distance away.

We are all delighted to welcome the Benn Conger Inn to the *CIBR* innkeeping family. Its location in Groton makes it an ideal stopping place for travelers on I-81, one of the most highly traveled north-south arteries in the East. I've taken special pains with the directions.

BENN CONGER INN, 206 W. Cortland St., Groton, N.Y. 13073; 607-898-3282. A 6½-bedroom village mansion in a quiet community in New York's southern tier. Cornell University and the Finger Lakes nearby. Lodgings available every day of the year. Restaurant closed every Monday and also December 24 and 25. Breakfast included in the cost of lodgings. Dinner and Sunday brunch served nightly except Monday. Golf, tennis, swimming, downhill and xc skiing, and backroading nearby. No pets. Margaret and Robert Oaksford, Innkeepers.

Directions: From I-81, use Exit 12. Turn south (left) on Rte. 281 for a short distance; turn west (right) on Rte. 22. Cross Rte. 38 (W. Cortland St.) making no turns. Benn Conger driveway is on the right.

BIRD AND BOTTLE INN
Garrison, New York

It was daffodil time at the Bird and Bottle Inn—not only daffodils but the first beginnings of other beautiful light and airy spring blossoms.

I had awakened to the joyous sound of the birds and had lingered under the covers for just a few more minutes, noting with appreciation the handsome overhead beams made of mellowed, weathered barnboard and the rest of the furnishings in my lodging room which was in one of the restored outbuildings of the inn.

There was much to do that day, so a few minutes later I ambled over the red brick walk to the main building of the inn for breakfast. Some birds flew overhead and one of them landed on the chimney of this yellow clapboard house that has played host to so many travelers and guests over the years. I opened the Dutch door with its heavy cast iron hardware and stepped into the main reception

area where the polished, wide pine floorboards seemed almost to reflect an oil portrait of a young lady dressed in colonial costume.

To my right was the low-ceilinged dining room where the previous night there had been the gleaming white napery with candles and many diners seated side by side, a very romantic idea, indeed. The menu on the blackboard had announced that there was ratatouille au froid, also smoked trout, French onion soup, and then a supreme of chicken, roast duckling Bigarade, and rognon de veau moutarde.

For breakfast Innkeeper Ira Boyar suggested the small dining room with a crackling fire against the chill of the early spring morning. There were fresh flowers on the table.

I had selected my breakfast order the night before from a menu that included all kinds of eggs, sausage, and fruit juice. I chose scrambled eggs and sausage and noticed some other houseguests were having beautiful french toast served with syrup or honey. We soon began to talk with one another because it's that kind of atmosphere.

Breakfast completed, I leaned for a moment on the window overlooking a little terrace and stream where a light spring rain was making punctuation points in the small puddles. The trees were in early bud and I could well imagine what magic the entire scene would reveal in another two or three weeks.

Ira suggested that I might like to see more of the bedrooms in the main building and as I walked up the stairs I realized that I was looking at the same colonial wallpaper that I have in my own dining room. However, it seemed much more appropriate in this setting, here on the second floor where the floorboards creaked a little and were slightly aslant.

All of the bedrooms are furnished in Early American antiques and have either a canopy or a four-poster bed. All have private baths and woodburning fireplaces. There are two double rooms and a suite which includes a cozy sitting room.

The Bird and Bottle goes back to the mid-1700s when it was a stagecoach stop on the New York to Albany route. Its nearness to West Point undoubtedly made it a meeting place for Benedict Arnold's emissaries to the British prior to his defection.

Today the colonial atmosphere is preserved with narrow clapboards (quite unusual), low ceilings, and rich paneling. The inn is beautifully decorated with many duck decoys, period wallpaper, pewter, old paintings, and many wooden accessories. It is indeed like stepping back into an earlier time.

BIRD AND BOTTLE INN, Garrison, N.Y. 10524; 914-424-3000. A 4-bedroom country inn, rich in antiquity located on Rte. 9, a few miles north of Peekskill, N.Y. A short distance from Boscobel Restoration, U.S. Military Academy at West Point, and Sleepy Hollow Restorations. From April 1 to Nov. 1 lunch and dinner served daily. From Nov. 1 to April 1 dinner served Wed. thru Sun. Sunday brunch served year-round. Ira Boyar, Innkeeper.

Directions: From NYC: cross George Washington Bridge and follow Palisades Pkwy. north to Bear Mtn. Bridge. Cross bridge and travel on Rte. 9D north 4½ mi. to Rte. 403. Proceed on Rte. 403 to Rte. 9, then north 4 mi. to inn. From I-84, take Exit 13 and follow Rte. 9 south for 8 mi.

The historical Albany Post Road which runs alongside the inn has been named a state and national landmark. This 6.3-mile segment runs from Continental Village to the juncture of Route 9, just north of the Bird & Bottle.

This is the only sizable portion of the original road that is little changed from the days of the mid-1700s. It was the original transportation artery by land from New York City to Albany. Portions of the road followed Indian paths; the path was widened to carry troops and stores north during the French and Indian War; it became the route of postal and stagecoach service; and was traveled on and protected by many outposts of Americans during the Revolution.

The southern end of the road, prior to the Revolution, was called Robinson's Bridge. It was described by General Heath as the "Gorge of the Highlands" and named by him "Continental Village." It came into prominence after the Battle of White Plains, which ended in a draw, with the enemy retiring to New York and the Continentals taking up positions north of the Croton River.

October 9, 1777, marks the burning and pillaging of Continental Village. A British attack was never again made against Continental Village throughout the Revolutionary War. While the greater historic interest centered on West Point as the "Gibraltar of America," the village continued to be an important military post and depot of supplies. Everyone connected with the Army of the Revolution, from George Washington down, passed through it or was stationed at it.

Continental Village Post Road was much traveled by Washington and his officers in 1779-80. He often crossed the Hudson from West Point inspecting its outposts, and used this turnpike in passing to and from the Eastern States. American soldiers were encamped up and down and along the Old Post Road during the Revolution.

Along the road are fifteen homes that were built in the latter 1700s up to the mid-1800s, one of which is the Bird & Bottle Inn.

Aged as the Old Albany Post Road is, it bears no marks of its long, enchanting history, changed but little since the American Revolution. Age, however, is not the main distinction of this road. It has borne many of the famous men of history— Washington, Franklin, Lafayette, Heath, Parsons, Putnam, Hamilton, John Jay, Enoch Crosby, and others—a virtual roll call of the guiding spirits in the War of Independence. Historic events have happened upon it, or near it. André traveled this road on his last somber journey, under guard of Major Talmadge and one hundred horses, when he was brought from North Castle to the Robinson House near Garrison.

The Old New York-Albany Post Road has seen the troops of

two wars, passage of the postal, stagecoach, and telegraphic service, and then, luckily, was bypassed when the Highland Turnpike and Route 9 were built.

It would be difficult to find any place of equal area where more Revolutionary history was written.

Ira Boyar
Bird and Bottle Inn
Garrison, New York

One favorite back road: leaving the inn by way of Greiner Road with its old limestone cliffs (the original shore of Lake Ontario) to Goodrich Road and into Clarence Center (six miles) and the Clarence Center Emporium and Ice Cream Parlor. Next door is Ruth VanKuren's Antique shop (a two-story old general store full of antiques). Then, heading east on Clarence Center Road past many dairy and corn farms to Akron, New York. Here one can stop to fish or swim at the Akron Falls Park. Then Route 5 to Kutter's Cheese Factory and Store (ten miles).

Bob and Judy Lenz
Asa Ransom House
Clarence, New York

CLARKSON HOUSE
Lewiston, New York

A light snow was falling on an early December evening when I first visited the Clarkson House in Lewiston, New York, a number of years ago. The Christmas tree lights were already blinking out their happy message, and there was a small group of sculptured figures depicting the Holy Family across from the inn. I ventured down the street to see the appealing miniature Christmas tree lights draped around each of the trees in the business district. It all made a very happy holiday effect.

This was my first visit to this corner of New York State dominated by the presence of Niagara Falls. I learned about the Clarkson House from my good friend, Robert Lenz, the innkeeper of the Asa Ransom House in Clarence, New York. Bob said that it was very special, and he proved to be right.

I found the Clarkson House to be an excellent restaurant— something I knew the moment I smelled a most delicious aroma which I discovered came from the charcoal grill right in the middle of the dining area, where the filets and lamb chops were sizzling away merrily. Around it, there is an unusual arrangement of booths and tables, and on the walls a collection of tools and gadgets used more than 100 years ago. "They haven't discovered the use for some of them!" said Marilyn Clarkson. There are old-fashioned kerosene lamps on the tables, and the walls have several good paintings interspersed with wall lamps.

On the first trip I discovered that Bob Clarkson is a great believer in having things under control. For example, there are 22 tables, all carefully spaced on the wooden floor which is scrubbed every day. This means that reservations are most advisable as only a limited number of diners can be accommodated.

Secondly, the menu has been judiciously pared down to a few entrees which are very carefully prepared and most tastefully arranged on the plates. There is an emphasis on beef, including sirloin, filet, and prime rib. There are also delicious French-cut lamb chops. A combination of beef filet and lobster tail, or half of a Maine lobster (flown in fresh) are also offered. That, plus four desserts, including cherries jubilee and baked Alaska, is the menu. I mustn't forget to mention that there was a little sign on one of those delicious-looking baked potatoes that said, "Eat all you like, I've been scrubbed and tubbed."

At that time the newest thing at the Clarkson House was a lobster tank which holds up to two hundred lobsters in artificial sea water. "We've always served lobsters," explained bob, "and now we can serve lobsters fresh from the sea!"

Perhaps the Christmas tree lights in Lewiston, which I first noticed in 1973, provided the inspiration for the Niagara Falls Festival of Lights, a five-week celebration featuring over 40,000 colored lights, handpainted storybook character displays, animated Christmas displays, and many seasonal decorations.

The focal point is the winter garden, three stories of lush indoor tropical vegetation complemented with a variety of decorations. A message tree and mailbox for Santa are other highlights of this holiday extravaganza.

THE CLARKSON HOUSE, 810 Center St., Lewiston, N.Y. 14092; 716-754-4544. A country restaurant, 7 mi. from Niagara Falls and Olde Fort Niagara. No lodgings. Dinner served daily except Mondays. Closed Christmas. Bob and Marilyn Clarkson, Innkeepers.

Directions: From I-190, exit at Lewiston and follow Rte. 104E for 1½ mi. Turn right on Rte. 18F and travel 2 blocks west to restaurant.

33

GLEN IRIS INN
Castile, New York

Cora Pizzutelli and I were leaning over the stone wall gazing at the 107-foot Middle Falls of the Genesee River in front of the Glen Iris Inn. The wonderful lyrical sound of the river is ever present, and the nearest point from which to view the falls is a terrace about 25 steps from the front of the inn.

"Our guests have always enjoyed the beauty and majesty of Letchworth Park," she said, "and there are many animals that are seen in great abundance including deer, raccoon, chipmunks, ground hogs, foxes, wild turkey, quail, grouse, and pheasants. Lots of people enjoy the great variety of wild flowers. An overnight stay here is nearly the equivalent of a weekend elsewhere."

Letchworth State Park is about eighteen miles long and about two miles wide. It follows the course of the Genesee River in what is best described as a miniature Grand Canyon. The full length is traversed by an auto road. There are several different turn-off points with spectacular views that the river has carved in a path through the land on its way north to Lake Ontario. There is not a single bit of commercialism to mar this enchanting experience.

The inn was the former home of William Pryor Letchworth and was built in the early 1800s. The bedrooms are very comfortably furnished and are reached by a twisting, turning staircase of dark chestnut wood that leads all the way to the third floor. Instead of

having room numbers, the rooms have the names of trees found in the park. All are furnished in the 19th-century style. A modern motel unit is located in a nearby grove for additional overnight guests.

Cora and Peter Pizzutelli, sensitive, nature-loving people, are the innkeepers. Each is deeply devoted to this beautiful inn. The feeling has run in the family, because both their son Peter, Jr., and their daughter Paula grew up in the inn. In fact, Paula, after graduating from the Cornell University Hotel School and gaining four years of experience in the accommodation business, has now permanently joined the inn staff.

Peter is a chef with years of experience, and the many different dishes that come out of the kitchen are always prepared under his watchful eye.

Cora's area of interest is the ever-growing gift shop within the inn.

The unusual combination of a beautiful country inn located next to a spectacular waterfall in a totally protected state park in a historical section of western New York State attracts large numbers of visitors to the area and to the Glen Iris Inn. Consequently, I cannot emphasize too strongly the advisability of having reservations in advance for either breakfast, lunch, or dinner, and also for lodgings. Cora tells me that every summer they regretfully have to tell people that there is no room in their inn.

Just as I was leaving the Glen Iris, I got one of the biggest thrills that I've had in more than ten years of visiting: a freight train rumbled over the great railroad bridge that spans the Genesee River just above the end, and it was a thrilling sight to see the locomotive and the cars chugging their way high above the riverbed. The engineer obliged with a few blasts on the whistle to top it off.

GLEN IRIS INN, Castile, N.Y. 14427; 716-493-2622. A 20-room country inn located at the Middle Falls of the Genesee River in Letchworth State Park. European plan. Breakfast, lunch, dinner served to travelers daily. Open from Easter Sunday through first Sunday in November. Footpaths, swimming, and bicycles nearby. Historical sites in park and spectacular views within walking distance. Peter, Cora, and Paula Pizzutelli, Innkeepers.

Directions: Inn is located off Rtes. 436, 19A, and 39 in Letchworth State Park, 55 mi. from Buffalo and Rochester.

GARNET HILL LODGE
North River, New York

I had taken an early morning walk and was now in the "Gazebo," located about one hundred yards from the front porch of the Log House at Garnet Hill Lodge. The view to the south was of the mountains and the lake, and I noted that it was somewhat different than the view looking west from the front porch of the Log House. The "Gazebo" is the newest addition and is used as a late-afternoon and evening gathering place and I was finding it a place of solitude at this very moment.

The time was 7:30 a.m. and there was a bit of haze on 13th Lake and its surrounding mountains. The mid-July half-moon was gradually fading from sight as the sun became the dominant force of the day.

Meantime, the tantalizing aromas of Mary Heim's breakfast were wafting across the terrace and mixing in with the natural sweet smell of grasses and trees.

"Doesn't it look wonderful!" George Heim, who had probably been up for hours taking care of the many chores of the inn, dropped into one of the rustic chairs beside me. "It's the ever-changing aspect of the seasons that never ceases to thrill me. In the springtime we have quite a few white-water enthusiasts and hikers and it's wonderful to see the woods come to life. I generally take our guests on hikes in all different seasons. It helps them gain knowledge of the area, and creates a common bond between them.

"You must come up, of course, in the autumn when this foliage is absolutely spectacular. The end of September is an excellent time. It's wonderful for hiking to the abandoned garnet mine, or to one of the distant ponds. In wintertime, it is breathtaking. We have miles and miles of cross-country ski trails and everything is literally buried in snow . . . "

I was already impressed, because the night before George and Mary had shown me some slides of Garnet Hill Lodge in all seasons and one of them showed snow up to the roof of the porch, so that it was possible to walk in through the second-floor window. The slides showed guests cross-country skiing, snowshoeing, and hiking, and the summer scenes included sailboating, canoeing, and fishing.

"Fishing is a big thing here," said George. "We have landlocked salmon and brook trout in 13th Lake, and the nearby lakes and streams have lake trout, rainbow, brownies, bass, walleyes, and pickerels. Another thing that impresses our guests is the unusual number of wild animals. In a morning walk down to the beaver pond, they can see beavers, deer, hares, loons, blue herons, foxes, weasels, and raccoons. The owls, hawks, and ravens are very popular with

birdwatchers. Many bring their tape recorders." I asked about black bear and he replied, "Oh yes, we have them, but they don't bother anybody."

Lodgings are in individual bedrooms, very clean and neat; about half have private bathrooms. The *chef de cuisine* is Mary Heim and the specialties include generous portions of pot roast, chicken, baked fish, and other hearty offerings.

In response to a question about the white-water trips, George said, "As the winter snows melt, the upper Hudson River offers one of the finest white-water rafting trips in the East. The gorge trip is fifteen miles long and the rapids and the scenery are really spectacular. Our guests who are here from April to June enjoy it very much. There are several outfitters in the area and we're happy to make arrangements with them so our guests can really enjoy this unusual experience."

GARNET HILL LODGE, 13th Lake Road, North River, N.Y. 12856; 518-251-2821. A 19-room rustic resort-inn high in the Adirondacks, 32 mi. from Warrensburg. Open year-round with the exception of two weeks in June and November. Mod. American and European plans available. Breakfast, lunch, and dinner served to transients. Swimming, boating, hiking, fishing, and xc skiing on grounds. Downhill skiing, long distance hikes, Hudson River white-water rafting trips, and beautiful Adirondack drives nearby. The area has many museums, art and craft centers, and historical points. No pets. No credit cards. Taxi service provided to bus stop 30 mi. away. George and Mary Heim, Innkeepers.

Directions: From the Northway (I-87) take Exit 23 and follow Rtes. 9 and 28 north 4 mi. Take left fork (Rte. 28) 22 mi. to North River. Take second left (13th Lake Road) 5 mi. to Lodge. For more explicit directions, write for brochure.

HOLLOWAY HOUSE
East Bloomfield, New York

It was a beautiful sunny day in western New York. The corn was up, covering the rolling hills off Route 20. The sky was blue without a cloud, and the silos and barns of this beautiful farming country were constant reminders of its rich yield.

This time, I was coming east after paying an overnight visit to the Asa Ransom House in Clarence, and entered East Bloomfield just about noontime. East Bloomfield is a village of elms, maples,

oak trees, and lovely old homes. It is a relatively short distance from Rochester.

At the Holloway House, Doreen Wayne explained that Jonathan Child, who was elected in 1834 as Rochester's first mayor, had opened a store in 1812 in part of Peter Holloway's tavern. In 1818 he married Sophia Eliza, the daughter of Colonel Nathaniel Rochester, who lived a mile west of the tavern when he established his city at the falls of the Genesee.

"In those days, of course, the road was just thin ruts created by stagecoaches and farm carts," said Doreen. "Now Route 20 moves along the northern edge of what we call in these parts the 'Bristol Valley.' A great many people find their way to our door, just as they did when Peter Holloway, the village blacksmith, built this as a tavern in 1808."

The inn was doing a very brisk business for lunch, but Fred and Doreen promised to visit with me as soon as things got quieter, and showed me to a corner in the Peter Holloway Room, which has a view of the village through the beautiful trees. The waitress recited the lunch menu for me and brought a wonderful variety of hot fresh breads for which the inn is quite famous. Doreen was able to visit for just a few moments and to tell me about the buffet dinner which is served on Friday nights during July and August.

"We have seafood, shrimp, scallops, oysters, creamed mushrooms, and various types of Newburg dishes. Everybody always 'oohs and aahs' over the way the big table is decorated. It is very popular with the people who live in the area. On Saturday night we have a prime roast beef dinner.

"Incidentally, we have two kinds of dinners, either a complete dinner or a plate dinner. The plate dinner includes the entrée, two vegetables, a salad, potato, our well-known Sally Lunn bread and homemade rolls. The complete dinner includes a choice of appetizers, entrée, choice of potato, two vegetables, a choice of salad and salad dressing, the Sally Lunn bread, homemade rolls, beverage, and a choice of dessert."

There are several very interesting nearby attractions, according to Doreen Wayne. First is the Wizard of Clay pottery and workshop which is housed in a complex of geodesic domes where all the pottery pieces are handmade on the potter's wheel, one at a time, by the "Wizard" and his staff of skilled craftsmen. It is located on Route 20A, three miles east of Honeoye Lake, and is open year-round. The second, within walking distance of the Holloway House, is the restored 1833 Bloomfield Academy bordering on the historic Civil War Park. Inside the academy is the unique "Communications Museum" which is particularly enjoyed by ham operators. It has one of the earliest collections of early radio apparatus — actual equipment associated with Marconi, De Forest, Armstrong, Edison, and other pioneers. A feature of this museum is a replica of a 1925 radio store completely stocked with hundreds of parts and tubes for building one's own radio set.

"Our guests particularly enjoy visiting these places after lunch," remarked Doreen.

THE HOLLOWAY HOUSE, Rtes. 5 & 20, East Bloomfield, N.Y. 14443; 716-657-7120. A country restaurant 8 miles west of Canandaigua, N.Y. No lodgings. Lunch served daily 12 to 2 p.m.; dinner — 5:30 to 8:30 p.m. Sunday — 12 to 7:30 p.m. closed Monday. Open April 1 thru Thanksgiving. Sonnenberg Gardens, golf courses, and Finger Lake Racetrack nearby. Fred, Doreen, and Mildred Wayne, Innkeepers.

Directions: From N.Y. State Thruway, take Exit 45. Follow Rte. 96S 3 miles to Victor, N.Y. At the third traffic light go south on Maple Ave. 5 miles to Holcomb. Turn right at light and then take second left to Rte. 5 and 20.

GREENVILLE ARMS
Greenville, New York

In the years since the late 60s and early 70s country inns have become very popular and are continuing to attract new friends and devotees every day. However, the country inn concept goes back many years before that, and the Greenville Arms has a family tradition of Catskill Mountain innkeeping extending at least forty years into the past.

It is a Victorian country mansion with several interestingly fashioned porches, cupolas, gables, and corners. It's well-shaded with tall trees, and beautifully landscaped with bushes and shrubs. Throughout, the atmosphere could best be described as "homey and inviting."

Another dimension to be found at the Greenville Arms is its role as a very comfortable resort-inn. Behind the main house with its several bedrooms with private and shared baths, is the Carriage House where there are more contemporary rooms, all with private baths. There is a large, beautiful lawn with shuffleboard, ping-pong, horseshoes, badminton, lawn bowling, and a swimming pool.

The innkeepers at Greenville Arms are two sisters, Barbara and Laura Stevens. They are carrying on in the family tradition, since Greenville Arms was originally owned by their mother, and their aunt and grandmother still own Catskill Mountain inns.

For a further insight into what Greenville Arms is really like, let me share a portion of a letter I received from Barbara: "A great deal of our business comes from nice people with *CIBR* under their arms. They are so enthusiastic and interesting and come from all over the country. They tend to share many common interests mostly because they have been staying at other inns along the way.

"Greenville Arms had the pleasure of hosting several family gatherings this year. One couple reserved the inn for a weekend so that they could relax and enjoy time with their wedding guests, another was celebrating an anniversary, and still another had two special birthdays. We had a family group that just hadn't managed to get together for many, many years. These families were truly wonderful. The idea of planning a family reunion at a country inn seems to be growing in popularity. We hope so, as we feel fortunate to have shared in each of those held at Greenville Arms.

"Our area had two new attractions this year that provided a lot of fun for our guests. A really good summer theatre group performed during July and August nearby and a touring company provided both day and evening cruises on the nearby Hudson River. Both provided delightful diversions."

The main house at the Greenville Arms was built in 1889 and

has the feeling of being almost frozen in time with the same type of furniture, decorations, and lifestyle. There are even button switches for some of the lights. One of the most delightful things for me was the many different types of bedspreads. Off the second floor is a porch that you always wanted and never had.

Dinner is a single entrée and is really typical Catskill Mountain home-cooking with lots of turkey, baked ham, roasts, and fresh vegetables from the garden.

Apparently, it is also a great place for family reunions.

GREENVILLE ARMS, Greenville, New York 12083; 518-966-5219. A 20-room Victorian country inn in the foothills of the northern Catskill Mountains, 25 miles south of Albany, 120 miles north of New York City. Modified American or bed-and-breakfast rates available year-round except weekdays in Jan., Feb., and March (bed-and-breakfast only). Rates include a hearty breakfast and specially prepared single-entrée country dinner. Pool and lawn sports on grounds. Antiquing, country auctions, historic sites, horseback riding, golf, tennis, xc and downhill skiing, ice skating, and snowshoeing nearby. Children are welcome. Pets accommodated in nearby kennels. No credit cards. Laura Stevens and Barbara Stevens, Innkeepers.

Directions: Exit N.Y. State Thruway at 21B (Coxsackie-New Baltimore). Turn left on 9-W south 2 mi. to traffic light. Turn right on 81 west, 13 mi. to Greenville. Turn left at traffic light on 32S. You will see Greenville Arms on the right. Via Taconic Pkwy: Exit at Ancram on Rte. 82W, over Rip Van Winkle Bridge and follow Rte. 23W to Cairo. Turn right on 32N, 9 mi. to Greenville.

LINCKLAEN HOUSE
Cazenovia, New York

I was back at the Lincklaen House. The hour was 11:15 P.M. I had arrived at approximately 10 o'clock and found the ubiquitous Helen Tobin still at the inn. We sat in front of the parlor fireplace for a nice hour-long chat. One of the things she mentioned was that people using Exit 34 on the New York State Thruway had the advantage of coming up Route 13 past Chittenango Falls, which is just a few minutes away from Cazenovia.

"These falls are actually higher than Niagara," she said, "and it is such a beautiful spot. During the wintertime the ice formations are spectacular."

Guests staying at the Lincklaen House and meeting Helen for the first time frequently say, "Oh, I feel as if I have known you for a long time." This is because Helen has genuine warmth and consideration, and the Lincklaen House reflects this feeling. It's this feeling, also, that keeps the paneled walls and ceilings as gleaming as the white tablecloths. She also insists on fresh flowers, crisp vegetables, hot popovers, hearty portions, lots of bath towels and, above all, a feeling of rapport with her guests.

"I try to talk with everyone while they're here," she said. "Many become good friends and I hear from them at Christmas." Speaking of Christmas, Helen has framed many of the Christmas cards from the Golden Lamb Inn in Lebanon, Ohio, and they hang in the lobby.

Lincklaen House has been called one of the best examples of

early 19th-century architecture in central New York State. Its Greek Revival lines are in harmony with other village buildings. It was built in 1835 as a stopover for travelers and named after the founder of the village. Over the years many famous guests have enjoyed its hospitality, including Franklin D. Roosevelt, Grover Cleveland, John D. Rockefeller, and John Dewey. Fortunately, the interior and exterior embellishments have remained untouched, and visitors are delighted upon discovering the intricate paneling and carving.

Cazenovia is one of the attractive towns along Route 20 in central New York State, and its situation on a beautiful lake is an added attraction for Lincklaen House guests.

The area has recreation for outdoor-minded guests in both summer and winter, and there is especially good downhill and cross-country skiing nearby.

"Being an innkeeper is so much fun," Helen said, as we walked through the dining room which was faintly lighted by the last glow of the fireplace. "It's taken quite a while to have things right, but returning guests make it all worthwhile. Some say they were here the day the deer came through the side door; others remember the day that Ann was accepted to Cornell. It's just great."

"Cazenovia is getting to be a very special event-minded community," Helen remarked. "We have the Winter Festival every February; the Lorenzo needlework exhibit the whole month of June; arts and crafts on our village green, plus a parade and fireworks over the Fourth of July; the Lorenzo driving competition, which takes place in July; the Franklin car reunion each year in August; and our own events here at the Lincklaen House at Christmastime.

"We serve afternoon tea here every day and it's the one time of the day that I make every effort to be back here to meet my guests and to introduce them to each other. It's one of the nicest times of the day at the Lincklaen House when we are all sitting around the fire or in the courtyard."

LINCKLAEN HOUSE, Cazenovia, N.Y. 13035; 315-655-3461. A 27-room village inn, 20 mi. east of Syracuse. Near several state parks, the Erie Canal Museum and the Canal Trail. European plan. Modified American plan upon request. Breakfast, lunch, and dinner served to travelers daily. Open year-round. Tennis, golf, bicycles, Alpine and xc skiing nearby. Helen Tobin, Innkeeper.

Directions: From west on N.Y. Thruway, take Exit 34A, follow Rte. 481 south, take Exit 3E and follow Rte. 92 east to Cazenovia. From east on N.Y. Thruway, take Exit 34 and follow Rte. 13 south to Cazenovia. From Rte. 81, take Exit 15 (LaFayette) and follow Rte. 20 East, 18 mi. to inn.

MILLHOF INN
Stephentown, New York

Gregory Tallet and I were off on a spin on my motorcycle. He had donned my extra helmet and his mother Ronnie Tallet had rushed in to the Millhof Inn for her camera so that we could be photographed before taking flight.

I had been looking forward to the twenty-mile trip from Stockbridge to Stephentown, New York, not only to see all the members of the Tallet family, who are the innkeepers at the Millhof Inn, but to view the new suite which had been added on to the original structure, along with some of the other features which Ronnie and Frank had told me about. It also provided me with the opportunity to learn about the progress of Debbie Tallet who is now at Rochester Institute of Technology studying hotel management. She has been working at the Yankee Clipper in Rockport, Massachusetts, during the past few years. Her sister Lisa, busy baking cookies for the Millhof's guests, also has the makings of an innkeeper.

The Millhof with its hand-carved and colorfully decorated railings and window shutters, is similar to many European inns that I have visited, particularly in Germany's Black Forest.

The word "millhof" really means millhouse, and this building was actually used as a sawmill for many years. Frank and Ronnie have made numerous alterations and additions, but the basic structure remains the same. Frank is from a French background and Ronnie was born in Yugoslavia, so that many of the furnishings and decorations are from the old country. Ronnie is quite an accomplished artist and has done a number of paintings which are displayed at the inn.

The European Alpine theme extends thoughout the inn and particularly to the lodging rooms, each of which is individually decorated and furnished with plants, books, and magazines. Frank has done almost all of the decorating and redesigning and, besides the new suite, in recent years he has also constructed the very attractive garden deck where breakfast is served in the summertime.

Ronnie does all of the cooking and among other things her blanquette de veau and chicken Alba are two of the most admired dishes.

"We're attracting people who want a quiet place, a place to relax," is the way Ronnie summed up the pleasant evolution of the Millhof Inn. "We have a community refrigerator for our guests and try to make things as comfortable and as pleasant as possible. The result is that guests are coming for longer stays. One couple actually got married in one of our lodging rooms.

"These have been wonderful years for us, especially since we put the swimming pool in. Although we are quite close to Tanglewood where the Boston Symphony plays every summer and Williamstown where there's an excellent summer theater, many of our guests find the atmosphere of rest and relaxation very pleasing. Many of them visit us for the first time traveling north and south on Route 22, but then come back for longer stays later on."

Now Gregory and I were speeding up the road to Hancock, Massachusetts, passing the Jiminy Peak Ski Area, and he told me what fun it is to ski there, and how he likes to ride the Alpine Slide in summer, and what it's like to grow up in a small village on the border between New York and Massachusetts. "I can tell the guests about all the back roads and also where to go cross-country skiing," he said.

"When I grow up there's two things I want. First, I want to be an innkeeper like my mother and father, and second, I want a motorcycle like yours."

MILLHOF INN, Route 43, Stephentown, N.Y. 12168; 518-733-5606. A 10-room middle European-style country inn. 14 mi. from Pittsfield and 12 mi. from Williamstown. A pleasant drive from both Tanglewood in the summer, and Jiminy Peak and Brodie Mountain in the winter. European plan. Full breakfast menu served daily. Afternoon tea served to guests. Many fine restaurants nearby. Open every day from May 26 through March 31. Swimming pool on grounds. Hiking, skiing, backroading, and all of the famous Berkshire recreational and cultural attractions nearby. No pets. Frank and Ronnie Tallet, Innkeepers.

Directions: From New York: exit the Taconic Parkway on Rte. 295. Travel east to Rte. 22 north. Turn east at Stephentown on Rte. 43. The inn is one mile on the left. From Boston: exit Mass. Turnpike at New Lebanon. North on Rte. 22 to Rte. 43, etc.

OLD DROVERS INN
Dover Plains, New York

Menus are some of my favorite reading, particularly menus from country inns. This time I was reading the portable menu at the Old Drovers Inn. It was hanging on one of the low beams next to the fireplace, but host Charlie Wilbur is prepared to move it to any corner of the dining room so that everyone may contemplate the culinary marvels awaiting his choice. There are the famous Old

Drovers cheddar cheese or cold lemon soups, also onion or Russian cabbage soup.

A second course could be, among others, a paté of duck livers, Portuguese sardines, or a shrimp cocktail. Choosing an entrée involves deciding between dishes like roast duckling, curry of turkey or lamb with chutney, beefsteak and kidney pie, shrimps rarebit, roast baby pheasant or partridge, or sweetbreads served in cognac.

The desserts that evening included one of the inn's famous sweets: fresh key lime pie. There was also strawberry meringue glacé, peach Melba, and pecan pie.

I've gone into some detail about his menu because luncheon and dinner are the main reasons why most people visit Old Drovers Inn. The atmosphere in the dining room is romantic, to say the least, with red leather benches, low wood ceilings, and an attractive combination of rough beams and stone walls. Lining the walls, just below the ceiling, is a collection of glass, copperware, and brass. An old musket hangs over the fireplace. Oversized glass hurricane lamps protect the candles on the tables, and it is great to come in on a chilly day to this beautiful room with a cheery fire crackling in the fireplace.

The atmosphere reminds me very much of English country house hotels I've visited.

The three somewhat sumptuous lodgings on the floors above are reached by a box-like staircase hung with marine prints. A most comfortable sitting room on the second floor has a fireplace, deep-cushioned chairs, and plenty of books and magazines. The Federal Room, where breakfast is served, is decorated with some interesting Hudson Valley murals.

There is a handsome, double-sized sleigh bed in the corner bedroom which also has its own fireplace and is wood-paneled. Another bedroom has twin beds with beautiful quilts, more handsome paneling, a tall chest of drawers, and a fireplace. The curved ceiling in one room indicates that before its conversion into a spacious bedroom, it must have been part of the ballroom. These rooms, by the way, are usually booked considerably ahead and are available only to guests who also plan to have dinner.

Dining at the Old Drovers Inn is an elegant, luxurious experience, and the prices reflect the skillful preparation of top-quality food and drinks, fine tableware, and expert service. Host Wilbur says, "Guests spending the night and taking dinner and a full breakfast should plan on spending $250 for two."

A dining experience like this must be savored in the most leisurely and unhurried fashion. But imagine, with all of this, I can still order browned turkey hash served with mustard sauce, and delicious, crispy, crunchy-on-the-outside-and-soft-on-the-inside popovers! Incidentally, Old Drovers' great turkey hash recipe is in the *CIBR Cookbook*.

OLD DROVERS INN, Dover Plains, New York 12522; 914-832-9311. A 3-room authentic 18th-century luxury country inn midway between New York City and the Berkshires just off New York Rte. 22. European plan. A full breakfast available to houseguests at à la carte prices. Closed on Tuesdays and Wednesdays and for 3 weeks prior to Dec. 30 each year. Luncheon served weekdays from noon to 3 p.m. Dinner served weekdays from 6-9 p.m., Saturdays and holidays from noon to 9:30 p.m., Sundays from 1-8:30 p.m. No credit cards. No amusements for children under 12. Charlie Wilbur, Host.

Directions: From New York follow Saw Mill River or Hutchinson River Pkwy. to I-684 which leads into Rte. 22 at Brewster. Go north to Dover Plains.

REDCOAT'S RETURN
Tannersville, New York

The year was 1976. I was visiting the Redcoat's Return for the very first time. Turning left at the traffic light in Tannersville off Route 23A, I followed Greene County Route 16 past some old mountain resorts, and after a couple of miles I could plainly see the inn to my right against the mountain backdrop. It was a white clapboard building with a friendly porch on two sides.

As I parked my car, an Irish setter bounded up to make me feel welcome. I felt even more welcome when I stepped inside the front door and found a roaring fire and an imposing moose head hanging over the mantelpiece. "Welcome to Redcoat's Return," said a voice on my left, and there was Peggy Wright. She and her husband Tom are the innkeepers of this rather fascinating country inn.

The first thing I did was to drop into a deep comfortable chair next to the fire and request a cup of tea. This gave me a chance to look around at this large living room which also doubles as a portion of the dining room. There were wooden shutters at the windows and a great many old prints, paintings, and photographs on the walls. Overhead the beams were exposed and it was a perfect place to be on a cold winter afternoon.

A tall sandy-haired man came striding into the room with his hand outstretched and said, "Hello, I'm Tom Wright. We're certainly glad to see you." I began to get a clue about the name of this inn from his very definite British accent, and when I inquired about it, he laughed and replied, "Oh, it is just our sense of humor. As you can see, I'm British, but I have been in this country a long time. Peggy and I thought this would be a great name for an inn in the Catskills."

"We were looking for a country inn to buy and came up here. We knew this just had to be the place," said Peggy. "We're 2000 feet high here and this section of the Catskills has some beautiful old homes and a private park nearby. When we saw the building and realized its potential, we all agreed we would leave the city and become country innkeepers."

While innkeeping may have been a new experience for the Wright family, Tom brings his background as a chef. He was with the Cunard Line for a number of years and on the *Queen Mary*. He was brought up in England and did his apprenticeship at the Dorchester Hotel in London. He does all of the cooking and some of his dishes include prime ribs with Yorkshire pudding, poached fillet of sole, roast duck in orange sauce, steak and kidney pie, and English-style fish and chips.

There are 12 rooms in this inn, all of them with wash basins, and several with private baths. "We've tried to preserve the best of what

is really appropriate for the building," explained Peggy, "and have made a few major changes that will provide more bathrooms." These lodging rooms are rather small and cozy and definitely of the country inn variety. There is an unusual small and intimate dining room on the first floor that has a very impressive collection of Hogarth prints including the "Rakes Progress" and other well-known works. It is a little room that inspires comment and conversation. This is in addition to the main dining room.

Most recently Tom and Peggy have built a beautiful gazebo on the front lawn as well as a formal croquet court. It is a lovely place to sit while you wait your turn. In the old days the hotel on this site had a gazebo and the Wrights have always wanted to replace it. It has a lovely pagoda shape and a cedar shake roof.

Perhaps I can arrange a croquet match between the staff of the Redcoat's Return and the Claremont Inn in Southwest Harbor, Maine.

THE REDCOAT'S RETURN, Dale Lane, Elka Park, N.Y. 12427; 518-589-6379. A 12-room English inn approx. 4 mi. from Tannersville, N.Y., in the heart of the Catskills Mts. Within a short drive of several ski areas and state hiking trails. European plan. Lodgings include breakfast. Dinner served daily except Thursdays; no lunches served. Open from Memorial Day to Easter. Closed 1 week in early Nov. Please call for details. No pets. Hiking, nature walks, trout fishing, croquet, skiing, swimming, ice skating, riding, tennis nearby. Tom and Peggy Wright, Innkeepers.

Directions: From the New York Thruway, going north, use Exit 20; going south, use Exit 21. Follow 23A to Tannersville; turn left at traffic light onto County Rd. 16. Follow signs to Police Center, 4½ mi. Turn right on Dale Lane.

The main attraction in Skaneateles, the inn notwithstanding, is the lake, and the best way to see it is to drive south down the east shore and then north up the west. Joining the two lakeside routes at the southern inlet is Glen Haven Road, a twisting, sometimes narrow passageway, named for a famous sanitorium and resort located here over a century ago.

Skaneateles Lake is spring-fed and in 1846, two abolitionist doctors founded the Glen Haven Hotel and Water Cure on the western shore of the inlet. The cure was a blend of hot and cold baths in the spring water, daily exercise, and strict diet, and was reputed to heal a variety of ills from rheumatism to nervous troubles. Men wore skull caps soaked in the water, and women, for reasons unexplained, were required to wear bloomers, controversial, if not downright scandalous. Nationally known by the late 1800s, the Cure boasted a 4-story, 75-room hotel, accommodating 200 guests, and several steamships ran regular routes between Glen Haven and Skaneateles. Automobile travel is blamed for a subsequent decline in popularity, and the hotel was torn down in 1911.

The inlet today is placid and sleepy, a well-kept secret. A small restaurant, named perhaps for it's famous precursor, overlooks the lake from the southeast shore, and just to the south, a tiny building furnished with potbellied stoves and antique wooden desks serves

*as the local public library, historical society, and school. As you wind
north along the west shore, a converted Pennsylvania Railroad car
stands in stark contrast to the Victorian houses nestled on the
hillsides, and the views of the lake are quite spectacular all the way
back to the village.*

*Take Route 41 south to Scott. Turn right on Glen Haven Road
and follow it north to the inlet, then northwest to Route 41-A. Take
41-A north to Skaneateles (approx. 45-50 miles).*

William and Joy Eberhardt
The Sherwood Inn
Skaneateles, New York

*A wonderful back-road walk near the hotel would be the
quarter-mile down the pier. As you feast your eyes on Tampa Bay,
you can stop to admire the gorgeous yachts at the Marina or step
back in time at St. Petersburg's small but excellent historical
museum, with artifacts dating back to the original Indian settlers
here. Next door is the MGM exhibit of the* HMS Bounty *used in
the movie* Mutiny on the Bounty. *Stroll a little farther and you come
to Spa Beach, where people sunbathe and go for a swim. Across the
street is the Senior Citizens Center named for Doc Webb, St. Pete's
pioneering retailer. It is no rocking chair operation. They have
dances and all kinds of active doin's there all year.*

*On the end of the pier is our famous inverted pyramid. This
remarkable building holds all kinds of interesting things. There is a
fine seafood restaurant called Pierside, and also an old-fashioned
ice cream parlor. From the observation deck on the roof, you can
see beautiful views of St. Petersburg and Tampa Bay. There is also a
fine laser sculpture which is beamed down the pier toward St.
Petersburg. This is lovely every evening. Surrounding this pyramid
are many shops and eating establishments. It is called The Isle of
Nations, and the offerings feature merchandise and foods from
around the world. There is also a stage that offers free entertainment
during the day. This is a very interesting walk or drive or, if you like,
you may travel by the tram that operates along the pier concourse.
It's a fun ride and it's free! This walk begins just a block and a half
from the Albemarle.*

The Tucker Family
The Albemarle Hotel
St. Petersburg, Florida

THE SHERWOOD INN
Skaneateles, New York

Talk about a clear day! I stood on the front steps of The Sherwood Inn looking as far down Skaneateles Lake as I could see. There were a few early-morning fishermen and, even as I watched, a couple of swimmers came to the beach located right in front of the inn. A few paces to the left the Skaneateles excursion boat was getting brightened up for its many day-trips to the other end of the lake. The two wren houses were already hives of activity, as well.

Skaneateles is on Route 20 which runs east and west in central New York State. It's a pleasant village oriented to the lake with several impressive old buildings whose integrity has been preserved although the town has been modernized. The center of activity is undoubtedly The Sherwood Inn.

This morning I returned to the lobby to find a very unusual display of crafts, all made by craftsmen from Skaneateles and vicinity. For example, there was a display of wooden blocks which were put together in the form of a small village. This is part of a continuing effort by the inn to bring Skaneateles crafts and arts to the attention of the traveling public.

In one corner of the lobby, the morning continental breakfast for inn guests was laid out with some tempting sweet rolls and pots of coffee and orange juice. On the piano, a print of the inn was displayed. These prints are also sold in a shop adjacent to the inn.

The two dining rooms, which were so busy the previous night, now were quiet. However, the sunporch was occupied by many guests partaking of a full breakfast.

Coming as quietly as possible down the main stairway was a family of four, including two little daughters. They had cameras and bags, and went out through the lobby to continue what was obviously a vacation trip.

There are eleven lodging rooms and three apartments at the inn. The honeymoon suite is done in shades of blue and the patterns of the quilt on the four-poſter canopy bed match both the draperies and the wallpaper. There is a beautiful view of the lake from almost every bedroom. Like many other New York state hostelries, The Sherwood Inn started its life as a stagecoach tavern and fortunately after seveal ups and downs has finally achieved an even greater reputation as a contemporary village inn and a holiday destination.

I was delighted to see that *Travel and Leisure* featured Skaneateles in a recent edition and the Sherwood Inn received a prominent portion of attention.

The article, which started off at the Sherwood Inn, paid particular attention to the Federal period antiques, oriental rugs and peg-board floors, with a special mention of the antique dollhouse and the fireplaces that send a warm glow into the lobby during the late fall and early winter. Other attractions in Skaneateles are also mentioned including some of the shops of the town and, of course, Skaneateles Lake, one of the most beautiful of the Finger Lakes.

THE SHERWOOD INN, 26 West Genessee St., Skaneateles, N.Y. 13152; 315-685-3405. A 15-room village inn on the shores of Lake Skaneateles in the Finger Lakes district of New York State. Continental breakfast included in room tariff. Lunch and dinner served daily to travelers. Open every day except Christmas. Tennis, swimming, golf, and indoor winter ice skating available nearby. Near Everson Museum, Barrow Art Gallery, and William Seward House. William and Joy Eberhardt, Innkeepers.

Directions: From New York State Thruway use Weedsport exit and follow Rte. 34 south to Auburn (6 mi.). Turn east on Rte. 20, 7 mi. to Skaneateles. Inn is located in center of village.

I do not include lodging rates in the descriptions, for the very nature of an inn means that there are lodgings of various sizes, with and without baths, in and out of season, and with plain and fancy decoration. Travelers should call ahead and inquire about the availability and rates of the many different types of rooms.

1770 HOUSE
East Hampton, Long Island, New York

"Acquiring the 1770 House was part of a longtime dream for us," recounted Sid Perle. "We spent many months searching outer Long Island for just the right place for the ideal country inn." Sid and I were seated in the main living room of the inn where some of the most recently acquired pieces are from the old Easthampton Post Office. They have been used very cleverly. There was one window that was labeled, "General Delivery." Another one for money orders now has a tiny television set that disappears completely, if necessary.

We were joined momentarily by Miriam Perle, who is the chef at the inn. She formerly ran a cooking school in Great Neck for twelve years and studied earlier at the Cordon Bleu in Paris.

The menu changes weekly and, with the exception of desserts, is a complete meal. The appetizers include such unusual items as cold asparagus tarragon, leek and mushroom tart, fettucini al pesto, and a French fish chowder. The salads are different every week, as are the salad dressings.

I asked Miriam about the main dishes. "Because we're here on the outer edge of Long Island where lots of fresh fish are available we always have a choice of two or three fish dishes. Tonight there is a lemon-herb weakfish and a fresh soft-shell crab amandine. We also have steamed sole Chinois, swordfish al pesto, and other Long Island fish specialties. By the way, tonight we are serving roast duck with a lemon ginger glaze." She knows my great love of roast duckling and knew that she had, indeed, made a conquest.

Downstairs in the Tap Room there is a beautiful beehive fireplace, and many old trivets and other artifacts on the wall. The atmosphere is quite similar to an English pub.

"Your readers might be interested in the fact that on Thanksgiving we have hors d'oeuvres and soup in the Tap Room, then everyone goes upstairs to the main dining room for dinner, and dessert is offered in the library—but not until we have all had a walk in the village!"

The bedrooms are delightful. Several of them have canopied beds and combinations of French and American Victorian antiques, including several bedside tables with marble tops. They are all very romantic, and one in particular on the ground floor overlooking the garden struck my fancy as being an ideal honeymoon suite.

Incidentally, guests at the 1770 House can also be booked at the Mill Garth in Amagansett, just a short distance away. It has fetching rustic cottages, some of which have their own cooking conveniences.

Sid said there have been several references to my quotation from

Owen Meredith, which is occasionally used on their menus:
> *We may live without friends, we may live without books,*
> *but civilized man cannot live without cooks.*

Sid put an arm around Miriam. "I always tell them that I'm the luckiest guy in the world because I'm married to one of the world's great cooks."

1770 HOUSE, 143 Main St., East Hampton, Long Island, N.Y. 11937; 516-324-1770. An elegant 6-room village inn near the eastern end of Long Island. Open all year. Dinner served Friday through Tuesday during the summer months. During the off-summer months, dinner served on Friday and Saturday only. During July and August, weekend reservations made for 4 days only and mid-week reservations for 3 days only. Convenient to many cultural and recreational diversions, including antiquing and backroading. Not comfortable for children under 14. No pets. The Perle Family, Innkeepers.

Directions: From New York City: take the Long Island Expressway to Exit 70, and then turn south to Rte. 27 East, which is the main street of East Hampton. The inn is located diagonally across the street from Guild Hall.

I do not include lodging rates in the descriptions, for the very nature of an inn means that there are lodgings of various sizes, with and without baths, in and out of season, and with plain and fancy decoration. Travelers should call ahead and inquire about the availability and rates of the many different types of rooms.

SPRINGSIDE INN
Auburn, New York

It was a beautiful summer night, and the lampposts that light the way through the larch, silver maple, and flowering crab trees along the circular roadway leading to the front of the Springside Inn were all decorated with gay hanging baskets.

I walked through the parking lot where the unusual number of cars reminded me that summer dinner theater is offered at the inn, and I could hear the strains of music from *South Pacific*. I passed the little duck pond and as soon as I walked through the front door of the familiar red building I was taken in tow by Barbara Dove.

"Oh, I'm so glad you're here this evening," she said. "Bill and I want to talk to you about the plans for our trip to Germany." It was a very busy evening so she showed me to a table in the Surrey Room, and much to my delight my waitress would be Melissa Dove, Barbara and Bill's daughter. Melissa said that her sister Lois was also on the staff.

From among the many temptations on the menu, including lobster Newburg and filet of sole Florentine, I chose the roast duckling. The first course was a nice big bowl of whole shrimp on a bed of ice with a delicious sauce.

This high-ceilinged dining room, where I had dinner on my first visit back in the late '60s or early '70s, was decorated with flags from France, Switzerland, Italy, Britain, and Canada. Melissa, Lois, and the other waitresses were wearing black dresses with the white bib aprons and white duster caps.

Barbara bustled back and said that there were a few rooms where guests had not yet checked in and would I like to see them? Off we flew. Each of the lodging rooms is decorated differently, with one in varying shades of pink with matching bedspreads and curtains. Another room has twin beds, Victorian furniture, and lamps with red bows. By way of contrast, the room on the top floor is done in shades of beige and yellow with formal valances at the window, a Tiffany-type lamp, hooked rugs, and twin beds.

On the way downstairs, we paused for a moment where the open staircase is L-shaped and once again talked about how many weddings are held at the Springside and how many bridal bouquets have been tossed from this particular point on the stairs.

The duck and I arrived at the table simultaneously (some more of Bill's magic), and I had a moment for a short conversation with Melissa.

"We have many guests from all over the United States and Canada," she remarked. "Many of them come from Toronto and Montreal. They seem especially pleased to get a jar of our homemade salad dressing to take home."

The Springside Inn on the northern end of Owasco Lake is one of the most beautiful spots imaginable. Autumn is particularly enjoyable for a drive along the lakeside roads where there are many farm stands offering apples, pumpkins, pears, and other Finger Lakes fruits and vegetables.

Later on, both Bill and Barbara joined me for a late dessert and we also peeked in at the dinner-theater where an attractive young actress was singing "I'm In Love With A Wonderful Guy." Bill explained that the dinner-theater was so popular that they're booked every night.

SPRINGSIDE INN, 41 West Lake Rd., Auburn, N.Y. 13021; 315-252-7247. A 7-room country inn, 1 mi. south of Auburn with a view of Owasco Lake. In the heart of the historical Finger Lakes. Lodgings include continental breakfast. Some rooms with shared bath. Open every day. Boating, swimming, bicycles on grounds. Golf, riding, Alpine and xc skiing nearby. Bill and Barbara Dove, Innkeepers.

Directions: From N.Y. Thruway, take Exit 40 and follow Rte. 34 south through downtown Auburn to Rte. 38. Follow Rte. 38 south to traffic circle at Lake and take 2nd exit right at West Shore of Owasco Lake. Drive 1/4 mi. to inn.

Note: literally moments before this book went to press I learned to my great sorrow of the untimely passing of Barbara Dove.

I shall always remember Barbara just as I described her in this account . . . . an enthusiastic, involved, warm individual who loved innkeeping.

THREE VILLAGE INN
Stony Brook, New York

It was about nine o'clock on a very soft summer's night. I walked through the low doorway of the inn to the terrace with its white wrought iron furniture and decided to take a short stroll before retiring. Through the wonderful old trees there was a cluster of lights which proved to be the marina with a great collection of cruisers, speedboats, luxury yachts, outboards, and sailboats. They gleamed white in the floodlight, and what was passive and quiescent tonight would be back in action tomorrow. I happened to meet other guests at the inn and we sat down on a handy bench and started comparing notes.

"We expected something good," they said, "but I don't think we expected to be so removed and serene. It is like a little country village. Imagine a clapboard colonial built by an old sea captain—low ceilings, green shutters, geraniums, and ivy climbing up the trees.

"Something that surprised us is the Long Island seafood. I have always known there were fish in Long Island Sound, but I never expected such a variety."

They plunged on. "I'll tell you what impressed us tremendously besides the paintings, prints, antiques, and old Long Island atmosphere . . . it's the history of the whole area. The Robertses, particularly Whitney, gave us a touch of it today, but I think we could stay here for at least three days and not experience it all. I just love that sweet little Caroline church with its ancient greystones and white picket fence."

The Three Village Inn is located in one of the most interesting and well-preserved towns on Long Island, about 60 miles from New York City. In recent years, very attractive cottages have been built facing the Yacht Club and marina.

From my very first visit I realized that Nelson (he's the head chef) and Monda Roberts have placed a great deal of emphasis on the food. They are very particular about some things, including not using foil for baked potatoes, and baking them in rotation through the evening. Vegetables are fresh whenever they are available. The menu is quite extensive and includes a great deal of beef, pork, veal, and lamb as well as the fresh seafood. The extra touch of serving sherbet with the main meal is something I have always enjoyed. Desserts include things such as apple crisp, homemade cakes, Indian pudding, and delicious fruit pies and tarts. They are all made in the inn's kitchen.

There had been several bedrooms added since my previous visit. The one in which I stayed was accessible to the handicapped. The total of rooms was now twenty-three.

"In the off-season we have a lot of people from Manhattan come out for a restful weekend, because everyone is working at such a pace these days," Monda told me. "During the week visitors to SUNY at Stony Brook are frequent guests. During the rest of the year we have visitors from Germany, Japan, Switzerland, England, and Australia—many of them connected with university functions. By the way, it is possible to come from Kennedy Airport to the Three Village Inn by limousine for a relatively reasonable rate. We can make arrangements."

Nelson and Monda Roberts and their son, Whitney, have been at the Three Village Inn since 1946, and since 1978 they have been the innkeeper/owners. It's given me a great deal of pleasure to be visiting it since 1974.

THREE VILLAGE INN, 150 Main St., Stony Brook, L.I., N.Y. 11790; 516-751-0555. A 9-room village inn with 23 adjacent cottage/ motel accommodations, 5 mi. from Port Jefferson, on Long Island's historic north shore. Near the museums of Stony Brook. European plan. Lunch and dinner served to travelers daily. Closed Christmas. Golf, swimming, and boating nearby. Special attention given to handicapped persons. No pets. Nelson and Monda Roberts, Innkeepers.

Directions: From L.I. Expressway, take Exit 62 and travel north on Nichols Rd. to Rte. 25A. Turn left on Rte. 25A and proceed to next light. Turn right onto Main St. and travel straight ahead to inn. Available from New England via L.I. ferries from Bridgeport during the summer. Ferry reservations advisable. (N.Y.: 516-473-0286; Conn.: 203-367-8571.)

SWISS HUTTE
Hillsdale, New York

Tom and Linda Breen are people of many enthusiasms. Happily enough most of them can be found here at this Alpine country inn located in the southwest corner of the Berkshires in a valley formed by mountains reminiscent of the Bavarian Alps where Linda was born. (I am happy to say I had a very pleasant visit with her brother in Munich a few years ago.)

Nestled among the firs and hemlocks, the inn's architecture has a distinctly Alpine feel that impresses first-time guests almost without fail. Dinner guests, as well as those enjoying overnight accommodations, have the pleasure of an unobstructed view of

Catamount ski area

Catamount Ski Area which is very spectacular in the wintertime, and equally so during the other seasons. The uphill lifts and the start of the cross-country ski trails are literally within walking distance of the inn's front door.

On a lovely July afternoon I took the short drive from Stockbridge to Great Barrington and then bore west on Route 44 towards New York State. After turning at the Swiss Hutte sign I followed the road down a gentle slope past the swimming pool, the tennis courts, and the putting green to the swift running brook where masses of flowers caught my eye.

Flowers are one of Tom's enthusiasms. He has not only a beautiful rose garden, but a perennial garden with over 150 different plants providing a serene country atmosphere. Many is the time I've found Tom in his chef's whites attending his beloved flowers, and at the same time keeping a watchful eye on preparations for the evening meal in his spotless kitchen.

A very attractive gazebo on the bank of the pond creates an almost Japanese effect. Large boulders placed around the shoreline are interspersed with plantings and after night falls there are gay colored lights illuminating the trees.

Accommodations at the Swiss Hutte are in the main inn where there are country inn-type rooms, and in chalet-type motel units, each with its own balcony and an excellent view of the mountains.

Apart from the natural beauty, perhaps the inn is best known for its food, another great enthusiasm shared by Linda and Tom. Both lunch and dinner are leisurely affairs with individually prepared dishes. Since the time of my first visit in early 1970 I have always enjoyed many of the mid-European specialties such as Weiner schnitzel; however, among other menu items are French pancakes filled with chicken, sweetbreads in Bèarnaise sauce, sauerbraten, and veal chops Normande. The French and Swiss specialties have received many awards.

Linda is very particular about the salads. "We feel that they must be fresh and cool and we try to have a perfect combination of oil and vinegar along with the condiments," she said. "They are delicious when they are eaten with fresh, hot French bread."

Among the desserts, which are included in the price of the main dish, are crème carmel, French apple torte cheesecake, and a super-delicious raspberry cream pie.

Other diversions to be enjoyed at the Swiss Hutte include tennis, swimming, hiking, downhill and cross-country skiing, and many other seasonal attractions. In summer, Tanglewood, Jacob's Pillow, and the Berkshire Playhouse are just a few miles away. The Berkshire and nearby New York State backroading is exceptional with dirt roads that lead through the forest right at the inn's front door.

SWISS HUTTE, Hillsdale, N.Y. 12529; 518-325-3333. A 21-room Alpine country inn overlooking Catamount ski area, 6 mi. from Gt. Barrington, Mass. Modified American plan omits lunch. Breakfast, lunch and dinner served to travelers daily. Closed month of April and from Nov. 15 to Dec. 15. Pool, tennis, putting green, Alpine and xc skiing on grounds. Tom and Linda Breen, Innkeepers.

Directions: From Boston, travel on Mass. Tpke. and take Exit 2. Follow Rte. 102 to Rte. 7. Proceed on Rte. 7 to Rte. 23. From New York City, follow Taconic Pkwy. and Rte. 23. From Albany, follow N.Y. Thruway and Taconic Pkwy. Inn is 10 mi. east of Pkwy. on Rte. 23.

COLLIGAN'S STOCKTON INN
Stockton, New Jersey

Obvious though it may seem, it was quite natural for me to be whistling a few bars of Richard Rodger's melody, "There's a Small Hotel," because here I was at the very "wishing well" that inspired the Lorenz Hart lyrics—the wishing well at Colligan's Stockton Inn.

Evidently there's been an accommodation here on this site since about 1710, although the present building, or most of it, dates back about 150 years. The stone walls have the wonderful weathered look that comes with Pennsylvania-New Jersey stone, and the mansard roof indicates once again a Victorian addition in later years.

The five dining rooms have the narrow windows, typical of their time, set into the thick walls. Five fireplaces bring a cheery atmosphere to the low ceilings and random-width floors.

I was making notes about all of these features when my good friend of many years, Todd Drucquer, came bounding in, and I was caught up by his wonderful ebullience as we started on a tour of what for him was a newly acquired inn. Todd is also innkeeper of the Pump House Inn in Canadensis, Pennsylvania *(CIBR)*.

"First of all," he said, as we walked into the tavern section, "this has been here for the entire life of the inn. It's where the local townspeople come at the end of the day and we don't want to change very much, because we think it's lovely just the way it is. It belongs to the town, and like an Englishman's pub it's 'their' place."

We went into the first of the dining rooms. "Everyone wants to know if we're going to do anything about the murals," he said. "We're not going to touch a single one, because they are absolutely priceless. They were painted a number of years ago on the plaster walls and they depict the countryside as it was during the early part of the 19th century. Here's a section showing the ferry landing down at the riverbank. The murals are one of the reasons I fell in love with this place."

We continued on into a large dining room with glass on two sides. "Actually there are three areas in the inn," he told me. "There's the old inn building itself, then this room which has an open feeling, and we have entertainment here. Outside, we have the Old World Garden with waterfalls, hanging plants, two trout pools that supply fresh trout for our table, and lots of *gemutlichkeit*. As you see, it's an open garden with a roof overhead and we're open for lunch and dinner from Memorial Day until Labor Day." The atmosphere here reminded me very much of suburban Vienna restaurants.

We returned to the front dining room, and I asked about the menu. "We serve American cuisine with continental overtones. There are dishes like crabcakes, prime ribs of beef, snapper soup, clam chowder, and pheasant, quail and venison in season. I'm bringing in some of the Pump House favorites, too, like shrimp in beer batter, stuffed fresh sole, and soft-shell crabs. As you well know, we think the cuisine is of prime importance."

During 1983 a few accommodations in the main building and adjoining carriage house will be made available.

So, Colligan's Stockton Inn, which has had a most interesting and varied career, can now look forward to many, many more years. Knowing Todd Drucquer's penchant for beautiful country inns and enticing menus, I'd say that he dropped a silver dollar in the wishing well himself. His wish came true.

COLLIGAN'S STOCKTON INN, Route 29, Stockton, N.J. 08559; 609-397-1250. A traditional inn located in a Delaware River village. Lunch and dinner served every day. Open all year except Christmas Day. All of the scenic and cultural attractions of nearby Bucks County, Pa., and New Jersey are within a very short distance. No pets. Todd and Penny Drucquer, Innkeepers.

Directions: From New York City: Take New Jersey Turnpike south to Exit 10, then follow I-287 north of Sommerville, exiting to Rte. 22 west. Go 2½ miles and then take Rte. 202 south, past Flemington to the Delaware River. Use the last exit in New Jersey marked "Rte. 29, Lambertville and Stockton." Go 3 miles north on 29 to Stockton. From Philadelphia: Follow I-95 north to the Delaware River. Cross the Delaware to the first exit in New Jersey marked "29 Trenton/Lambertville." Follow 29 north through Lambertville, approximately 17 miles to Stockton.

THE MAINSTAY
Cape May, New Jersey

Long before the words, "bed and breakfast" came into vogue in the United States, Tom and Sue Carroll, as young as they may seem, were among the innovators of a unique travel style. I met them in the early part of the '70s and in the intervening years I have had many enjoyable visits with them and have documented their progress in the pages of this book.

At the time of my first visit, The Mainstay was located a few blocks away from its present site in a very pleasant Victorian summer home. However, for the last few years it has occupied an Italianate Victorian villa built in 1856 by wealthy southern planters as an elegant gambling club. Apocryphal though the story may be, it is said the first operator of the club, a Mississippi showboat minstrel, employed a lady to rock on the front porch and watch for the police. The legend goes that if she rocked violently the gamblers inside would quickly stash their evidence and when the police arrived they would be having a harmless musicale.

After such a flamboyant beginning the house was sold in 1896 to a sedate Philadelphia family who added the back wing and entertained some of the great and near-great of Philadelphia society during the many years that followed.

Today The Mainstay is a lovely guest house in one of the most unusual remaining Victorian environments, the town of Cape May. I understand that there are over 600 Victorian buildings in Cape May in various stages of restoration and preservation.

"Breakfast at Nine, Tea at Four," is the title of a small booklet containing among other things a short history of the inn and several very enticing breakfast menus. Breakfast is the only meal served at the inn; in warm weather it is offered on the broad veranda, and on cool mornings, in the dining room. "Tea at Four" pertains to the tea that is offered after the house tours that are given four days a week for both inn guests and interested visitors. The booklet also contains recipes for breads and tea dainties.

Overnight accommodations vary. Rooms are named for famous Americans who visited Cape May and many of them are quite large and furnished in ostentatious Victorian splendor. There are also several cozy little rooms that were once used for servants' quarters.

Tom and Sue renovated the beautiful old house next to the Mainstay which has at least four more bedrooms available, all decorated in the Victorian manner. Each of these rooms has its own bathroom. The Clara Barton room (yes, she visited Cape May) has a queen-sized walnut bed, a matching dresser, and a bay window overlooking the original edifice of the Mainstay. The Bret Harte room, named for the American novelist, has four windows across the front, a queen-sized bed, a sitting area, and an entrance to the main porch. Still another room in the new section is named for Stephen Decatur. A new sitting room has also been added.

I stayed in the Abraham Lincoln room which commemorates his visit to Cape May in 1849. He was the first of five presidents to vacation in Cape May during the 19th century.

"Many people ask us since we live in this Victorian atmosphere if we consider ourselves Victorians," Sue commented. "We definitely do not. We love the decorations and all the other evidences of Victoriana but we are totally 20th-century people."

So, the Mainstay continues to grow and prosper. I would suggest reservations be made well in advance.

THE MAINSTAY INN, 635 Columbia Avenue, Cape May, N.J. 08204; 609-884-8690. A 12-room inn in a well-preserved Victorian village just one block from the ocean. Breakfast served to house-guests. Open every day from April to October; weekends in March and November. Boating, swimming, fishing, bicycles, riding, golf, tennis, and hiking nearby. Not suitable for small children. No pets. No credit cards; personal checks accepted. Tom and Sue Carroll, Innkeepers.

Directions: From Philadelphia take the Walt Whitman Bridge to the Atlantic City Expy. Follow the Atlantic City Expy. to exit for Garden State Pkwy., south. Go south on the Pkwy. which ends in Cape May. The Pkwy. becomes Lafayetts St.; turn left at first light onto Madison. Proceed 3 blocks and turn right onto Columbia. Proceed 3 blocks to inn on right side.

THE WOOLVERTON INN
Stockton, New Jersey

It was a lovely September Sunday noon at The Woolverton Inn. I had driven up from Washington and followed I-95 through Wilmington and Philadelphia, keeping my eye peeled for some unexpected detours. Turning off on Route 32 north along the Delaware Canal, I crossed the river at Lambertville, and followed the river road on the New Jersey side north to Stockton.

Sunday noon at The Woolverton Inn is a sad-happy time. It is sad for the guests who have had such a wonderful weekend and must leave to return to the city before the traffic gets too heavy. The "city" in this case could be either New York or Philadelphia since Stockton is almost midway between the two. It is a happy time for those fortunate guests who have still another day or two to enjoy the ideal September weather and take their leisure in the Delaware Valley on the many back roads, bicycle paths, or pleasant country walks.

I found Deborah Clark (known to almost everyone as "Debo") in the kitchen and she sat down to have another half cup of tea before clearing away the breakfast dishes and continuing on with the daily duties of an innkeeper. "It's been a wonderful weekend," she said, buttering another piece of the still-warm breakfast breads. "We had members of a wedding party staying here, including the parents of both the bride and the groom who came from distant points. In fact, they made arrangements and reservations to return in the early spring."

I think that's one of the key reasons why The Woolverton Inn has already made so many new friends. The setting of course aids immeasurably.

The construction is of undressed stone, except for the walls around the doors and windows which are chiselled smooth. They are at least two feet thick. All of the parlors and bedrooms are carefully furnished with period antiques and each one expresses an early American individuality. One of the most popular is the master suite which has a canopy bed; however, all of the bedrooms are a delight.

Debo, who is the innkeeper-hostess, explained that the inn does not serve any meal except breakfast. "There are many well-known restaurants in the area," she explained. "However we make special arrangements to be sure that even late arrivals need never go to bed hungry.

"This is one of my favorite times of year," she exclaimed, "the deer slip quietly across the lawn to eat the fallen apples in the orchard and our guests like the fun of walking along the river tow path or relaxing on the porches and patio overlooking the garden. And nearby are a great many craft and antique shops, as well. We've already lighted fires in the living room and library and many of our guests are rediscovering what fun it is to read books and enjoy the warmth of the fireplace."

THE WOOLVERTON INN, R.D. 3, Box 233-A, Stockton, New Jersey 08559; 609-397-0802. A 10-room pastorally-oriented inn on the east side of the Delaware River within just a few moments of historic Bucks County, Pa. Open year-round. Breakfast is the only meal offered on a regular basis and is included in the price of the rooms. Bocci and croquet on grounds. Swimming, tubing, canoeing, tennis, golf, horseback riding, and wonderful history-laden back roads including visits to Washington's Crossing nearby. No pets. George and Ann Hackl, Proprietors; Deborah Clark, Innkeeper.

Directions: From New York City: Take New Jersey Turnpike south to Exit 10, then follow I-287 north of Sommerville, exiting to Rte. 22 west. Go 2½ miles and then take Rte. 202 south, past Flemington to the Delaware River. Use the last exit in New Jersey marked "Rte. 29, Lambertville and Stockton." Go 3 miles north on 29 to Stockton and turn right on Rte. 523, up hill ¼ of a mile to a sharp left-hand turn—the inn sign. The inn is the second driveway on the right. From Philadelphia: Follow I-95 north to the Delaware River. Cross the Delaware to the first exit in New Jersey marked "29 Trenton/Lambertville." Follow 29 north through Lambertville, approximately 17 miles to Stockton.

One of the most picturesque parts of our area centers around the only covered bridge left in New Jersey. Taking Route 523 south from Flemington you arrive in Sergeantsville, where homebaked breads, quiches, and other goodies can be purchased at the crossroads Country Store. At the intersection, take a right; drive about one mile past beautiful farms and you will come to the Covered Bridge, which spans the Wickecheoke Creek, one of the major streams in the area feeding into the Delaware River. Take a left just before the bridge and meander down Lower Creek Road (it is unmarked). Although the land is all privately owned, people generally do not mind considerate visitors taking advantage of the many lovely picnic spots. About two miles down the road, on the left after the road crosses the stream, there is a wonderful swimming hole in the lee of high, hemlock-covered sandstone palisades. The stream is heavily stocked with trout in the spring. In another mile, the road joins the River Road in Stockton (Route 29). Take a left and on your right will be the old stone Prallsville Mill standing at just the point where the Wickecheoke Creek crashes over a waterfall to join the majestic Delaware River. Along the river, an old railroad bed has been taken up to make a splendid walking trail. Returning to Route 29 you will almost immediately come on Woolverton Road on the left (again unmarked, but it is directly across from "Stockton Auto Body" on the right). The Woolverton Inn is up at the top of the hill on the left.

Deborah Clark
The Woolverton Inn
Stockton, New Jersey

Most of our guests drive to Cape May via the Garden State Parkway. However, a more interesting road is Route 9, which runs almost parallel to the Parkway. From the Ocean City Exit on the parkway, drive onto Route 9, probably one of the oldest roads in New Jersey. Here and there all along the road are interesting examples of 18th- and 19th-century architecture. Route 9 is also dotted with "mom and pop" antique shops, some specializing in "junktiques," but others with some surprisingly fine pieces.

Located on the west side of Route 9, in Swainton, is Leamings Run Botanical Garden, a beautiful island of peace in south Jersey. There are 27 beautifully designed gardens, ponds, a fernery, and a Colonial farm with an herb garden. At any time from June through October, visitors can view this wonderful place.

A bit farther south on Route 9 in the Cape May courthouse is our county historical museum. Housed in a lovely 18th-century building is a very interesting collection of furniture, farm implements, old prints, maps, and articles pertaining to the history of south Jersey. There is also a genealogical library.

Route 9 becomes Route 109 and joins the parkway just before it comes into Cape May.

Tom and Sue Carroll
The Mainstay Inn
Cape May, New Jersey

Our very favorite back road is one that we have shared with many, many guests. The destination is a small historic village nestled in the Helderberg Mountains. The eleven-mile drive is truly scenic, with lovely Catskill Mountain views all the way. The village itself was once a prosperous milling community. The beautiful homes and churches are a true find for anyone with an interest in 18th- or 19th-century architecture. My favorite reason for visiting the village is the State Preserve, located just at the end of town. The Preserve is like a well-kept secret! There are trails to walk leading to a quiet, peaceful lake, and an absolutely gorgeous waterfall that's perfect for walking under and up in the summertime! We like to direct people on alternate routes going and returning. Both routes offer antique shops and country stores that shouldn't be missed. One country store boasts an inventory of over 1,000 items—anything anyone could possibly want from fresh cut flowers to new snow tires!

Barbara and Laura Stevens
Greenville Arms
Greenville, New York

THE CAMERON ESTATE INN
Mount Joy, Pennsylvania

Betty Groff was telling me about the history of The Cameron Estate Inn: "Doctor John Watson built the mansion in 1805," she explained, as we strolled through the impressive wooded area that surrounds the inn. "It later became the country home of Simon Cameron, Lincoln's first secretary of war who was also a four-time U.S. senator and ambassador to Russia. He and his son Donald, who succeeded Simon as senator and also served as secretary of war under President Grant, entertained many notables of American history here."

We stopped for a moment and she pointed out the many trout darting about in a woodland stream. "We stock this stream with trout which our guests may fish for," she said, "and the chef will cook their catch to order." We stopped for a moment on an old stone bridge and she continued the narrative, "As you know, Abe and I live right here in Mount Joy and we've been operating the Groff Farm Restaurant for quite a few years. But we've always wanted to own an inn and we've had our envious eye for a long time on this estate which was owned by Elizabethtown College and used as a conference center."

Agreeing to meet for dinner later on, Betty and I separated at the front door of the inn, a most impressive early 19th-century red brick mansion with attractive dormer windows on the third floor. I speculated mentally that the broad veranda which runs around three sides of the inn probably had been added later in that century.

Stepping inside, I found the interior to be exactly what one would have expected in a mansion: large living rooms, a library, generously sized bedrooms, some with canopy beds and a great many with fireplaces. There are many oriental rugs and period furnishings chosen by Abe and Betty to define the historic significance of the inn. These are fitting complements to the fine paneling and marble embellishments.

Dinner that evening in the main dining room was once again a baronial experience, with excellent service, delicate china, and fine silverware against pristine napery. The menu included filet of brook trout belle meuniere, calves liver Americaine, Wiener schnitzel, veal steak sauté "Simon Cameron," medallions of pork in a sauce chasseur, and breast of chicken in a piquant tarragon sauce—an interesting contrast to the dinner offered at Groff's Farm Restaurant.

Imagine my surprise and delight to find that whilst I was enjoying the splendid repast and good conversation, my room had been made ready for the night with the covers of my bed turned down.

CAMERON ESTATE INN, R.D. #1, Box 305, Donegal Springs Road, Mount Joy, Pa. 17752; 717-653-1773. An elegant 14-room inn in a former mansion 4½ mi. from both Mount Joy and Elizabethtown, Pa. Eight rooms with private baths. Convenient to all of the attractions in the Pennsylvania Dutch country as well as the Hershey and Lancaster museums, art galleries, and theaters. It is located halfway between Gettysburg and Valley Forge. Breakfast is included with the cost of the room; lunch and dinner served every day except Sunday and Christmas. Open from Jan. 11 to Jan. 2. Not recommended for young children. No pets. Abram and Betty Groff, Innkeepers.

Directions: Traveling west on the Pennsylvania Tpke. take Exit 21. Follow Rte. 222 S to Rte. 30 W to Rte. 283 W. Follow Rte. 283 W to Rte. 230 (the first Mount Joy exit). Follow Rte. 230 through Mount Joy to the fourth traffic light. Turn left onto Angle St. At first crossroads, turn right onto Donegal Springs Rd. Go to the stop sign. Turn left onto Colebrook Rd. Go just a short distance over a small bridge. Turn right, back onto Donegal Springs Rd. Follow signs to inn—about ½ mi. on the right.
Traveling east on the Pennsylvania Tpke. take Rte. 72 at Lebanon Exit to the Square in Manheim. Turn right on W. High St. This becomes the Manheim-Mount Joy Rd. Follow directly into Mount Joy. At the first traffic light, turn right onto Main St. Follow Main St. to the next traffic light. At light turn left onto Angle St. Follow above directions from Angle St.

THE CENTURY INN
Scenery Hill, Pennsylvania

It is now many years since I first visited the Century Inn and once again in the brisk dusk of a late October evening I walked up the front walk past the pillars on the stone-paved porch and through the front door. The beautiful antique-blessed interior and front sitting room with the Whiskey Rebellion flag is just as it was during the time of my first visit when I met Gordon and Mary Harrington and we talked all through dinner and far into the night of the things which inn-seekers enjoy so much: history, music, art, and the lovely countryside.

Gordon and Mary are gone now, although fortunately there are some pencil sketches of them in the inn. Their place has been taken by their son Gordon, Jr., and his black-eyed Welsh wife Meggin and their young son Gordon Franklin Harrington III.

Beyond that, the Century Inn remains what it has been for so many years: the pride of the community and a place sought out by true lovers of country inns. They've been coming for many years to enjoy stuffed pork chops, roast turkey, seafood, whipped potatoes, sweet potatoes, absolutely scrumptious cole slaw and homemade pies.

All of the dining rooms and bedrooms reflect the true passion for collecting which was really started by Gordon's mother and father. Now there are even more things than ever being proudly shown.

"I think the heart and soul of the Century Inn is found right here in our little Tap Room," he said expansively. I had to agree that the atmosphere was certainly conducive to good conversation and good fun, and echoes of the inn's early days can be found in the beautiful stenciling on the walls, the exposed beams from which hung many different types of lamps, a rack of old-fashioned muskets and firing pieces, and a piece of Pennsylvania Dutch folk art which is really a wall clock in disguise.

The inn was decorated for Halloween with many arrangements of corn stalks and colorful autumn leaves. A very fierce pumpkin glared at me from one of the tables. I peeked into the kitchen where a few of the ladies of the village who have been employed at the inn for many years were preparing the Saturday evening meal. I nodded to them and continued on into the Keeping Room with its huge fireplace and truly astonishing collection of old tools and artifacts hung around the mantel. This is a cozy dining room of the inn and many a lovely meal have I enjoyed in this pleasant atmosphere.

Breakfast is served as it has been for many years at the very back of the inn in a beautiful dining room which has broad expansive windows looking down into a woodland and hills beyond.

The Century Inn was built before 1794 and is the oldest continuously operating tavern on the National Pike, most of which is today's U.S. 40. Consequently, the inn has played an important role in the history of southwest Pennsylvania. General Lafayette stopped here on May 26, 1825, and Andrew Jackson was a guest twice, once on his way to his inauguration as President of the United States.

After a sumptuous dinner in the candlelit dining room and more good conversation with Gordon, Meggin, and their friends, I retired to my second-floor bedroom. Knowing how much of themselves Gordon and Mary Harrington had put into this inn, I was certain that they would be most pleased to realize that Gordon Franklin Harrington III, was already off to a good start as the third-generation innkeeper!

THE CENTURY INN, Scenery Hill, Pa. 15360; 412-945-6600 or 5180. A 10-room village inn on Rte. 40, 12 mi. east of Washington, Pa., 35 mi. south of Pittsburgh. European plan. Breakfast served to houseguests only. Lunch and dinner served to travelers daily. Closed approximately Dec. 21 until March 20. Contact inn for exact opening and closing dates. No pets. No credit cards. Personal checks welcome. Meggin and Gordon Harrington, Jr., Innkeepers.

Directions: From the east, exit the Pa. Tpke. at New Stanton. Take I-70W to Rte. 917S (Bentleyville exit) to Rte. 40E and go 1 mi. east to inn. From the north, take Rte. 19S to Rte. 519S to Rte. 40E and go 5 mi. east to inn or take I-79S to Rte. 40E and go 9 mi. east to inn. From the west, take I-70E to I-79S to Rte. 40E and go 9 mi. east to inn.

BARLEY SHEAF FARM
Holicong, Pennsylvania

It was daybreak. I didn't even have to open my eyes to discern this fact since some Canada geese honking in a nearby field were sharing this information with all who cared to listen (and even some of us who didn't)! I burrowed down underneath the decorator sheets, pulled the woolly blanket over my head and pretty soon they stopped honking, although I did hear a plaintive "baa" from one of the sheep.

Ann Mills had laughingly warned us the previous evening that this might happen. We had gathered around a table in the old 1740 section of this stately Pennsylvania farmhouse. "We have pigs, chickens, and a special kind of sheep called Horned Dorsets," she explained. "Many of our guests are enjoying their first contact with real farm animals and it's quite a thrill for them to realize that very often the eggs they are eating for breakfast are straight from the nests. We also have beehives and wildflower honey which many of our guests take home with them. Almost everything comes from the farm and I bake the bread fresh every day. Breakfast is the only meal we serve."

According to a carefully footnoted history, compiled in 1977 by James Wright, Barley Sheaf was a part of a William Penn land grant and was originally built during the time that the Lenape Indians lived in this area. There has been quite a succession of owners, but in recent

years it was the Bucks County home of the eminent playwright George S. Kaufman. Apparently Moss Hart and Kaufman enjoyed many hours of collaboration here during the 30s. The Marx brothers were frequent guests, and I understand that Harpo was a special friend of the Kaufmans.

There is a very tastefully lettered wooden sign on Rte. 202, just outside of Buckingham, which directs guests down an avenue of trees with fields on each side. At the end is a magnificent copper beech tree which has sheltered one end of the farmhouse for many years.

Three playful and accommodating dogs usually usher guests into the house with its highly polished wide floorboards and collection of antique furniture. A house cat named Winston is usually on the scene as well.

The nine bedrooms are all of ample size, and are very tastefully furnished. Three of them have a shared bath.

In some of these rooms and also in the breakfast and living rooms there are some early American paintings and also some by Ann Mills.

I was deeply impressed by the Pennsylvania barn, the herb garden, the grassy lawns, and other outbuildings. I have a particular affinity for barns of all kinds and some Pennsylvania barns have a quality that really sets them apart from their fellows. The grounds have a parklike atmosphere bounded by wooden fences, and bordered during my visit by colorful peonies. A little beyond was a patch of woods and a field planted with soybeans and corn.

I took a dip in a rather sizable swimming pool which Don Mills said was one of the oldest in Bucks County.

Breakfast in the sunny dining room is bounteous. "After all, we're a farm and we think bed and breakfast at a farm should include a real farm breakfast," said Ann.

BARLEY SHEAF FARM, Box 66, Holicong, Pa. 18928; 215-794-5104. A 9-room bed-and-breakfast inn, 8 mi. from Doylestown and New Hope, Pennsylvania. Near Delaware River, Bucks County Playhouse, George Washington's Crossing. Breakfast only meal served; bag lunches on request. Open March 1 thru weekend prior to Christmas. Croquet, badminton, swimming pool, farm animals on grounds. Tennis, boating, canoeing, and horseback riding nearby. Near all of the natural and historical attractions of Buck's County, Pennsylvania. Recommended for children over 8. No credit cards. Don and Ann Mills, Innkeepers.

Directions: Barley Sheaf Farm is on Rte. 202 between Doylestown and Lahaska.

EAGLES MERE INN
Eagles Mere, Pennsylvania

For me, Eagles Mere is one of the last unspoiled vacation spots in the East. It is high in the Land of Endless Mountains, north of Williamsport, Pennsylvania. The village could be the subject of a good book.

"These lovely summer homes that you see nestled among the trees were built by people whose families have been coming up here for many years," explained Kathleen Oliver. "The summer people are very active in our community affairs and supply support for many of the community programs in which our inn guests can also participate."

Kathleen, who with her husband Bob is the innkeeper at the Eagles Mere Inn, went on, "There's much to do here both summer and winter. The lake provides swimming, canoeing, sailing, and fishing, and on winter weekends the volunteer fire department operates a toboggan slide with a 1200-foot ride down the hill to the lake on specially constructed toboggans. The speeds get up to 45 miles per hour."

However, the big news at the Eagles Mere Inn is that Kathleen and Bob have completed the renovations of the old Crestmont Inn property located on the highest knoll in the area. The ancient inn building has been completely torn down and the adjacent Evergreen Lodge now has 21 attractive Colonial-style bedrooms, each with a private bath. These have all been most tastefully furnished. Downstairs in the large living room is a native stone fireplace for the guests to enjoy. Meals are served at the main inn.

Perhaps the most exciting new development is the six new Har-Tru tennis courts and a pro-shop with a resident pro, providing a chance to take some tennis lessons and also an excellent opportunity for serious players. The Dickerson Championships are held each year over the July 4th weekend, and the sanctioned Eagles Mere Championships are held annually during the third week in August. In the winter, the pro shop becomes the cross-country ski headquarters.

There is also a swimming pool and a par-3 "pitch-and-putt" golf course that can be played with a 9-iron and a putter.

Sunset Cottage, a cozy place for honeymooners with a stone fireplace and warm surroundings, has been completely renovated and is available by the week from spring through fall.

I was particularly intrigued by the fact that the row of garages, once used to house the old flivvers of summer guests fifty years ago, have been turned into a series of craft shops, open on weekends, where the ladies of the surrounding mountain area bring their handmade quilts, homemade jams, antiques, and much more, providing for a day of enjoyable browsing.

Ultimately Eagles Mere offers an opportunity for a retreat to some wonderful, natural, unspoiled bliss. There are miles of marked hiking trails, and one of the loveliest leads around the perimeter of

the lake, only minutes from the inn. Other more strenuous hikes have been carefully mapped out.

I must say I never thought that Kathleen and Bob would get so much accomplished in such a short time. They've done it, and they've done it well. Congratulations.

EAGLES MERE INN, Mary and Sullivan Aves., Eagles Mere, Pa. 17731; 717-525-3273. A 30-room (all with private baths) small village inn high in the Allegheny Mountain range about an hour's drive north of Williamsport. Tennis, heated swimming pool, pitch-and-putt golf, xc skiing on grounds. Golf, hiking, horseback riding nearby. Modified American plan in season; European plan (room and breakfast) out of season. Breakfast and dinner served to travelers. Luncheon in season. Open every day from May 1 to Nov. 1; open from Friday dinner through Sunday breakfast in winter. Closed December 24-27. No pets. No credit cards. Robert and Kathleen Oliver, Innkeepers.

Directions: Exit 34 (Buckhorn) from I-80. Follow Rte. 42 north 32 mi. to Eagles Mere. Turn right on Mary Avenue to inn.

EVERMAY-ON-THE-DELAWARE
Erwinna, Pennsylvania

It was six o'clock in the morning at Evermay-on-the-Delaware. The sun was coming up over the river and the geese were heralding the first streaks of daylight.

I had a grandstand seat to the first act of the new day from the window of my third-floor bedroom. It had a very intimate feeling and was furnished with Victorian furniture and an oriental rug, as were the other third-floor rooms.

I raised the window, more easily to hear the first sounds of the happy birds as they swooped from tree to tree along the banks of the Delaware River, building nests and lifting paeans of praise to morning. At that early hour there were very few cars on the river road and I felt very much as if I were in my own private world. What music would best accompany such a scene? I decided that Grieg's "Morning" from the *Peer Gynt Suite* would be best.

Long before Ron Strouse and Fred Cresson, innkeepers of the Sign of the Sorrel Horse in nearby Quakertown, discovered and explored the full potential of this lovely property, Evermay had existed as an accommodation as far back as 1871. The original part of the house was built in 1700 by a prominent family in the valley. A 1905 photograph in the parlor of the inn shows that it has hardly been changed since that date.

I made two visits to Evermay in 1982; the first was in January when it was still being refurbished and redecorated.

Painters were painting and carpenters were carpentering and

Ron and Fred, busy as they were, took a few moments to show me everything from top to bottom and also gave me a running history of the building. At that time Victorian beds and bureaus were waiting to be moved into each successive bedroom and public room as they were completed.

Now, a few months later, the miracle had indeed been wrought and everything was in tiptop condition.

Besides the snug rooms on the top floor, Evermay also has larger second-floor, master-sized bedrooms, many with fireplaces.

One of the reasons for the inn's immediate popularity undoubtedly is the cuisine. Dinner is prix-fixe, usually five courses and a choice of two or three entrées. Ron and Fred request that gentlemen wear coats and ties in the dining room and since there is only one seating at 7:30 P.M., reservations are necessary.

At Evermay, the price of the room includes breakfast and also afternoon tea. "Many of our guests arrive late afternoon after driving from New York or Philadelphia," explained Fred, "and we serve a proper tea which will hold them until dinner."

Located as it is on the banks of the Delaware River in Bucks County in a classic Victorian-style building with a tradition of hospitality, it's hard to imagine a more fitting scenario for a country inn.

EVERMAY-ON-THE-DELAWARE, Erwinna, Pa. 18920; 215-294-9100. A 16-bedroom riverside inn in upper Bucks County. Breakfast and afternoon tea included in the room tariff. Box lunches available for houseguests. Dinner served nightly at 7:30 P.M. by reservation. Convenient to all of the Bucks County natural and historical attractions including handsome mansions, museums, and historical sites. Xc skiing, backroading, and canoeing nearby. No amusements for small children. No pets. Ron Strouse and Fred Cresson, Innkeepers.

Directions: From New York City: take Rte. 22 to Clinton; Rte. 31 to Flemington; Rte. 12 to Frenchtown. Cross river and turn south on Rte. 32 for 2 mi. From Philadelphia: follow I-95 north to Yardley exit and Rte. 32 north to Erwinna. There are several other routes also.

I do not include lodging rates in the descriptions, for the very nature of an inn means that there are lodgings of various sizes, with and without baths, in and out of season, and with plain and fancy decoration. Travelers should call ahead and inquire about the availability and rates of the many different types of rooms.

GATEWAY LODGE
Cooksburg, Pennsylvania

Everybody who loves country inns should meet Linda Burney. The best way to meet Linda is to visit Gateway Lodge, owned by Linda and her husband Joe. Located next to Cook Forest State Park, the Lodge is in the gorgeous Clarion River country of western Pennsylvania.

I, who thought that I had covered most of Pennsylvania in the last eighteen years, had never been to Cooksburg. Although I had had some inkling about Gateway Lodge, I was delighted to find that it was a log cabin modeled after the homes that were built by settlers in this part of Pennsylvania in the 18th century. The second floor has the traditional garrison overhang from which the settlers could fire their rifles at unfriendly Indians who might be trying to break in on the first floor. This is found in early New England houses as well.

But let's return to Linda. She is a wonderfully warm and enthusiastic person who believes sincerely that Gateway Lodge is paradise regained.

"Joe and I come from farther north," she said. "We were on a vacation here a few years ago, came by for a visit, fell in love with the place, and before I knew it we had moved in lock, stock, and barrel and had become innkeepers almost overnight."

"When we first started out we were going to have a cook, but I said to Joe, 'Well, nobody has died from my cooking yet, so why don't I try?' I did the dinner and Joe would do the breakfast. The first night we had three people—we served chicken and biscuits, and I forgot to make the biscuits!

"We have only two choices on the menu each evening. The first person who calls for a reservation each day can set the menu. Today we are having stuffed steak, but we also serve stuffed pork chops, country-style spareribs, chicken and biscuits, and lasagna. The second person who calls can set the second choice on the menu for the evening.

"We splurge on desserts and offer a choice of four or even six. Tonight we have a choice of walnut pie, chocolate lover's delight, custard pie, apple pie, or cherry cheesecake."

I asked her about what guests did during their stay. "In the summertime they love the hiking—we have more than 27 miles of trails—and there is canoeing, innertubing down the Clarion River, horseback riding, and just getting back to nature. Everything is very rustic and natural. In the fall there is such beautiful foliage that it is unbelievable, and in the winter there is snowshoeing, cross-country skiing, snowmobiling, and tobogganing.

"It's great for kids. They find thousands of things to do even though we don't have a TV. They discover the deer and the chipmunks, and they go fishing."

The big living room of the main lodge has log walls and a beautiful big fireplace with lots of deep, comfortable chairs gathered around it. The bedrooms have beds with chestnut headboards and all have dust ruffles and comforters. The rooms were undergoing extensive alterations during my visit. At this time there is one bathroom for the ladies and another one for the gentlemen "down the hall."

Like the Doe Run Inn in Kentucky, Gateway Lodge is a rustic country inn reminiscent of the days of Colonial America. It is situated in forests of virgin pine and hemlock, and everything has been designed to harmonize with this wonderful natural environment.

GATEWAY LODGE, Rte. 36, Cooksburg, Pa. 16217; 814-744-8017. A 9-bedroom rustic cabin situated in the heart of the western Pennsylvania forest. Two bathrooms "down the hall." Adjacent to Cook Forest which has beautiful backroading and many trails. All types of seasonal outdoor recreation available. Open year-round, except Thanksgiving week and December 20 to 27. No credit cards. Linda and Joe Burney, Innkeepers.

Directions: Because Cooksburg is accessible from all four directions, locate Cook Forest State Park on your map of Pennsylvania and find Rte. 36. It is about 40 minutes north of I-80.

FAIRFIELD INN & GUEST HOUSE
Fairfield, Pennsylvania

When the Fairfield Inn marked its 225th anniversary on Thursday, September 2, 1982, Innkeeper David Thomas held a special candlelight dinner with chamber music and a bill of fare that featured Colonial recipes and roast turkey.

The main building of the inn, an impressive three-story Pennsylvania stone building with wood balconies on the front, is on the main street of the village. It is famous not only for having extremely enjoyable country food and pleasant service, but also for being in every sense of the word a meeting place and a center of social activity for the region.

Lodging rooms are in what the local townsfolk call the Cunningham House which David painstakingly restored and furnished just a few years ago. There are four bedrooms furnished mostly with original antiques. Some of them look out over the village scene and others in the rear have a view of the mountains. "For years the building sat empty and idle, and fortunately no one did anything to it," David said with a twinkle in his eye. "As a result the random-width floorboards, carved mantels, raised-panel doors, and other features are still quite intact. An officer of the Sixth United States Cavalry was cared for here in 1863."

The building began its long career as the plantation home of the Miller family who settled here in 1755. The rear portion of the building dates from 1757 and the front stone section was built about the same time that Squire William Miller laid out the town.

It became an inn in 1823, when Squire Miller's niece and nephew, Mary and James Wilson, purchased the property, and it has been in continuous operation ever since.

The present owner, David Thomas, has made the inn a proper setting for many events throughout the year, including a Festival of Christmas held the first and second weekends of December. Reservations for this event are open on the first Monday in November and are filled almost within hours.

The inn is also the scene of the "Pippinfest," held on an autumn weekend, that involves everyone in the village. Senior citizens have a quilt show and, among other things, there is an apple-dessert baking contest, square dancing, bonfires, old movies, and block parties. In the spring of the year the inn sponsors a Monday evening lecture series that includes such esoteric topics as John Bell pottery and 18th-century garden-design quilts. There are also adult cooking classes and a gourmet cooking class for local 4-H members.

The menu of the inn specializes in foods from "scratch." There are such old-fashioned delights as chicken and biscuits, many types of apple dishes, and a special Dutch dressing.

Bean soup is always on the menu because it commemorates the occasion when the townswomen made bean soup in iron kettles to feed the starving soldiers after the battle of Gettysburg.

Visitors are also fascinated with the story about Jeb Stuart stealing 700 horses from the valley in 1862.

With bright, energetic David Thomas as the keeper of this inn, it is well on its way toward its second 225 years of service to travelers and local folk alike.

FAIRFIELD INN & GUEST HOUSE, Main St., Fairfield, Pa. 17320; 717-642-5410. A country restaurant near Gettysburg with 4 lodging rooms available (shared baths). Breakfast, lunch, and dinner served daily. Closed on major holidays, Sundays, and first week in Sept. and Feb. Dinner reservations advised. Nearby region is rich in history, including Gettysburg Battlefield, Caledonia State Park, and Totem Pole Playhouse; 3 mi. from Ski Liberty. No pets. David W. Thomas, Innkeeper.

Directions: Fairfield is 8 mi. west of Gettysburg on Rte. 116.

1740 HOUSE
Lumberville, Pennsylvania

Harry Nessler, relaxed in grey flannels and sport coat, and accompanied by his two dogs, was waiting for me at the front door of the 1740 House. "Good morning," he said, "I see you've been taking a constitutional."

I had indeed. I'd awakened about six o'clock and decided not to lose a moment of my working holiday. My room in the inn was originally an old stable and the walls were of heavy stone. There were massive beams overhead. Through one window I could see unspoiled woods on the far side of the Delaware River and Canal, and I could see the southern tip of Bull's Island. The swimming pool was visible through the other window. Each of the lodging rooms here either opens onto a terrace or has its own balcony.

I decided that this would be a good morning to take a stroll over the footbridge from Lumberville to Bull's Island. In the growing light of the morning, the oak, walnut, and sycamore trees around the inn were beginning to take shape, and I noted with approval the arrangement of plantings that Harry had made including laurel, forsythia, rhododendron, and myrtle.

After enjoying the fresh, clear quietness of the country morning, I walked back along the canal towpath, where the cardinals, grosbeaks, and doves were already busy searching out their morning meal.

That thought sent me back to the inn at a faster pace, and Harry suggested that we go right in and have breakfast.

We made our own toast from homemade bread and enjoyed delicious jams, fruit juice, croissants, pastries, cold cereal, and Pennsylvania Dutch hot hard-boiled eggs. This breakfast is included in the room tariff. Other guests came in, and one of them asked Harry about the exact place where Washington crossed the Delaware.

"It's about ten miles south of here," he said, "and Valley Forge is only about 45 minutes away." He reached into his pocket and said, "I hope you'll take a copy of this brochure. It's called 'Highways of History' and it's the best thing to take with you if you're touring Buck's County. There are well over a hundred historic sites and buildings within an easy drive. The best way is to take the three tours, one day at a time."

There are a few unique features at this country inn that reflect its "one-of-a-kind" innkeeper. For one thing, weekend reservations must include two nights. Usually these are booked well in advance. Another feature worth noting is that dinner is served between 7:00 and 8:00 p.m. in the small dining room, and it's necessary for everyone—even houseguests—to have reservations.

Harry also has definite ideas about the ambience of his inn. "It's an extension of the things I hold dear—good taste, good food, and good manners. We welcome everyone who shares these enthusiasms. I like to think of all the people who come to this inn as my houseguests."

1740 HOUSE, River Rd., Lumberville, Pa. 18933; 215-297-5661. A 24-room riverside inn, 6½ mi. north of New Hope, in the heart of

historic Bucks County. Lodgings include breakfast which is served to houseguests daily; dinner served daily except Sundays and Mondays, by reservation only. Open year-round. Pool and boating on grounds. Golf and tennis nearby. Harry Nessler, Innkeeper.

Directions: From N. Y. C., travel south on N.J. Tpke., and take Exit 10. Follow Rte. 287 north to another Exit 10. Proceed west on Rte. 22 to Flemington, then Rte. 202 south over Delaware Toll Bridge. After an immediate right U-turn onto Rte. 32N, drive 5 mi. to inn. From Pa. Tpke., exit at Willow Grove and proceed north on Rte. 611 to Rte. 202. Follow Rte. 202 north to Rte. 32 and turn north to inn. From Phila., take I-95 to Yardley-New Hope Exit, follow 32N through New Hope and 7 miles to inn.

I do not include lodging rates in the descriptions, for the very nature of an inn means that there are lodgings of various sizes, with and without baths, in and out of season, and with plain and fancy decoration. Travelers should call ahead and inquire about the availability and rates of the many different types of rooms.

HICKORY BRIDGE FARM
Orrtanna, Pennsylvania

Nancy Jeane Hammett put her finger to her lips, and indicated that I was to remain behind. On tiptoes she walked very quietly to the edge of the brook. All was very still and quiet except for a slight rustling in the tree branches. She motioned for me to follow and when I joined her she pointed out the young trout in the brook. "Many people came here just for the fishing," she whispered.

We had just returned from a short walk along the brook which tooks us over a rustic bridge and through the woods past a cornfield to two additonal buildings with accommodations for the Hickory Bridge Farm overnight guests.

The work that had been started the year before in the old farmhouse was now completed. There were additional bedrooms furnished with 19th-century farm furniture, including beds with lovely old quilts, beautiful old chests, braided rugs, antique dolls, a sewing machine which is treadle-operated, handpainted furniture, marble-topped bureaus, and the like. Nancy Jeane and her husband Dr. Jim are great collectors, so the dressers and chests had many odd little knickknacks.

There are three bedrooms in the farmhouse and a little breakfast room off the kitchen where there's a bowl of fruit and buns for breakfast. "Our guests take breakfast out on the deck overlooking the covered bridge," explained Nancy Jeane.

There's a great deal more to Hickory Bridge Farm than what I've described above. Many things have been happening during recent years and perhaps this letter from Nancy Jeane will help to fill us all in:

"October has fled with the leaves, and everything at Hickory Bridge Farm is almost too quiet. The past month was our best of the year. The Apple Harvest Festival at our nearby South Mt. Fairgrounds was the greatest ever and our festival here outgrew our family so we moved to the streets of Fairfield. We had a big time at the festival; I made baskets, the kids had their own crafts, we sold apple cake, and Dr. Jim and our sons ran the wheels off our antique truck taking all the kids for free rides.

"The Adams County Fruit Growers Association asked if they could hold their annual USA Apple Queen contest here again this year.

"Because of public demand, our dining room is now open on Saturday evenings by reservation. We have many faithful customers who particularly like to come here for a quiet supper on the farm. Our breakfasts at the farmhouse continue to be a great success. Guests love to talk across the table with people from all over the country.

"We've been fortunate in having a good growing season and a bountiful garden. Here it is November and I am still picking leaf lettuce and parsley. Dr. Jim fixed up our root cellar in the old part of the farmhouse and we keep apples, potatoes, and squash until spring."

So the seasons and the years roll on at the Hickory Bridge Farm and what began as a hobby for Nancy Jeane and Dr. Jim, who is the local general practioner, has now become a family enterprise with Nancy Jeane and Dr. Jim who maintains that he is an expert on replacing light bulbs; Mary Lynn Martin, the manager; Mary Lou Hammett running the gift shop (she is son Jim's wife), and Kay Hammett in charge of the dining room (she is son Dave's wife).

It is really an inspiration to pay a visit to Hickory Bridge Farm.

HICKORY BRIDGE FARM INN, Orrtanna, Pa. 17353; 717-642-5261. A country inn on a farm 3 mi. from Fairfield and 8 mi. from Gettysburg. Near Gettysburg Battlefield National Park, Caledonia State Park, and Totem Pole Playhouse. Open year-round. 7 lodging rooms available in 2 cottages and the farmhouse; 7-day advance deposit required. Breakfast included in rates. Hiking, biking, hayrides, square dancing, fishing, hunting, and country store museum on grounds. Golf, swimming available nearby. The Hammett Family, Innkeepers.

Directions: From Gettysburg take Rte. 116 west to Fairfield and follow signs 3 mi. north to Orrtanna.

THE PUMP HOUSE INN
Canadensis, Pennsylvania

Seventeen years ago the Drucquer family who had lived and worked in New Jersey for a number of years were touring the Poconos looking for some property for a second home. As they came up the road from the center of Canadensis toward Skytop they saw a farmhouse for sale. It sat on seven acres of rolling land with huge trees, a sizable lawn and, as an extra bonus, a view of the mountains from the front porch.

"As I think back now," mused Todd Drucquer, "The idea came to almost all of us at the same time — what a wonderful place for a country inn!"

To make a long story short, they purchased the property, refurbished it, decorated it with loving care, and the Pump House Inn is now a way of life for Todd and his wife Penny, his brother Mark, his father Henri, and Todd's two growing sons, Chris and Cole.

Almost from the start, the Pump House has had a reputation for innovation. For example, the first menu reflected the Drucquer family's French heritage. Another novel idea was to create a dining room that actually had a waterfall in it. "This came about because there was one large rock that we just couldn't move," Todd said. "So we decided to make it into an indoor waterfall. It's very beautiful and romantic by candlelight."

Chef Gregory Redling has carried on the tradition of fine cuisine established at the Pump House from the very first year. The

dining room serves the cuisine of the provinces of Marseille, Le Havre, and Dijon. The hor d'oeuvres selection includes ballotine aux quatre poissons, sauce verte, marines des artichauts nouvelle.

The entrées feature roast rack of lamb Persille, sautéed veal with lemon and lime sauce, and sautéed calves' liver with papaya, leeks, and cream.

In addition to the French menu there are such hearty British offerings as veal kidneys and lamb chops, chicken and sausage pie, and beef tartar.

The dining rooms, including the Library and the original Pump House dining room, have crystal goblets, fresh flowers, and starched linens setting the mood for very special evenings. The Grill has a lush garden feeling.

All of these are under the watchful eye of John Keeney, the resident manager, whom I first met many years ago when I was traveling through that part of the Poconos with my son Keith.

A new penthouse suite has been added to the bedrooms above-stairs and a guest cottage on the property has been completely renovated and redecorated. It has a beautiful cozy living room with a welcoming fireplace, two bedrooms, a sunporch, and terrace. Todd Drucquer explains that it's ideal for either one or two couples.

Guests have the beauty and serenity of the entire Pocono area at their disposal with good cross-country and downhill skiing in the snow months and several excellent nearby golf courses during the remainder of the year.

The Pump House is a sophisticated country inn in the Poconos. It has received accolades from many well-known publications, including *Gourmet Magazine* and the *New York Times*.

As this book was being prepared for the printer, Todd telephoned me that he and Penny had just purchased Colligan's Stockton Inn in Stockton, New Jersey, which they would operate simultaneously with the Pump House. "With John and Gregg on the scene," he said, "you know the Pump House will always be in good hands. Penny and I will be dividing our time between the two inns."

THE PUMP HOUSE INN, Canadensis, Pa. 18325; 717-595-7501. A 7-room country inn with a separate guest cottage high in the Poconos, 1½ mi. north of Canadensis village and 16 mi. northeast of Stroudsburg. European plan. Dinner served Tues. through Sun. from Apr. through Oct. Dinner served Wed. through Sun. — Nov., Dec., Feb., March. Closed Christmas and New Year's Day; month of Jan. Bicycles, downhill and xc skiing, and golf nearby. The Drucquer Family, Owners; H. Todd Drucquer, Innkeeper.

Directions: From the north, follow I-84 to Rte. 390 south. Inn is located 13 mi. south on Rte. 390. From the south, follow I-80 to Rte. 191. Travel north on Rte. 191 to Rte. 390 north. Follow signs to Canadensis. Inn is 1½ mi. north from light to Canadensis.

INN AT STARLIGHT LAKE
Starlight, Pennsylvania

Mozart in the morning—the Concerto for Flute and Harp. The lighthearted strains put a new spring in my step as I came downstairs at the Inn at Starlight Lake. I stood for a moment in the living room with its big stone fireplace, making a mental inventory of some of the fascinating bric-a-brac—a bust of Dante, a small piece of framed stitchery with the legend "The Blessing of the House is Contentment."

I admired a great stack of wood in one corner and all the books and magazines that would take anyone two years to read. I examined a collection of prints of scenes from what I presumed was Dumas's *Three Musketeers.* There were plants, photographs, musical instruments, and a group of pastel portraits of bright young people with the McMahon look about them.

The Inn at Starlight Lake is situated on a back road on a lake in the rolling hills of northeastern Pennsylvania. It's been in operation since 1909 and originally was intended to be a summer refuge for New Yorkers. In May 1974, Jack and Judy McMahon acquired it and resolved to preserve its early character.

The inn is a rambling, old-fashioned comfortable place with the accumulated furniture of years. Along with the usual sports offered at resort-inns—swimming, boating, canoeing, sailing, tennis, and hiking—there are extensive cross-country ski trails that run many miles into the natural forests of the area. The inn has a certified PSIA ski school.

It's a place for families with kids and very pleasant for honeymooners. It's wonderful for just wandering off and watching for deer, and returning and taking part in such old-fashioned diversions as sing-alongs, informal dramatics, and charades. There is an "oldie but goodie" movie program too.

Jack has added some fancy equipment and the Starlight Radio Theatre is growing in talent and enthusiasm. This is old-fashioned radio drama with many of the guests taking part. The radio plays are recorded and played back to everybody's delight.

Because they've raised their own children—Cecilia, Will, Patty, and Johnny—right here on this lake (which by the way does not permit motor boats), the McMahons are quite conscious of the fact that children need diversions at all times, so there are several sources of amusement on the grounds, including a game room for rainy days.

Accommodations are in the main building and also in adjacent cottages which have been winterized and redecorated. The inn is very popular for family reunions and for groups of couples who might enjoy vacationing together.

The menu has a number of German specialties including Jager schnitzel and Wiener schnitzel. Some other dishes I sampled were cream of cauliflower soup, Hungarian goulash, sauerbraten, buckwheat cakes, and blueberry pie. "We like holidays here," said Judy, "when families gather for Thanksgiving and Christmas. We're open and everyone's welcome."

All of this and W.A. Mozart in the morning.

THE INN AT STARLIGHT LAKE, Starlight, Pa. 18461; 717-798-2519. A 30-room resort-inn located 5 mi. from Hancock, N.Y. Modified American plan. Breakfast, lunch, dinner served daily between May 15 and April 1. Closed Easter if it falls within above dates. Swimming, boating, canoeing, sailing, fishing, hunting, tennis, hiking, bicycling, xc skiing, and lawn sports on grounds. Canoeing, hunting, fishing, golfing nearby. No pets. Judy and Jack McMahon, Innkeepers.

Directions: From N.Y. Rte. 17, exit at Hancock, N.Y. Take Rte. 191S over Delaware River to Rte. 370. Turn right, proceed 3½ mi. turn right, 1 mi. to inn. From I-81, take exit 57 to Rte. 6 east to 171. Go 10 mi. north to Rte. 370. Turn right, proceed 12 mi. Turn left, 1 mi. to inn.

It is true that all roads leading to the Inn at Starlight Lake are back roads. It's impossible to get here without finding yourself on some little-traveled, curving, up-and-down-road. Pointing out a few: Coming from New York City or the northern New Jersey area, one can approach Hancock from NY Route 97, which snakes along the Delaware and passes the replica of Old Fort Delaware. The Delaware River is one of our national treasures. In its upper portion it has changed little, scenically, since the last century. The upper Delaware branches into two parts at Hancock and forms some wonderful areas to travel by. You could really arrive by canoe with a little planning.

Coming from the south through Pennsylvania, one could drive through Honesdale, a charming 19th-century county seat with several historic points of interest, and take either Route 191 N, or Route 670-247 N to Route 370 through miles of . . . well . . . just COUNTRY.

Coming from the north, one can take Route 92 S (NY) to Route 171 (Pa.), and, at Lanesboro, see a national engineering landmark, the Starrucca Viaduct, built in 1848, the oldest train bridge still in use in America. The area is filled with railroad lore for the true railroad enthusiast and the casual observer — Honesdale, site of the first steam engine and gravity railroad, and Susquehanna, site of the first railroad depot and hotel combined in America, now a restaurant. While people are here, we are always pleased to give them hand-out maps and route them along these byways. The roads, by the way, are great for cyclists, too.

Judy and Jack McMahon
The Inn at Starlight Lake
Starlight, Pennsylvania

I have many favorite drives through the countryside. Some are long and some are short. One of my favorites is about ten miles long and is lovely any time of year. We start at the inn entrance and go north along Route 191 for about a mile to Pine Grove Road. Making a right turn on Pine Grove Road, we cross over the Wallenpaupack Creek and pass by Pine Grove Cemetery. This burial ground was used by the earliest settlers in the South Sterling area and is still used to this day. Traveling along at a leisurely pace, you will enjoy seeing Panther Lake and Lake Russell via the Lake Russell Road, which is a dirt-and-gravel road, but very smooth. The rhododendron and the ferns are profuse. Several deserted barns and apple orchards add to the charm of this idyllic drive through the woods.

When we reach Route 447, we turn left and proceed north for about two miles to our Pine Grove Road again. Turning left we head

back toward the Sterling Inn through some beautiful farmland and vistas of the nearby mountains. The whole trip is just under ten miles and takes about half an hour.

Norman, I can't describe the pleasure I get taking this short trip. I've taken many of our guests on this little excursion and have pleasantly surprised many of our guests who have been coming for years.

Mary Kay Logan
The Sterling Inn
South Sterling, Pennsylvania

SIGN OF THE SORREL HORSE
Quakertown, Bucks County, Pennsylvania

I'm happy to say that I caught Ron Strouse in one of his infrequent moments of relaxation in the midst of a busy day. He joined me at the breakfast table for a late cup of coffee and we talked about the Sign of the Sorrel Horse, its history, and his thoughts about the menu.

"Records trace it to 1784 when the innkeeper was a Revolutionary War soldier," he commented. "My partner, Fred Cresson, and I have tried to furnish it with antiques and collectibles that are in harmony with the deep-set windows, the native stone walls, and the beamed ceilings. Just recently we removed a front porch, which was probably a later addition, so that the original simple lines of the inn are much more visible.

"We have six lodging rooms which we've furnished as authentically as possible. There's a little passageway at the top of our twisty staircase that has a small common area for the use of our house-guests and we keep fresh flowers and fruits in every room. Of course, there are no televisions or telephones.

"As far as our menu is concerned, it's mostly French with some northern Italian dishes. We like light things, very few red meats, but many veal and chicken dishes, and quite a lot of fish and seafood. The menu changes about once a month and includes some *nouveau cuisine* and light sauces. We only use what's fresh and everything is all prepared to order. We go to the markets in Philadelphia and deal with the butchers for fresh things, and change the menu according to what's available."

I remarked that I arrived the evening before at dinnertime and the aspect of this old inn with candles on the table all lit for dinner was indeed a warming sight. It is located a few miles out of Quakertown on a road with the romantic name of "Old Bethlehem Pike."

There are two small dining rooms in which the tables are comfortably spaced, and the white interior walls and rough stone exterior walls provide a most appropriate background for growing plants and handsome colonial paintings. They are an interesting study in textures.

The Sign of the Sorrel Horse also has a few other surprising amenities, including a small but welcome swimming pool, a trellised terrace, a couple of goats, lambs, and geese, and herb and flower gardens located in one corner of a wooded area.

Set among the rolling hills of Lake Nockamixon about 35 miles from Philadelphia and 70 miles from New York City, it's within a convenient drive of New Hope, the Bucks County Playhouse, and many historic sites and sights.

One extra point: coming from Quakertown, have faith and follow directions. I turned left off Rte. 313 and followed Rte. 563 north for about two miles to the first real crossroads, and after turning left, the inn was only a quarter-mile beyond.

Ron and Fred are also the proprietors of the newly-restored Evermay-on-the-Delaware Inn located a short distance away in Erwinna. It is also included in *Country Inns and Back Roads.*

SIGN OF THE SORREL HORSE, Old Bethlehem Rd., RD #3, Quakertown, Pa. 18951; 215-536-4651. A 6-room restored inn 5 mi. from Quakertown. European plan. Continental breakfast served to houseguests. Dinner served Wed. thru Sat. and Sunday brunch. Open March 1 to Jan. 15; closed Christmas Day. Swimming pool on grounds. Not suitable for children. No pets. Ronald Strouse and Frederick Cresson, Innkeepers.

Directions: From Quakertown, follow Rte. 313 east to 563 north 2 mi.; turn left onto Old Bethlehem Rd. for ¼ mi. Inn is on left.

OVERLOOK INN
Canadensis, Pennsylvania

Although it was midsummer and we were seated by the pool with fleecy white clouds lazily floating overhead and birds singing in the gently swaying trees, I asked Lolly Tupper what it would be like on a typical October Saturday afternoon here at the Overlook Inn.

"Oh, every one of our lodging rooms would be filled and 'country-inners' would be sipping tea or hot mulled cider and munching doughnuts or homemade cookies. You'd probably find them in animated conversation with new-found friends, playing backgammon, chess, or cribbage, and a few would be at the television set in the library cheering on their favorite college football team. By the way," she said with a touch of a smile, "the art of conversation has now been revived at country inns!"

The Overlook Inn is located in the high Pocono Mountains in northeastern Pennsylvania. The fragrant pine, blue spruce, and locust forests stretch out in all directions, and the cardinals, quail, and robins find them equally as inviting as the rhododendron and mountain laurel.

The lodging rooms are comfortably furnished with antiques and collectibles, and the beds are covered with beautiful handmade quilts.

The innkeepers are Lolly and Bob Tupper who seem almost to have been born to their roles. Bob is a big man with a wonderful sense of humor and a booming laugh. Lolly is quieter and has the knack of making guests feel as if they really are in a very special place.

"I wish you'd come and visit us during the holidays," she continued. "You know we start off with a Thanksgiving Day buffet with turkeys, hams, and all the traditional trimmings. At Christmas we put a big evergreen on the porte cochere and it's literally covered with Christmas lights. The guests love it because as soon as they get within sight of the inn they can see the lights. New Year's Eve we have a midnight buffet, and then a brunch on New Year's Day. Naturally, we're 'thinking snow' because our guests can go downhill or cross-country skiing in just a few minutes."

Standing up, she exclaimed, "Oh, it's time for afternoon tea, would you like a cup right here at the pool and maybe a biscuit or two?" I agreed, although I must say I was looking forward to dinner which I knew would include rabbit with a super French sauce or perhaps a quail with wild rice.

She turned back just a moment, "Do you realize that it's six years ago on a rainy October Saturday afternoon that you first came to visit us at Overlook? I remember because it was pouring, and we were anxious to meet you."

Well, rainy or not, it was certainly one of the happiest days of my life.

OVERLOOK INN, Dutch Hill Rd., Canadensis, Pa. 18325; 717-595-7519. A 21-room resort-inn in the heart of the Poconos, 15 miles from Stroudsburg, Pa. Mod. American plan. Dinners served to travelers. Open every day of the year. Pool, shuffleboard, bocci, horseshoes, hiking on grounds; golf, tennis, Alpine slide, ice skating, downhill and xc skiing, indoor tennis, antiquing, backroading, summer theater nearby. No children under twelve. No pets. Jackets requested at dinner. Bob and Lolly Tupper, Innkeepers.

Directions: From the North (New England, New York State, and Canada): use I-84 and take Route 390 south through "Promised Land" about 12 mi. to traffic light in Canadensis. Make right hand turn on Rte. 447 north—go 1/3 mi. to Dutch Hill Rd. turn right— inn is 1½ mi. up hill. Look for new sign on right. From New York City: take George Washington Bridge to I-80 west. Turn off at Pennsylvania Exit 52. Follow Rte. 447 north—straight through Canadensis traffic light—about 1/3 mi. past light to Dutch Hill Rd. Follow above directions from Dutch Hill Rd. From Philadelphia: Pennsylvania Tpke. to Northeast extension to Exit 35. Follow I-80 East to 380 West to Mt. Pocono Exit 8. Turn right on 940 to dead end. Make right and quick left. You're still on 940. Follow 390. Make left. Follow 390 to traffic light in Canadensis. Make left ¼ mi. to Dutch Hill Rd. Turn right 1½ mi. up hill.

STERLING INN
South Sterling, Pennsylvania

I could not resist it any longer—I had been listening to the gurgling waters of the Wallenpaupack Creek for about twenty minutes on a warm, lazy afternoon. I was sitting on a lawn chair about fifty paces from the back of the Sterling Inn, just two feet from the bank of the creek. The smell of the freshly-cut lawn mingled with the scent of the forest on the other side of the water.

I kicked off my shoes, rolled up my pants, and waded out to stand on the flat, smooth shelf of rock in the middle of the creek. The water was clean and cool. There was a little pool about twenty-five feet away, deep enough for me to sit in and have the water come up to my chest. A flash of red and another of blue signaled a cardinal and a bluejay darting into the woods, deep in the Pocono Mountains of Pennsylvania.

I climbed back on the bank and was drying my feet when one of the other guests came and plunked down on a nearby chair. "I think this is one of the best-kept, neatest places that I have ever visited," she said. "It's as American as apple pie and fresh vegetables. The rooms are so comfortable, and I'm very glad I came. Don't you just love it here?"

Even if her enthusiasm hadn't been catching, I would have had to agree.

This was the friendly and unpretentious atmosphere that Alice Julian had in mind over a half-century ago when she acquired the Sterling Inn. That is the way her daughter and son-in-law, Carmen and Henry Arneberg, kept it, and the same way that the present owners, Ron and Mary Kay Logan are keeping it today.

The Sterling Inn is on a back road in the Poconos. There are enticing hiking and walking trails on the inn property and nearby. One of them, Ron told me, leads to a waterfall on the ridge behind the inn. There is a very pleasant nine-hole putting green, a swimming area with a sandy beach, and a little pond with willow trees and a few ducks.

Lodgings are to be found in several very attractive buildings in the parklike atmosphere. The Wayside, Lodge, Meadowlark, Spruce, and Spring Run are all beautifully situated with extremely attractive rooms, all with private baths.

The menu includes such entrées as roast lamb, pot roast and standing rib roast, because Mary Kay Logan says, "This is the kind of food that people serve only when they are having guests for dinner." All the baking is done in the warm, friendly kitchen.

In many ways this Pocono Mountain inn personifies the things that I find most delightful in country inns. For example, fresh flowers are on the dining room tables at all times, and there are books and magazines in all parlors and sitting rooms. When guests advise the inn of their arrival time, the inn automobile will meet buses and airplanes. Special diets can also be accommodated.

For the first time in its half-century history the inn is now open year-round and the setting is like a winter postcard. Outdoor activities include cross-country skiing and lessons, ice skating, sledding, winter hikes, and roasting chestnuts or marshmallows by the open fire. Major ski areas are within a short drive from the inn.

Now it is possible to enjoy the Sterling Inn in both winter and summer.

STERLING INN, Rte. 191, South Sterling, Pa. 18460; 717-676-3311. A 60-room secluded country inn resort in the Pocono Mountains, 8 mi. from I-84 and 12 mi. from I-380. American plan. Reservation and check-in offices close at 10 P.M. Breakfast, lunch, and dinner served to travelers daily. Jackets required for dinner. Open year-round. Swimming, putting green, shuffleboard, all-weather tennis court, scenic hiking trails, xc skiing and lessons, ice skating, and sledding on grounds. Golf courses, horseback riding, major ski areas nearby. No pets. Visa and Mastercard accepted. Ron and Mary Kay Logan, Innkeepers.

Directions: From I-80, follow I-380 to Rte. 940 to Mount Pocono. At light, cross Rte. 611 and proceed on Rte. 196 north to Rte. 423. Drive north on Rte. 423 to Rte. 191 and travel ½ mile north to inn. From I-84, follow Rte. 507 south through Greentown and New-foundland. In Newfoundland, pick up Rte. 191 and travel 4 mi. south to inn.

THE PINE BARN INN
Danville, Pennsylvania

Even though I see Marty and Barbara Walzer at least once a year, I always get such a kick out of his yearly letters to me about what's going on at the Pine Barn Inn, I think I'll share a great deal of his most recent letter.

First let me explain that the Pine Barn Inn is located in central Pennsylvania a few miles from Lewisburg (the home of my college, Bucknell).

The residents of that area of Pennsylvania think most kindly of the Pine Barn as a restaurant, and travelers speak highly of the accommodations which, even though they are somewhat "motel" in style, are furnished with attractive cherry reproductions and have many thoughtful touches that I always enjoy finding in a country inn, such as plants, and magazines and books for guests to read. The menu includes roast beef and roast leg of lamb, as well as homemade pies, breads, rolls, and salads.

The inn began life in the 1870s as a wonderful Pennsylvania barn and later served for a long time as a riding stable and then as a private home. It was transformed in 1950 to The Pine Barn Inn and in 1967 it was purchased by Shube and Marty Walzer. Today it is a restaurant and inn of considerable reputation.

Now for the portions of Marty's letter:

"The biggest news, of course, revolves around Christopher, but that news is only that he continues to be a normal, healthy two-year-old who never ceases to entertain us. He's definitely showing the proper innkeeper's traits.

"Shube (Marty's father), is visiting now, but is already homesick for the Florida weather. There's no indication that he will pursue any gardening here this spring, so I guess it's time for me to learn the difference between a dandelion and a daffodil. I think that Barbara bought Holland's entire 1982 production of tulips, and I have spent the fall digging six-inch holes around both our house and the inn.

"Because I headed a community drive to raise a million dollars for a new community center, I've now been asked to head the committee to build it, so there goes any free time for the next nine months.

"Spurred on by Jane Fitzpatrick's (Red Lion Inn, Stockbridge, Massachusetts) enthusiasm and encouragement, Barbara and I sponsored a benefit Holiday Party and Art Exhibit that raised $6,000 for the center." (He enclosed newspaper clippings.)

"Barb has just completed the redecoration of one of our private dining rooms, now called the Library. There are beautiful prints by a Pennsylvania artist and some oak floor-to-ceiling bookshelves. I finally found a place for my 1941 set of the *Book of Knowledge*.

"Our staff remains the same except that they are one year older and better paid.

"We purchased three of the homes on the street below us and expect to open one of them about the end of February as a guest house with six rooms. It will have a TV/library room.

"The wildest thing that happened this year was when Barb and I purchased the cupola from the highest peak of the Crestmont Inn to put on the grounds of our home nearby. When we get it set up, we'll welcome visitors." (Crestmont is now part of the Eagles Mere Inn, *CIBR*).

"I've got to go watch the football game and root against Dallas, so I'll send you a few more notes later on." (He never did.)

THE PINE BARN INN, Danville, Pa. 17821; 717-275-2071. A picturesque country restaurant with 45 attractive motel rooms in central Pennsylvania. European plan. Breakfast, lunch, and dinner served daily except Christmas, July 4th, and Memorial Day. Near several colleges and historic sites. Golf, tennis, waterskiing, sailing, and canoeing nearby. Pets allowed in some rooms. Martin and Barbara Walzer, Innkeepers.

Directions: From Exit 33 of I-80, go south 3 mi. to Danville. Take a left at the first traffic light. Proceed 10 blocks and follow signs to Geisinger Medical Center. Pine Barn adjoins the Center.

THE TAVERN
New Wilmington, Pennsylvania

"The sheltered cot, the cultivated farm,
The never-failing brook, the busy meadow,
The decent church that topped the
*   neighboring hill,*
The Hawthorn bush, with seats
*   beneath the shade,*
For talking age and whispering lovers made.

These words from Oliver Goldsmith in many ways express the beautiful countryside and ambience of New Wilmington, which is in the rolling country of northwest Pennsylvania.

The year was 1973. For years I had been fascinated with the "plain people" who live in eastern Pennsylvania. These include the Amish, Dunkards, Moravians, and Schwenkfelders. I had always enjoyed the back roads of Lancaster and Berks counties and admired the picturebook farms and industrious people.

Now at the western end of Pennsylvania, I was once again in "Dutch country." I had heard there was a sizable community of Amish here, but I was surprised at the scope.

The purpose of my visit was to meet Mrs. Ernst Durrast and visit The Tavern in New Wilmington. When I drove through the town, I saw the familiar black buggies and plain dress of these pious folk who originally fled from Europe in the 18th century to obtain religious freedom.

"Oh, yes," Mrs. Durrast remarked over a cup of tea, "this is Amish country, and they are a people who are quite proud of their ancestry. I hope that while you're here you'll drive out to the countryside to see those neat farms and spotless buildings." We talked about New Wilmington and Westminster College and some of the joys of living in western Pennsylvania.

"Well, I've had this inn for forty-five years," she said, "and I just can't imagine living anywhere else. This is a lovely little town. I like it especially because there's a constant flow of young people from the college."

The talk then shifted to the startling number of entrées on the luncheon menu. Just for fun, I counted twenty-seven, plus an appetizer, vegetables, fritters, salad, rolls, dessert, and a beverage. It was real country fare, including gourmet beef balls, creamed chicken on a biscuit, cabbage rolls, grilled smoked pork chops, ham steaks, and cheese soufflé with creamed chicken. Two warm honey buns with whipped butter are always served.

As I could see, lunch was a substantial meal. Mrs. D. explained to me that a great many of her noontime patrons are older people and prefer to eat their main meal at midday.

Dinners include the majority of the luncheon offerings plus about twelve other main dishes. There's often a most unusual combination of white meat of chicken and lobster tail served in a special sherry sauce. How does that sound?

There's a small lodge across the village street with a few sleeping rooms available. One of these is frequently occupied by my dear friends Claire and Lucy Dee Dee of Grand Rapids, Michigan. They first recommended Mrs. Durrast's splendid establishment to me back in 1972.

New Wilmington is just a few minutes from I-80, the east-west highway that traverses northern Pennsylvania. It's about two hundred and forty miles from the Poconos where there are at least three country inns that I have found most comfortable.

"It wonders me," said Mrs. Durrast, borrowing a quaint Amish saying, "why it has taken you so long to find us."

THE TAVERN, Box 153, New Wilmington, Pa. 16142; 412-946-2020. A bustling country restaurant on the town square with 5 sleeping rooms in a lodge directly across the street. European plan. Lunch and dinner served daily except Tuesdays. Reservations required. Closed Thanksgiving and Christmas. Sports and cultural events at Westminister College nearby. No credit cards. No diversions for small children. Mrs. Ernst Durrast, Innkeeper.

Directions: From I-80, take Exit 1-S, and follow Rte. 18 south to Rte. 208. Proceed east on 208 to town square. From I-79, follow Rte. 208 west for 14 mi. to New Wilmington.

Southern New England

Eastern Time Zone

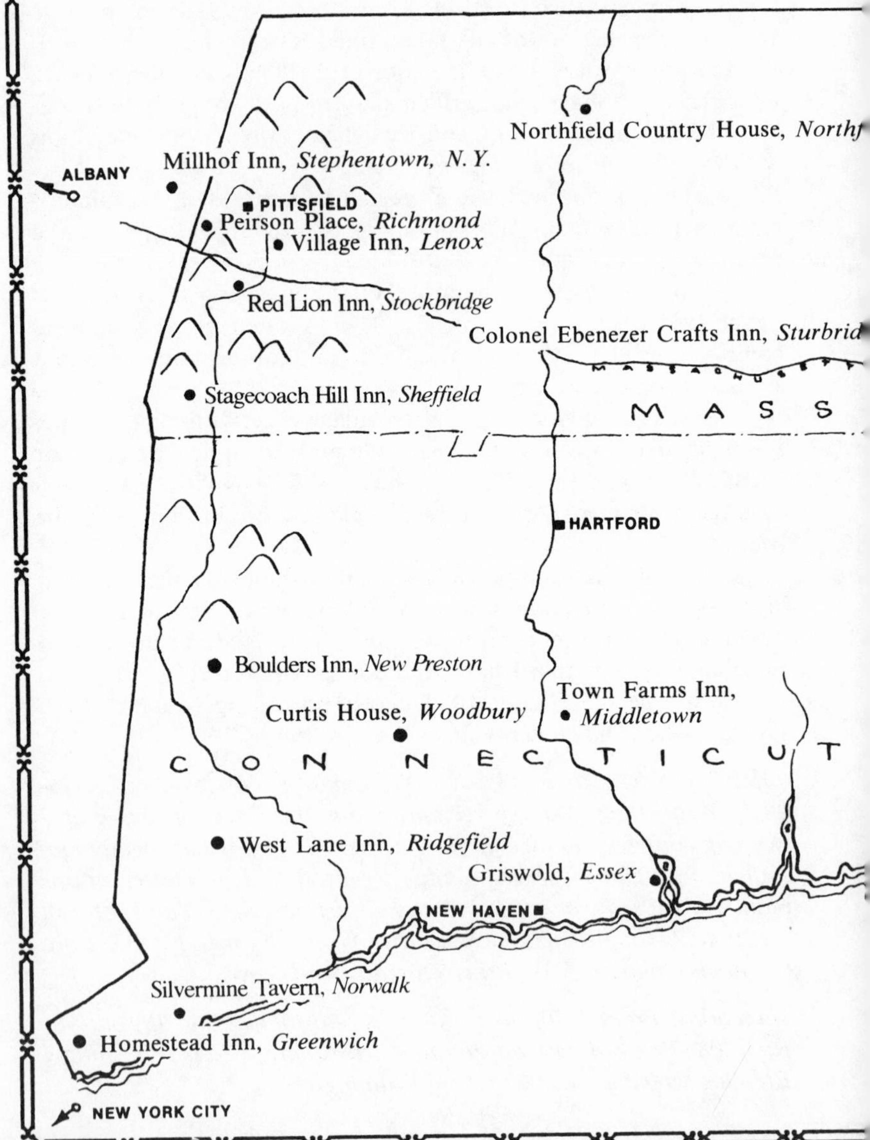
Northfield Country House, Northf
Millhof Inn, Stephentown, N.Y.
ALBANY
PITTSFIELD
Peirson Place, Richmond
Village Inn, Lenox
Red Lion Inn, Stockbridge
Colonel Ebenezer Crafts Inn, Sturbrid
MASSACHUSETT
Stagecoach Hill Inn, Sheffield
MASS
HARTFORD
Boulders Inn, New Preston
Town Farms Inn,
Middletown
Curtis House, Woodbury
CONNECTICUT
West Lane Inn, Ridgefield
Griswold, Essex
NEW HAVEN
Silvermine Tavern, Norwalk
Homestead Inn, Greenwich
NEW YORK CITY

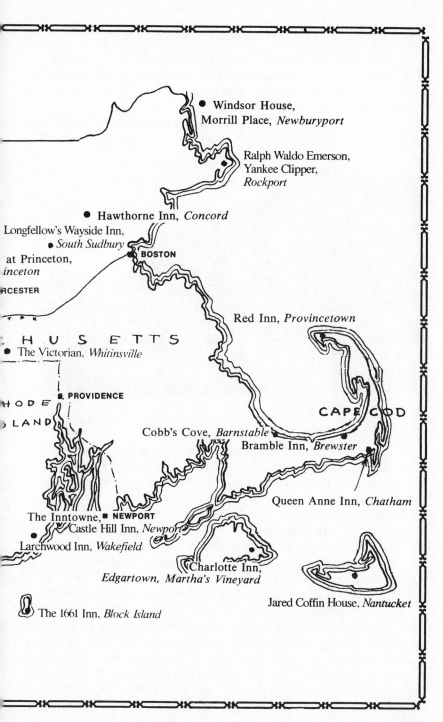

Windsor House,
Morrill Place, *Newburyport*

Ralph Waldo Emerson,
Yankee Clipper,
Rockport

● Hawthorne Inn, *Concord*

Longfellow's Wayside Inn,
● *South Sudbury*

at Princeton,
inceton

RCESTER

Red Inn, *Provincetown*

BOSTON

● H U S E T T S

● The Victorian, *Whitinsville*

HODE

LAND

■ PROVIDENCE

CAPE COD

Cobb's Cove, *Barnstable*

Bramble Inn, *Brewster*

Queen Anne Inn, *Chatham*

The Inntowne, ■ NEWPORT
Castle Hill Inn, *Newport*

Larchwood Inn, *Wakefield*

Charlotte Inn,
Edgartown, Martha's Vineyard

The 1661 Inn, *Block Island*

Jared Coffin House, *Nantucket*

105

CURTIS HOUSE
Woodbury, Connecticut

"Yes, since the inn opened in 1754, I believe we are the oldest inn in Connecticut." The speaker was redhaired Gary Hardisty, himself a lifelong resident of Woodbury and a member of a family that has operated the Curtis House since early 1950.

"There have been quite a few changes and alterations over the years, and many different owners. However, since four of them, all

unrelated, were named 'Curtis' I believe that this is an appropriate name."

The Curtis House by any name is a real country inn experience. I visited it on a chilly Saturday afternoon in January after a pleasant snowfall the night before. Everything combined to make it idyllically New England. The countryside was at its best in a white mantle, and the 18th-century homes and churches in the towns and villages in northwest Connecticut, gleamed in the bright sunshine.

The drive from the Massachusetts Berkshires (Woodbury is in the Connecticut Berkshires) took about ninety minutes and I was eagerly anticipating lunch. As I opened the old front door, the heavenly odors of hearty New England cooking wafted toward me.

I walked through a narrow hall past the stairway to the lodging rooms on two floors above, and entered the low-ceilinged, heavily beamed dining room. Waitresses were bustling about carrying trays laden with beef pot pie, Yankee pot roast, roast beef hash, and scallops. The room was filled with happy people, including quite a few families of students at the local prep schools. I was given a quiet table in the corner, and my visit to the Curtis House began in earnest.

My luncheon included a delicious fresh fruit and sherbet cup, hot muffins, and a beef pie. From the desserts I chose an apple crisp which was served with vanilla ice cream. I noticed that the dinner menu offered these things and much more, including sweetbreads, roast beef, and quite a few dishes such as broiled bluefish.

I was delighted to discover that there were eighteen lodging rooms in this old inn, many of them with canopied twin or double beds. Twelve of the rooms have private baths. There are four more modern rooms in the nearby Carriage House.

Later, I chatted with Gary Hardisty in the living room with the fireplace and wide floorboards. He pointed out that the large inn signs outside were the work of Wallace Nutting who included many of the Woodbury buildings in his book, *Connecticut the Beautiful*. Gary mentioned that Woodbury was one of the antiquing centers of New England and there were many, many antique shops on Routes 6 and 47. The Glebe House which was the birthplace of the American Episcopal Church is only a ten-minute walk from the inn.

Gary explained that as a rule dinner reservations are not accepted, with the exception of New Year's Eve, Mother's Day, Easter, and Thanksgiving.

I learned that almost everything on the extensive menu is prepared from scratch and the inn does all of its own baking. Those warm muffins at lunch really hit the spot.

After spending the remaining part of the afternoon browsing through the village, I left Woodbury and the Curtis House as the setting sun created great red and orange streaks over the snowy hills and the lights of the inn were already casting their warm beckoning glow. This is the way it's been for well over 200 years.

CURTIS HOUSE, Route 6 (Main St.), Woodbury, Conn., 06798; 203-263-2101. An 18-room village inn, 12 mi. from Waterbury. Open year-round. European plan. Lodgings include continental breakfast. Lunch and dinner served daily except Christmas. No pets. Lodgings not adaptable to young children. Antiquing, skiing, tennis, platform tennis, horseback riding nearby. The Hardisty Family, Innkeepers.

Directions: From N.Y. take Sawmill River Pkwy. to I-84. Take Exit 15 from I-84 in Southbury. Follow Rte. 6 north to Woodbury. From Hartford take I-84 to Exit 17, follow Rte. 64 to Woodbury.

THE BOULDERS INN
Lake Waramaug, New Preston, Connecticut

Carolyn Woollen drew another cup of delicious tea from the samovar and I helped myself to two lumps of sugar and a dollop of cream. She passed me a plate of homemade breads and cakes.

For a moment we just sat there looking out across Lake Waramaug, now comfortably covered with a good blanket of snow and basking in the brilliance of colors and hues created by the sinking sun. Blue waters, white sails, and ruddy swimmers give this same lake an altogether different look in summer.

Carolyn put her finger to her lips and then her hand to her ear, "If we listen quietly I think we can hear the Canada geese talking to each other."

There was a stamping of feet at the back door and I could hear the clatter of cross-country skis being stacked in the corner. Some red-cheeked guests came trooping across the living room and gathered around the fireplace warming their hands and exclaiming about the wonderful time they had had on the trails.

In the 1980 edition of this book I reported on the progress that Carolyn and her husband Jim and their children Peter, Mary, and Byron had made during their first full season at the inn. At that time their objective had been to provide a small intimate retreat where care, attention, and a homelike atmosphere would blend with the physical setting and facilities. Now I was ready for another update:

"Oh, we've all had a wonderful time. In addition to attending to our guests, we've extended our outdoor dining area with two terraced decks overlooking the lake. We did this in time for last summer's guests and the shady area under the pine trees proved a very popular place for dining.

"We installed fireplaces in our cottages which certainly make them very cozy. They all have either patios or balconies.

"Summer and fall are well-established here by a tradition of vacationers and by those enjoying the autumn foliage, but more and more of our guests are coming during the colder months because it's an area of such incredible beauty. I think it's quite reminiscent of the Scottish hills and it's hard to realize that New York is just eighty miles south of us. Guests can skate on the lake, toboggan on our old ski hill, and hike the mountain trails which actually start from the back door. We're only twenty minutes away from the Mohawk Mountain ski center. For guests who are more inclined toward reading or conversaton, we have a whole corner of the living room set aside as a library."

I picked up the menu to see what chef Marty Carlson was

offering this season and found two familiar favorites: Duck Breast Maconnaise and Chicken Paprikash. "Each night a list of several specials supplements the standard menu," Carolyn explained, "this keeps Marty's creative juices flowing and offers constant variety to guests. His versatility is exciting."

The cross-country skiers and hikers would have a hearty meal at the Boulder Inn tonight.

One brief snatch of conversation caught my ear: "You know, Emily, it's so good here right now, can you imagine what it's like in the summer!"

BOULDERS INN, Lake Waramaug, New Preston, Ct. 06777; 203-868-7918. A 14-room year-round resort-inn, 20 mi. north of Danbury, 40 mi. west of Hartford. From Memorial Day to Labor Day, three meals a day served to travelers as well as guests. Monday dinner an informal meal for houseguests only. Lodging during this period on the modified American plan. From September through May, breakfast is served every day; dinner, Tuesday through Saturday. Open on Thanksgiving, closed Christmas Eve and Christmas Day. Tennis, swimming, boating, sailing, fishing, antiquing, hiking on mountain trails, bicycling, xc skiing, sledding. Golf, horseback riding, and downhill skiing nearby; 20 min. from chamber music concert series July through August. Not suitable for children under 6. The Woollen Family, Innkeepers.

Directions: From I-84, take Exit 7 and follow Rte. 7 north to Rte. 202 (formerly 25) through New Milford. Proceed 8 mi. to New Preston then 1½ mi. to inn on Rte. 45.

A suggested wandering from Boulders Inn through the Litchfield County hills: from the Boulders driveway, turn left and go south on Route 45 to New Preston. Turn right in front of Pavilion Hall and go west on the New Preston Hill Road approximately eight miles to Route 7 at Bulls Bridge (the covered bridge is 100 yards west of the highway). Turn north on Route 7, noting along the way the Fellerman Glass Studio, the town of Kent, Kent Falls and Cornwall Pottery ("Pottery Exhibit"). Four miles north of Cornwall Bridge turn right on Route 128. Cross the covered bridge into the hamlet of West Cornwall (the Deck Restaurant, Ingersol Shaker Furniture, Farnsworth Books & Antiques). Continue east on 128 to Route 4, east on 4 to Goshen, then south on Route 63 to Litchfield (North Street and South Street are bordered by classic 17th- and 18th-century mansions). For horticulturists, a three-mile ride south on Route 63 brings one to White Flower Farm (open April through October); or, head west out of Litchfield on Route 202 for seven miles to Route 341. Turn right and bear west three miles to Route 45; left on 45 and south 1½ miles to the Boulders.

Carolyn and Jim Woollen
The Boulders Inn
New Preston, Connecticut

About five miles from the Homestead Inn in Greenwich, going east on the Post Road, is Valley Road, one of the old historic routes along the Mianus River. This rolling road runs along the water's edge and is framed by stacked stone fences. Some of the houses are built of stone and have the flavor of earlier times.

In 1688 the first gristmill was built on the upper Mianus River beside the bridge (now called Palmer Hill Bridge) connecting Valley Road with Palmer Hill Road. This bridge is the beginning of Dumpling Pond, where the British staged one of their biggest raids on Greenwich in 1779. General Tryon's lobsterbacks (a local name for the red-coated British soldiers) were plundering the town. Several of them came to the mill and demanded that the miller's wife feed them. The miller's wife, a fervent rebel, told the soldiers that dinner was not done, and while they waited she secretly removed the dumplings she had been cooking and threw them into the pond. Since then it has been known as Dumpling Pond.

Nancy Smith and Lessie Davison
The Homestead Inn
Greenwich, Connecticut

One of the prettiest local rides to see the "wonder of nature" (fall foliage) is to go north out of the Curtis House driveway to the first traffic light. Turn left onto Route 317 and travel up hill and down dale to the town of Roxbury, approximately five miles. Natives say that on a clear day, from the top of one of the hills, the Empire State Building in New York City can be seen. While I have never personally witnessed this phenomenon, the panorama, I believe, cannot be equaled anywhere. Our colors are every bit as vibrant as those in our sister states of Vermont and New Hampshire and while our hills may not be as high, they have their own special grandeur. There is, too, on the top of one of the hills, a private "grass strip" airport still in operation and looking much the same as it did when originally opened around 1932 by a still-local family. At one time parachute jumping was taught at this field and Sunday afternoon exhibitions were given.

Gary Hardisty
Curtis House
Woodbury, Connecticut

SILVERMINE TAVERN
Norwalk, Connecticut

"Meet Miss Abigail," said Frank Whitman. "She's the only woman permitted by Connecticut law to stand within three feet of a bar."

I spoke courteously, but Miss Abigail just stood there in her crinoline and lace, looking inscrutable. The walls behind her and, in fact, in all of the dining rooms were covered with old farm implements and tools, as well as American primitive paintings.

Frank and I continued our tour of the Silvermine Tavern. "The Tavern was named for the town," he said. "That name, in turn, came from an old as-yet-unfounded rumor about a silver mine

discovered by an early settler. The old post office was here at the four corners."

We passed through two low-ceilinged sitting rooms brimming with antiques. There were fireplaces in each and one had an old clock with wooden works. Frank pointed out the beams from the original inn as well as the old-fashioned colonial hinges on the doorway. Some of the oil paintings of the colonial ladies and gentlemen looked rather forbidding.

The inn was decorated for Christmas with an eighteen-foot Christmas tree on the porch and an antique four-passenger sleigh beside it. The tree and the sleigh were visible from all of the dining rooms and the centerpiece of the decorations. There was also a large gingerbread house made by Lothar, the inn baker.

I followed him up a winding staircase and found typical country inn bedrooms without television or telephones. These are also to be found in other buildings.

"You can imagine that we're quite popular with honeymooners," he said. "They like to wander the country roads and to feed the ducks and swans on the Mill Pond."

The Tavern at various times has served as a country inn, a gentleman's country seat, and a town meeting place. It has a very large outdoor dining area overlooking the Silvermine River and the Mill Pond with ducks and swans. Summer terrace dining among the oaks, maples, pines, and poplar trees is very popular with playgoers to the Westport Playhouse and the Stratford Shakespeare Theatre nearby. I like the Silvermine in the winter also, when the many fireplaces are crackling and the candles create a romantic feeling.

Some of the New England dishes on the menu include Indian pudding, bread pudding, honeybuns, native scrod, lobster, scallops, and oysters. On Thursday night there is a buffet that includes roast beef, corned beef, and fried chicken. On Wednesday and Friday night during the summer there is a barbecue, and there is a Sunday brunch buffet which has as many as 25 different offerings on the big tables.

When my tour of the Tavern and all the buildings at the Crossroads was over, I went back to ask Miss Abigail if she'd care to join me for dinner. I suggested the chicken pie. No reply. I pointed out that all the breads and desserts were homemade—even the ice cream. Still she remained inscrutable.

But I didn't feel too badly when Frank assured me that she hasn't spoken to anyone in years.

SILVERMINE TAVERN, Perry Ave., Norwalk, Ct. 06850; 203-847-4558. A 10-room country inn in the residential section of Norwalk. Long Island Sound and beaches 6 mi. away. European plan includes continental breakfast. Lunch and dinner served to travelers daily. Open year-round. Closed Christmas Day and Tuesdays during winter. Golf, tennis, and fishing nearby. Francis C. Whitman, Innkeeper.

Directions: From New York or New Haven via I-95, take Exit 15. Pick up the new Rte. 7 going north. At the end of Rte. 7 (approx. 1 mi.) turn right, go to first stoplight, turn right. At next stoplight by firehouse turn right onto Silvermine Ave. Proceed down Silvermine Ave. about 2 mi. to Tavern. From I-84 and Danbury take old Rte. 7 south to Norwalk. Watch for Kelly Greens ½ mi. south of Merritt Pkwy. on the left, turn right on Perry Ave. opposite Kelly Greens. Follow Perry Ave. 2 mi. to Tavern. From Merritt Pkwy. take Exit 39 south on old Rte. 7 and follow directions above.

GRISWOLD INN
Essex, Connecticut

The Griswold Inn is proof of the old saying "Nothing succeeds like success." When I mentioned this to innkeeper Bill Winterer, he laughed modestly and said, "I'm not so sure we're successful, but I know we're working very hard at what we're doing and we love it."

Bill first visited Essex and saw the inn when he was an officer candidate at nearby New London Coast Guard Academy. After a few years in the world of high finance, he and his wife Vicky decided to start life anew here as innkeepers.

"Can you imagine," he said, "Only five families have owned this building since 1776. It was the first three-story structure in Connecticut and except for a couple of small changes, it remains the same. The Tap Room was built in 1738 and was the first schoolhouse in Essex. It was rolled on logs down the main street to its present location by a team of oxen."

"Our revolutionary activities began here in Essex in 1776 when the *Oliver Cromwell,* a ship of war commissioned by the Continental Congress, was built in the Essex shipyards," said Bill. "However, the greatest excitement came during the War of 1812 when the entire Essex fleet was destroyed in the harbor by British ships. The British officers occupied the Griswold Inn, and I understand the commanding officer spoke of it as being 'long on charm but short on plumbing.' I think we have the plumbing under control today."

Today, the Griswold Inn has within its many dining rooms and parlors a remarkable collection of marine paintings, prints, ship models, firearms, binnacles, ships' clocks, a potbellied stove, humorous posters and prints, a genuine popcorn machine, and heaven-knows-what-all.

One of the dining rooms was constructed from an abandoned New Hampshire Bridge, and in still another, the walls rock back and forth creating the impression of being on board ship. Fresh flowers, warm woods, open fires, and candles abound, and for the guests' edification, there are different kinds of entertainment almost every evening.

All of the twenty-two guest rooms at the "Gris" have private baths and are furnished in early Essex. A lovely home next door to the inn has been converted into two suites. On the street floor of this building, a comfortable living room with a woodburning fireplace and a game room will provide houseguests with space for conviviality and relaxation.

The menu is basically American with a wide selection of fresh and salt-water fish, also beef and lamb dishes, which have been popular in this country since its very beginning. A Hunt Breakfast is

served every Sunday which includes great, long tables of fried chicken, herring, lamb, kidneys, eggs, grits, creamed chipped beef and the inn's own special brand of 1776 sausage.

Bill and Vicky, along with their children, are great lovers of holidays and as a result the Griswold has special holiday celebrations throughout the year, including an annual children's Halloween parade, the Thanksgiving festival, a concert of baroque Christmas music by the Eastern Brass Quintet, a gala New Year's Eve party, and further celebrations on Groundhog's Day, Valentine's Day and George Washington's birthday. Each of these holidays is commemorated by decorations on the evergreen tree perched on top of the famous potbellied stove in the Tap Room. At Easter the tree is decorated with bunnies and eggs.

The Winterers are also the proprietors of the Town Farms Inn in nearby Middletown and the Dock n' Dine Fish House at Saybrook Point.

GRISWOLD INN, Main St., Essex, Conn. 06426; 203-767-0991. A 22-room inn in a waterside town, steps away from the Connecticut River, and located near the Eugene O'Neill Theatre, Goodspeed Opera House, Ivoryton Playhouse, Gillette Castle, Mystic Village, Valley Railroad and Hammonasset State Beach. European plan. Complimentary continental breakfast served daily to inn guests. Lunch and dinner served daily to travelers. Hunt breakfast served Sundays. Closed Christmas Eve and Christmas Day. Day sailing on inn's 44-foot ketch by appointment. Bicycles, tennis, and boating nearby. Victoria and William G. Winterer, Innkeepers.

Directions: From I-95 take Exit 69 and travel north on Rte. 9 to Exit 3, Essex. Turn right at stoplight and follow West Ave. to center of town. Turn right onto Main St. and proceed down to water and inn.

WEST LANE INN
Ridgefield, Connecticut

"Basically, I think we have three different types of guests that find their way to our little inn." Maureen Mayer and I were seated on the broad front porch of the West Lane Inn enjoying a generous continental breakfast. "By the way," she added, "if you'd like a bigger breakfast, we have an a la carte breakfast menu that offers, among other things, grapefruit, sliced bananas, berries, yogurt, corn flakes, and poached eggs."

One of the things that sets West Lane Inn apart is the many additional amenities this attractive woman innkeeper provides for her guests. For example, there is a clock in every bedroom as well as a computerized phone system, a radio-TV, individual heating and air conditioning controls, and a one-day laundry and dry-cleaning service. On this visit the big news was that Maureen was now providing six more generous-sized rooms in a New England clapboard building a few steps back of the main inn.

"I have seen the need for these additional accommodations for some time," she explained. "Among our guests are families being relocated to the Ridgefield-Fairfield-Danbury area who need a comfortable, roomy place in which to stay while they look for a new home. Many come and stay for a week or two. I decided that they would be much more comfortable if we had accommodations that reflected the feeling of the area, so we have rooms with decks overlooking our lawn and the forest in the rear. Some of these have fireplaces and kitchen facilities. You see, guests can literally establish a little home for a short time. One of our bathrooms is designed for the handicapped."

I observed that Ridgefield itself would be an ideal suburban place in which to live. Within commuting distance of New York and driving distance of the many corporations which are relocating in Fairfield County, Ridgefield is a most pleasant town with large graceful trees and excellent small shops. "There's also a very active community here," Maureen remarked. "We have a historical society, a library, the Ridgefield Symphony, the League of Women Voters, and various men's service clubs, sports groups, and business groups."

West Lane Inn is set back from the village street with a broad lawn enhanced by azaleas, tulips, roses, and maple and oak trees. It was originally built as a mansion in the early 1800s and the bedrooms are unusually commodious.

The other types of guests are commercial travelers, both men and women, and vacationers who enjoy country-inn hospitality. "I think we understand commercial travelers very well and we've done everything possible to have them feel that this is really a 'home away from home.' I believe you met a gentleman from Yorkshire, England, here a couple of years ago.

"As far as the country-inn travelers are concerned, we're at sort of a crossroads for north-south, east-west travel, and many couples on their way to or from New England come back and stay every year."

The West Lane could well be a model for other bed-and-breakfast inns everywhere. Every lodging room is spotless and the furnishings and decorations are all part of a harmonious color scheme.

One of the things that also appeals to me is the 100%-cotton sheets on every bed in the inn. When was the last time you slept in a bed that had 100%-cotton sheets? Outstanding.

WEST LANE INN, 22 West Lane, Ridgefield, Conn. 06877; 203-438-7323. A 20-room inn in a quiet residential village in southwest Connecticut. Approx. 1 hour from N.Y.C. Open every day in the year. Breakfast and light snacks available until 10:30 P.M. Convenient to many museums and antique shops. Golf, tennis, swimming, and xc skiing and other outdoor recreation available nearby. No pets. Maureen Mayer, Innkeeper.

Directions: From New York: follow I-684 to Exit 6, turn right on Rte. 35, 12 mi. to Ridgefield. Inn is on left. From Hartford: Exit I-84 on Rte. 7 south and follow Rte. 35 to Ridgefield.

THE HOMESTEAD INN
Greenwich, Connecticut

My arrival at the Homestead coincided literally with that of Lady Lancashire.

No, Lady Lancashire is not a member of Princess Diane's ladies-in-waiting, nor will you see her listed in *Burke's Peerage*. However, she has had some mention in the American press. Lady Lancashire is a copy of a ship's figurehead that for many years stood proudly atop a grape arbor on the property that is now the Homestead Inn in Greenwich.

When Nancy Smith and Lessie Davison purchased the inn a few years ago, they discovered the original, literally larger-than-life wooden carving was missing. However, it has since been discovered on display at the Museum of the City of New York. How it got there from Greenwich is, as I understand it, a mystery.

"Of course it was impossible to relocate her, but Nancy and I were determined that some representation of the Lady should be at the Homestead." Lessie handed me a cup of tea and a piece of beautiful chocolate cake.

"So, we commissioned a copy from Greg Fisher who is a marvelous woodcarver located in Old Mystic. We could hardly wait, although it was two years in the carving." This was Nancy's contribution.

Finding the right tree was the first challenge, but Greg found it in Presque Isle, Maine. All the details and careful planning finally resulted in this beautiful carving standing six feet tall and weighing 800 pounds. "It took four men to carry her across the threshold of the inn," Nancy said.

Now, in addition to the Lady Lancashire, the Homestead has thirteen bedrooms, all of them with a distinctly different decorative theme. They are splendidly furnished, including many antiques and such comforts and appurtenances as clock radios, electric blankets, two pillows for every head, lots of books and magazines, and very modern bathrooms that contain the only make-up mirrors I've ever seen in a country inn.

A continental breakfast included in the room charge is served to overnight guests.

The inn is located in the residential area of Greenwich and is set back from the road in its own orchard and gardens, highlighted by magnificent hydrangea bushes.

The restaurant at the Homestead is called "La Grange" and the French cuisine is the creation of Jacques Theibeult from Paris. The dinner menu features many French dishes including veal, duckling, lamb, and beef. Both lunch and dinner are served.

Reflecting the sensitivities and tastes of Lessie Davison and Nancy Smith, two attractive and talented women who a few years ago saw the possibilities of restoring the Homestead property, the inn today manages to be an interesting mix of old New England and a suburban sophistication.

Greenwich itself abounds in things to do. There are first-run cinemas, excellent sports facilities, including a municipal golf course,

public tennis courts, and a number of marinas. There is a small historic museum, delightful shops, and frequent local art and music events.

The inn is convenient to many corporate headquarters in Fairfield County.

Now, in addition to the two elegant women innkeepers, there is one more — Lady Lancashire.

THE HOMESTEAD INN, 420 Field Point Rd., Greenwich, Conn. 06830; 203-869-7500. A 13-room inn located in the residental area of a suburb, 45 mins. from New York City. Lunch served Mon. thru Fri. Dinner served daily except Christmas, New Year's, Good Friday, and perhaps others. Located a short distance from Connecticut countryside and shore scenes. Accessible by train from New York City. No amusements for children under 12. No pets. Lessie B. Davison, Nancy K. Smith, Innkeepers.

Directions: The inn is 3 min. from Rte. I-95. Take Exit 3 in Greenwich, turn left and go under the Turnpike and then left again in about two blocks, just before the railroad overpass. Go 2 blocks to the stop sign, turn left on Field Point Rd. and continue to the inn on the right.

TOWN FARMS INN
Middletown, Connecticut

A pleasant mid-December light snow was gently falling as I followed the river road from Middletown toward the Town Farms Inn. In the late afternoon dusk, I saw the mellowed red brick building tucked in right beside the railroad tracks, with the river on the other side busily making its way to the sea.

I walked into the parlor where a bright fire in the fireplace was already sending forth a cheery glow. In one corner was a striking Christmas tree with small glistening white lights, red bows, and gold garlands and ornaments. I settled down in a deep sofa and immediately ordered a cup of tea—it seemed most appropriate in this elegant atmosphere that reminded me of similar scenes in the English Lake district.

This time it was Vicky Winterer who was able to join me for a few moments before we both went over to nearby Essex to share the excitement of the tree-lighting ceremonies at the Griswold Inn.

"This has really been a very happy autumn for us," she said. "The most significant step we have taken is the installation of Walter Hawley as innkeeper. He has been invaluable and, as you know, is extremely knowledgeable about food. Both Bill and I are very pleased with him."

Indeed, I am well acquainted with Walt's many abilities since I have known him for some years, first when he was at the Inn at Princeton and later at the Inn on the Library Lawn.

"This past October we began a series of special festival dinners," Vicky continued. "First a wine-tasting dinner and then a game festival at which three or four different wild meats and birds were served. We are topping it off with a special traditional Christmas festival next week.

"It's been over a year since our reopening after the fire, and it took us several months to get everything tidied up once again. While we were at it we tuck-pointed the entire building and repainted the public rooms, but as you notice we have stayed with the faithful old colors that have really become very much appreciated by our patrons."

We strolled into the American Indian room with its low ceilings and beautifully mellowed exposed beams. The ladder-back chairs add a harmonious note. Twin fireplaces were decorated with Christmas garlands and white lights, and all of the candelabras were entwined with garlands of holly. There were red roses in vases on each table.

This room creates an intriguing contrast to the River Room which is almost two stories high with magnificent chandeliers, a

Palladian window, and a full view of the river and shore beyond.

The inner wall of the River Room has a mural depicting a circa 1865 scene on the river. The light blue walls were adorned with green garlands, and on a little balcony at one end a string trio was tuning up for the evening's entertainment. "We find chamber music most appropriate, but we also have other types as well," Vicky remarked.

My attention was drawn to the dessert trolley absolutely loaded with scrumptious, creamy, delightful offerings that convinced me Walter Hawley was not very far away. The menu at Town Farms Inn includes a definite nod towards French cuisine with, among other things, a roasted Muscovy duck; fresh boneless trout seasoned with mushrooms, shallots, and capers; small venison steaks embedded with red peppercorns, sautéed and wrapped in a herbed crêpe; and a venison, rabbit, and wild duck *estouffade* braised with a selection of vegetables and served in a brioche.

"You must come back next summer and have lunch on the terrace overlooking the river," quoth Vicky. "Bill and I love to come over here, sit under the colorful Cinzano umbrella, and watch the river traffic. When the occasional train goes by everybody applauds. On Friday nights we have dancing on the terrace."

TOWN FARMS INN, Silver St., Middletown, Conn. 06457; 203-347-7438. A riverside restaurant just a few minutes from the center of Middletown. Lunch and dinner served daily except Christmas Eve and Christmas Day. Wesleyan Univ. nearby. Long Island Sound about 40 min. away. Bill and Vicky Winterer, Innkeepers.

Directions: From I-91 follow Rte. 9 south to Middletown and take Exit 12. Follow signs to Town Farms.

121

COBB'S COVE
Barnstable Village, Cape Cod, Massachusetts

"That's the beach and harbor area out there, it's just a short and pleasant walk." Evelyn Chester and I had arrived at the top floor of Cobb's Cove, which is a very small, quiet inn in Barnstable Village on the north shore of Cape Cod. This particular room had a studio-type window which swept from the eaves almost to the top of the cathedral ceiling. Many of its features were also to be found in the other five lodging rooms, including massive exposed beams and posts, and natural wood walls and ceilings. Each has a full bath including a whirlpool tub, a dressing room, private telephone lines which are available for extended stays, and air conditioning. The bedroom furniture, draperies, and adornments harmonize beautifully with the colors and textures of the handsome wood. There are big fluffy towels reminiscent of those supplied by the paradors in Spain.

"At night it's fun to turn off the lights and look at the Cape Cod sky lit by the stars and moon, and to see the twinkling lights of towns in the distance," she remarked, as we returned to the first floor and the Keeping Room.

We were ushered through the dining room by an impressive cat named Fordham and a West Highland terrier, who answered to the name of Annie Laurie. There was a long trestle table where Evelyn and Henri-Jean, who was at the moment in the kitchen preparing dinner, serve their houseguests. Floor-to-ceiling bookshelves displayed works on many subjects, sharing space with a wide variety of shell, mineral, and fossil collections. In one corner was a baby grand piano, and the strains of Handel wafted from a hi-fi system.

Henri-Jean radiating good humor and the savory aromas of bluefish Provençale, came out of the kitchen, and we all sat down in front of one of the most unusual fireplaces I've ever seen. "It's a

Count Rumford fireplace," explained Henri-Jean. "You'll notice that it's quite shallow, but it was designed hundreds of years ago by a gentleman whose personal history would make a good book or movie. The design is such that it keeps the entire room bathed in generous heat. We have a book about the fireplace and its originator."

That was the beginning of a long and most enjoyable conversation which continued throughout the remainder of the beautiful sun-bathed December afternoon on Cape Cod. I heard all about how Henri-Jean, who is a civil engineer, designed, cut out, assembled, and physically built this beautiful Colonial salt-box manor on its 1643 historical site. "Actually, Evelyn and I worked side by side in every phase of its design and construction," he said, sending a most loving look in her direction. "We've been open since 1976, but have maintained a restrained profile, acquiring our guests by personal referral. What we have here is a basic enjoyment of life and people, because everyone who visits us has something to share."

There is much to share, both at Cobb's Cove itself and in that particular section of Cape Cod. "We are on the low-key side of the Cape," asserted Evelyn with a smile. "Because it's more people-oriented rather than a resort section, most of the small craft shops, like the weavers and the pottery and the Bird Barn, are open year-round. We have many guests who come in the so-called off-season, and in many ways that's the best time. The beaches are even more beautiful because there's hardly anyone on them, except the seagulls. There are lots of opportunities for walking and bicycling."

I'm looking forward to many visits and evenings of sitting around the Keeping Room fireplace after a good dinner at Cobb's Cove. It would be a good place to write a book.

COBB'S COVE, Barnstable Village, Rte. 6A, Cape Cod, Ma. 02630; 617-362-9356. A 6-room secluded inn on Cape Cod's north shore. Lodgings include a full breakfast. Houseguests can arrange for dinner. Open every day in the year. Within a short distance of Cape Cod Bay and the Atlantic Ocean, the U.S. National Seashore, and Sandy Neck Conservatory, as well as many museums, art galleries, craft shops, and other attractions of the Cape. Active sports nearby. No facilities to amuse children at the inn. No pets. Credit cards not accepted. Evelyn Chester, Innkeeper.

Directions: From Rte. 6 (Mid-Cape Hwy.) turn left at Exit 6 on Rte. 132 to Barnstable. Turn right on Rte. 6A, approximately 3 mi. through Barnstable Village, past the only traffic light and turn left just past the Barnstable Unitarian Church. After approximately 300 yds., look for small wooden sign on left at a gravel driveway saying: "Evelyn Chester."

CHARLOTTE INN
Edgartown, Massachusetts

I awakened at 6:30 A.M. on a splendid September morning at the Charlotte Inn in Edgartown on Martha's Vineyard Island. The sun peeked around the corner through the french doors, and with each passing moment the furnishings and decorations of my room became visible. "Was this, indeed," I asked myself, "the ultimate country inn bedroom?"

This particular bedroom happened to be in the handsome Carriage House that Gery Conover had designed especially for this site in the Charlotte Inn garden.

The cathedral ceiling was supported by two 6x8 beams whose brown stain contrasted with the white plaster ceilings and green wallpaper with its delicate silver pattern. Overhead a stately brass chandelier hung from the ceiling. A traditional square French antique clock silently noted each passing second.

A very pleasant wing-backed chair was accompanied by a brass floor lamp, and over a Chippendale low chest was a handsome oval gilt mirror. There were a few adornments on the wall reflecting Gery and Paula Conover's great interest in art of all kinds. On the right hung a set of three framed line drawings of as many breeds of chickens. To my left was an 18th-century print showing a New England brick building.

I'm tempted to go on with a further description of this new apartment that is typical of the other bedrooms throughout the inn and the annex; but just before press time I received a letter from Gery Conover, Jr., who proudly announced that one of the old Edgartown circa 1800 houses across the street has now become a part of the Charlotte Inn.

"It has a fantastic garden so we have decided to call it the 'Garden House.' We will be decorating it in a 'French Country' look. This house will also provide our houseguests with a private lounge of their own where they may enjoy the fireplace, play games, watch TV and get acquainted."

Like many other Edgartown houses, the Charlotte Inn is a classic three-story white clapboard with a widow's walk on top. It was the former home of a Martha's Vineyard sea captain. Lodgings are individually furnished with their own private baths, and are very quiet. Guests may enjoy a continental breakfast served in their rooms. Several rooms have working fireplaces and there are many four-poster beds. There are lots of fresh flowers, books, magazines, good reading lamps, and a most romantic atmosphere.

Lunch and dinner at the Charlotte Inn is taken at the Chez Pierre dining room, run by Bernard and Eniko Delisle. The menu is both continental and American with such items as broiled swordfish served with caviar, fresh sea scallops sauteed with morels, and Nantucket pheasant in a black-plum sauce. Chez Pierre is open year-round, except during winter months when it's only open on weekends.

Gery and Paula, with considerable assistance from Gery, Jr., and Timmy, also maintain a prestigious art gallery displaying outstanding oils and watercolors by such artists as Carolyn Blisch, Ray Ellis, and Philip Jameson.

All of this plus what may be the ultimate country inn bedroom? I'll leave that to you.

CHARLOTTE INN, So. Summer St., Edgartown, Martha's Vineyard Island, Ma 02539; 617-627-4751. An 18-room combination inn-art gallery and restaurant located on one of the side streets in the village of Edgartown, just a few short steps from the harbor. European plan. Rooms available every day of the year. Continental breakfast served to inn guests. Chez Pierre restaurant open for lunch and dinner from mid-March through New Year's Day, also winter weekends. Boating, swimming, beaches, fishing, tennis, riding, golf, sailing, and biking nearby. No pets. Gery and Paula Conover, Innkeepers.

Directions: Martha's Vineyard Island is located off the southwestern coast of Cape Cod. The Woods Hole-Vineyard Haven Ferry runs year-round and automobiles may be left in the parking lot at Woods Hole. Taxis may be obtained from Vineyard Haven to Edgartown (8 mi.). Check with inn for ferry schedules for all seasons of the year. Accessible by air from Boston and New York.

THE BRAMBLE INN GALLERY AND CAFE
Brewster, Cape Cod, Massachusetts

May is a great time to visit Cape Cod when it is relatively unpeopled by enthusiastic vacationers and the myriad, frequently overlooked, back roads and small shops can be enjoyed to their fullest.

On a May morning, I awakened in the front bedroom of the Bramble Inn. Through the window I could see the beautiful soft green colors of a newly leafed willow tree and the blossoms of a lovely old Cape Cod apple tree. The grass was green, the sky was blue, and the air was soft with promise.

I first visited Karen Etsell and Elaine Brennan, the innkeeprs, in 1976 and reported that the Bramble Inn Gallery and Cafe (hereafter known as the Bramble Inn) was a wonderful addition to *CIBR*. From the very beginning I found the inn delightful. The walls and woodwork are sparkling white and the floorboards of differing widths have been refinished with a warm brown patina. There are lots of hanging plants and ivy that provide more natural accents. The basic colors are green and pink, and in the cafe there are green placemats and pink napkins held in place by flowered rosebud napkin rings.

The main decor of the first floor is provided by a collection of watercolors, oil paintings, lithographs, pastels, and wood lathe art. Also scattered among these are photographs taken by Elaine. These adornments are all for sale.

The menu at the Bramble Inn offers delicious hearty entrées, as well as lighter dishes. The baked filets of sole are stuffed with chopped shrimp and almonds and covered with a rich Mornay sauce. Another popular offering is the Carbonnade de Boeuf Bourguignon. It is served with a green salad and freshly baked bread. On the lighter side the menu also has crêpes, the Bramble Inn quiche, and the famous Cape Cod Bramble, an old-fashioned delicacy of chopped

raisins and cranberries gently sweetened and wrapped in a tender pastry and topped with vanilla ice cream.

The Bramble Inn has gained tremendous recognition through Karen's and Elaine's very successful book, *How To Open A Country Inn.* This has really created some interesting changes and new developments in the lives of these two attractive and capable women.

Karen sent me a most informative brochure that indicated that in January she gave a lecture at the University of Massachusetts in Amherst on "the business of country innkeeping." I was certainly proud to learn that.

During 1982 Karen and Elaine bought the attractive 1849 House next door to the present Bramble Inn. The architecture is Greek Revival, as is that of the Bramble, and it is painted white with green shutters and has masses of pink and white petunias in the flowerbeds. With a completely refinished interior, this house provides five additional lodgings rooms, two with private baths.

"One of the things that we have been wanting for some time is a common room for our guests," Elaine commented. "Now we have one." Karen added, "It is an extremely gratifying experience to create something to fill a need and then have the public respond to it so well. Our neighbors, the townspeople of Brewster, were so pleased with the beautification of the property that we received a certificate of recognition from the Historic District."

There's one item that should be added to the Bramble Inn menu: perseverance and progress. Both are available in abundance.

THE BRAMBLE INN GALLERY AND CAFE, Route 6A, Main St., Brewster, Cape Cod, Ma. 02631; 617-896-7644. A 7-room village inn (two with private bath) and art gallery in the heart of one of Cape Cod's northshore villages. Lodgings include continental breakfast. Open May through Oct. Lunch and dinner served daily except Sundays from mid-June through Labor Day. Swimming, sailing, water sports, golf, recreational and natural attractions within a short drive. Adjacent to tennis club. This is a small, intimate inn and does not meet the needs of most children. No pets. Credit cards accepted for meals and purchase of art work. Personal checks for lodgings. Elaine Brennan and Karen Etsell, Innkeepers.

Directions: Take Exit 10 from Rte. 6. Turn left (north) and follow Rte. 124 to the intersection of Rte. 6A (4 mi.). Turn right, one-tenth mile to inn.

COLONEL EBENEZER CRAFTS INN
Sturbridge, Massachusetts

For some years I have been hoping to find an inn in central Massachusetts which could be an ideal overnight stop for travelers from the west to Boston or Maine, or from New York City and the south to New England. Oddly enough, I found it almost under my nose in Sturbridge, Massachusetts, containing one of the Bay State's most enduring and worthwhile attractions: Old Sturbridge Village, a community of early 19th-century New England which has been reproduced with taste and style.

The ten room bed-and-breakfast Ebenezer Crafts Inn (guests are invited to have luncheon and dinner at the nearby Publick House), was originally built by David Fiske in 1786. Placed by Mr. Fiske on a high point of land, the house still overlooks the rolling hills adjacent to Sturbridge. It was named for one of the early patriots of Massachusetts, Colonel Ebenezer Crafts, who later migrated to Vermont's northern kingdom where the town of Craftsbury Common commemorates his contributions to the community.

The congenial host and hostess at the Ebenezer Crafts Inn are Patricia and Henri Bibeau, who were most accommodating during my stay, and provide inn guests with a continental breakfast and an afternoon tea which is served either on the terrace overlooking the new swimming pool or in the warm living room or sunporch.

Each of the lodging rooms has its own bath and shower, and at the time of my visit, there was a bowl of apples in each room for everyone to enjoy. Pat commented that she frequently turns down the beds in the evening and also leaves cookies. Both are nice country inn touches.

The rooms are very light and airy and are furnished either in antiques or good reproductions. There were a number of chenille bedspreads, including one called "The Pride of Sturbridge."

The living room really invites guests to get acquainted and I was delighted to find a generously supplied bookcase and also stacks of the *National Geographic* which makes wonderful bedtime reading.

The exterior landscaping for the inn includes a beautiful new brick patio where guests may have morning breakfast or afternoon tea surrounded by plants and an herb garden. A new stone stairway leads from the patio to the pool area and shrubbery has been planted to form a live sundial around the flagpole. This is certainly a first in *CIBR* inns!

I must admit that I was taken by the quiet, hideaway feeling at this inn. The Indian-red stain of the narrow clapboards which are accented by the white trim, proved an ideal setting for the elm, maple, oak, and apple trees and the many beds of flowers.

Because guests at the Colonel Ebenezer Crafts Inn take a great many of their meals at the nearby Publick House, it is of interest to know that luncheons and dinners there include excellent New England clam chowder, as well as New England dishes such as

lobster pie, broiled native scallops, double-thick lamb chops, deep dish apple pie—à la mode or with cheddar cheese—and Indian pudding served with vanilla ice cream.

CIBR readers with reservations at the Ebenezer Crafts Inn should check in at the main desk of the Publick House which is in the village of Sturbridge.

COLONEL EBENEZER CRAFTS INN, c/o Publick House, Box 187, Sturbridge, Ma. 01566; 617-347-3313. A 10-room bed and breakfast inn in a historic village 18 mi. from Worcester. Old Sturbridge Village nearby. Lodging rates include continental breakfast and afternoon tea. (Lunch and dinner available at nearby Publick House.) Open year-round. Swimming pool on grounds. Tennis nearby. Buddy Adler, Innkeeper.

Directions: From Massachusetts Tpke.: take Exit 9, follow signs to Sturbridge on Rte. 131. From Hartford: follow I-84, which becomes I-86. Take Exit 3.

LONGFELLOW'S WAYSIDE INN
South Sudbury, Massachusetts

I'll never, NEVER forget that night. There must have been at least forty innkeepers from *CIBR* enjoying a roast goose dinner in the upstairs dining room of Longfellow's Wayside Inn. We were having the fun of getting together and the opportunity to recognize innkeeper Frank Koppeis as the New England Innkeeper of the year.

We had gathered at lunch earlier that afternoon, and had spent a very pleasant few hours talking over innkeeping problems and exchanging ideas, and then had gone on a tour of the special sights at the Wayside, including the Old Gristmill, the Martha and Mary Chapel where so many people were married every year, the Little Red Schoolhouse, and the many very special, well-preserved bedrooms of this hostelry which actually dates back well into the 18th century.

Between the soup and salad I became aware of a sound in the hallway beyond the dining room and then, without warning, the door burst open and there immediately paraded into the room about seventeen men and boys wearing Colonial costumes and playing fifes and drums! The sound of their music and the jauntiness of their spirit filled the dining room and everyone arose and applauded vigorously. Of course, we had all been filled with the fascinating history of Sudbury and the fact that the militiamen had marched off to nearby Concord on April 18, 1775, to participate in the events that are so well-known to every student of American history.

Now with this great stirring music being played by piccolos, fifes, and drums and with the musicians, even the young boys, all dressed in Colonial costume, there was no doubt that we felt as if "we were there."

This is the Sudbury Ancient Fife and Drum Company and they stayed on long enough to play about four numbers and joked with us considerably and told us a little bit about what they do and the fact that they have been playing in this band for a long time and make appearances all over the country. They marched off to the tune of "The Girl I left Behind Me," which has been a popular tune since long before the American Revolution. I'm happy to report that the Fife and Drum Company play on the road in front of the inn Wednesday evenings during the summer, which also serves as a practice session for them.

What else can I say now about Longfellow's Wayside Inn? Incidentally, this building which has had many trials and tribulations of its own, is now in the hands of a foundation that is interested in preserving it in perpetuity. It was discovered by Henry Longfellow during the 19th century and I'm sure that all of us are familiar with the almost-epic poem that deals with some of the habitués of that time. In the early twenties Henry Ford also heavily endowed it.

There are a few lodging rooms available, but please, to avoid disappointment, make reservations well in advance. The dining room specializes in good New England fare such as baked Cape Cod scallops, Indian pudding served with ice cream, muffins made from meal stone ground at the Gristmill, and Massachusetts duckling in orange sauce.

It's a great experience even when the Fife and Drum Corps is *not* making an appearance!

LONGFELLOW'S WAYSIDE INN, Wayside Inn Rd., off Rte. 20, South Sudbury, Mass. 01776; 617-443-8846. A 10-room historic landmark inn, midway between Boston and Worcester. Within a short distance of Concord, Lexington, and other famous Revolutionary War landmarks. European plan. Lunch and dinner served daily except Christmas. Breakfast served to overnight guests. Francis Koppeis, Innkeeper.

Directions: From the west, take Exit 11A from Mass. Tpke. and proceed north on 495 to Rte. 20. Follow Rte. 20 7 mi. east to inn. From the east, take Exit 49 from Rte. 128. Follow Rte. 20 west 11 mi. to inn.

COUNTRY INN AT PRINCETON
Princeton, Massachusetts

"Darling, will you marry me?"

I'm a real romantic, because I was enormously intrigued when Ron and Maxine Plumridge told me that quite a few such proposals have been made in this quiet, discreet, private little dining room called the Library Den. I could see that the atmosphere was perfect with the candlelit table by the window and the Chinese Ming red wall coverings creating a most intimate setting. The expectant couple could watch the moon rise, as I was doing on this particular evening, and pick out the lights of Boston in the distance.

The inn is set on a high point of land in this sequestered eastern Massachusetts village. It is in the midst of broad lawns, country gardens, a real pine grove, woodlands with granddad maples, and fieldstone walls. There is a generous terrace around three sides.

The building, a late-Victorian country mansion, was built in 1890 by Charles Washburn, whose growing family had wonderfully good times here for many years.

Today, Maxine and Don, with just a trace of their Canadian heritage audible in their voices, have transformed this house into an elegant, late-Victorian country inn. Guests immediately sense something romantic and exciting as soon as they step across the threshold into the reception area. Shining floors, handsome rugs, collector's antiques and reproductions, and a warm sense of welcome are some of my first impressions.

There are six bedrooms, some are spacious parlor-suites, each uniquely decorated with authentic antique bedroom furniture. Two of them are the largest bedrooms I've ever seen in any real country inn. Since breakfast is served in the privacy of the guest bedrooms, all have small tables with views of the countryside or forest.

Incidentally, the inn was originally restored a few years ago by two very ambitious women, and was included in *Country Inns and Back Roads*. Now, I'm delighted to include it once again because Don and Maxine have done an admirable job in the last eighteen months. They love innkeeping and the inn certainly reflects their feelings.

Dinners are prepared by chef Christopher M. Woodward with an emphasis on classic French cuisine. At the time of my visit, the entrées included fresh salmon fillet stuffed with a scallop mousse and wrapped in a sculptured puff pastry. There was also roast veal in a Dijonnais sauce and Cornish game hen garnished with cranberries and finished with a cranberry liqueur. Salad is served following the meal, and desserts are most tempting.

The Washburn Dining Room looks out over the terrace at the

panoramic view. The Garden Dining Room is light and airy and decorated in earth tones to complement the many plants that abound.

I couldn't help but return to the subject of the romantic little Library Den dining room. "Why are there so many proposals here?" I asked.

Maxine replied, "Well, generally the couples have seen the inn and had dinner here at an earlier date. The gentleman telephones and makes arrangements to reserve the Library Den for a later visit. It is at this private dinner that he proposes."

"Are there many acceptances?" I asked.

"Oh, yes, and they come back here for their honeymoons as well!"

COUNTRY INN AT PRINCETON, 30 Mountain Rd., Princeton, Ma. 01541; 617-464-2030. A 6-bedroom late-Victorian mansion, 50 mi. from Boston and 14 mi. north of Worcester. Open all year except Christmas. Dinner reservations Wed. thru Sun. evenings. Sunday brunch. Closed Mon. and Tues. Near Wachusett Ski Resort and Audubon and Wildlife Society. Tennis, swimming, fishing, hiking, downhill and xc skiing nearby. Not suitable for children. No pets. Don and Maxine Plumridge, Innkeepers.

Directions: From Boston, follow Rte. 2 west to Rte. 31 south. From Conn. and Mass. Tpke., follow Rte. 290 north to Rte. 190; then take Exit 5 and continue on Rte. 140 to Princeton. At Rte. 62 turn left 4 mi., and turn right at post office and flashing light. With the town common on your left, the inn is 200 yards up Mountain Rd. on right.

MORRILL PLACE
Newburyport, Massachusetts

The scene bordered on the idyllic. I was on the screened-in summer porch of the Morrill Place with Monroe purring contentedly on the wicker couch beside me while we both watched Buns, the resident bunny rabbit, eating the nasturtiums in the window box. Innkeeper Rose Ann Hunter was reading to me from John P. Marquand's account of Newburyport. "Newburyport appears at its best," she read, "on a clear October day, for October is usually the

most genial month in northeastern Massachusetts. Our October skies are clear and soft blue. Such leaves as are left on the elms are an unobtrusive russet yellow.

"In October, you will find that Newburyport still offers an illusion of security, a blending of past and present, and the serene sort of disregard for the future that is one of the greatest charms of an old New England seaport.

"Newburyport is not a museum piece, although it sometimes looks it. It has some of the most perfect examples of early Colonial and Federal architecture in America, but it is a vital, tolerant place and still able to keep up with the times, if you get to know it."

I was seeing Newburyport through the eyes of this very enthusiastic young woman who moved here a few years ago. In addition to having shown me through the graceful Newburyport mansion which has been turned into a warm and receptive guest house, she was kind enough to take me on a comprehensive tour of the town and the Parker River National Wildlife Refuge on Plum Island.

"Morrill Place was built in 1806," Rose Ann said, "by Kathyrn and William Hoyt. The owners include three Newburyport sea captains—that's why there's a widow's walk. We have fourteen guest rooms and we are always open, even through the holidays. There are twelve working fireplaces."

We were joined for a moment by Kristen, who is an energetic eight-year-old.

Earlier in the afternoon, my house tour started at the front of the house in the formal living room which is adorned with oriental *objets d'art.* I marveled at the double-hung staircase with the six-inch risers. "This was built at the time when women wore hoop skirts," Rose Ann explained. "Double-hung staircases are rare, even in Newburyport."

Many of the bedrooms have fireplaces and were being redecorated with distinctive period wallpapers. I saw my first "Indian shutters" which, when closed, left a narrow horizontal open slit. "In the 18th century, the real danger was from marauding pirates," she explained.

My room was named after Daniel Webster who was a frequent visitor to the house. There was a remarkably preserved print of Mr. Webster over the fireplace, and the furnishings were typical of other bedrooms, including an antique deacons' bench, two twin beds, each embellished with a pineapple motif, a lovely old chest of drawers, and a Boston rocker.

Our tour, as so many do, ended up in the kitchen where we had a refreshing cup of tea and I learned that the breakfasts include juice, coffee or tea, cereal, fresh baked rolls and English muffins, topped off by "mother's strawberry jam."

How could I help but like the Morrill Place with a cat named Monroe and a rabbit named Buns?

MORRILL PLACE, 209 High St., Newburyport, Ma. .01950. (617-462-2808.) A 10-room guest house on one of Newburyport's beautiful, residential avenues. Most rooms share bath with one other room. Lodgings include continental breakfast, only meal offered. Open every day in year. Within a very convenient distance of all of the Newburyport historical and cultural attractions, and Plum Island Wildlife Refuge. Other recreational facilities nearby. Rose Ann Hunter, Innkeeper.

Directions: From Boston follow I-95 north and take Historic Newburyport exit and follow Rte. 113. This becomes High St. Follow it for about 2 miles. Inn is on right hand side at corner of Johnson and High St. From Maine: Exit I-95 for Historic Newburyport and follow above directions.

Martha's Vineyard is full of many beautiful roads worthy of exploring. It is hard to pick out one that is outstanding. One suggestion is the less-traveled road that circles Lambert's Cove on the west side of the island. Lambert's Cove Road is about four miles long. It is winding, hilly, and narrow, which makes it difficult to travel any faster than 20 mph., and this is just as well as then nothing is missed. Some of its highlights include a lovely farm, many stone walls, several fresh-water swimming holes, and dense trees that reach over the road and shade it almost entirely. On this road one can also find one of the island's nicest beaches. A two-to-three-minute walk through the woods on a sand path will lead you to a beautiful beach where the sand is whiter and finer than you'll find anywhere.

Gery Conover
Charlotte Inn
Edgartown, Martha's Vineyard, Massachusetts

From Morrill Place, I made a left-hand turn leading west for about a mile to Atkinson's Common. I took the extreme right road following it to the end. On the left side behind the stone wall there is a lovely little park, Mosley Pines. Just beyond the park, leading north, I crossed over the old Chain Bridge, which was first opened to travelers in 1792 and is the first structure built over the Merrimac River.

At the fork in the road I went left; just a short distance down the road is the home of Robert Frost. On the left is Lowell's Boat Shop, which has been tucked away on the riverbank since 1793.

I proceeded along the shore, and the winding road took me past lovely period homes with private boat docks, as well as the Congregational Church where I made a sharp left turn.

I went about three miles until I arrived at a stop sign at the end of River Road, and along the way noted the colors of fall were gone and the browns and greys of winter prevailed. In the distance flocks of white gulls were heading toward the river. They swooped down and gently landed on the ashen-blue water.

I kept bearing left and just past Wallbee's Boatyard, I could see the town line of Rock Village, established in 1642 and unspoiled by time. There is another bridge crossing over the Merrimac. Continuing on Church Street, the river was on my right and I went left, past a small burial ground. After a short distance I came to Route 113, turned left and headed east toward Newburyport.

In a short time I arrived at West Newbury Commons, a typical village green, and just beyond is Long Hill Orchard where there are apples, cider, and other amenities. Farther beyond, on the right, was my last stop, the Mill Pond Recreational Area for boating and hiking. I stayed on Route 113 leading east and it brought me back to Morrill Place.

Rose Ann Hunter
Morrill Place
Newburyport, Massachusetts

As for a "back-road" route to the Whistling Oyster, one could turn south on Route 1, instead of north (after exiting I-95), and follow the signs to the Yorks. Follow York Street (Route 1A) and find several historical spots (including the Olde Gaol), and then continue along 1A through York Harbor into York Beach and onto Shore Road in York for the lovely, truly scenic drive along the coast.

Just over the town line south on Shore Road (forgot this one) is Henry Strater's little gem of a museum—the Museum of Art of Ogunquit. Off Main Street (on Hoyt's Lane) is Ps Galleries which is tops. In other words, one could walk less than two miles and spend an entire day visiting excellent galleries.

John Parella
The Whistling Oyster
Ogunquit, Maine

HAWTHORNE INN
Concord, Massachusetts

In previous editions of this book, I have suggested that Gregory Burch is a real Renaissance man, equally at home at the easel, with sculptor's clay, at an archeological dig, or entertaining his guests at the morning breakfast table.

All of that is true except for one important change: Gregory Burch and Marilyn Mudry were married in the garden of the inn in August 1981, so that the Hawthorne Inn can now boast a Renaissance woman as well as a man. Furthermore, as this book went to press a Renaissance baby girl has arrived on the scene and has been named Ariel Zöe Burch.

The town of Concord is unique because it has three famous periods in its history, any one of which would be a sufficient claim to distinction. The first began more than three hundred years ago when the early Puritans made it the first Massachusetts settlement away from the Tidewater. Concord was the scene of the first battle of the Revolutionary War and, finally, in the 19th century, it was the home of Emerson, Alcott, Thoreau, and Hawthorne, the great authors of the period known as the "flowering of New England."

The Hawthorne Inn is located in the historic zone of Concord, just down the road from the Alcott House on the road out of Concord toward Lexington. It is tucked back a short way from the road among the beautiful 100-year-old maples and larches that were planted by Nathaniel Hawthorne.

The inn is located on land that once belonged to Ralph Waldo Emerson, as well as the Alcotts and Hawthorne. Bronson Alcott planted his fruit trees and made pathways to the mill brook, and the Alcott family tended their crops of vegetables and herbs here. Two of the original trees are still standing and can be seen on the west side of the inn.

Marilyn and Gregory have cleared out the wooded area in the back of the house and landscaped it. There are friendly inn dogs that are constantly going for walks with guests.

The rooms have antique furnishings, handmade quilts, and oriental and rag rugs. There are original art works, both ancient and modern, antique Japanese Ukiyoye prints and sculpture by Gregory. There are floor to ceiling bookshelves in the Common Room which is warmed by a cozy fire in the chilly season.

The doors of the five bedrooms have name-plaques and scented wreaths. There are dried flowers in the rooms, am-fm clock radios, fresh fruit, poetry books, and herbal sachets. Guests are offered tea or coffee as they check in.

Breakfast is taken in the Common Room and features home-

baked breads, fruit juice, a selection of teas or a special blend of freshly ground coffee. In season there are fruits from the gardens and vines of the inn, and honey from the inn's own beehives.

The inn is directly across the road from Hawthorne's house, the Wayside, and next door to it is the Alcotts' Orchard House. The Concord grape was developed at Grapevine Cottage, adjacent to the inn.

I believe that the generous and warm atmosphere at the Hawthorne Inn would be a marvelous experience in any setting, but when we add all of the ambience of Concord, Lexington, South Sudbury, and the other eastern-Massachusetts communities it becomes an exceptional opportunity to experience some of the best of America's past.

THE HAWTHORNE INN, 462 Lexington Road, Concord, Mass. 01742; 617-369-5610. A 5-room bed-and-breakfast village inn approximately 19 mi. from Boston. Breakfast to houseguests is the only meal served. Closed in January and February. Within walking distance of all of the historic and literary points of interest in Concord. No pets. No credit cards. Limited facilities for young children, but ideal for young people who have an appreciation for history and literature. Gregory Burch, Marilyn Mudry, Innkeepers.

Directions: The Hawthorne Inn is in the historic zone of Concord, ¾ of a mi. east of the town center. From Rte. 128-95 take Exit 45 west for 3 mi. Bear right at the single blinking yellow light. The inn is one mi. farther on the left (south side), directly across from the Wayside (home of Hawthorne and Alcott).

PEIRSON PLACE
Richmond, Massachusetts

"I've spent years researching the history of this property," said Margaret Kingman. "It's a historical landmark in Berkshire County. We have two houses here plus a great many outbuildings—the beautiful big barn behind us, and 150 acres of wooded hillside.

"Many of our guests are fascinated by the fact that my great-grandfather, my mother, and I were all born in the same room in the Peirson House and that my family has owned the property since the land was acquired from the Indians in 1762."

The Peirson Place is really very unusual and Margaret has created an intimate bed-and-breakfast inn that is markedly different from other accommodations in the Berkshires. She has many guests who have been returning each year because they enjoy the shaded quiet of the Victorian gazebo, the tranquility of the woods, and the quietude at the pond.

"Many of our guests follow the birdwatchers' path and also enjoy riding bicycles and swimming, and the use of our sauna," she remarked.

The most interesting news from the Peirson Place is the fact that one of the main buildings, called the Cogswell Guesthouse, now remains open during the winter to accommodate the cross-country skiers on the woodland trails. There are combinations of rooms that can be divided or combined for a maximum of ten guests, and two of those have private baths. There's a guest lounge and a dining room where breakfast and tea will continue to be served all winter, just as they are in the summer, as well two pullman kitchen units available.

Margaret and I strolled about the grounds and she pointed out the fact that the Cogswell House was built in 1762 by Joseph

Cogswell. "A few years later Nathan Peirson built a tannery on the land starting a connection through a later marriage between the Cogswells and the Peirsons. Joseph Cogswell and his four sons were Minutemen serving at Bennington, Bunker Hill, and Valley Forge."

The main house was built in 1788 on the site of the first tannery, and the Cogswells and the Peirsons reunited when Nathan's oldest daughter married the grandson of Joseph Cogswell.

In addition to the Cogswell Guesthouse, which is also open from November to May, the Peirson Place has accommodations in the Peirson House which has very sumptuous rooms. There are more frugal, but most interesting quarters—hosteling in the barn. "We make refrigerator space available for guests who wish to picnic by the pond and there are dozens of good restaurants here in the Berkshires."

I think the *esprit* at the Peirson Place was best displayed when I joined a group from Montreal at the breakfast table during late August. Of course the conversation turned immediately to the subject of music because most of the guests had direct connections with the Montreal Symphony and were here when Zubin Mehta was conducting at Tanglewood. It was a very lively breakfast in which the conversation flowed generously in both French and English.

PEIRSON PLACE, Richmond, Mass. 01254; 413-698-2750. A country house 6 mi. from Pittsfield on Rte. 41 near all the scenic attractions of the Berkshire Hills including Tanglewood, Hancock Shaker Village, and marvelous backroading in 3 states. The main house (Peirson Place) which includes adjacent cottages is open from May to Nov. There are both private and shared baths. Cogswell Guest House is also open from Nov. to May to accommodate cross-country skiers on woodland trails. It has 5 rooms that can be divided or combined for one, two, or three couples. One-day rentals are not accepted on weekends during Tanglewood season. Pond, sauna, badminton, darts, boating, on grounds. Tennis, golf, horseback riding, etc., nearby. No pets. No facilities to amuse children under 12. The Kingman Family, Innkeepers.

Directions: From Boston: Take Massachusetts Turnpike to Exit 1. Follow Rte. 41 north through Richmond. Peirson Place on left-hand side. From New York: Leave Taconic State Parkway at Rte. 295 and continue east to Rte. 41. Turn left.

JARED COFFIN HOUSE
Nantucket, Massachusetts

It was a joyous reunion. We were gathering not only from all over New England, but also from New York, Pennsylvania, New Orleans, and even California. We were all (myself excepted) innkeepers from *CIBR* gathering on the ferry at Woods Hole to set sail for Nantucket to enjoy a two-day informal conference.

With a warning blast on the whistle, the *Nebska* cast off and we were on our way. It seemed almost no time at all, what with all of the visiting and catching up we had to do, before we were arriving in Nantucket and playing the game of picking out the landmarks as the boat made its way into the breakwater and dock. Penny Drucquer of the Pump House Inn delighted in the high-spired churches and the waterfront buildings. Cliff Rudisill from the Village Inn said that this was his first time on the island and he was really looking forward to it.

Although a taxi and the inn station wagon were available, most of us walked the three blocks from the ferry slip to the Jared Coffin. The first-time visitors marveled at the well-preserved late 18th- and early 19th-century homes.

Nantucket was seriously damaged by the Great Fire of 1846. This, coupled with the discovery of gold in California and oil in Pennsylvania, caused the depletion of the whaling oil industry on the island and the young people left in great numbers to seek their fortunes in other places. This explains why the island has remained somewhat low-key with very few new buildings constructed in the late 19th century, so that Nantucket was bypassed by the Victorian movement.

We walked up the stone steps of the inn and there were innkeepers Phil and Peggy Read waiting to give us a joyful greeting. Some of us were assigned rooms in the main house and others in the various historic homes acquired by the inn during the past few years.

The newest of these is an 1841 Greek Revival house located across the street from the inn, which increases the room capacity to 58. This building will contain twelve rooms with queen-sized canopy beds and private baths, and, as is the case with so many of the other JC bedrooms, there are wide pine-board floors, oriental carpets, and many non-working fireplaces. There will also be a living room and an adjoining room which can serve as a conference room for groups of twelve to sixteen persons or as a lounge for houseguests. There are spacious lawns with two large shade trees creating a cool and pleasant spot.

Our conference was a great success, attributed in no small measure to the deft handling of all details by the JC staff. We had an ample opportunity to tour the island by bus and the May weather was absolutely perfect. Being ahead of the great influx of summer homeowners and guests who arrive in July and August, it was obviously an ideal time to visit Nantucket.

The bicycling, beachcombing, and endless walking about the town provided all of us with hearty appetites and there was much "oohing and ahhing" over such JC specialties as quahog chowder and bay scallops. Phil described the menu as classical American cuisine for which the inn has received several awards and much recognition.

Our conference was over almost before we realized it. Once again we gathered at the rail of the ferry as the fascinating silhouettes of Nantucket—the two church towers and the wonderful old well-cared-for summer homes—receded into the distance.

JARED COFFIN HOUSE, Nantucket Island, Mass. 02554; 617-228-2400. A 58-room village inn 30 mi. at sea. European plan. Breakfast, lunch, dinner served daily (food service in Tap Room only in Jan., Feb., Mar.). Strongly advise verifying accommodations before planning a trip to Nantucket in any season. Swimming, fishing, boating, golf, tennis, riding, and bicycles nearby. Philip and Margaret Read, Innkeepers.

Directions: Accessible by air from Boston, New York, and Hyannis, or by ferry from Woods Hole and Hyannis, Mass. Automobile reservations are usually needed in advance: 617-540-2022. Cars are not recommended for short stays. Seasonal air service from New York and ferry service from Hyannis are available May thru October: 617-426-1855. Inn is located 300 yards from ferry dock.

THE QUEEN ANNE INN
Chatham, Cape Cod, Massachusetts

It's just possible that I was talking to one of the most enthusiastic, if not one of the youngest, innkeepers of my acquaintance. She was wearing yellow jogging pants, a blue striped top, and blue jogging shoes. Her name was Sonja Weinkopf and she was then all of twelve years old. Her father and mother, Guenther and Nicole, are the innkeepers of The Queen Anne Inn which can be found in Chatham on Cape Cod.

That was 1980. Now Sonja is 5½ feet tall, blond, and a really good-looking fifteen-year-old "Fraulein." The inn guests see her every morning serving breakfast to them in July and August and when they don't see her she is learning all about the front desk and bookkeeping.

Just as Sonja has changed, so has The Queen Anne. It has blossomed from a ruin only four years ago, and is pleasing an increasing number of guests every year.

In the winter of 1978 Guenther began restoring and renovating the building and has been bringing what appears to be the best of European innkeeping tradition into a perfect marriage with some of the delightful ambience of the outer Cape.

There is a capacious deck on the rear side of the inn overlooking a spacious lawn where some chairs and benches have been placed under the trees making it a very inviting prospect for reading and enjoying quiet moments. Attractive guest cottages are nestled among the trees.

During the winter of 1982-83 balconies were added to all the rooms on the garden side, holding to the Victorian style. The lofts under the roof of the north wing were set up as large suites, also with balconies, and will have the most beautiful view over Oyster Pond Bay. All guest rooms will have matching new linen and antiques, and a fireplace will warm the dining area.

The garden will be expanded and a small swimming pool will be added along with a few hot tubs.

Because it's a Cape Cod inn, naturally, the menu has many seafood offerings including baked oysters, finnan haddie, and the Nantucket Fireman's Supper served on Wednesday nights. The Austrian influence is reflected in a Viennese *tafelspitz,* Hungarian *gulyas,* and other continental specialties.

The big event every Tuesday evening is a clambake held in the garden where Maxine Mather, the native innkeeper, will continue with her parties for houseguests. Guenther says Maxine spins yarns "longer than any old salt fisherman could dream of."

The Queen Anne is also the proud owner of a rather large Boston whaler on which guests thoroughly enjoy their excursions to the outer Cape beaches and islands.

There is a pond down the road where guests can swim and a beach where there is sand, surf, and waves. The outer Cape is a great place for bicycles.

One of the most unique additions has been the herb garden at the inn which has one of the most complete herb plantings I've ever seen, rivalling that of the Asa Ransom House. Everything is used in the kitchen from the lemon balm to the thyme, including dill, fennel, hyssop, pennyroyal and tarragon.

THE QUEEN ANNE INN, 70 Queen Anne Rd., Chatham, Mass. 02633; 617-945-0394. A 30-room village inn on Cape Cod on the picturesque south shore. Full American, modified American, or European plans. Open May 1 thru New Year's Eve. Breakfast, dinner, Sunday brunch, and Tuesday clambake served to travelers. Near all of the Cape's scenic, cultural, and historical attractions. Water skiing, deep-sea fishing, sailing, bicycles, backroading, beach walking nearby. No recreational facilities for children on grounds. Nicole and Guenther Weinkopf, Innkeepers.

Directions: From Boston: Take Rte. 3 south to Sagamore Bridge crossing Cape Cod Canal. Continue on Rte. 6 to Exit 11; take Rte. 137 south to Rte. 28, turn left. This is Chatham's Main Street. Turn right into Queen Anne Rd. From New York: Take I-95 north to Providence, R.I.; I-195 to Wareham, and Rte. 6 to Sagamore Bridge (see directions above).

NORTHFIELD COUNTRY HOUSE
Northfield, Massachusetts

"What I really enjoy most about being an innkeeper is our guests. They come from all parts of the world and it is such a wonderful feeling to have them here, introduce them to each other, and then to sit back and watch the meld work."

One of the qualities I am always delighted to find in innkeepers is enthusiasm, and Jan Gamache of the Northfield Country House has enthusiasm to spare. Fortunately, the inn is small enough so that she has ample opportunity to get to know all of her guests quite well. "It is an intimate little country inn," she said. "I think it is just the right size, because it gives all of us a chance to share our thoughts and experiences. We sit around the fire on chilly evenings or out on the porch in the summertime, and the conversations are so stimulating. I actually miss our guests after they leave."

I had visited Northfield Country House earlier in the year, but because there is a waiting list for inns to be included in *CIBR*, it was almost the end of the year before I could return and confirm with Jan that the inn would be in the book for 1983.

The inn was wonderfully decorated for Christmas; in the entranceway a child's hobby horse sported a big red bow and there were wonderful green garlands cascading down the staircase balustrade. Poinsettias were everywhere. A Christmas tree in one corner of the living room was gaily decorated with colorfully wrapped gifts underneath. Over the mantel were garlands of greens interspersed with white lights. Carved into the mantelpiece was the message "Love warms the heart as the fire the hearth." My eye was immediately attracted to a very handsome collection of decoys.

There were wing chairs in the corners and a view out of the window into the forest. The unusually large fireplace had three couches arranged around it and I can well imagine that guests found it all much to their liking.

Much to their liking as well would be the very attractive country inn bedrooms, each one individually decorated with an assortment of interesting, comfortable, homey furniture, and most with working fireplaces. On the beds were attractive down comforters.

Besides a really mammoth country breakfast commencing with a Scandinavian dish called *meusli,* a combination of oatmeal, cream, nuts, coconuts, fruit, and whipped cream, dinner is offered to house-guests and others with advance reservations. It is a single entrée, five-course meal usually featuring a roast or baked fish. Everything is homemade. On the night of my visit the main dish was a shrimp and artichoke casserole and the dinner was accompanied by, as it is every evening, fresh popovers.

Northfield is an extremely pleasant and as yet unspoiled New England village, just a few miles below the Massachusetts-New Hampshire line. It has been for many years the site of Northfield-Mt. Hermon secondary school.

Jan summed up her feelings about being an innkeeper: "We feel that the inn is for our guests' enjoyment and we invite them to make themselves totally at home. We are open year-round and our guests frequently stay for many days because there is so much to do in this beautiful countryside in all seasons. There is a ski-touring center nearby and four major downhill areas within an hour's drive. Most of all we want our guests to take time out for the simple pleasures of country life at its best."

NORTHFIELD COUNTRY HOUSE, School St., Northfield, Ma. 01360; 413-498-2692. A 7-bedroom secluded country inn in the Connecticut River Valley a few mi. south of the N.H. line. Open year-round, except closed Thanksgiving, New Year's Eve, 1st week of Jan., and 1st 2 wks. in Aug. Room includes full breakfast. Dinner served to houseguests and others by advance reservation. Tennis, swimming, xc skiing on grounds. Antique shops, flea markets, auctions, boating, fishing, golf, Old Deerfield Village, Mohawk Trail, and marvelous backroading nearby. No pets. No credit cards. The Gamache Family, Innkeepers.

Directions: From I-91 use Exit 28A, follow Rte. 10 north to Northfield Center. Turn left toward Keene. Continue through main street of town and turn right on School St. (at firehouse). Go 9/10th of mi., crossing one blacktop country road and turn right at inn sign.

RALPH WALDO EMERSON
Rockport, Massachusetts

The telephone call came from Ohio and the man on the other end had this to say: "I've lived out here in the Midwest all of my life, and one of the things I've always wanted to do was to travel to New England and spend some time by the ocean. Where would I go to find lots of ocean and rocks to climb, where it's real 'New England'?"

I thought instantly of the Ralph Waldo Emerson. Its broad veranda has an unobstructed view of the ocean and it has some of the best climbing rocks that can be found anywhere.

The "Emerson," as it's called in Pigeon Cove, is made for people who are fascinated by the sea. It is possible to walk from that broad front porch across the lawn, through the natural rock garden, across a little dirt road to the rocks on the shore. And what rocks they are! A marvelous collection of boulders and great slabs of granite which are relics of the ice age. Among them are hundreds of small tidal pools. The sea gulls dive and zoom continually. Offshore there are dozens of little buoys which indicate where the lobster traps are in the waters below.

I tried to explain all of this as lucidly as possible. He asked me if they served typical New England food. "Well," I replied, "How do lobster, clams, fresh saltwater fish, and homemade cakes sound to you?" He agreed.

I told him about Pigeon Cove and strolling along the tree-shaded streets with the rambler roses and the New England houses. I explained about the lanes that led down to the sea to provide access to the rockbound coast, and how much they reminded me of lanes in Sussex and Surrey, which for centuries have provided a path between the fields and into the woods.

To his inquiry about whether children would like it, I replied that when I was there last, a fair number were in evidence. "They enjoy the pool at the ocean," I pointed out.

I explained that the Emerson was really the result of putting two resort hotels together and making them into one. It is more like a hotel than an inn as far as the atmosphere is concerned, but because it is owned by the Wemyss family who also operates the Yankee Clipper, there is very much of the feeling of personal hospitality. I most enjoy sitting on the broad veranda which overlooks the ocean during the clement months, and the comfortable living room during the rest of the year. There are lots of opportunities to get acquainted with other guests, and Gary Wemyss is very much the genial innkeeper.

Before he rang off, he asked whether Ralph Waldo Emerson, the famous New England essayist, had ever stayed at the inn. "They say he did," I answered. "In his diary he made this entry: 'Returned from Pigeon Cove where we made the acquaintance of the sea for seven days. 'Tis a noble, friendly power and seemed to say to me: "Why so late and slow to come to me? Am I not here always thy proper summer home"?'"

"Well," he replied, "if it is good enough for Ralph Waldo Emerson, I think it certainly will be good enough for me. I am going to make my reservations for July right now."

RALPH WALDO EMERSON, 1 Cathedral Ave., Rockport, Mass. 01966; 617-546-6321. A 36-room oceanside inn, 40 mi. from Boston. Modified American and European plans. Breakfast and dinner served daily from July 1 to Labor Day; bed and breakfast only during remainder of the year. Pool, sauna, and whirlpool bath on grounds. Tennis, golf nearby. Courtesy car. No pets. Gary and June Wemyss, Innkeepers.

Directions: Take I-95 to Rte. 128 to 127 (Gloucester). Proceed 6 mi. on Rte. 127 to Rockport and continue to Pigeon Cove.

"European Plan" means that rates for rooms and meals are separate. "American Plan" means that meals are included in the cost of the room. "Modified American Plan" means that breakfast and dinner are included in the cost of the room. The rates at some inns include a continental breakfast with the lodging.

THE RED INN
Provincetown, Massachusetts

Provincetown in September! The clean sea air has a pungent quality. The sun takes a few minutes longer to make its morning debut, but it is every bit as warming and as generous as in August, inviting noon and afternoon swimming at the numerous nearby Cape Cod beaches. The Provincetown shops may not open until 10 or 11 A.M., but it is much more fun browsing. The back streets with their twisting and turning lanes seem more private and personal when there are fewer people about.

When I shared some of these thoughts with Ted Barker during a leisurely luncheon at the Red Inn he responded with enthusiasm. "September is really ideal. Our staff takes a deep breath and begins to enjoy Provincetown, too. There is elbow room and the village returns to its quiet, private status. Marci and I like to walk up Commercial Street to 'do' the shops and see some of our village friends."

Marci and Ted Barker and various members of their family have made the Red Inn a genuine Cape Cod institution. In a tourist-oriented locality where new restaurants arrive with the birds in spring each year and permanently close their doors in the fall, the Red Inn has thrived with each passing year.

"I believe the fact that we are a family-run restaurant makes a big difference in our service," said Marci, who joined us for a moment at our table overlooking the harbor. "Do you know I counted sixteen members of our family who were working at the inn at the same time during the summer. There were sons, daughters, in-laws, nephews and cousins—a real 'old time feeling' that made it lots of fun."

Marci and Ted already had been operating the inn for quite a number of years before I made my first visit in 1974. This sense of permanency is one of the features that I look for in deciding which of the many fine inns and restaurants would be most appropriate for this book. My policy for the last several years has been to add only inns that offer lodgings.

During the past years I have written extensively about the menu, which includes various cuts of western beef, a great variety of seafood dishes, and lobster (which seems harder to get with each passing year). I also raved about the super desserts including brandied peaches, strawberries Romanoff, strawberry shortcake, made with an oven-baked biscuit and generous amounts of strawberries and honest-to-goodness freshly whipped cream. My favorite is a baked apple with a filling of brown sugar and cranberries topped off with whipped cream or vanilla ice cream.

150

Ted and Marci emigrated to Provincetown from Vermont a few years ago, and still maintain a great love for backroading. "Here on the outermost point of the Cape there is only one road out and the very same road back," laughed Marci. "However, as you think about Provincetown there are many little side roads or cross streets and ways that offer tidy examples of American-European-influenced architecture. There is a strong Portuguese ethnic influence here and there are many little stores that reflect this."

"In Truro there are several off-the-highway byways that offer glimpses of marshlands, creeks, and wetlands that support all manner of wildlife on the bay side," Ted pointed out. "On the ocean side there are side roads leading directly to the high dunes of the National Seashore and the great expanses of the unspoiled shoreline as far as the eye can see."

Well, luncheon was over and so was my yearly visit at the Red Inn. I took one long last look at the harbor and the flocks of seabirds looking for a meal on the wet banks as the tide receded.

"Come on, we'll walk up town with you," said Ted. "It feels good to take the afternoon off."

THE RED INN, 15 Commercial St., Provincetown, Mass. 02657; 617-487-0050. A waterside country restaurant with a striking view of Provincetown Harbor. No lodgings. Open for lunch and dinner every day of the year. During winter a late lunch/early dinner is offered. Within walking distance of all Provincetown lodging accommodations and recreational activities and attractions. Guided "whale-watching" excursions. Ted and Marcie Baker, Innkeepers.

Directions: Follow Rte. 6 to end of Cape Cod.

STAGECOACH HILL
Sheffield, Massachusetts

I like to arrive at Stagecoach Hill just at dusk as the carefully tended stone walls along Route 41 become vague shapes, and occasionally my headlights reveal some deer out in the meadow. This route is aptly named Undermountain Road, for along this stretch I feel as if I am driving directly underneath the imposing, protective influence of Mount Race.

Entry is through ponderous Victorian doors and up a short flight of stairs to a lounge area, dimly-lit by candles flickering in red jars. Except in the warm summer months, additional light is provided by fires on two raised hearths.

More candles grace the dining rooms, which are most inviting

with their red tablecloths, white napkins and gleaming silverware. The walls have sporting and hunting prints and a generous sprinkling of photographs and prints of the English royal family, including Queen Victoria, Queen Mary, King George, and Prince Charles and Lady Diana.

The innkeepers are John and Ann Pedretti who have lived in the Berkshires for a number of years. Oddly enough, they moved to England for two years in the early 1970s, and since Ann is from Lancashire, England, they're both very pleased to have found such an English inn in such a beautiful setting. In some ways, it reminds me of a traditional English inn in Ann's own Lancashire country called, "Hark to Bounty."

In addition to doing all of the cooking, Ann also does the extremely neat lettering on the blackboard menu which on my last visit showed such interesting main courses as baked scallops, duckling Bigarade, steak and kidney pie, and roast prime rib of beef served with Yorkshire pudding. "I learned to cook several different veal dishes because John is from northern Italy and he loves them. I also do a New England oyster pie," she said. (The recipe for this pie is in our *CIBR Cookbook.*)

In looking at the menu, I realized that it offered a choice of either an à la carte or table d'hôte, or a mixture of each. Certain appetizers are offered at no additional charge, as well as certain desserts.

The "Coach," as it's known locally, is an ideal distance from either Boston or New York. Its situation in the Berkshires makes it ideal for a visit in any season, because there are several ski areas within a very short drive, and also good cross-country skiing. In summer, all of the Berkshire recreational and cultural advantages are most accessible.

In addition to rather rustic overnight accommodations in the old red barn and another small outbuilding on the property, country-inn style bedrooms are available in the main house. These are all furnished with gay curtains, matching bedspreads, and appropriate furniture. One of these is a suite with its own kitchen. Plans are also afoot for a swimming pool to be built in the beautiful orchard.

Breakfast is not offered to guests at Stagecoach Hill; however, there is always a pot of coffee available.

STAGECOACH HILL INN, Undermountain Rd., Sheffield, Mass. 01257; 413-229-8585. An American country inn with British overtones located on Rte. 41 midway between Salisbury, Conn., and Gt. Barrington, Mass. Three lodging rooms in main building. Lunch and dinner served daily. Closed Christmas Day. Near So. Berkshire ski areas, Tanglewood, Jacob's Pillow, and all summertime and winter attractions. Proposed swimming pool on grounds. John and Ann Pedretti, Innkeepers.

Directions: From Mass. Tpke., take Exit 2 and follow Rte. 102 west to Stockbridge. Take Rte. 7 south to Great Barrington, then follow Rte. 41 south to inn.

THE RED LION INN
Stockbridge, Massachusetts

"What is your favorite country inn?"

That's a question I hear literally hundreds of times a year. Quite truthfully I have no favorite. I love them all. If I didn't, I'm sure that I couldn't include them in this book. However, there is one country inn to which I feel very close. That's the Red Lion Inn in Stockbridge.

I feel very close to it for many reasons, not the least of which is that I can see it through my office window, just a half-square away. (A little play on words, there.)

I'm close to it for many other reasons as well, because, like all of the residents of my village, I have a proprietary interest in the Red Lion. We who live in Stockbridge were dismayed to learn in 1967 that the old inn, originally erected in 1793, enlarged and improved over many years, then almost completely destroyed by fire in 1896, was possibly going to be torn down and replaced by a gasoline station. We were very much relieved when Jack and Jane Fitzpatrick, owners of Country Curtains, acquired the property, reopened it in 1967, and turned it into a thriving concern.

Like the visitors to Stockbridge, I have spent many a pleasant time rocking on the broad front porch and enjoying lunch at the Widow Bingham's Tavern with my friends. I have attended at least three conferences of *CIBR* innkeepers at the Red Lion over the past eighteen years. Like many other village inns it is the center of a great deal of our social activity, including wedding receptions, political gatherings, anniversary parties — in general, a meetingplace for villagers.

From the start, the Fitzpatricks have made the Red Lion a family affair, with Jack and Jane being joined by their two daughters Nancy and Ann. They are all very much involved.

Ann is the innkeeper at Blantyre, an imposing brick mansion of a former estate just a few miles from the center of Stockbridge. Blantyre has sumptuously proportioned bedrooms and two proper courts for playing croquet, as well as a swimming pool and tennis courts. Arrangements may be made through the Red Lion for accommodations there, except in the winter when it is closed.

One of the most enjoyable times at the Red Lion is at Christmas when the inn is decorated "to the nines" with Christmas greens and trim and 2,000 feet of laurel roping. The ceiling-high tree in the lobby shimmers with hundreds of handmade ornaments.

Ann Fitzpatrick's candy sculptures are restored to their familiar spots throughout the public rooms. During the holiday season, there is afternoon harp music, a visit from Santa, and a concert by bell

ringers. Children can hang decorations they have made on the children's tree in the hallway by the gift shop. The Christmas spirit continues with a group of carolers who gather on the front porch at Epiphany. Incidentally, the Red Lion Christmas trees adorning the top of the porch are kept lighted till long after Christmas.

Betsy Holtzinger, the innkeeper, easily recognizable by her shining blond hair, pointed out to me recently that Stockbridge is a five-season town: winter, spring, summer, autumn, and fall foliage. "It is the first country-inn experience for many people," she commented, "and we want to make it a memorable one. The Berkshire Theatre Festival, the Boston Symphony at Tanglewood, and Jacob's Pillow Dance Festival are open in the summer. In the winter we've got lots of downhill and cross-country skiing. Fortunately, the Norman Rockwell Museum, which contains many of his original paintings, is open every day except Tuesday year-round."

RED LION INN, Stockbridge, Mass. 01262; 413-298-5545. A 95-room historic village inn dating back to 1773 in the Berkshire mountains. European plan. Breakfast, lunch, and dinner. Open year-round. (From Nov. 1 to May 1, only 30 rooms open.) Adjacent to Tanglewood, Norman Rockwell's Old Corner House Museum. The Berkshire Playhouse, Jacob's Pillow, Chesterwood Gallery, Mission House, and major ski areas. Outdoor heated pool. Tennis, golf, boating, fishing, hiking, mountain climbing, and xc skiing nearby. Jack and Jane Fitzpatrick. Owners; Betsy Holtzinger, Innkeeper.

Directions: From the Taconic State Pkwy., take Exit 23 (N.Y. Rte. 23) to Mass. Rte. 7. Proceed north to Stockbridge. From the Mass. Tpke. Exit #2 Lee, follow Rte. 102 to Stockbridge.

THE VICTORIAN
Whitinsville, Massachusetts

I was having lunch at the Victorian on the sun porch, which has been beautifully decorated and furnished in a kind of Sadie Thompson-cum-Art Nouveau motif. We sat in the fabulous white wicker South Sea Island chairs amidst a collection of hanging plants which Martha Flint identified as Swedish ivy, Wandering Jew, and

Boston fern. "Everybody wants to sit out here," she said. "It's so wonderfully bright, especially with windows on three sides."

The cover of the luncheon menu, like the dinner and dessert menus, was adapted from designs of the 1920s showing very modish men and women looking as if they had all stepped out of a page of a French fashion magazine of the time.

It was the *inside,* however, that interested me most, and the choice today included several types of omelets, including crabmeat and cream cheese, spinach and sour cream; a variety of salads, crêpes, coquilles St. Jacques, and eggs Victorian.

While I was at it, I also took a peek at the dinner menu featuring "Medallions of the Huntress," which the menu described as two small filets of beef with a classic brown sauce. There were also prime ribs of beef, scallops gratinée, duckling served with sweet and sour sauce and garnished with a peach mousse, veal Oscar, filet of sole, and shrimp scampi.

"Our first course, which is included with each dinner, is described by the waiter or waitress. We prefer to serve salads after dinner in the continental manner," Orin explained.

The dessert menu included crêpes, cheesecake, apricot sherbet, brandy Alexander pie, chocolate mousse, and lime Bavarian pie. An additional menu described the various kinds of coffees and after-dinner specialties, such as Irish coffee, café Amaretto di amore, café chocolat anisette, and café Caribbean; all of these had short descriptions to help the relatively uninitiated, such as myself.

The Victorian is an imposing mansion that sits regally above the road on a grassy slope. There is rich wood paneling everywhere and appropriate, somewhat massive Victorian furniture. Unusual touches include hand-tooled leather wainscoting in a charming third-floor room with lovely arched windows, and intricately tiled floors in the bathrooms.

Some of the eight bedrooms have walk-in closets, and one has a dressing room with full-length mirrors mounted on the mahogany doors. Little "extras" at the Victorian include apples in the guests' rooms, turn-down service, hot mulled wine, and a continental breakfast for houseguests.

I'm certain that the Whitin family, who built this beautiful mansion during the 19th century and for whom the town is named, would thoroughly approve of the warm spirit of hospitality that pervades it today.

THE VICTORIAN, 583 Linwood Ave., Whitinsville, Mass. 01588; 617-234-2500. An 8-room (6 with private baths) Victorian mansion in a quiet town 15 mi. from Worcester, Ma. and 40 mi. from Narragansett Bay in R.I. European plan. Dinner served to travelers daily except Mondays. Lunch served to travelers Tues. thru Fri. Open on Sun. at 5 p.m. Overnight guests receive continental breakfast. Lawn games, ice skating, fishing on grounds. Golf and tennis nearby. Pets accepted. Orin and Martha Flint, Innkeepers.

Directions: From Providence, follow Rte. 146 north and take the Uxbridge exit. From the traffic light in Uxbridge, proceed north on Rte. 122 approximately 1½ mi. to Linwood Ave. (there will be a sign on the corner saying "Whitinsville — Left"). Bear left here. The inn is a few hundred yards around the corner. From Worcester, follow Rte. 146 south to the Whitinsville-Purgatory Chasm exit. Proceed into Whitinsville and keep right at the set of traffic lights onto Linwood Ave. The inn is on the left at the other end of Linwood Ave. — about 1½ mi.

The back road I want to tell you about is Route 16. It starts up north of Boston by the airport and comes down through Newton and Wellesley. It was voted one of the most beautiful highways in America some years ago. The part that is pertinent to the Victorian is where it comes through our neighboring town, Uxbridge. On Route 16 in Uxbridge, there are six or eight operating textile mills. One of them, the Stanley Woolen Mill, has been owned and operated by the same family (the Wheelocks) for over 170 years, longer than any other mill in America. Another mill just down the street is Bernat's, one of the biggest names in yarns. There are five yarn suppliers in Uxbridge, and it is well known as a yarn center, both for knitting and for looms.

The Stanley Woolen Mill offers a mill tour every day, and all the mills have outlet stores where one can find tremendous values in unique fabrics and yarns. It is a weaver's paradise, and there are bargains on woolens by the yard or even by the blanket. The Wheelocks are trying to have Uxbridge declared something like a museum town, because the textile industry is not dead here. It's a microcosm of what New England used to be like when the industrial revolution first hit America.

We also have a wonderful ornithological area near Route 16 called Heritage Park, the focal point of which is called Rice City Pond. This is a famous birdwatchers' area. Also, the West River attracts many fishermen because if its fine trout fishing, and that's

just over there, too. Near the West River is a good place to hunt
pheasant, quail, and ducks, which my birdwatching friend says
brings people out from all over the state.

Orin and Martha Flint
The Victorian
Whitinsville, Massachusetts

A lovely alternate route to the Yankee Clipper is Route 127,
leaving the first rotary after the bridge on Route 128 and following
signs for Annisquam. This is a much-traveled local road, but is one
that most people overlook on their way to Rockport, as it is not
the most direct. There are lovely vistas of the ocean from little
coves and beaches. The beautiful Annisquam River flows under the
highway, and views of the Annisquam Yacht Club and Wingersheak
Beach are breathtaking, especially at sunset. The charming, un-
spoiled, very old New England village of Annisquam is off this road.
Because many tourists have not found it, Annisquam remains a
quiet, local community, but is well worth a visit. This alternate
route to the Yankee Clipper goes around the northwest side of the
island. It takes a little longer to reach us this way, but when traffic
to Rockport is heavy, it provides a lovely change and eventually
you will arrive in Rockport.

Fred and Lydia Wemyss
The Yankee Clipper
Rockport, Massachusetts

In some ways Fred Wemyss sums up the hospitality at the
Yankee Clipper with one of his typical limericks:

> "A seasoned old traveler named Flynn
> Said, 'of all of the places I've been
> To wine in, to dine in,
> To have a good time in,
> You can't beat an old country inn.'"

THE VILLAGE INN
Lenox, Massachusetts

The village of Lenox with its tree-lined streets has an interesting history dating from Colonial days continuing through the 18th and 19th centuries. In many ways the Village Inn reflects quite a few of those historical events. The building itself dates back to the American Revolution and has been operated for over 150 years as an inn.

It is a two-and-a-half-story yellow clapboard building with a basic Federal design that has been adapted to meet various needs over many years. Two rear wings were once well-constructed barns moved from another part of Lenox and joined to the inn about 100 years ago. They form an L-shaped sheltered terrace with a lawn on which there are a number of beautiful maples, a small fountain, and an American flag. Plantings of iris, daffodils, petunias, roses, and tulips brighten the picture throughout the warmer weather.

This has been a portentous year for the Village Inn because Ray Wilson and Cliff Rudisill have instituted many changes which I think make it even more attractive. Their interest in music and art is reflected by the music recitals and art shows which are now offered almost year round in the living room and the lobby. One such recital was by John Gilmore, a tenor with the Metropolitan Opera.

Fresh-cut flowers reflect the current season and there are many rich varieties in the Berkshires. Just off the dining room an antique gift shop has been added which includes a coin silver collection, Shaker pieces, and many handsome quilts. In the dining room and on the front porch classical music is almost always in evidence.

One of the biggest changes has been the addition of the evening meal which has a wide selection, including prime rib, fresh swordfish, lobster, cornish hen, roast pork, and even a New England boiled dinner. Desserts feature fresh berries in season (both Cliff and Ray pick strawberries and raspberries during the summer), as well as Indian pudding, homemade custards and cakes, including the always enjoyable three-layer carrot cake. During the Tanglewood season the inn offers an after-concert menu with light fare.

Afternoon tea is served everyday with homemade scones, finger sandwiches, and desserts. In keeping with the spirit of innkeeping, the Village Tavern features live enterainment on weekends and it is a good opportunity for inn guests and local folks to enjoy good music. It's a cozy place to gather.

On the second floor, authentic New England rooms and suites are available for overnight or more leisurely guests. These have low ceilings, country furniture, and authentic wallpaper. Most have their own bathrooms, but some baths are "down the hallway." I noticed a real old ball-and-claw bathtub and Ray explained that they had not been replaced because people admire them. There is an attractive corner room with two twin spool beds and a very pleasant view of the village. I took particular note of the mounted prints of all the U.S. presidents adorning the long narrow hallway which otherwise might be dull. Cliff said that many of the guests enjoy learning for the first time who was president at the time they were born.

The Village Inn is just a short walk from the bus stop and many of the inn guests from New York and Boston and even points farther distant find this an ideal way to travel to Lenox.

THE VILLAGE INN, Church St., Lenox, Mass. 01240; 413-637-0020. A 25-room inn in a bustling Berkshire town 4 mi. from Stockbridge, 8 mi. from Pittsfield, and 1 mi. from Tanglewood. Lenox is located in the heart of the Berkshires with many historical, cultural, and recreational features. Breakfast, lunch, and dinner served daily to travelers. Open every day of the year, except Christmas Day. Swimming in pleasant nearby lakes. All seasonal sports including xc and downhill skiing available nearby. No pets. Personal checks accepted. Cliff Rudisill and Ray Wilson, Innkeepers.

Directions: After approaching Lenox on Rte. 7, one of the principal north-south routes in New England, exit onto Rte. 7A to reach the village center and Church Street. When approaching from the Mass Tpke. (Exit 2) use Rte. 20N about 4 mi. and turn left onto Rte. 183 to center of town.

WINDSOR HOUSE
Newburyport, Massachusetts

"Actually," said Judith Crumb, putting a rather English flavor into her diction, "We are offering two different types of dinner here at the inn. The first is Supper With the Innkeeper, a rather informal affair served in the kitchen, and Fritz and I eat with the guests. There's usually a four- or five-course meal and unless there are dietary restrictions it's chef's choice. It gives Fritz a great forum to try out new dishes or repeat family favorites, and he often gives cooking hints as he adds the final touches.

"Our Edwardian Feasts are truly regal occasions. We suggest formal attire, we all wear evening clothes and there is court music playing in the background. The Feast itself starts at 7:30 and consists of at least ten courses—fish, poultry, and meat courses are mixed with aspics and savories and sweets.

"We only accept reservations for one type of dinner per day and so they should be made well in advance. We can feed up to six guests for Supper with the Innkeeper and we can seat from two to six for the Edwardian Feast, but we accept only one party. Menus are submitted if the guest requests."

The Windsor House was built in 1796 as both a residence and a ship's chandlery office. The kitchen was the original shipping and receiving room, as can be seen from the big outside doors.

The brick wall of the fireplace is a part of a fire wall that extends to the top story and separates the old warehouse section from the living section. The posts and beams throughout the entire house were built by ships' carpenters.

The kitchen is really the pulse of the Windsor House. Not only do the guests gather around in the morning to enjoy Fritz's pre-prandial skills, but as Judith says, "It's the place where we all gather *any* time during the day and tell tales and get acquainted."

Guests at the inn continually write me complimentary notes about the breakfast that is included with the room tariff. Judith speaks of it as "a proper two-course English breakfast," although she points out that unlike the Britons, "Our toast is served warm instead of cold. Most breads are baked in the kitchen and there is a traditional English breakfast cake and English County Fair egg bread which is particularly yummy. Fritz has several culinary inspirations at breakfast time including a Rink Tum Tidy or Nantucket soufflé. There are lots of herbed eggs and each order is cooked to the guest's preference."

Three of the lodging rooms have private baths and three have shared baths. There are two family-suite combinations available, and trundle beds for small people. One of these suites has its own entrance at the street level and is ideal for elders or guests who might find stairs a problem.

On the very top floor it is possible to look out of the bedroom windows and see the houses that survived the Newburyport fire of 1811.

The Windsor House is within a pleasant stroll of the fascinating Newburyport waterfront.

WINDSOR HOUSE, 38 Federal Street, Newburyport, Ma. 01950; 617-462-3778. A 6-room inn located in the restored section of Newburyport. Open year-round. Breakfast served to all guests; dinner by 3-day advance reservation. Located in the Merrimack River Valley 3 mi. from Plum Island, and the Parker River National Wildlife Refuge. A short walk from the restored 19th-century retail area, restaurants, and museums. Also nearby: deep sea fishing, swimming, art galleries, antique shops, family ski area, horseback riding, and year-round theater. Some trundle beds available for children; no cribs or playpens. Parents must provide for infant care. Small dogs welcome. Can meet bus or planes at local airport. Judith and Fritz Crumb, Innkeepers.

Directions: From Boston and Maine: From I-95 use Exit to Rte. 113, turn right onto High St. (Rte. 1A) and proceed three miles to Federal St., turn left. Inn on left across from Old South Church (Rte. 1A is scenic drive from either Boston or New Hampshire).

YANKEE CLIPPER
Rockport, Massachusetts

The granite boulders loomed around me as I gingerly negotiated the rocky path, grateful that I had worn my rubber-soled deck shoes. With the aid of some strategically placed rope railings, and following Fred Wemyss's directions, I picked my way down to the water's edge. On this warm September morning it was like a totally different world. There were small tidal pools in which I could see bright green moss and several species of marine life. Overhead a few gulls dipped and swooped, bright spots of white against the clear blue sky. I sat with my back against a warm granite boulder, enjoying the sun and salty sea air.

I would shortly be joining all of the Wemyss family for lunch, including Gary and June who are at the Ralph Waldo Emerson, Barbara and Bob Ellis who are the innkeepers at the Yankee Clipper, and Fred and Lydia, who are the owners of both inns.

This was also the occasion for another reunion with my dear friend Debbie Tallett from the Millhof Inn *(CIBR)* who has spent several summers at the Yankee Clipper. Debbie, who has literally grown up in the inn business has been studying hotel management. Barbara said that she has done a wonderful job in the kitchen and her homemade breads and carrot cakes are very popular.

The inn complex consists of several buildings. One is the original building overlooking the water where the dining room and many large bedrooms with sea views are located. A few paces away there is the Quarterdeck where some of the rooms enjoy an unobstructed view of the ocean and gardens. The penthouse atop this building provides a magnificent vista.

Still another of the lovely old Rockport buildings is called Bullfinch House and is noted particularly for its architectural beauty. It is of Colonial Greek design named for its designer who also created the Boston Statehouse.

The furnishings in all of the bedrooms include many mahogany four-poster beds and double and single pineapple beds as well. Many will accommodate families of three or more quite comfortably.

The Sunday night buffet at the Yankee Clipper consists of seafood Newburg on patty shells, chicken a la king, or perhaps beef Stroganoff; tossed salad, green peas, tomato aspic, or molded fruit salad and various condiments. The lobster dinners are one of the most continuingly popular reasons for people returning to the Yankee Clipper.

There's much to occupy the time of both the active and more contemplative guests at the Yankee Clipper. A beautifully heated, salt-water pool is sheltered by lovely garden walls and beautiful shade trees. Many guests spend the greater part of the day in the comfortable deck chairs looking out over the sunlit waters of the bay. Be sure to bring a camera and your palette. For the more actively inclined, there is golf, tennis, boating, and fishing—not to mention wonderful strolls around the village of Rockport.

YANKEE CLIPPER, P.O. Box 520, Rockport, Mass. 01966; 617-546-3407. An intimate 28-room inn on the sea, 40 mi. from Boston. Modified American plan from May 15 to July 1 and Labor Day to Nov. 1. Breakfast, lunch, and dinner served during July and August. Meals served to travelers by reservation only. The Quarterdeck is open Thur. through Sun. Nov. 1 to April 1 on a bed-and-continental-breakfast basis. (Closed Dec. 24 and 25.) No pets. Heated outdoor pool, ocean view, shoreline walks. Many antique shops and other stores within walking distance. Fred and Lydia Wemyss, Proprietors; Barbara and Bob Ellis, Innkeepers.

Directions: Take I-95 to Rte. 128 to 127 (Gloucester). Proceed 6 mi. on Rte. 127 to Rockport and continue to Pigeon Cove.

ROCKPORT, MASSACHUSETTS

Rockport has been an artists' colony for over forty years. Once it was a sleepy fishing village, but then it was "discovered" by artists during the Depression of the thirties. Some of the most important people in painting have either visited or lived in Rockport. Now it attracts all kinds of creative people, including photographers, writers, and craftsmen, as well as artists.

INN AT CASTLE HILL
Newport, Rhode Island

I was enjoying a few moments of quiet on the porch of one of the harbor houses at the Inn at Castle Hill watching the water traffic on Narragansett Bay. In the foreground, a young fisherman wearing very high orange boots was taking in his nets, and in the middle distance I counted at least seventeen sailboats, including one of the famous twelve-meter yachts that are used in the America's Cup Races. In the far distance there was the presence of the famous Newport Bridge which soars over the bay to Jamestown.

Each one of the harbor houses is beautifully furnished with its own bathroom and is roomy enough to accommodate three people comfortably. All of them were newly decorated and the bright white walls and gay curtains and bedspreads were just perfect for the waterside atmosphere.

In addition to these lodgings, there are several rooms in the main mansion of the Inn at Castle Hill. This was once the property of the eminent naturalist Alexander Agassiz who built Castle Hill one hundred years ago as a summer residence. It has remained unchanged in character and many of the original furnishings, including oriental rugs and the handcrafted oak and mahogany paneling, are still intact. "This was done before Newport really became a chic society hideout," said Paul McEnroe, the innkeeper at Castle Hill. "Agassiz built this mansion for himself and was really one of the forerunners of Newport's later resplendence."

Paul and I strolled along the grassy bank to the deck of the main house where luncheon was served in full view of the ever-changing panorama of sea, sky, and ships. The menu included several very enticing offerings including a variety of omelets, crêpes, quiches, and salads.

Our conversation naturally led to the dinners at the inn, and Paul explained that the inn takes a limited number of diners each night and "they must be spaced just right. Dinner takes from two to two-and-a-half hours, so we naturally cater to people who are not in a hurry. Our dinners are now 98 per cent by reservation, and we only hold a table ten minutes. We always request that they not be late in order to avoid any misunderstandings.

"The evening meal is oriented to French cuisine and includes hot and cold hors d'oeuvres, soups, salads, fish, fowl, lamb, veal, and beef all cooked and served in the continental manner."

The European flavor of the Inn at Castle Hill is considerably reinforced by the road which leads from Ocean Drive through a small section of woods. It reminds me of the Barbizon Forest, about two hours south of Paris, which inspired a school of French painters, including Millet. When I remarked to Paul about this resemblence to inns I have visited in Europe, he responded enthusiastically, "That's exactly what we've tried to achieve. After all, this inn was built as a mansion and we're trying to recreate the elegance of Newport's past by having a menu, service, and furnishings that best suit our ideals. Jackets are required for dinner and no jeans, not even designer style, are allowed in the dining rooms. I'm sure that's the way it was eighty years ago."

Our regular readers will note that the dining rooms are now closed from January 3rd to Easter. However, rooms are available all winter with continental breakfast being served.

INN AT CASTLE HILL, Ocean Drive, Newport, R.I. 02840; 401-849-3800. A 20-room mansion-inn on the edge of Narragansett Bay. European plan. Continental breakfast served to houseguests only. Lunch and dinner served daily to travelers. Dining room closed from Jan. 3 to Easter. Guest rooms open all winter. Lounge open winter weekends. Near the Newport mansions, Touro Synagogue, the Newport Casino, and National Lawn Tennis Hall of Fame, the Old Stone Mill, the Newport Historical Society House. Swimming, sailing, scuba diving, walking on grounds. Bicycles and guided tours of Newport nearby. No pets. Paul Goldblatt, Manager. Paul McEnroe, Innkeeper.

Directions: After leaving Newport Bridge follow Bellevue Ave. which becomes Ocean Dr. Look for inn sign on left.

LARCHWOOD INN
Wakefield, Rhode Island

The Larchwood is a large mansion in the village of Wakefield, dating back to 1831, set in the middle of a large parklike atmosphere with copper, beech, ginkgo, pin oak, spruce, mountain ash, maple, Japanese cherry trees, evergreens, dogwoods, and a very old mulberry tree. In all there are three acres of trees and lawn.

The interior has many Scottish touches, including quotations from Robert Burns and Sir Walter Scott, and photographs and prints of Scottish historical and literary figures. One of the dining rooms has murals showing farms and seascapes of southern Rhode Island. On a recent trip I discovered a little sign I'd never seen before that said: "The Larchwood Inn where innkeeping is still in keeping." I detected a touch of innkeeper Frank Browning's sense of humor.

We were all in good humor that evening at dinner which began with an experience I've never had at any other inn. The waiter brought in a large silver tray with a choice of at least *four* different salads. "This has proven to be something that our guests enjoy very much," said Frank with a broad smile. "You're always talking about doing something 'memorable' and I think this fills the bill."

Since it was midsummer and real ocean weather, the conversation turned to the many beaches that are found throughout southern Rhode Island. "Most of these beaches are available without any permits," explained Frank. "Our houseguests frequently return on sunny afternoons with bright sunburns and stories about beaches they're sure no one else has discovered.

"One of the interesting parts of our summer dinner business is from people that are cruising on their boats. Our inn is about a mile and a half from Ram Point Marina which is at the head of Point Judith Pond. It is the largest and best facility in the area. We frequently get calls from people at the marina asking for reservations and directions. We often transport them back to their boat."

Because of the Scottish heritage which dates back to the previous owners, Mr. and Mrs. Hugh Cameron, Robert Burns's birthday is one of the big nights at the Larchwood Inn. "It's more popular than New Year's Eve," Frank remarked. "We're always booked six weeks in advance and we have a professional piper for the evening, a gentleman named John Alder who piped in the Queen of England at Newport a few years ago."

While I was looking at the menu Frank pointed out that a new feature was a lighter supper which included quiche Lorraine and quiche with crab, as well as various types of omelets and hot prime ribs of beef or sliced turkey sandwiches. "We're serving these in addition to our regular dinners," he said, "because many people would like something a little lighter or they come in later after a party. Of course we still have shrimp, lobster, swordfish, scallops, and langostinos."

The biggest news from the Larchwood is the addition of the "Holly House," a 150-year-old building across the street from the inn which provides eight more completely renovated and refurnished bedrooms to those already available in the inn itself. Guests at the Holly House can enjoy breakfast, lunch, and dinner at the Larchwood Inn dining room.

By the way, the Larchwood Inn is a few miles from Point Judith, Rhode Island, where the ferry leaves for Block Island. The Larchwood makes a nice overnight stop.

LARCHWOOD INN, 176 Main St., Wakefield, R.I. 02879; 401-783-5454. A 19-room village inn just 3 mi. from the famous southern R.I. beaches. Some rooms with shared bath. European plan. Breakfast, lunch, dinner served every day of the year. Swimming, boating, surfing, fishing, xc skiing, and bicycles nearby. Francis Browning, Innkeeper.

Directions: From Rte. 1, take Pond St. Exit and proceed ½ mi. directly to inn.

Newport has long been regarded as one of America's favorite year-round resorts, with history dating back to Colonial times. With its numerous architectural masterpieces representing several periods, the city is proud of its heritage. The restoration and preservation of its historic buildings have enabled Newport to share this heritage with its visitors and become a true museum of architecture.

One of the most pleasant aspects of Newport is its delightful weather any month of the year.

THE INNTOWNE
Newport, Rhode Island

During the more than seventeen years I've been making an annual project out of rewriting this book, there have been a number of interesting innovations and permutations among the many innkeepers with whom I've become acquainted.

Paul and Betty McEnroe are a case in point. I first met them in 1965 when they were innkeepers at the De la Vergne Farms Inn in Amenia, New York, which was included in the very first edition of *CIBR*. They, in turn, told me about Rodney and Ione Williams and the Inn at Sawmill Farm, which has been one of my regular visiting places since the late '60s.

The inn in Amenia was unfortunately destroyed by fire, and Paul and Betty relocated in Newport as the innkeepers of the Inn at Castle Hill. Meanwhile, being both creative and enterprising, they recognized the possibilities in converting a dilapidated old brick building of some architectural integrity in downtown Newport into an inn. It was quite natural for them to turn to Rodney and Ione, who are extremely well-known designers and decorators, to help with the project.

The result is an elegant Colonial inn in the heart of historic Newport which, like the Inn at Sawmill Farm, is a model for country inn decor and ambience.

"Ione was really involved in choosing all of the draperies, bedspreads, and wallpaper, even to the harmonizing colors in the lampshades," explained Betty McEnroe. "She carefully 'choreographed' — I think that's the best word for it — each room according to its size and the placement of the windows. We all agreed we wanted to achieve a feeling of lightheartedness and gaiety, but in a Colonial setting."

The lobby-living room area has some handsome antiques including an old grandfather's clock in a beautiful inlaid antique case, and one wall is a bookcase decorated with ivy plantings and a beautiful model ship. It's like being in a living room of a very elegant house of two hundred years ago.

The Inntowne is a perfect complement to the rest of historic

Bowen's Wharf

Newport. It is open twelve months of the year and it's most convenient for visiting Bowen's wharf with its many shops and boutiques. Furthermore, it's easy to drive around the city for a tour of the many mansions, some of which, along with the Tennis Hall of Fame, are open year around.

Betty and Paul serve continental breakfast in the engaging atmosphere of a little antique shop. As Betty says, "Our guests can enjoy the homemade muffins, juice, and coffee and then can purchase the bone china cup and saucer, the chair they sat on, the table they ate on, the oriental rug from the floor, or portraits from the wall."

The Inntowne does not accept reservations by mail, so please telephone only between the hours of 9:00 a.m. and 5:00 p.m. A tentative reservation can be made awaiting confirmation with deposit.

THE INNTOWNE, 6 Mary St., Newport, R.I. 02840; 401-846-9200. An elegant 20-room inn in the center of the city of Newport overlooking the harbor, serving continental breakfast only. Open every day. Reservations by telephone only between 9 a.m. and 5 p.m. Convenient for all of the Newport historical and cultural attractions which are extremely numerous. No recreational facilities available; however, tennis and ocean swimming are nearby. No pets. Not adaptable for children of any age. Betty and Paul McEnroe, Innkeepers.

Directions: After crossing Newport bridge turn right at sign: "Historic Newport." Drive straight to Thames Street; Inntowne is on corner of Thames St. and Mary St., across from Brick Marketplace.

THE 1661 INN
Block Island, Rhode Island

During the last few years the accounts of my visits to Block Island and The 1661 Inn also contained reports on the progress of the restoration by the Abrams family of the Manisses Hotel, a Victorian building just a few steps from the main building of the inn. It is one of the vestiges of the great days at the turn of the century when Block Island was a fashionable resort. It had fallen into considerable disrepair. However, in 1978 the first steps were made to convert the cellar into a very intriguing restaurant and the outdoor terrace into another dining area.

In 1982 the restoration of the Manisses was finally completed. Let me share a portion of an ebullient letter from Joan Abrams: "We're so excited because this has really been a 'dream project.' Each bedroom and bathroom is decorated entirely differently and almost all of the furniture is of the 1872 era. We had copies made of the original beds, in queen and king sizes, however, for the comfort of our guests. Some of the smaller rooms have the original Manisses beds. We have also been able to save some of the original lighting fixtures which have been restored and all of the lighting is from the late 19th century. There are flowers and hanging plants and large plants throughout the hotel.

"The exterior has been stained a very light grey and we have beaufitul flower gardens growing right up to the front porch. The deck where you and I had lunch has been finished with a wood floor just as it used to be. By fhe way, we'll be serving high tea every afternoon in the lobby overlooking the gardens.

"We dress our waitresses in long Victorian dresses and the waiters in ruffled vests and ties."

In 1984, The Manisses will have its own complete section in this book.

The 1661 Inn, an old, white house partially hidden from the road by thick hedges, has been operated by the Abrams family, including their daughter Rita and her husband Steve Draper, for fourteen years and continues to serve its frequently-returning guests very well. Three of the rooms overlooking the dining deck are enlarged, all of them with magnificent views of the ocean. Decks are being added to rooms on the second floor as well.

Because there is so much activity on Block Island for outdoor-minded people, including bicycling, beach walking, fishing, swimming, and the like, breakfast and dinner turn out to be very important times. There are many regional dishes including johnny cake, Indian pudding, blackberry flummery, Block Island clam chowder, flounder, lobster, and swordfish. Everything is made on the premises, and the baked stuffed flounder with mussels and clams is a real joy.

As I mentioned earlier, I've been watching the progress at The Manisses and noting with pride the increased popularity of The 1661 Inn during the past few years. I think the entire Abrams family is to be congratulated for a splendid accomplishment. My question to Joan and Justin is: "What next?"

THE 1661 INN, Box 367, Block Island, R.I. 02807; 401-466-2421 or 2063. A 25-room island inn off the coast of R.I. and Conn. in Block Island Sound; 11 private baths. Open from Memorial Day thru Columbus Day weekend. Breakfast served to travelers daily. (Guest House open year-round; continental breakfast included in off-season rates; dinner upon request.) Lawn games on grounds. Tennis, bicycling, ocean swimming, sailing, snorkeling, diving, salt and fresh water fishing nearby. Block Island is known as one of the best bird observation areas on the Atlantic flyway. The Abrams Family, Innkeepers.

Directions: By ferry from Providence, Pt. Judith, and Newport, R.I. and New London, Ct. Car reservations must be made in advance for ferry. By air from Newport, Westerly, and Providence, R.I., New London and Waterford, Ct., or by chartered plane. Contact inn for schedules.

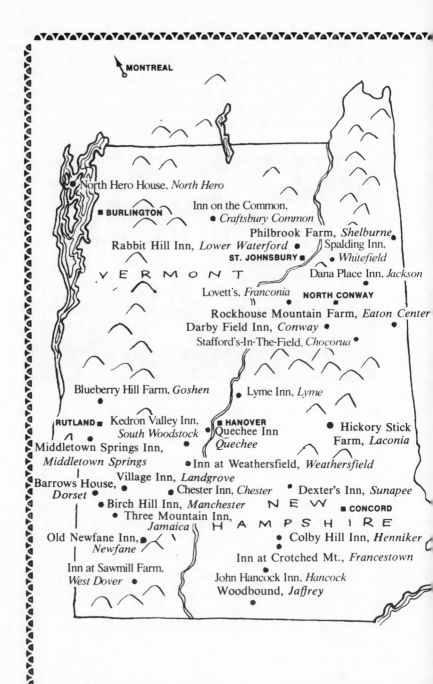

MONTREAL

North Hero House, *North Hero*

■ BURLINGTON

Inn on the Common,
● *Craftsbury Common*

Philbrook Farm, *Shelburne*

Rabbit Hill Inn, *Lower Waterford* ●
)) Spalding Inn,
ST. JOHNSBURY ■   ● *Whitefield*

V E R M O N T
Dana Place Inn, *Jackson*

Lovett's, *Franconia*   NORTH CONWAY

Rockhouse Mountain Farm, *Eaton Center*

Darby Field Inn, *Conway* ●

Stafford's-In-The-Field, *Chocorua* ●

Blueberry Hill Farm, *Goshen*
●

Lyme Inn, *Lyme*

RUTLAND ■ Kedron Valley Inn,
South Woodstock   ■ HANOVER
Quechee Inn
Quechee

Hickory Stick
Farm, *Laconia*

Middletown Springs Inn,
Middletown Springs

Inn at Weathersfield, *Weathersfield*

Barrows House,   Village Inn, *Landgrove*
Dorset ●   ● Chester Inn, *Chester*   ● Dexter's Inn, *Sunapee*

● Birch Hill Inn, *Manchester*   N E W   ■ CONCORD
● Three Mountain Inn,
Jamaica   H A M P S H I R E

Old Newfane Inn, ●   ● Colby Hill Inn, *Henniker*
Newfane

Inn at Crotched Mt., *Francestown*

Inn at Sawmill Farm,
West Dover ●   John Hancock Inn, *Hancock*
Woodbound, *Jaffrey*

Northern New England

Eastern Time Zone

M A I N E

● Country Club Inn, *Rangeley*

CALAIS ■

■ BANGOR

● Waterford Inne,
E. *Waterford*

Pentagoet Inn, *Castine*

Grey Rock Inn,
Northeast Harbor

Whitehall Inn, *Camden*

Claremont Inn,
Southwest Harbor

● Pilgrims Inn,

Squire Tarbox,
Westport Island

Goose Cove Lodge, *Deer Isle*

Homewood Inn,
Yarmouth ●

Bradley Inn, *New Harbor*

PORTLAND ■

Charmwoods, *Naples*

Black Point Inn, *Prouts Neck*

Captain Lord, Old Fort Club, *Kennebunkport*

Whistling Oyster,
Hartwell House, *Ogunquit*

Dockside Guest Quarters, *York*

175

BARROWS HOUSE
Dorset, Vermont

Charlie Schubert and I were taking a few minutes to stroll the grounds at the Barrows House and the first thing that he called to my attention was the beautiful new gazebo which he described as: "The talk of Dorset." I could see for myself that several guests were enjoying the beauty and serenity as we passed by.

I might add that Charlie has been promising me this gazebo for some time, so I'm glad it's a reality.

"The big project this year involved the creation of two bedrooms and a sitting room out of the attic space in what we call the Truffle House," he explained. "Marilyn has received so many compliments on the decor of these rooms that she is tempted to hang out her decorator's shingle. We've also completely renovated the Carriage House and transformed it into a really super accommodation.

"It is hard to realize that we've been here for ten years," said Charlie, "and I guess it's actually twelve since we first talked to you in Stockbridge about the possibilities of having a country inn.

"Oh, there have been some interesting times all right," he said. "I think that the winter of the gas shortage was the year that Marilyn and I really came of age as innkeepers. We had ordered a lot of cross-country equipment for the ski shop, made arrangements for the swimming pool to be dug that spring, and started renovating and adding new apartments in all the various old outbuildings we have here. Then, as we all remember vividly, the snow didn't come and the gasoline disappeared!"

All of that seemed far away today. The pool looked beautiful to me with the gaily colored umbrellas, the snack bar, and the

"changing room," which was designed to look like a small country barn. The tennis players changed partners and started another set.

Charlie excused himself for a few moments to greet some arriving guests and I sat there in the early twilight enjoying the quiet and peace of this Vermont country town.

Dorset has always been a town in which I feel at home. I have been well-acquainted with it for more than thirty years. The streets are tree-shaded, the houses are traditionally late Colonial and early Victorian; there is a village green, a post office, and general store. I have played many a round of golf on the rather sporty course and enjoyed many an evening of theater at the Dorset Playhouse. Incidentally, Charlie Schubert himself is an actor and during the winter he has appeared in quite a few plays given by the local company.

There is indeed a spirit at the Barrows House which I find so frequently among people who have left the city to take up a new life as country innkeepers. As busy as Charlie and Marilyn are in this thriving inn, they always seem to have time to stop and pass the time of day with their guests, help them plan an antiquing trip through the Green Mountains, arrange for a fourth at doubles or even accompany them out on the cross-country ski trails.

"Sometimes," Marilyn Schubert says, "this can be deceiving. It looks like the life of a country innkeeper is all fun and games. Believe me, maintaining 28 rooms in 6 houses, a ski shop, swimming pool, tennis courts, a full service dining room, and keeping up with all of our guests is a time-and-a-half job. Don't get me wrong, I'm not complaining. It is great fun, but there are lots of times that Charlie and I never even see each other during the day. But we love it and we wouldn't do anything else."

BARROWS HOUSE, Dorset, Vt. 05251; 802-867-4455. A 28-room village inn on Rte. 30, 6 mi. from Manchester, Vt. Modified American plan omits lunch. Breakfast and dinner served daily to travelers. Swimming pool, sauna, tennis courts, paddle tennis, bicycles, skiing facilities, including rental equipment and instruction on grounds. Golf, tennis, trout fishing, and Alpine skiing nearby. No credit cards. Charles and Marilyn Schubert, Innkeepers.

Directions: From Rte. 7 in Manchester, proceed 6 miles north on Rte. 30 to Dorset.

KEDRON VALLEY INN
South Woodstock, Vermont

Paul and Barbara Kendall and their two active sons Chip and Dave are living symbols of the new Vermont—young people with knowledge and spirit that see great opportunities in preserving the Vermont of yesteryear while at the same time providing modern, sensible conveniences which make it even more attractive. The KVI is tucked away in a mountain fastness near Calvin Coolidge's birthplace.

Chip and I were down earlier than anyone else. He was going on an all-day hike in the mountains, and I didn't want to miss a moment of what promised to be a resplendent Vermont day. While we munched cornflakes, his brother Dane came in, and I asked them what it was like living in an inn.

"Oh, it's fun," Chip said, "we get to meet all kinds of people, and sometimes I show them where to fish, or how to get to some of my favorite places in the mountains . . . and even a hidden covered bridge."

"Of course, we have to work hard here in the summertime," Dane said, "Chip helps my father in the kitchen, and I bring bags in from people's cars. My mother is always sending me on errands, too."

"Lots of people come here because it's so quiet," Chip continued, "some of them have never heard a brook before."

"Yeah, a lot of them are big eaters," Dane said, somewhat pointedly. (I guess he saw me eating the tenderloin tips and two pieces of their grandmother's pie last night.)

Chip started for the door. "Hey, I hear mother and dad coming down—let's get out before we have to help with the breakfast." They were gone.

I wrote the above paragraphs in the 1968 edition of this book, and everything is true now except that there is a great deal more going on at the Kedron Valley Inn. Besides lounging near cozy fireplaces, the winter activities include paddle tennis, ice skating, cross-country skiing, and sleigh rides on the premises, and downhill skiing at several nearby ski areas.

A few years ago the inn became involved in a very old Vermont tradition, that of maple sugaring. Much of this is done in the old-fashioned way using a team of horses with a sled for gathering the sap. Chip Kendall, who is now 25, is in charge of the sugaring operation. Twenty-four-year-old Dane is in charge of maintenance.

On a recent visit, during the first snowfall of the season, the inn never looked better. The porches had been rebuilt and all the

wood trim painted but, unfortunately, the box elder tree is no more. Besides the two sleeping rooms with fireplaces, there are three more sleeping rooms with old-fashioned woodburning stoves that add additional heat and more atmosphere. There are now ten rooms with fireplaces, Franklin stoves, or antique parlor stoves.

The past fifteen years have seen continuing development of opportunities for summertime diversions: one is the acre-and-a-half pond with a sandy beach and diving board, and another is the Kedron Valley Stables, with mounts for beginners and experts, private lessons, wagon rides, picnic trail rides, and horse trekking.

In line with the continuing and growing interest in horses, the KVI has for the last few years sponsored an "Inn-to-Inn" riding adventure which includes overnight stops at several farms as well as two other inns in this book. There are also weekend riding vacations with western or eastern tack, consisting of two full days of guided trail riding on dirt roads and through woodland trails.

KEDRON VALLEY INN, Rte. 106, South Woodstock, Vt. 05071; 802-457-1473. A 34-room rustic resort-inn, 5 mi. south of Woodstock. Near Killington, Mt. Ascutney ski areas. European plan. Breakfast, lunch, and dinner served daily from early May to Nov. 1. Closed Sunday evenings Nov. to mid-March. Closed from mid-March to early May. Christmas Day buffet served from 1 to 5 p.m. Swimming, riding, sleigh rides, carriage rides, paddle tennis, hiking, and xc skiing on grounds. Tennis, golf, and bicycles nearby. Paul and Barbara Kendall, Innkeepers.

Directions: Take Exit 1 from I-89 and follow Rte. 4 to Woodstock. Proceed south on Rte. 106 for 5 mi. Or, take Exit 8 from I-91 and follow Rte. 131 for 8 mi. Proceed North on Rte. 106 for 12 mi.

BIRCH HILL INN
Manchester, Vermont

Jim and Pat Lee and I were enjoying a cup of tea in the low-ceilinged living room of Birch Hill Inn. From the windows on three sides the fields, now deep under a blanket of Vermont snow, stretched down into the valley and up to the hills beyond. It was a warm, comfortable place with a spinet piano, an ongoing, never-ending jigsaw puzzle, and innumerable books and magazines. Over the big fireplace was a print of George Washington's triumphal

entry into New York City after the Revolutionary War. I noted much interest in art, music and history in this lovely old farmhouse, the main part of which is 190 years old. Four generations of Pat's family have lived here and that is one of the things that makes this inn special.

I caught a glimpse of some cross-country skiers and asked Jim about the extent of the trails.

"We worked at clearing our trails all summer and now have a network of about eight miles for both hiking and cross-country skiing. I'm happy to take the guests out at any time, and you'll see for yourself that the combination of woods and views is at times almost overwhelming."

"Well so much for cross-country skiing, what about the summertime?"

Jim's face lit up. "For one thing, we offer a kidney-shaped swimming pool and a view in all directions of the surrounding mountains. We have great walking trails, which are the cross-country ski trails in the winter. We have our own trout pond stocked with six- to seven-inch rainbows and the guests are allowed to catch and release the fish. It's an ideal spot to practice fly casting. Nearby, the golf is first-rate at the Equinox Golf Club and there's tennis, biking, and fabulous backroading in the mountains."

Pat picked up the conversational ball. "Our accommodations include a full breakfast. We like to serve homemade muffins, french toast, or egg-in-the-hole, and other hearty things. After breakfast we let our guests know what we will be serving for dinner that evening, and they can make a reservation if they'd like.

This perked up my interest and I asked about the menu. "Well, we always have homemade soup, tomato bisque for example, and home-baked bread. Our single entrées could be veal Marsala, butterflied leg of lamb, or chicken breasts Parmesan. Sometimes Jim cooks Cornish hens or a turkey on the outdoor grill. We have lots of fresh vegetables right from our garden, and always a flavorful salad. Our emphasis is on thoughtfully prepared food, including a delectable dessert to top off each evening meal. We all eat together and we really enjoy getting to know our guests as we sit around one big table.

Accommodations at this informal, family-style inn are in five extremely comfortable and cheerful bedrooms in the main house all of which have views toward the mountains, farm, and pond. They are well decorated with paintings and furniture from the family home. A nearby cottage on the grounds has been converted into an ideal family-style accommodation as well.

BIRCH HILL INN, Box 346, West Road, Manchester, Vt. 05254; 802-362-2761. An extremely comfortable country home that has been converted into an inn. Five bedrooms in the main house plus a family cottage a few paces away. Located about 5 min. from downtown Manchester Center. Breakfast included in the cost of the room. Dinners offered to houseguests only by reservation, every night except Wed. Swimming pool, xc skiing, trout fishing, and walking trails on grounds. Alpine skiing at major areas nearby as well as tennis and golf facilities; great biking. Open after Christmas to mid-April, and May to late Oct. (be sure to make reservations). No pets. No credit cards. Pat and Jim Lee, Innkeepers.

Directions: From New York City: Taconic Parkway to U.S. 22. Turn east from Rte. 22 at your own choosing, and go north on Rte. 7 to Manchester. Fork left just beyond the Johnny Appleseed book shop on West Road and look for Birch Hill Inn 2 mi. on right. From Boston: Take the Massachusetts Tpke. to I-91 to the second Brattleboro Exit and continue to Manchester on Rte. 30.

BLUEBERRY HILL
Goshen, Vermont

I first visited Tony Clark at Blueberry Hill in midsummer of 1972, when the idea of opening up an inn exclusively for cross-country skiers was just taking shape in his mind.

The inn is very definitely family-style. Everyone sits around the big dining room table and there is one main dish for each meal, which is cooked in the farmhouse kitchen. This main dish is likely to be something quite unusual, depending on the cook's gourmet proclivities.

The bedrooms are plain and simple with hot water bottles on the backs of the doors and handsome patchwork quilts on the beds. To be there is truly like visiting a Vermont farm in the Vermont mountains.

I'd like to share with you a letter from Tony, telling about *summer* at Blueberry Hill: "We're open from June through October, as well as from December through March for skiing. Summertime here in the Green Mountains is just fabulous. Our vegetable and flower gardens are the best they've ever been. Guests gave a hand taking down two nearby barns. Our little summer restaurant went off very well, with Laura doing a super job with busy crowds on Saturday nights. I, by the way, do the omelets on Sunday nights.

"There's great fishing in our streams, hiking, and biking, and nearby tennis, and always a refreshing dip in the pond (I'll bet you didn't even know we had one!). Many guests who don't have their own gardens enjoy helping us pick the vegetables from ours. They can even help clear trails."

In late July, for the last few years, there has been an annual cross-country footrace and Blueberry Festival. The course covers 6.5 miles on the paved and gravel roads, leading the runner down through the cool shaded heart of Goshen, Vermont, up a series of hills and back through the woods and pastures with beautiful views of the Green Mountains. Following the race, the Blueberry Festival, open to competitors and spectators alike, features a chicken barbeque with salads, homemade breads, and blueberry baked goods. An old-time square dance wraps up the evening's festivities.

Besides being one of the oldest and best-known ski touring centers in Vermont, Blueberry Hill is now very popular with summer and fall back-packers and hikers. There are many, many trails, most of which are used for cross-country skiing in the wintertime. It's possible to use the inn as a central point for such activities or to include it on an itinerary. It's always important to phone ahead for reservations and information.

Reservations for winter accommodations should be made as early as possible, as the inn is often booked solid for weeks at a time in winter. Reservations open on September 1.

BLUEBERRY HILL, Goshen, Vt. 05733; 802-247-6735. A mountain inn passionately devoted to cross-country skiing, 8 mi. from Brandon. Modified American plan for overnight guests. All rooms with private baths. Open from June to November when public restaurant is open for dinner; and December to April. Closed Christmas. Swimming, fishing, and xc skiing on the grounds. Tony Clark, Innkeeper.

Directions: At Brandon, travel east on Rte. 73 through Forest Dale. Then follow signs to Blueberry Hill.

CHESTER INN
Chester, Vermont

Chester is an old Vermont village with a surprisingly exciting history and many 19th-century homes and buildings, including a striking group of stone houses at the eastern end of the town. It has one of the longest main streets of any village I've ever visited.

Situated at the slender village green is a Victorian building that reflects many architectural influences. The porch runs across the entire first floor and there is a second balcony over the center section. This is the Chester Inn.

The innkeepers for the past few years have been Tom and Betsy Guido who, with their sons, Gregory, 9, and Zackry, 6, moved to Vermont from Cleveland. They brought with them endless amounts of panache, a wonderful love of art of all kinds, and a burning desire to run a country inn.

Reflecting over my early visits, I'd say that they had succeeded admirably. Today, the Chester Inn is a busy place in all seasons.

Seated around the pool that shares a lovely grassy area in the back of the inn, Betsy and Tom shared a few of their thoughts about innkeeping which I believe in many ways tell us a great deal about the inn itself.

"Vermont has changed so much from days past," exclaimed Betsy. "It's no longer just a place to go for skiing, but has four distinct seasons. I love the quietness of spring when all of a sudden one day the ground wakes up and shoots forth an array of blossoms and sprouts.

"Summer has become a real Vermont vacationland. Our area abounds with church suppers, flea markets, and country crafts."

"Hiking and bicycling are very popular, too," noted Tom. "And what better place for backroading than Vermont?" .

"Autumn is wonderful and it starts in late September," Betsy continued. "We took our boys and the dogs and climbed Fox Chair Mountain just outside town. There's a stone formation on the top resembling a chair where foxes sit and howl at the moon. The view is breathtaking and the color spectacular. The town below us looked like the set of a toy train layout."

Tom broke in, "Oh, there's no time like winter. Our fireplace burns day and night, and people make themselves at home around it. We even have people who come in off the street to ask to sit by the fire and warm their toes and enjoy the peacefulness."

Tom excused himself to go into the kitchen to start to prepare the evening meal and Betsy half whispered to me, "You know Tom is very proud of what has been accomplished in the kitchen and he receives lots of compliments. Everything we make here is homemade and the entrées and vegetables are cooked to order.

"I wish you could be here at Christmastime. We have an eleven-foot Christmas tree decorated with red bows and white lights. I love Christmas. There's a fairylike atmosphere that happens here with lots of natural greens over the chandelier in the dining room and above the mantel, and cascading down the stairs. After our Christmas Eve buffet when Tom is dressed as Santa Claus, we have caroling, eggnog, and Christmas cookies in the lounge."

Sounds like a merry Christmas in all seasons at the Chester Inn.

CHESTER INN, Chester, Vt. 05143; 802-875-2444. A 30-room village inn on Rte. 11, 8 mi. from Springfield, Vt. Convenient to several Vt. ski areas. Lodgings include breakfast. Dinner served to travelers daily except Mon. Lunch served in the Fullerton Tavern daily except Sunday. Closed from late October to mid-November and April to mid-May. Pool, tennis, sauna and excercise room, guest privileges at nearby racquetball club, and bicycles rented on grounds. Golf, horseback riding, Alpine and xc skiing nearby. No pets. Tom and Betsy Guido, Innkeepers.

Directions: From I-91 take Exit 6. Travel west on Rte. 103 to Rte. 11.

INN AT SAWMILL FARM
West Dover, Vermont

It was one of those wonderful, magic nights when everything seemed to be falling beautifully into place. We were about 55 in number and the dining room at the Inn at Sawmill Farm was filled almost to overflowing with innkeepers from *Country Inns and Back Roads* enjoying a meeting being hosted by Ione, Brill, and Rodney Williams.

Even for the innkeepers who are frequently a blase lot at times, the menu was a culinary adventure not only in the starter department, but in the main dishes as well. I shared a table with Ione Williams, Paul McEnroe from the Inn at Castle Hill in Newport, his wife Betty who is the innkeeper at the Inntowne Inn in Newport, and Rose Ann Hunter from the Morrill Place in Newburyport. We decided to share all the dishes, so there was much passing of clams Casino, the special game paté, and other first courses. This was followed by shrimp bisque soup that everyone declared to be superior. I ordered sweetbreads, but delighted in sampled morsels of the rack of lamb with an Indian sauce and other examples of chef Brill Williams' cuisine. When he came to the dining room in his immaculate white uniform, we all gave him a standing ovation.

The Inn at Sawmill Farm is well known not only among country-inn enthusiasts but also among country innkeepers themselves, and much time was spent touring the public rooms, the patio, tennis courts, the big pond and the beautiful grounds, as well as "oohing" and "ahing" over various lodging rooms, many of which are of post-and-beam construction with colorful chintzes and a generous application of barn board.

After dinner the story of Sawmill Farm was told by Rod and Ione and of how they had created the inn out of what Ione described as "a beautiful old farmhouse and barn." Their son Brill was trained by Ione in the kitchen and is now the head chef and officially one of the owners.

My acquaintance with the Williamses began in the late '60s, and since that time I have observed that in the lodging rooms added in various outbuildings of the original farm the textures of barn siding, beams, ceilings, floors, and the picture windows combine to create a feeling of rural elegance. Rod and Ione are particularly qualified to create such a scene since he is an architect and she is an interior designer.

Several times during our overnight stay, I found a great many of the innkeepers gathered around the superb conversational piece in the main living room—a handsome brass telescope mounted on a tripod providing an intimate view of Mt. Snow rising majestically to the north.

As we all regretfully made our goodbyes the next day, one innkeeper said she thought it was such a lovely idea for the inn to keep its beautiful outdoor Christmas decorations so that at night the white lights on the bushes and trees created a wonderful fairyland atmosphere. Rod acknowledged her comment and said that the inn always kept these lights in place until Eastertime.

During the past year Rodney and Ione built their own home nearby (very handsome, indeed) and their former quarters in the original farmhouse were renovated, decorated and furnished, thus adding four more bedrooms to the inn. Three are studio rooms with fireplaces and there's another two-room suite, also with a fireplace.

INN AT SAWMILL FARM, Box 8, West Dover, Vt. 05356; 802-464-8131. A 23-room country resort-inn on Rte. 100, 22 mi. from Bennington and Brattleboro. Within sight of Mt. Snow ski area. Modified American plan omits lunch. Breakfast and dinner served to travelers daily. Closed Nov. 7 through Dec. 7. Swimming, tennis, and trout fishing on grounds. Golf, bicycles, riding, snowshoeing, Alpine and xc skiing nearby. No children under 8. No pets. No credit cards. Rodney, Brill, and Ione Williams, Innkeepers.

Directions: From I-91, take Brattleboro Exit 2 and travel on Vt. Rte. 9 west to Vt. Rte. 100. Proceed north 5 mi. to inn. Or, take U.S. 7 north to Bennington, then Rte. 9 east to Vt. Rte. 100 and proceed north 5 mi. to inn.

THE MIDDLETOWN SPRINGS INN
Middletown Springs, Vermont

Christmastime at the Middletown Springs Inn . . . what a joy! Snow was piled at least sixteen inches deep on the tops of the hedges and the old-fashioned wheelbarrow on the lawn assumed a shape fantastical. Mel Hendrickson had carefully shoveled out a path to the handsome Victorian front door flanked by colorful Christmas decorations and I could see the lights from a Christmas tree in the main living room.

Before my hand had touched the graceful brass knob, the door was flung open and there were Mel and Jean Hendrickson. "Welcome to the Middletown Springs Inn and Merry Christmas!" I was immediately taken in tow and ushered into a handsome library which was warmed by an old-fashioned cast iron stove. A cup of tea and freshly made cake were placed before me, and I knew at long last I had arrived home.

The guest visiting here for the first time is surprised and then really overwhelmed by one important feature of this inn—its truly amazing collection of *dolls*.

Jean's grandmother started the collection, which was continued by her mother and now by Jean. There are dolls everywhere—dolls of every description, shape, nationality, and occupation. It is a veritable museum of dolls. There are Dionne quintuplet dolls, Little Women dolls, Henry VIII and all of his wives—there is a doll for practically every occasion and it would be very easy to go on for paragraphs describing them, but let me tell you about Mel and Jean.

After having raised six children, they would certainly have been entitled to take life more casually. But the opportunity came to convert this Victorian mansion into an inn about three years ago and Mel and Jean viewed it as an entirely new career. They plunged in with hearts high and a youthful outlook. Now they have integrated themselves into the community. "We love it," says Jean.

There are seven very tastefully decorated Victorian bedrooms with many interesting, unusual touches, and of a certainty many dolls and other fascinating knickknacks.

A full breakfast is served which might include blueberry pancakes, sticky buns, country-style oatmeal, scrambled eggs with onions, or blueberry coffee cake. This is included in the price of the room.

The evening meal (served only to houseguests) has a single main dish such as a roast, or chicken baked with ham and cheese, and homemade desserts including "mile-high" strawberry pie.

When the Hendricksons moved from Baltimore to Middletown

Springs, they brought not only this fabulous collection of dolls and antiques, but also dozens and dozens of photographs of the family, including their grandparents and grandchildren, all of which are in evidence throughout the inn. It is really like being in someone's home.

This spirit is particularly true in the big kitchen where eventually everyone gathers. Attached to the refrigerator were at least five "thank you" notes painfully printed with colored crayon from their grandchildren who had joined the Hendrickson family for a reunion over Thanksgiving.

Boy, can you imagine what it's like to have Mel and Jean for grandparents and to visit them with all of the wonderful surprises in their big country home!

THE MIDDLETOWN SPRINGS INN, Middletown Springs, Vermont 05757; 802-235-2198. A 7-room Victorian mansion on the green of a lovely 18th- and 19th-century village. Shared baths. Breakfast included; arrangements can be made for dinner. Open year-round; however, call in advance for reservations. Within easy driving distance of all central Vermont summer and winter recreation in Mt. Killington, state parks, summer theater, etc. Lawn sports on grounds; swimming, golf, tennis nearby. Not suitable for young children. Jean and Mel Hendrickson, Innkeepers.

Directions: From Manchester Center, Vermont, follow Rte. 30 to Pawlet and turn north on Rte. 133 to Middletown Springs. From Poultney, Vermont follow Rte. 140 to East Poultney and on to Middletown Springs.

Going south from the inn on Route 133, drive 4½ miles to Wells Road, past Morgan Mountain on the left (Morgan, of horse fame, had his first house at the foot of this mountain) and "The Purchase," another mountain, on your right. Actually, you are between these mountains in a broad valley. At Wells Road, you turn right and pass between Moosehorn Mountain and Broad Hill, down a sweeping curve into the village of Wells, about five miles on this leg. In Wells, you intersect Route 30—turn right on Route 30 up past Lake St. Catherine, a magnificent lake nestled at the foot of St. Catherine Mountain with an escarpment rising high above you to the mountain itself. In Poultney, ten miles later, you cross Route 140, turn right, and in another nine miles you are back at the inn.

Route 140 runs beside the Poultney River. Wherever you see areas where cars are parked or have parked, there is a swimming hole in the river. These range from cold "jaccuzis," where the water flows over you at the foot of natural rock dams, to deep holes that you jump or dive into from a height of ten to fifteen feet over the river. There are six such spots on the way from Poultney to the inn.

Mel and Jean Hendrickson
The Middletown Springs Inn
Middletown Springs, Vermont

Now for the truly back road experience: Just finding us, many exclaim, is an experience. We suggest turning off Route 11 into

Peru, Vermont. There one finds the J.J. Hapgood Store, one of the oldest and friendliest general stores around. From there take the Hapgood Pond Road, which passes Hapgood Pond State Park, containing a great nature trail and pretty setting. Then the road becomes gravel and meanders through the National Forest. Then, suddenly, a sharp turn and one discovers a valley in the mountains— Landgrove. Across the flats and over the west branch of the West River where the "ole swimmin' hole" once was, you'll see the cross-roads. On the right is Landgrove Church, which has services only in the summer. Directly in front of you is the old one-room school-house, which is now the Town Hall and Library. Turn left here. For those interested in old headstones and their related literary art, take time to stop on your left at the burial sites of some of Landgrove's early settlers. The Village Inn is around the next bend.

Jay and Kathy Snyder
The Village Inn
Landgrove, Vemont

While taking a ride to Bennington, Vermont, early this summer, Ronnie and I came across Route 346, just north of us, and were richly rewarded for our curiosity. It is a well-paved road used mostly by the "locals," and not by the general traveler. The mountain views were spectacular and the tranquility of the farms and meadows felt as if time had passed them by.

Upon reaching Bennington, a stop at Bennington Pottery is a must and usually a bargain; also there's a great little restaurant for lunch, and the Bennington Museum, where one can see the Grandma Moses collection.

Frank and Ronnie Tallet
Millhof Inn
Stephentown, New York

THE INN AT WEATHERSFIELD
Weathersfield, Vermont

The ancient Greeks believed that each of us is predestined to live our lives in a pattern devised by the gods. If indeed that is true, then Mary Louise and Ron Thorburn were each destined to become innkeepers, because seldom have I found two people who are well-suited, both in temperament and skill, for this honorable profession.

Fortunately for lovers of inns, The Inn at Weathersfield, as ancient a structure as "any in the land" provides them with a perfect setting for their roles. Located in the mountains of eastern Vermont, just west of the Connecticut River, the original farmhouse was built nearly two centuries ago. It was enlarged in 1796, a carriage house was added in 1830, and graceful pillars on the front porch, built by a homesick southern minister around 1900, supply the rather surprising "southern Colonial" look. The inn is set back from the highway and has eleven large guest rooms and a two-room suite all furnished with period antiques. Each room has a private bath, some have canopied beds, and most have working fireplaces. The dining room has exposed beams and a big fireplace.

Mary Louise and I were in the Keeping Room in front of a crackling fire enjoying a mug of mulled wassail, a cider made from locally grown and pressed apples. "Did you know that our fruit shrub with maple syrup and sherbert added was featured on the cover of the June, 1982, *Gourmet?* We were so excited."

She continued, "Innkeeping has been wonderful and we've put almost all of our ideas into motion. We serve breakfast on silver trays in the bedrooms and I am able to present some of my really special recipes, including chicken Weathersfield. Dinner is served in the dining room, which is a wonderful place for everyone to get to know each other. Ron loves it because it's filled with our books, and he has his piano and plays almost every night."

As we walked into the dining room she continued, "We have facilities here for people to bring their own horses and carriages, and we also have guests who ride horseback down from the Kedron Valley Inn.

"Our big news is that the addition to the rear of the inn is completed and we have more bedrooms and a new guest lounge."

She handed me a minature ceramic saying, "We give one of these to every one of our guests. It's created by my daughter Heather. No one leaves the Inn at Weathersfield without a pleasant reminder of how much we enjoyed having them."

The reader can realize that I have only scratched the surface of all of the wonderful warmth and ambience of this cordial Vermont country inn. As I said at the beginning, it's almost as if the Thorburns and The Weathersfield Inn were destined for each other. Now there is a happy conviction of completeness.

THE INN AT WEATHERSFIELD, Route 106 (near Perkinsville), Weathersfield, Vermont 05151; 802-263-9217. A 12-room Vermont country inn located just a few miles west of I-91 and north of Springfield. European plan, with breakfast and a high English tea included in the cost of the room. Dinner also served. Closed for dinner, Sunday, Monday, and Tuesday (although also available on other evenings during the high season). Horseshoes, badminton, croquet on the lawn; sleigh riding on grounds. Also a natural amphitheater with music and theater offered during the summer. Many footpaths and back roads. Bicycles available. Berry and apple picking, golf, downhill skiing, (Ascutney and Okemo), xc skiing, horseback riding nearby. Children under 8 years old are not conveniently accommodated. No pets. Mary Louise and Ron Thorburn, Innkeepers.

Directions: If traveling north on I-91, use Exit 7 at Springfield and follow Rte. 106. Traveling south, take Exit 8 and follow Rte. 131 to Rte. 106 and turn south. From Boston, leave I-89 and follow Rte. 103 across New Hampshire west into Vermont where it becomes Rte. 131 and then go south on Rte. 106.

RABBIT HILL INN
Lower Waterford, Vermont

Lower Waterford is truly picturebook New England. The village is situated along just one street and consists of the Rabbit Hill Inn, the village church, the 150-year-old post office, the library, (which has an honor system of signing out books), and about eight early 19th-century, classic New England homes. The view from Rabbit Hill Inn is of the magnificent Presidential Range of New Hampshire in the distance. What a sight it is with the sun lighting up its snow-clad peaks.

This is what Eric and Beryl Charlton saw a few years ago when they came to this Connecticut River valley in search of a country inn. "We knew this had to be our place," exclaimed Beryl. "It really is quite different from my home, Stratford-on-Avon, and Eric's, which is Newcastle-on-Tyne."

Eric continued, "Besides the lovely natural views, we were both intrigued by the history of the inn, which is really the story of the community." A building known as the Briar Patch was opened as a tavern and general store in 1795 by a man named Samuel Colby. Then the main building was built in 1825 as a home and a workshop for making winnowing machines. In 1834 it became an inn for the first time because lower Waterford was on a heavily traveled road between Portland and the interior of New England and Montreal. Maple syrup was one of the earliest exports.

"Most inns more than 150 years old have had both good and bad years, and during the 1950s, the carriage house and ballroom, built in 1855, were turned into a motel—horrors."

Today, the Carriage House has re-metamorphosed back to its original, graceful form. Even the arches have been restored.

"It has been wonderful," said Beryl. "We've found a builder who specializes in restoration and uses square-cut nails and the same kind of joints that were in the original building. He is a real purist. We found flooring from a house that was built in St. Johnsbury in 1800, latches from a house dismantled in Upper Waterford, and two local women cut stencils for decorating the hallways and rooms. We've replaced a lot of furniture by degrees. It is very difficult 'de-moteling' a place."

Before I get carried away with this restoration let me explain that all of the inn's country bedrooms have their own private baths, and all but two have a view of the mountains. The bedrooms are generously furnished with antiques and a collection of coal miner's lamps that originally came from England. There are lace-trimmed canopy beds and wallpapers, and other decorations in the country-inn theme.

Rabbit Hill is ideal for outdoor-minded guests. Besides the inn's own cross-country ski trails, there's alpine skiing, fishing, sailing, canoeing, walking, and mountain climbing.

A word or two about the dinner menu is in order; there are some excellent soups and appetizers including a cold salad of cucumber, orange, raisins, almonds, and yogurt spiced with a curried dressing. Entrées include mushroom goulash which is a sauté of mushrooms, green peppers, tomatoes, and onions flavored with paprika; and steak Farci which is a pan-broiled sirloin steak stuffed with mushrooms, bacon, shallots, and gruyere cheese served in a red wine sauce.

Dinner is served in the candlelit dining room which also overlooks the great mountains of New Hampshire.

One final thought. When you visit Rabbit Hill be sure to bring your camera.

RABBIT HILL INN, Pucker St., Lower Waterford, Vt. 05848; 802-748-5168. A 20-room country inn with a view of mountains on Rte. 18, 10 mi. from St. Johnsbury, Vt. Modified American, European plans. Open all year except 2 weeks in April and November. Breakfast and dinner served to travelers. Fishing, xc skiing on grounds. Tennis, swimming, walking, alpine skiing, sailing, backroading nearby. The Charlton Family, Innkeepers.

Directions: From I-91: Exit 20 east through St. Johnsbury, follow Rte. 2 east and signs to Rte. 18. From I-93: Exit Rte. 18 junction, turn north (left) on Rte. 18.

THE INN ON THE COMMON
Craftsbury Common, Vermont

Ever since my first visit to this inn in the summer of 1975 I've thought of it as a moveable feast. Perusing the previous copies of *CIBR,* I've discovered that Penny and Michael Schmitt have had something new and exciting to report every year.

The village of Craftsbury Common was founded in 1789 by Ebeneezer Crafts, who moved here from Massachusetts after the Revolutionary War. A great many of the buildings around the Common, which is an open, fenced piece of land, were built in the late 18th and 19th century and are still standing. The inn buildings were constructed in the early 1800s and are graceful examples of Federal architecture. There are antiques throughout generously combined with all the modern comforts. Each guest bedroom is individually decorated and supplied with fresh flowers or plants, extra pillows, and terry cloth bathrobes.

Penny Schmitt supervises the dinner which is served only to houseguests and sometimes includes fresh rainbow and brook trout available "only when the postmaster goes fishing." Breakfasts are quite elaborate with many types of omelets—cheese, herb, mushroom, onion, tomato, or even an "everything" omelet which is all of the above.

This would be quite enough for most inn-goers. However, in 1978 a swimming pool was added and an excellent tennis court and that was the first year of "cut throat" croquet played with imported English mallets and balls. That was also the year that the old building across the road from the inn was renovated and new bedrooms were added.

Nearby is the Craftsbury Sports Center, a complete ski-touring facility. There is a trail that goes in front of the inn, over the fields to the center, and cross-country skiing guests have a moveable feast of their own!

In 1979 the Center took on even greater dimensions with activities on nearby Lake Hosmer including a sculling camp, a running camp, a soccer camp, and provisions for kayaking and canoeing. Inn guests are invited to be spectators at various events, if not actually participating.

In 1982 the dining room and the porch were enlarged, keeping the outer arches and lattice-work intact, and a wall of insulated glass was added. It did not change the building line at all.

There are now two beautiful long tables in the dining room, and frequently Michael is the host at one, and Penny is the hostess at the other. There is a beautiful view of the rose garden which is lighted at night.

Almost at press time I received a note from Penny and Michael to the effect that they have just purchased a house on the Common. "We are going to add bathrooms by eliminating some of the small rooms. Each of the buildings will have its own sitting area for the guests, lots of comfortable furniture, a TV in the parlor and a guest kitchen in both the Annex and the New House."

Yes, over the years The Inn on the Common has indeed become a moveable feast, but may I hasten to add there's ample opportunity for sitting in the inn garden, watching sunsets, walking on country roads, reading books, and enjoying the peace and quiet of the Northeast Kingdom countryside.

THE INN ON THE COMMON, Craftsbury Common, Vt. 05827; 802-586-9619. A 15-room resort-inn in a remote Vermont town 35 mi. from Montpelier; 5 rooms with private bath, 10 sharing 5 baths. Modified American plan omits lunch. Breakfast and dinner served to houseguests only. Open 365 days a year. Attended pets allowed. Swimming, tennis, croquet, lawn bowling, xc skiing, snowshoeing, on grounds. Golf, tennis, swimming, sailing, horseback riding, canoeing, fishing, xc and downhill skiing, skating, hiking, and nature walks nearby. Michael and Penny Schmitt, Innkeepers.

Directions: From the south take I-91 to St. Johnsbury exit. Take Rte. 2 west, to Rte. 15 west, to Hardwick. Then take Rte. 14 north for 8 mi., turn right and go 3 mi. up long curving hill to inn. From Canada and points north, use Exit 26 on I-91 and follow Rte. 58 W to Irasburg. Then Rte. 14 southbound 12 mi. to marked left turn, 3 mi. to inn.

NORTH HERO HOUSE
North Hero, Vermont

I was seated on the deck of my room at the North Hero House looking down on the grassy dock at a young mother who was cuddling a child in her arms, and it took me back more than thirty years to a similar scene at another Vermont lake where a young mother was playing with a baby boy and crooning endearments into his ear. (He's now a father and recently presented me with a granddaughter.)

There are children of all ages at the North Hero House. This isn't strange at all, because Roger and Caroline Sorg brought their very young children with them in the early 1970s when they acquired this attractive inn on the shores of Lake Champlain. In those days David and Lynn were very, very young and eager to play with other children.

Now David is in his last year at the University of Vermont and will continue on in the hospitality business. He is in complete charge of the dining room at North Hero House every summer. Lynn is now a sophomore at UVM studying dental hygiene and is very much in evidence at the inn during the summer months.

For the entire Sorg family it has been a wonderful adventure and North Hero House has become a model for resort-inns. It has grown from the single old original inn building to include three additional buildings. This has represented many summers and winters of hard work for the entire family.

I have been revisiting the North Hero House for many years and have had lots of happy moments on the tennis courts, on the lake, on the front porch, jogging, canoeing, windsurfing, bicycling, and waterskiing with the Sorgs. Dr. Roger Sorg is a dentist in Flemington, New Jersey during the other nine months of the year.

For those people with boats, North Hero Island can be reached by water, as it is part of the inland waterway stretching from Key West, Florida, to the St. Lawrence Seaway.

This past summer Lynn inaugurated early Saturday morning breakfasts on the grassy dock, and those who joined before the regular dining room breakfast hours were rewarded with magnificent blue skies, sparkling water and gentle breezes. Next summer early morning voyages are planned on the float-boat with juice, coffee, and coffee cake included.

Antiquing is one of the most-enjoyed pastimes for guests at North Hero House. Auctions are numerous and always fun. It's a short drive to Mt. Mansfield and Stowe to enjoy a lovely gondola ride; and at Smuggler's Notch, the famous Trapp Family Lodge with its beautiful flower gardens may be visited.

Montreal is not far and arrangements can be made at the inn for a private limousine tour of the city. One of the most worthwhile trips is a visit to the Shelburne Museum where there is a collection of Early Americana housed in 35 lovely old dwellings on 45 acres.

Well, I am planning on being back at the North Hero House in 1983, this time probably for lunch and maybe some windsurfing. I know that Caroline has already added some new goodies to the menu, including baby silver salmon baked in parchment and a chunky tomato-dill soup.

Actually, I can hardly wait.

NORTH HERO HOUSE, Champlain Islands, North Hero, Vt. 05474; 802-372-8237. A 23-room New England resort-inn on North Hero Island in Lake Champlain, 35 mi. north of Burlington and 65 mi. south of Montreal. Modified American plan. Breakfast, lunch, and dinner served daily to travelers. Open from late June to Labor Day. Swimming, fishing, boating, waterskiing, ice house game room, sauna, bicycles, and tennis on grounds. Horseback riding and golf nearby. No pets. No credit cards. Roger and Caroline Sorg, Innkeepers.

Directions: Travel north from Burlington on I-89, take Exit 17 (Champlain Islands) and drive north on Island Rte. 2 to North Hero. From N.Y. Thruway (87 north), take Exit 39 at Plattsburg and follow signs "Ferry to Vermont." Upon leaving ferry, turn left to Rte. 2, then left again to North Hero. Inn is 15 min. from ferry dock on Rte. 2 By water: follow sectional maps to North Hero-City Bay. Enter bay and proceed westerly directly to North Hero House. Reservations highly recommended.

OLD NEWFANE INN
Newfane, Vermont

I first heard of Eric Weindl and his wife Gundy because of the cuisine at the Old Newfane Inn. However, my visit convinced me that this historic hostelry has several other highly attractive aspects that make it an ideal objective for country inn enthusiasts.

Eric, like his fellow countryman Guenther Weinkopf at the Queen Anne Inn in Chatham, Massachusetts, originally came from a small village near Munich, and both he and Gundy speak English with a very intriguing southern German accent.

I was visiting in the middle of a warm August afternoon, just a few minutes before Eric would find it necessary to start preparations for the evening meal. The three of us were seated on the side porch overlooking the village green, the fountain, the maples and oaks, and the Windham County Courthouse.

The Courthouse was built in 1825, the same year the inn was moved to its present location from the top of Newfane hill, which at that time was really the center of the village. The Town Hall is a mixture of Greek Revival and Colonial, and there are several other buildings around the square that are much older.

I had just been escorted on a tour through every one of the ten meticulously decorated and furnished lodging rooms. It was like visiting a Vermont farmhouse of a hundred years ago. There were elaborate samplers and wall hangings such as I have never seen before. The second-floor rooms, at one time part of a ballroom, are light and airy and there's a very pleasant little side balcony overlooking the green.

Eric, who was trained as a chef in one of the best hotels in Switzerland, warmed up to the subject of the Old Newfane Inn menu, "I think we could be characterized basically as Swiss-Continental," he said. "Our maitre d' does such dishes as chateaubriand or one of several flaming specialties at the tableside, which is always a lot of fun."

"This I can tell you," said Gundy, "Eric is a very good-natured man who loves good fun, but he takes cooking very seriously and is most particular about everything on the menu, including frog legs, shrimp scampi, lobster, tournedos of beef, and medallions of veal. He is too modest to say this, but people drive for many, many miles just to enjoy dinner with us. You see, I'm the hostess so I meet them all."

Dinner was served in the low-ceilinged dining room with its mellowed beams overhead and windows along one side. The floor-boards of varying widths were highly polished and there were pink tablecloths with white undercloths, candles on the table, and pistol-handled knives. The maitre d' was wearing an elegant-looking tuxedo, and the waitresses were wearing black uniforms trimmed in white.

I was entranced with the salad which was very simple and served with one of the most extraordinary, but simple, dressings I have ever tasted—just my preference for salads. I've never tasted better calves' liver which was served in a Tyrolean sauce, and I had the opportunity to sample the medallions of veal served with creamy mushrooms that were delicious. Everything could be cut with a fork.

Because both Eric and Gundy are highly involved throughout the day with food and dining room preparation, casual visitors cannot be accommodated for tours of the inn. If you have a reservation and find the front door locked, ring the bell and they will be delighted to show you to your room.

OLD NEWFANE INN, Court St., Newfane, Vermont 05345; 802-365-4427. A 10-room village inn 12 mi. west of Brattleboro, on Rte. 30. European plan. Lunch and dinner served to travelers during summer. Closed for rooms on Mondays. Open mid-Dec. to first of April; May to end of Oct. Closed Thanksgiving, Mother's Day. Near many downhill ski areas, Marlboro Music Festival. Backroading, tennis, swimming, nearby. No facilities for children under 7. No credit cards. Eric Weindl, Innkeeper.

Directions: From New York: Follow 684 to 84 to Hartford; I-91 to Brattleboro, Exit 2. Follow Rte. 30 for 12 mi. to Newfane. From Boston: Follow Rte. 2 to Greenfield. I-91 to Brattleboro, Exit 2; follow Rte. 30 to Newfane.

One of our favorite drives is one which we often recommend to our guests. It takes them on Route 30 north through Dorset and on up the Rupert Valley to the village of Pawlet. The valley is dotted with dairy farms and cornfields. A worthwhile stop is the "Pawlet Potter," where everything from small pots to large lamps can be seen. Across the street a cup of coffee or snack can be purchased at the old "railroad station."

From here our road goes east through Danby Four Corners to the town of Danby; lots of antiques here. A short jog on Route 7 will take you to the Peel Gallery of Art, where the works of thirty artists are displayed in a remodeled barn. Don't miss this!

Head back to Manchester on Route 7 south. Although this is not a back road, it takes you through lovely country. If you can spot it, Morse Hill Road goes to the right about eight miles from Danby. This is a short-cut back to Route 30, close to our West Road. It has beautiful views and one can see across the village of Manchester all the way to the Berkshires. This loop is about 25 miles, round trip.

Jim and Pat Lee
Birch Hill Inn
Manchester, Vermont

As to our back road contribution, may I offer the twenty-mile stretch from Dorset to Pawlet on Route 30, then Route 133 that runs from Pawlet to Middletown Springs in Vermont? This country road is eye-catching any time of the year, but during the Fall Foliage Festival, it's downright breathtaking with rolling hills, picturesque farms, tiers of brilliant maples, and simply a photographer's delight.

Charles and Marilyn Schubert
Barrows House
Dorset, Vermont

I think that my favorite back road is Route 58 from Lowell to Montgomery through (and over) Hazen's Notch. It's only about twelve miles long, a very curvy dirt road, almost no buildings on it, but wonderful views north to Jay Peak and great solitude. It is the northern termination point of the Bayley-Hazen military road, which was built from about 1770 to 1800 or so, in various stages. Its southern point in Peacham is paved, but pretty. The Hazen Notch road, as we call it, gives you a sense of wilderness and adventure and a little sense of what it must have been like when the settlers came. What a daunting task they faced in just the simple act of road

building! But what scenery—rushing brooks beside the road, dark quiet forest, a balancing rock—it is wonderful to leave your car and just walk around—great wildflowers, mysterious noises in the forest, and usually all sorts of wildlife crossing the road—deer, weasel, fox, and if you look north over the valley, you can often see hawks soaring. Maybe I don't want you to print this—I don't think that everyone will like the Notch—it is a little scarey to drive, if you're not used to narrow winding dirt roads—and there are no tourist attractions up there at all.

Michael and Penny Schmitt
The Inn on the Common
Craftsbury Common, Vermont

THE QUECHEE INN AT MARSHLAND FARM
Quechee, Vermont

Barbara Yaroschuk was telling a group of California innkeepers about the Quechee Inn at Marshland Farm (henceforth known as the Quechee Inn) in the mountains of central Vermont: "Summer is one of the nicest times in Vermont. Many people think of Vermont only for foliage and skiing, but summer is wonderful. A Vermont morning with the sun on the dew and the birds flying from our barn to nest in the trees, and the flights of water fowl from the wildlife preserve—just beautiful. Our inn was built in 1793, the farmstead of Colonel Joseph Marsh, the first lieutenant governor of Vermont, and we have one of the largest barns in the state on our property."

The occasion was a meeting of *CIBR* innkeepers at the Wine Country Inn in California's Napa Valley, and we were all seated on

the outer deck enjoying some brilliant morning sunshine as it burned off the valley mists that were obscuring the nearby high hills and vineyards.

This was quite a contrast to my visit to The Quechee Inn when the snow had been so high that I could not see the tops of the fences. That's when the term "Vermont winter" comes to mind. The inn is a cross-country skiing and learning center and there is lots of skating and downhill skiing as well as snowshoeing nearby. It's fun to spend an afternoon on the trails, and to return to a mug of mulled cider in front of the living room fireplace. While eating popcorn and cracking nuts, guests can muse over the very tempting dinner menu that features such dishes as leg of lamb, veal Marsala, roast duckling, and trout.

In summertime inn guests enjoy privileges at the Quechee Club and they can play two of the best golf courses in New England. The clubhouse has an outdoor pool and there is a beautiful little lake in the middle of the golf course, just right for the Sunfish, sailboats, and paddleboats. There are ten tennis courts.

For outdoor enthusiasts, there is much good hiking and bicycle riding and the inn is only about fifteen minutes from Woodstock, one of the most beautiful villages in New England.

Much of the interior of the inn reflects its late colonial ancestry and many of the bedrooms have been enhanced with four-poster and brass beds, and decorated with bird and flower prints. The view from the windows look out over the lawns, rolling countryside, corn fields, and the Wildlife Preserve. Two extremely handsome prints of the original owners are a focal point in the dining room.

The Quechee Inn is a dream come true for Mike and Barbara Yaroschuk and their children, Scott, Christine, and Cathy. As in the case of most family-owned country inns, there are chores and duties for all concerned.

I'm happy to report that Barbara, Mike, and the Quechee Inn hosted a splendid two-night meeting of *CIBR* New England innkeepers last fall. We not only enjoyed getting together, but had sufficient time to walk through the spectacular Quechee gorge and visit the shop of Simon Pearce, world-renowned Irish designer and blower of glass. We could actually see the artisans at work.

THE QUECHEE INN AT MARSHLAND FARM, Clubhouse Rd., Quechee, Vt. 05059; 802-295-3133. A 22-room country inn in central Vermont just a few minutes from Woodstock, Dartmouth College, and many other Vermont attractions. Breakfast and dinner served daily to travelers. Closed two weeks in April and November. Spectacular foliage, sugaring, hiking, fishing, canoeing, bird-watching, and cidering available. Historic sites, antique shops, covered bridges, and especially the Quechee Gorge all within short distance. Tennis, golf, swimming, squash, sauna, sailboats, xc and downhill skiing nearby. Michael and Barbara Yaroschuk, Innkeepers.

Directions: From intersection of Interstate 91 and 89, take 89 north to Exit 1 (Rte. 4, Woodstock-Rutland). West on Rte. 4 for 1.2 miles. Right on Clubhouse Road to Inn.

THE VILLAGE INN
Landgrove, Vermont

This time I traveled to Landgrove from Weston taking the road that leads west, passing the Weston Playhouse, over the bridge and up the hill. At the fork I took the road marked "Peru" and "Landgrove."

This is an ideal backroad. For one thing, it becomes a dirt road almost immediately, something that is now hard to find in Vermont and it passes through some good woods and marshlands where I could see beaver lodges. At one point I crested a hill to discover a beautiful 19th-century home with spectacular flower plantings enjoying unexcelled views of both Stratton and Magic Mountain, two well-known central Vermont ski areas. It's possible to turn off to Danby, Vermont, on another dirt road leading to the right. Preoccupied as I was with the beautiful bucolic Vermont scenery, before I realized it there were the familiar red clapboard buildings with the white trim of the Village Inn in Landgrove.

It's interesting that my visits to Jay and Kathy Snyder have almost always been at noon, and we have had several lunches seated by the swimming pool giving us a chance to talk "shop" and for me to catch up on the details of all of the improvements and news of the inn. This time I learned that the Snyders' elder daughter Kim, who is 14, is now at the Northfield-Mt. Hermon School. "We all miss her a great deal," said Kathy. "However, she calls home *regularly!*" Kim is one of the main waitresses during the summer, and her younger sister Heidi, 13, will be following in her footsteps very shortly. Meanwhile, Heidi brings the ponies over from across the road and the young children who are guests get rides in the pony cart or on a saddle.

The Snyders were filled with other news of the inn, including the horsedrawn sleigh rides, now offered during the wintertime. "We usually start off at sunset," said Jay, "and then continue on the snowy roads getting back in time for dinner. It is a nice country experience. We have some very interesting midweek package plans, all of which include combinations of Alpine and Nordic skiing and our skiing guests are also very enthusiastic about the hot tubs."

We finished a leisurely lunch and then roamed around the inn grounds while Jay and Kathy pointed out different types of hybrid day lilies, including one very special lavender species, in the extensive flower beds.

There is an extensive vegetable garden, and Kathy laughingly told me that one year she and Jay had gotten their signals mixed. "He would come out and plant a row of something, and then I would come and, not realizing, I would plant the same row with something else. The result was that we had carrots coming up with the lettuce. There are some wonderful peas that are good enough to eat raw and many species of onions and other garden goodies."

The Village Inn has been owned and operated by the Snyders for more than twenty years. It first opened its doors as an inn in 1939 and for many guests the main interest was skiing. However, in recent years the Snyders have developed an all-season resort-inn, that is particularly attractive to families with children of all ages.

Summertime amenities on the grounds include tennis courts with a ball machine, a nine-hole pitch-and-putt golf course, a heated pool, volleyball, hiking trails, and fishing.

In winter the outdoor-minded guest can enjoy downhill skiing at five major areas nearby, plus cross-country skiing, snowshoeing and sledding in the woods right behind the inn. There is also an ice skating pond.

THE VILLAGE INN, Landgrove, Vt 05148; 802-824-6673. A 21-room rustic resort-inn in the mountains of central Vermont, approximately 4½ mi. from Weston and Londonderry. Lodgings include breakfast. Breakfast and dinner served to travelers by reservation during the summer except Wed. dinner. Open from Nov. 23 to April 15; July 1 to Oct. 17. Swimming, tennis, volleyball, pitch-and-putt, xc skiing, fishing on grounds. Downhill skiing, riding, indoor tennis, paddle tennis, antiquing, backroading, alpine slide, golf, summer theatre nearby. Children most welcome. No pets. Jay and Kathy Snyder, Innkeepers.

Directions: Coming north on I-91 take Exit 2 at Brattleboro, follow Rte. 30 to Rte. 11 and turn right. Turn left off Rte. 11 at signs for Village Inn. Bear left in village of Peru. Coming north on Rte. 7 turn east at Manchester on Rte. 11 to Peru. Turn left at signs for Village Inn. Bear left in village of Peru.

THREE MOUNTAIN INN
Jamaica, Vermont

Seventeen-year-old Claire Murray who had just returned home from Vermont Academy in Saxton's River, Vermont, was escorting me through the Three Mountain Inn. I happened to pay a visit at a time when her mother Elaine and her father Charles were both away from the inn, but I couldn't have picked a better-informed guide.

After a very pleasant tour of the many attractive, real country-inn bedrooms, many with flowered wallpaper, comfortable beds, and a Vermont farmhouse feeling, we returned to the beautiful big sofa in front of the Dutch oven fireplace, and over a cup of tea she told me what it's like to move from the city to the country and have a family-owned country inn.

"We think it's just fabulous," she remarked enthusiastically. "My father is really a wonderful host, and my mother has been having a lot of fun developing new recipes and supervising in the kitchen. Sarah, my younger sister, who is nine years old—she's playing soccer with her friends this afternoon—just loves the idea of being in an inn. She says it's like having company all of the time."

"I'm sorry that my mother isn't here now because she could tell you more about our breakfasts and dinners. I do know that we have

locally caught corncob-smoked trout and she makes all of the soups and quiches. One of my favorites is chicken paprikash and, boy, does she make great desserts and special ice creams!"

I asked her what she liked most about living in a country inn. "First of all, I really enjoy this house," she said. "It was built around 1780 and I never thought that when we were living in the city we would actually have a home like this, and of course everyone loves this fireplace room and they keep 'oohing and aahing' about the wide-planked walls and floors. I guess the biggest thing for me, though, is the downhill skiing. We are within minutes of Stratton, Bromley, and Magic Mountain. But I also like the cross-country skiing and we can take off from our backyard. I never thought I would ever live in a house with a swimming pool, and we have one of those, too. Our guests can play tennis nearby and go fishing or even horseback riding."

The sequel to this visit took place a few months later when I stopped back and had a wonderful dinner at the Three Mountain Inn and had a chance to meet Charles and Elaine Murray and also Sarah. There's a third older daughter named Kelley. They are all enthusiastic outgoing people who have taken to the new world of country inn-keeping with great zest. The meal was every bit as good as Claire had promised me, and I think Charlie summed up their feelings by saying, "Elaine and I feel confident that we're on our way to making the Three Mountain Inn one of the finest small romantic country inns in Vermont."

My original visit happened two years ago, and now Claire is attending the University of Vermont and thinking in terms of a major in psychology. In a recent letter she said she was looking forward to making the varsity lacrosse team. She expects to return to the inn this summer. She also hoped that I saw the Three Mountain Inn story on "PM Magazine" earlier in the winter.

THREE MOUNTAIN INN, Route 30, Jamaica, Vermont 05343; 802-874-4140. An 8-room inn located in a pleasant village in southern Vermont. Modified American plan. (Rates include breakfast and dinner.) Dinners also served to other than inn guests nightly except Wednesday. Closed April 15 to May 15; Labor Day to Sept. 15; Oct. 31 to Thanksgiving. Swimming pool on grounds. Tennis, golf, fishing, horseback riding, nature walks and hiking trails in Jamaica State Park, downhill and xc skiing, Marlboro Music Festival, Weston Playhouse, all within a short drive. No pets. No credit cards. Charles and Elaine Murray, Innkeepers.

Directions: Jamaica is located on Rte. 30 which runs across Vermont from Manchester (U.S. 7) to Brattleboro (I-91).

"European Plan" means that rates for rooms and meals are separate. "American Plan" means that meals are included in the cost of the room. "Modified American Plan" means that breakfast and dinner are included in the cost of the room. The rates at some inns include a continental breakfast with the lodging.

JOHN HANCOCK INN
Hancock, New Hampshire

One of the things I enjoy doing is browsing through copies of *Country Inns and Back Roads* that were published several years ago. For example, in 1974, writing about the John Hancock Inn I quoted innkeeper Glynn Wells who was saying, "When Pat and I talked to you a couple of years ago in Stockbridge you may remember that we said we were looking to buy a country inn that actually felt like our own home. Here in Hancock we know we found it."

My account continued, "Glynn Wells was speaking as the three of us were strolling down the main street in this southern New Hampsire village after a splendid dinner at the inn. He continued, 'What we're doing now has really became a tradition with a great many of our guests—strolling the village streets and looking at these fine old homes with picket fences and big trees. Some of them

walk to the village green past the bandstand to gaze at the graceful spire of the Congregational church. It's all part of the unwinding that many guests tell us they can do here.'

"We stopped to pass the time of day with a neighbor who was tending her flowers, and talked of the upcoming Old Home Day the following week. 'Oh, I wish you were going to be here,' Pat exclaimed. 'That's the day when former residents return. What began as a family picnic a century ago has grown to a wonderful town-wide celebration complete with parade, band concert, and all kinds of sports and fun. I've been waiting for it all year.'"

That was 1974, and since that time Glynn and Pat and their two children, Susan and Andrew, have not only successfully operated a country inn but have also become an integral part of this small community. The children are making significant contributions.

Susan is managing the Garden Spot, a secluded little corner in the outdoor area of the inn where one can get a light afternoon snack after lunch is over and before dinner starts. A gazebo is planned for one corner. It will be pleasant for weddings and receptions. Andrew is the second cook for dinner during the summertime. He is taking a food service course at school.

The John Hancock is a prime model for a village inn. It is the continuing center for community activity and is small enough so that villagers and visitors alike have the opportunity to get acquainted. It is New Hampshire's oldest continuously operating inn and all of the lodging rooms have been appropriately furnished. Many have double and twin canopy beds.

Over the years I've shared some of Pat Wells' letters with my readers and here is an excerpt from her most recent epistle:

"I think that the whole business of innkeeping has been an act of faith for us. Back in 1972 the realization that we were going to be somewhere else was the controlling factor that led us to Hancock. God has been good these years. We believe that with his strength and guidance we can make the inn what it richly deserves to be—a haven for others, a source of pride for the town, and a deep and rich experience for our family. It is all that, I believe, but never *could* be without the faith that has supported us in every kind of problem.

"We find that many guests are including the John Hancock Inn in a kind of a New England sampler. They plan a circle trip that includes Boston and its many attractions, the seacoast of Maine, the higher mountains of northern New Hampshire and then a stay in our land of picturebook villages, twisty roads among the hills, and inviting vistas that comprise the Monadnock region. Happily, many come back for longer stays after a brief taste."

THE JOHN HANCOCK INN, Hancock, N.H. 03449; 603-525-3318. A 10-room village inn on Rtes. 123 and 137, 9 mi. north of Peterborough. In the middle of the Monadnock region of southern N.H. European plan. Breakfast, lunch, and dinner served daily to travelers. Closed Christmas Day and one week in spring and fall. Bicycles available on the grounds. Antiquing, swimming, hiking, Alpine and xc skiing nearby. Glynn and Pat Wells, Innkeepers.

Directions: From Keene, take either Rte. 101 east to Dublin and Rte. 137 north to Hancock or Rte. 9 north to Rte. 123 and east to Hancock. From Nashua, take 101A and 101 to Peterborough. Proceed north on Rtes. 202 and 123 to Hancock.

WOODBOUND INN
Jaffrey, New Hampshire

Even after more than seventeen years of writing about country inns, I'll have to admit that it's always a thrill to get an *overseas* telephone call for further information about inns in any of our *Country Inns and Back Roads* series. This time there was a telephone call from Venezuela, and the man on the other end of the line (he sounded as close as the next town) said that he had a large family and wanted to stay for a few weeks at a place where everybody could enjoy themselves both with indoor and outdoor recreation and where there were other families with children.

He said they were interested in diversions such as swimming, sailing, canoeing, boating, and fishing and that he and his wife also enjoyed golf and tennis. "We've never taken a vacation in the United States before," he said, "and I realize that this is a pretty unusual request, but we wanted a place that would be 'peculiarly American.'"

After a few more questions, I narrowed the choice down to the Woodbound Inn which seemed to just about fill the bill for our South American neighbor. All of the recreation he mentioned was available plus a great many more things, including handcraft workshops, square dances, cookouts, beach lunches, along with such indoor recreation as ping-pong, pool, shuffleboard, electronic games, and even a music machine.

In addition to the Woodbound's 1,200-yard par 3 golf course with nine holes, there are four full-length 18- and 9-hole golf courses nearby. As far as fishing is concerned, there is a half-acre trout pond developed in a natural setting, and Lake Contoocook has wide-mouth bass, perch, and pickerel.

The Woodbound especially welcomes families and has cottage units that are designed particularly for them with maid service and meals at the inn. There are regular programs and activities for children and a baby-sitting service as well.

When I told the gentleman from Venezuela all of this and about how I had enjoyed my stays at Woodbound over the years he felt that this would be just perfect for his purposes.

Well I'm glad to say that the story has a happy ending. They were able to book rooms at Woodbound and, in fact, had such a marvelous time that they are planning to come back again!

Families can also enjoy winter sports here, including downhill and cross-country skiing on the grounds, ice skating, tobogganing, sleigh-riding, and even snowshoeing.

The newest excitement at Woodbound centers around a pair of chestnut Belgian horses, Tom and Jerry. They are providing the guests with carriage rides, hayrides and sleigh rides right from the inn porch. The old 1820 barn has been turned into a horse barn and some carriage sheds have been added.

There are also early morning nature walks with a local ecologist. These take place on a unique half-mile nature trail covering three separate ecological environments with an unusual number of uncommon flora. It seems as if there is always something new at the Woodbound Inn.

WOODBOUND INN and COTTAGES, Jaffrey, N.H. 03452; 603-532-8341. A 44-room resort-inn on Lake Contoocook, 2 mi. in the woods from West Rindge or Jaffrey. Within walking distance of Cathedral of the Pines. Both American and Mod. American plan available. Overnight European plan available in spring and late fall. Special rates for retirees in June and fall. Breakfast, lunch, and dinner served daily. Open all four seasons. Par 3 golf course, swimming, beach, sailing, water skiing, tennis, hiking, children's programs, downhill ski area, 22 miles of groomed ski-touring trails, tobogganing, lighted skating rink, summer carriage rides, hayrides, and sleigh rides. Ed and Peggy Brummer, Jed and Mary Ellen Brummer, Innkeepers.

Directions: From Boston, follow Rte. 2, then Rte. 119 to Rindge where there are directional signs to inn. From New York, follow I-91 to Bernardston, Mass. Proceed on Rte. 10 to Winchester, then Rte. 119 to Rindge and watch for signs to inn.

This is our favorite back road, starting right on inn property. Between Woodbound Inn and the outdoor Cathedral of the Pines, there is a town road about one-and-three-quarter miles long which is "Closed Subject to Gates and Bars," most of which may be traveled by auto at your own risk, but is used for the most part as a hiking trail. The whole surrounding area is covered with thick woods growth. However, behind the brush and trees lining the roadway are the cellar holes of houses and barns, stone-wall-lined cow lanes, dug wells, and a network of stone walls enclosing one-time fields, pastures, and cultivated areas for three farms. About halfway along the road is a schoolyard protected by stone walls, and the foundations of the one-room schoolhouse, chimney, and wood-shed. We know the names of some of the owners, the names and numbers of children that went to the school in certain years, tax records show the amount of livestock, we have old photos of some occupants, and a sketch of the school, along with a description of a big red mansard-roofed house that stood on one cellar hole.

To those guests who appear interested, we issue a challenge to see how many cellar holes, etc., they can locate, usually on their way to the Cathedral of the Pines, one of the best views in the area.

One owner, by name of Winch, lost his buildings in a fire in 1879, built a new house in Jaffrey, got divorced, left for California, and Jaffrey history says he was never heard of again. Poor Winch!

The Brummer Family
Woodbound Inn
Jaffrey, New Hampshire

One of the prettiest drives in New Hampshire, if not New England, is the old Route 202 and 9 which runs almost in front of the inn. Before the construction of new Route 202 and 9, passing through the center of Henniker, the old route was the present Main Street. This parallels the Contoocook River and joins the new route near Hillsborough. Along this short stretch is a millpond, a restricted fly-fishing stream, a whitewater canoeing river, and it is beautiful in every season. This makes a great alternate route when leaving the inn and going west, or when coming to the inn from the west on Routes 9 or 202. On the outskirts of Hillsborough look for the West Henniker sign and follow this for 4½ miles to the inn.

The Glover Family
Colby Hill Inn
Henniker, New Hampshire

One of my favorite back roads in the area takes you over two covered bridges, past another, and past the trailheads to South Moat and Boulder Loop. From the inn you return to Route 16 and turn left and left again onto the Kancamagus Highway (Route 112). Proceed 6.4 miles west on the Kancamagus and turn right at the sign for the Covered Bridge campground. You will pass over the first bridge, over the Swift River. Shortly thereafter on the left is the head to the Boulder Loop trail. This is a very scenic three-mile loop that takes you along some ledges overlooking the Swift River Valley. Farther down the Dugway Road, on the left, is the trailhead to the top of South Moat Mountain. A bit farther down, and on the left, is Red Eagle Pond, then the road turns into Still Road. At the end, turn right onto West Side Road. About one mile down the road, and on the left, just before the dairy, is another covered bridge (no longer in use). Turn left right after the dairy and you will pass through the next covered bridge and over the Saco River. At the end of the road, turn right to go through Conway and back to the inn, or left and go into North Conway.

Marc and Marily Donaldson
Darby Field Inn
Conway, New Hampshire

COLBY HILL INN
Henniker, New Hampshire

I was standing in front of the long window which now takes up one wall of the new dining room addition at the Colby Hill Inn. The view was exactly what is shown in Jan Lindstrom's sketch opposite. This had been the major change since my last visit here and in addition to providing more tables, the atmosphere was enhanced by the wide pine-board floors and lovely new pine furniture. A wood chunk stove provides comfortable and welcome warmth when needed.

"Oh, I see you're watching our birds," said Don Glover, joining me. "Many of our guests are confirmed bird watchers. Yesterday one of them said that he saw a bob-o-link which I haven't seen for many years. The new wider window really provides a much more intimate view of the birds." Don and his wife June were friends of mine at Bucknell University, and a few years ago they, along with their son Don, Jr., and his wife Margaret, acquired this classic New Hampshire inn. Speaking of our college days, Don said he had had a recent visit from a mutual friend, also a Bucknellian, Stevie Stephanou.

The inn is on the outskirts of the small village of Henniker which, among other things, is the home of New England College. The ceilings are low, the walls are hung with oil paintings and prints, and the furnishings are country antiques. A grandfather clock ticks away in one corner. There are birds during all seasons and a gorgeous flower garden during spring and summer. In earlier times, the living room fireplace was used for baking bread.

Lodging rooms at the inn are typical country New England. Many have candlewick bedspreads, hooked rugs, old bowl-and-pitcher sets, which are reminiscent of the days when water was brought in from the outside. Some of them have shared bathrooms and all of them have that wonderful, old "home" feeling.

"This is great cross-country skiing terrain," said Don. "There are forty miles of trails in this vicinity and a great many of our guests, including the children, come up for long weekends or even, when possible, during the week."

At that moment I caught the aroma of freshly baked bread coming from the kitchen, so Don and I wandered back to where Don, Jr., was getting things ready for dinner. Don, Jr., and I had a short conversation about the expanding menu. "We serve chicken Colby House," he said, "and this, along with our fresh seafood, has been received very well. We have specials almost every day and usually a fresh fish of the day. My mother has her own little baking corner here and she does the chocolate cakes, the cinnamon buns, the biscuits, and the applesauce. We have a lot of things on the menu that have grown in our garden, including juice from our own tomatoes. She also made some jelly from wild grapes that grow out behind the barn."

One of my favorite things at this inn is a delightful swimming pool sheltered by an ell formed by the two huge barns adjacent to the inn. It is most welcome on hot days of the southern New Hampshire summer.

This inn is enjoyable in many seasons because this section of New Hampshire has many lakes, state parks, golf courses, summer theaters, and antique shops which add to the attraction for vacationers or weekenders.

COLBY HILL INN, Henniker, N.H. 03242; 603-428-3281. A 12-room inn on the outskirts of a New Hampshire college town. European plan. Two rooms with shared baths. Breakfast served to houseguests only. Dinner served to travelers Tuesdays through Sunday, except Thanksgiving, Christmas, and New Year's Day. Open year-round. Swimming pool on grounds. Tennis and xc skiing one short block; alpine, 3 mi.; golf, canoeing, hiking, bicycling, and fishing nearby. No children under 6. No pets. The Glover Family, Innkeepers.

Directions: From I-89, take Exit 5 and follow Rte. 202 to Henniker. From I-91, take Exit 3 and follow Rte. 9 through Keene and Hillsborough to Henniker. At the Oaks, W. Main St., one-half mile west of town center.

THE DANA PLACE INN
Jackson, New Hampshire

Betty Jennings and I were standing in the middle of her garden and she was explaining that the entire output is used on the menu at the inn. "Well, there is the squash, the tomatoes, the parsley, lettuce, the carrots," she said, "and then we have a few herbs which are increasing in number every year."

We meandered through the grounds along the Ellis River, and she explained how the cross-country ski trails can also be used for walking during the summertime. The path led around the great boulders, through an orchard and came out at a pool formed by a natural basin in the river. "This is where we cross over in the winter," she said. "It is possible to ski from here right on down into Jackson, and a great many of our guests do it. Also, the people from Jackson come up for our lunches. It is just the right kind of a distance."

It was early September and I dipped my hand into the pool and found the water was still warm. I was tempted to dive off the rocks at the deep part. It looked so clear and inviting.

The Dana Place is a historic inn. There has been an inn here since the late 1800s. At one time it was a farm, as is evidenced by the many apple trees. Like so many New England dwellings, it has been through additions, with buildings snuggled up against each other. Now its L-shape has many comfortable, homey bedrooms of different sizes and shapes.

The location within the White Mountain National Forest offers opportunities for mountain climbing, hiking, walking, and has some access to alpine trails above the timber line for the avid and experienced climber. The lower mountains invite those who prefer easier walking and enjoy the pleasure of beautiful woodland paths and cross-country skiing. Guests can order picnic lunches for walks or drives through the countryside or into the mountains.

Betty and I continued our stroll and talked for a moment about the menu at the Dana Place. "We think of ourself as sort of 'country gourmet,'" she said. "For example, our perennial favorite is Chicken Gloria and was featured in a new book of recipes published by *Bon Appetit* Magazine. Our chef does some wonderful things with soups, including a cold peach soup that is served in the summer. We added Mud Pie to the menu and it's already a legend in its own time. It's coffee ice cream in chocolate cookie crust with whipped cream and my homemade fudge sauce. I still do all the desserts, including the french chocolate custard served with whipped cream. By the way, we make hot mulled cider from our own apples."

By this time we had completed our big circle next to the river, through the woods and open fields and were walking toward the inn with its white clapboard buildings. The green mountains provided a contrasting background.

I asked about the Jennings' children whom I have known for the past twelve years or so.

"Page is at Simmons College majoring in Physical Therapy. Chris is the sports editor for the *York County Coastal Star* in Kennebunk, Maine. He has six schools to cover and does most of his own photography in addition to the writing. We refer to him as 'the Red Smith of York County.'"

Betty sighed contentedly and said, "It is really beautiful here most of the year. I love the summers and fall, but to me there is nothing like seeing all this covered with snow and having lots of cross-country skiers gathering together at night around the fireplace. I am so glad we are innkeepers."

DANA PLACE INN, Route 16, Pinkham Notch, P.O. Box LB, Jackson, N.H. 03846; 603-383-6822. A 15-room resort inn, 5 miles from Jackson, N.H. in the heart of the White Mountains. Rates include lodging and full breakfast. Lunches served on winter weekends only. Dinners served to travelers daily from mid-June to late Oct. and from mid-Dec. to late March. Closed Thanksgiving Day. Two tennis courts, natural pool, trout fishing, xc skiing, birdwatching, on grounds. Hiking trails, indoor tennis, 5 golf courses, downhill skiing nearby. Malcolm and Betty Jennings, Innkeepers.

Directions: From Rte. 16, north of Jackson Village toward Pinkham Notch. The Dana Place is a flag stop for the Trailways through-bus to and from Boston.

THE INN AT CROTCHED MOUNTAIN
Francestown, New Hampshire

The first thing that comes to mind when I think of this inn is the fabulous view.

One of the intriguing things about this view, which can be enjoyed from a great many lodging rooms as well as from the dining room, living room, the terrace, and the swimming pool, is that it gets better with each visit.

When I mentioned this to Rose Perry, she laughed merrily and said, "Oh, we think so, too. Even though John and I have been looking at this view for many years, it becomes more and more meaningful to us."

There were many other most intriguing aspects besides the fabulous view with which this very attractive Indonesian-Chinese woman acquainted me. Rose's father is a hotelier in Singapore, and she lived a number of years in Hong Kong. Rose and John met while attending Paul Smith College, which is a hotel school in the Adirondacks. In complete charge of the kitchen, she does most of the cooking, and I was surprised at the unusual number of main dishes, many of which are her own recipes.

The inn was originally built as a farmhouse in 1822. The original owner had strong political convictions and constructed a secret tunnel from his cellar to the Boston Post Road, incorporating his home as a way station to shelter runaway slaves on their escape to the north.

During the late 1920s it was to become one of the most spectacular farms in New England, boasting an internationally recognized breed of sheep, champion horses, and Angora goats.

The house was destroyed by fire in the mid-30s, rebuilt, and John and Rose came on the scene in 1976.

I first visited Crotched Mountain early in June when the late New England spring is at its most delicious with apple blossoms

and lilacs, and I was smitten by the wonderful panorama stretching out for miles.

On September 25th, the time of my second visit, the fall colors were magnificent as only they can be in the Monadnock region, where occasionally the full range is reached before October first.

It was during this visit that I enjoyed a leisurely dinner and had the opportunity to see John and Rose Perry and the inn in a different light. There was a glowing fire in the low-ceilinged parlor of the little pub where after-dinner guests and other couples dropped in during the evening.

My lodging room had a fireplace, and windows overlooking the mountains and valleys; also a door through which I could step directly outside to the swimming pool.

The next morning I took a few moments to wander around on the broad green lawn and look out over the valleys. "It looks this way in Indonesia," Rose said, as she joined me for a few minutes. "It's just like the mountains and valleys in Djakarta. The floating mist on the mountains has an Indonesian look."

As I walked toward the car, John remarked that this was a different world in the winter when Crotched Mountain skiers would be walking the short path to the lift line, and the cross-country skiers would be headed into the woods.

The views are many at the Inn at Crotched Mountain.

THE INN AT CROTCHED MOUNTAIN, Mountain Rd., Francestown, N.H. 03043; 603-588-6840. A 14-room mountain inn (4 rooms with private baths) in southern New Hampshire 15 mi. from Peterborough. Within a short distance of the Sharon Arts Center, American Stage Festival, Peterborough Players, Crotched Mtn. ski areas. European plan. Open from Memorial Day to Oct. 31; from Thanksgiving to the end of the ski season. Breakfast, lunch, and dinner available to travelers in summer; breakfast or dinner, during winter and fall (telephone for reservations and exact schedule). Closed Easter. Swimming pool, tennis courts, volleyball on grounds. Golf, skiing, hill walking, and backroading in the gorgeous Monadnock region nearby. No credit cards. Rose and John Perry, Innkeepers.

Directions: From Boston: follow Rte. 3 north to 101A to Milford. Then Rte. 13 to New Boston and Rte. 136 to Francestown. Follow Rte. 47 2½ mi. and turn left on Mountain Road. Inn is 1 mi. on right. From New York/Hartford: I-91 north to Rte. 10 at Northfield to Keene, N.H. Follow 101 east to Peterborough, Rte. 202 north to Bennington, Rte. 47 to Mountain Rd. (approx. 4½ mi.); turn right on Mountain Rd. Inn is 1 mi. on right.

THE DARBY FIELD INN
Conway, New Hampshire

It's a long way from Orense in northern Spain to the White Mountains of New Hampshire, and yet in one short conversation Marily Donaldson and I traversed North America and the Atlantic Ocean to share our impressions of this section of northern Spain. Marily had lived there as a child and her eye lit up when she learned that I had visited Orense and a Spanish national inn (parador) located there.

This was all part of a very lovely late summer afternoon during which Marily and I, accompanied by her son Jeremiah and daughter Heather, were strolling around the grounds of the Darby Field Inn and stopping frequently as she pointed out the mountains which are visible from almost all of the inn rooms.

"Over there is South Mountain, and that's Mount Washington just to the right. We can also see Adams and Madison and Whitehorse Ledge in the center." There were several other mountains of various heights and hues all combining to create a wonderful feeling of being lifted into the sky. Marily must have noticed the glazed look in my eye, because she remarked, "I see that you, too, are a mountain person."

The Darby Field Inn, run by Marily and her husband Marc, sits on the border of the White Mountain National Forest where guests can cross-country ski, snowshoe, and hike to nearby rivers, waterfalls, lakes, and open peaks. Fortunately, there's a very pleasant swimming pool on the terrace providing guests with not only a cooling dip in the hot days of summer, but still another view of the mountains.

We wandered through the garden where there were corn in tassel, lettuce, snow peas, peppers, cabbages, and Brussels sprouts, all of which are enjoyed by inn guests. These are a fitting accompaniment to the hearty inn fare.

We walked into the main house, passing through the dining room with its bright white tablecloths and blue over-cloths already being laid for dinner.

I took a quick glance at a menu for the evening and decided that although the veal Piccata and chicken Marquis looked very inviting, I would settle for broiled lamp chops for that evening.

In the living room was a great stone fireplace flanked by floor-to-ceiling bookshelves and all kinds of comfortable furniture arranged in conversation groups.

Marily was called away for a moment, so Jeremiah and I continued on a tour of the bedrooms, some of which have wood-panelled walls and brass beds. Others have flowered country wall-

paper and a cozy feeling. There were lots of flowers and books.

Back in the living room once again, Marily rejoined us and I inquired about the name Darby Field.

"He was a notorious Irishman who was credited with being the first white man to ascend Mount Washington," she replied. "This was in June of 1642 and took eighteen days. He did get to the top and later on opened a tavern nearby."

She pointed out three volumes of scrapbooks in which she and Marc had carefully gathered brochures from inns all over New England.

"It seems that our guests these days are almost always real 'inn people.' We have many pleasant conversations with guests who are very curious about other inns that we have visited and what the life of an innkeeper is really like."

THE DARBY FIELD INN, Bald Hill, Conway, N.H. 03818; 603-447-2181. An 11-room White Mountain country inn, 3 mi. from Conway, N.H., within convenient driving distance of all of the Mount Washington Valley cultural, natural, and historic attractions, as well as several internationally-known ski areas. Modified American plan. Open April 27 to Sept. 4; Sept. 9 to Oct. 22; Nov. 18 to Mar. 26. Swimming pool and carefully groomed cross-country skiing trails on grounds. Tennis and other sports nearby. Marc and Marily Donaldson, Innkeepers.

Directions: From Rte. 16: Traveling north turn left at sign for the inn (½ mi. before the town of Conway) onto Bald Hill Rd., and proceed up the hill 1 mi. to the next sign for the inn and turn right. The inn is 1 mi. down the dirt road on the left.

From the front door of Lovett's Inn, you can turn left and wander into the village of Franconia, meandering out on Route 116 and the Easton Valley. A stop at the Robert Frost place to visit his home and walk a nature trail will evoke memories of some of his more famous poems. Continue on through the Easton Valley, nestled at the foot of Cannon Mountain and Mount Kinsman, and enjoy lovely open fields and working farms. Choose a number of lovely hiking trails to Bridal Veil Falls and Mount Kinsman.

Choose the Sugar Hill Road on the right and find yourself in the charming village of Sugar Hill with magnificent views of the Presidential Range. Stop to observe the Stewart Farm Maple Syrup operation and continue on to visit the Sugar Hill Historical Museum with its Carriage Barn, offering you a glimpse into the past history and culture of the area. Perhaps a stop at Harman's Cheese Store for a pound of wonderful cheddar cheese will seem tempting.

Or choose to stay on the Easton Road and find a charming swimming hole close to the Easton Town Hall for summer picnics and a clear view of Mount Kinsman. At the end of the Easton Road, you might turn left and go down to the Lost River Gorge, carved out by the ancient glacier that covered most of our continent. In Woodstock, turn right and drive back up through Franconia Notch, enjoying its natural mountainous beauties, the Old Man in the Mountains, numerous waterfalls, basins, and the Flume. An absolute must is a visit to the New England Ski Museum located at the base of Cannon Mountain, perhaps to be followed by an aerial tramway ride to the top of this rugged ski mountain. A short trip down the hill on Route 18 will bring you home once again to Lovett's Inn.

Charles Lovett
Lovett's by Lafayette Brook
Franconia, New Hampshire

A back road to a country inn: northbound from Boston on Interstate 93, take Exit 24, east on NH Route 3 to Ashland, and then Holderness to Route 113, which takes one around Squam Lake to Center Sandwich. Then follow 113 to North Sandwich to 113A to Wonalancet and Tamworth. Turn left on 113 in Tamworth to NH Route 16 north at Chocorua. Follow NH 16 north to Pinkham Notch and the Dana Place. Squam Lake is where On Golden Pond was filmed, and 113 follows its west shore closely for several miles with some excellent views of the lake. The Squam Lakes Science Center is an interesting stop and is located just outside of Holderness on 113. Center Sandwich has to be the personification of the New England village, with its white church spires, village green, and mill pond.

Route 113 from Center Sandwich through North Sandwich and 113A to Wonalancet and Tamworth is a winding back road with miles of stone fences, lovely mountain vistas, beaver bogs, white picket fences, beautiful farms, and innumerable unpaved side roads and woods paths just begging to be explored. As you head north on NH 16, keep an eye out on the left at the top of the hill for the famous view of Mount Chocorua and Chocorua Lake, a must shot for any photographer worth his silver bromide! That's if you have any film left.

Betty and Mal Jennings
Dana Place Inn
Pinkham Notch, Jackson, New Hampshire

DEXTER'S INN AND TENNIS CLUB
Sunapee, New Hampshire

My car headed up the dirt road through the New Hampshire forest, and I reflected that September is *the* time to be at Dexter's. I could see the first touch of changing colors in the leaves, and the wildflowers were positively brilliant.

As I crested the hill with the pleasing panorama of mountains stretched in front of me like the sides of a green bowl, I felt the full warmth of the September sun reflected by the yellow clapboard walls of the inn. Through the trees, past the terrace, I could see a few of the tennis courts were being used and I caught a glimpse of a young woman in a colorful bathing suit with one leg dangling in the pool.

As usual, I found Frank Simpson into one of the never-ending chores of innkeeping. This time he was raking the autumn leaves. We both share the same last name, but there the resemblance ends. Frank is a tall rugged-looking man with black hair and a face that looks as if it were chisled out of New Hampshire granite. Frank and his wife Shirley and their now-grown children have made a tradition out of his New England inn which is just a few miles from Lake Sunapee.

Frank was very anxious for me to see the five lovely rooms in the annex to the inn directly across the street from the main building.

As we moved from one bedroom to another, I began to share Frank's enthusiasm. The rooms are beautifully furnished with antiques, many four-poster beds, lace curtains, and lovely views of the mountains. I immediately asked Frank to be sure to put me in one that night because they appealed to me so much.

We walked back through the side porch into a typical farmhouse living room with a piano and lots and lots of books and magazines. There were original oils and watercolors on the walls.

We settled down in the lounge for a chat with Shirley, and quite naturally the talk centered on tennis.

"We have more tournaments now," Shirley told me. "The weekend after the Fourth of July is the Senior Sixties. You can tell your readers to get in touch with us for more information; the competition is very keen.

"Our tennis courts are all-weather so we can play as early in the spring as possible and even on warmish days late in the fall."

Frank had joined in. "We have cross-country skiing on over twelve miles of trails," he said, "and you'll see many of our guests using them for walking in the summer and fall."

He continued, "We discovered that in recent years quite a few energetic, eager people are visiting us because they love the outdoors and enjoy walking and hiking. They can walk right here on our property or make longer and more demanding hikes in the nearby mountains. Of course we pack them a lunch. I think this is part of the new genre of vacationers. They love country inns and especially want to get as close to nature and 'real things' as possible."

Dexter's is a resort-inn where there is something for almost everybody to enjoy. Many guests stay for quite a few days and even weeks at a time. It's a good place for children because there is a recreation room and a barn keyed for young people who need a place of their own.

DEXTER'S INN AND TENNIS CLUB, Box R, Stagecoach Rd., Sunapee, N.H. 03782; 603-763-5571. A 17-room country inn in the western New Hampshire mountain and lake district. Mod. American plan; European plan available in June and Sept. only. Breakfast, lunch, and dinner served to travelers by advance reservation; closed for lunch and dinner on Tues. during July and Aug. Lunches served only July, Aug.; Dec., Feb. Open from early June to mid-October. Open on a limited basis from late Dec. through mid-March. Suggest a phone call well in advance. Closed Thanksgiving and Christmas Day. Pets allowed in Annex only. Limited activities for children under 12. Three tennis courts, pool, croquet, shuffleboard, 12½ mi. of xc skiing on grounds. Downhill skiing and additional xc skiing nearby. No credit cards. Frank and Shirley Simpson, Innkeepers.

Directions: From North & East: use Exit 12 or 12A, I-89. Continue west on Rte. 11, 6 mi.-just ½ mi. past Sunapee to a sign at Winn Hill Rd. Turn left up hill and after 1 mi., bear right on Stagecoach Rd. From west: use Exit 8, I-91, follow Rte. 103 east into N.H.-through Newport ½ mi. past Junction with Rte. 11. Look for sign at "Young Hill Rd." and go 1½ mi. to Stagecoach Rd.

LYME INN
Lyme, New Hampshire

The Lyme Inn rests at the end of a long New England common, and although the village feels quite remote it is, nonetheless, just ten miles from Hanover, New Hampshire, the home of Dartmouth College, and inn guests have the opportunity to enjoy some of the sporting and theatrical events taking place there. It is just a few

minutes from the Dartmouth skiway and there's plenty of cross-country skiing nearby.

The ten rooms with private baths and five rooms with shared baths have poster beds, hooked rugs, hand-stitched quilts, wide pine floorboards, stenciled wallpaper, wingbacked chairs, and all kinds of beautiful antiques which guests frequently become very attached to and purchase. I feel certain that children would not be comfortable because there is no entertainment particularly designed for them.

I timed my most recent visit so that I could arrive in time to have breakfast with Innkeepers Fred and Judy Siemons, and speaking of breakfast, the inn is well known in that particular department. Besides an à la carte breakfast there are at least eight other full breakfasts with everything from cheese omelets, poached eggs, English muffins, and french toast, to a north country breakfast featuring pancakes.

The main dishes on the dinner menu include hasenpfeffer, Wiener schnitzel, rack of lamb, and hunter-style veal. (Judy's recipe for hasenpfeffer is in our *CIBR Cookbook*.)

Judy was overflowing with news about the inn. "Our third dining room now has our Garrison stove and what a difference it makes both in heat and warming up the atmosphere. We found a wonderful source of braided rag rugs and have replaced many of our older rugs and covered previously bare floors with some of the nicest braided rugs I've ever seen. We've also added quite a few Hitchcock chairs and tables to our dining rooms.

My attention was drawn to the unusual collection of framed samplers on the wall of the dining room. "Oh, I am definitely into samplers," exclaimed Judy. "I am always anxious to know more about them and sometimes our guests are able to be of assistance.

"Samplers are a form of American folk art," she continued, "and I find that the real old ones are fast disappearing. A friend of mine who lives nearby does most of our framing and we are doing everything we can to preserve them, including using acid-free paper."

In November, 1982, over sixty innkeepers from *CIBR* all enjoyed a lovely dinner at the Lyme Inn as part of a conference that was held at the nearby Queechee Inn. It was a wonderful opportunity not only to savor the inn cuisine, but also to visit the antique-laden bedrooms and sitting rooms.

I would estimate that it takes about three days to really enjoy this part of New Hampshire. The Dartmouth College Theater, the back roads, local shops, fairs, auctions, and the great emphasis on handcrafts in the area, plus the skiing, both cross-country and downhill, would encourage many guests to extend their holidays.

As my always-interesting visit drew to a close, Fred made a point of telling me that they have a great many Canadian visitors. "It's not very far from Montreal," he said, "and many of our friends from north of the border say that we are very similar to the English and Canadian inns that they like so much."

LYME INN, on the Common, Lyme, N.H. 03768; 603-795-2222. A 15-room village inn (10 rooms with private baths), 10 mi. north of Hanover on N.H. Rte. 10. Convenient to all Dartmouth College activities, including Hopkins Center, with music, dance, drama, painting, and sculpture. European plan year-round. Breakfast and dinner served daily to travelers, except dinner on Tuesdays. Closed three weeks following Thanksgiving and three weeks in late spring. Alpine and xc skiing, fishing, hiking, canoeing, tennis, and golf nearby. No children under 8. No pets. Fred and Judy Siemons, Innkeepers.

Directions: From I-91, take Exit 14 and follow Rte. 113A east to Vermont Rte. 5. Proceed south 50 yards to a left turn, then travel 2 mi. to inn.

HICKORY STICK FARM
Laconia, New Hampshire

I carefully separated the first bite of my first breast of roast duckling at Hickory Stick Farm, and prepared to transfer it to my expectant mouth. I could plainly see the succulent textures and colors. The outside was crisp and beautifully browned, and the meat underneath the skin was moist with just enough juice. I placed the tender morsel in my mouth and was immediately transported.

I take a lot of ribbing among the many innkeepers of my acquaintance for having a penchant for roast duckling. I've eaten it everywhere, from Longfellow's Wayside Inn in South Sudbury, Massachusetts, on New Year's Eve, to the Inn at Rancho Santa Fe, California. Now, I was in the Shangri-la of the world of roast duckling, the place where other roast duckling specialists want to go when they have roasted their last duckling—Hickory Stick Farm in Laconia, New Hampshire.

It's located on the top of a hill outside of Laconia, (see directions below) in a very busy section of the resort area of New Hampshire, dominated by Lake Winnipesaukee.

The entrance to this old converted farmhouse is through a lovely old-fashioned door leading into a beamed, low-ceilinged room with a brick fireplace which, at the time I was there, had some antiques on display. The floors are of brick or stone and there are antiques and gift items scattered about in several rooms which precede the entrance to the restaurant itself. The stenciling on some of the walls was done by Mary Roeder and is after the manner of Moses Eaton, Jr., who used to travel around southern New Hampshire in the early 1800s as a journeyman stencil artist. I believe some of his original work is in the Hancock Inn in Hancock, New Hampshire.

Mary and Scott Roeder (his brother Steve is at the Dockside Restaurant in York, Maine) showed me to a table with a most pleasant view of the fields, woods, and valleys with Mount Kearsage, Ragged Mountain, and Cartigan in the distance.

Besides the duckling, the menu had many other items on it such as veal a la Hickory Stick, seafood, and steaks, but it was to the duckling section that my eye was immediately drawn. I could have ordered a quarter of a roast stuffed duckling, a half, or a whole one for two, three, or four persons. They are all served with a country herb dressing and orange sherry sauce. Scott asserted that at least 75 percent of all of his entrées served are for roast duckling.

As the duckling on my plate disappeared, Scott went on to elaborate on the message that can be found on each table about how the ducklings are cooked. "This process involves roasting at a low temperature for about eight hours, which extracts about a pound of grease from each bird," he explained. "The ducks are then refrigerated, and as orders are received from the dining room, they are placed in a very hot oven for fifteen to twenty minutes.

The most interesting news from Hickory Stick is the fact that Scott and Mary have now made arrangements to provide two very attractive guest rooms in the inn. These would be available during the entire summer season of the restaurant, and during the remainder of the year they would be available except when Scott and Mary are on short vacations. Breakfast will also be provided. Because there are only two, I am sure they are going to be booked up well in advance. Please make advance reservations and avoid any inconvenience.

HICKORY STICK FARM, R.F.D. #2, Laconia, N.H. 03246; 603-524-3333. A hilltop country restaurant 4 mi. from Laconia in the lake country of New Hampshire. Two attractive lodging rooms with breakfast available most of the year. Please telephone ahead. The Shaker Village in Canterbury is nearby, as well as the Belknap recreational area and other New Hampshire attractions. Open from Memorial Day to Columbus Day. Dinners served from 5:30 to 9 p.m. Sunday dinner served all day from noon to 8 p.m. Extended hours during fall foliage season—call ahead. Scott and Mary Roeder, Innkeepers.

Directions: Use Exit 20 from I-93. Follow Rte. 3 toward Laconia approx. 5 mi. over bridge over Lake Winnisquam. A short distance past this bridge, turn right on Union Road immediately past Double Decker, a drive-in restaurant, and follow Hickory Stick signs 1½ mi. into the woods. If you do not turn onto any dirt roads, you are on the right track. From Laconia, go south on Rtes. 3 & 11 (do not take Rte. 106) and turn left on Union Road (about ½ mile past the Belknap Mall) and follow signs.

LOVETT'S BY LAFAYETTE BROOK
Franconia, New Hampshire

It was a warm Sunday afternoon in July and some of the guests at Lovett's were swimming in the natural brook across the country road from the inn. The maple tree, one of the first to turn to its fall colors in this section of the country, was providing cool green shade for guests engaged in animated conversation.

Lovett's is a sophisticated country inn with a spectacular view of Cannon Mountain with its many ski trails. There is considerable emphasis on excellent food and service, and the inn is well into its second generation of one-family ownership.

The main house of Lovett's actually dates back to 1790. It was built by Nicolas Powers, the original homesteader, and he was one of the petitioners to the state asking for aid to build a road through Franconia Notch.

Many of the guests have been returning for years, their fathers and mothers having come before them. "It is," one guest remarked, "almost like a club."

Summer in Franconia has many delights—antiquing, horse shows, summer theater, flower shows, auctions, and country fairs. Most of the ski areas run their lifts during the summer and autumn. Shopping seems to intrigue Lovett's guests, and there is a sprinkling of country stores and craft shops throughout the mountains.

Still another of the interesting side trips for Lovett's guests is a visit to the Robert Frost Museum which is not more than a ten-minute drive away. It can be identified by the legend, "R. Frost" on the mailbox.

On the campuslike grounds of the inn there are poolside chalets and others with mountain views and living rooms, many of them with fireplaces. These are furnished in bright contemporary fashion and are preferred by guests who enjoy the idea of being at the inn, but not so much a part of it. There are also several traditional country inn bedrooms in the main house and in two nearby houses.

Of the two swimming pools, one has rather chilly mountain water that comes right off nearby Cannon Mountain, and the other has a solar heater; one of the first in the area, I am sure.

With Lovett's impressive reputation for its food, it is difficult to make a choice from the tempting menu.

When I pressed Charlie Lovett to tell me which dish was most favored, he had this to say, "We're particularly proud of our cold wild blueberry soup, hot mussel bisque, and hot curried fresh sorrel soup, our eggplant caviar, and our pan-broiled chicken in brandy, herbs, and cream. People also tell us they enjoy our braised sirloin of beef Beaujolais, and lamb served with our own chutney."

While I sat with Charlie in the sheltered ell overlooking the solar heated pool, he told me the good news about the New England Ski Museum which is now established in Franconia Notch next to the tramway, "where it all began," he said.

"It is for all the New England states and will contain much memorabilia and history of some of the great early Austrian ski instructors, such as Hans Schneider, who really provided the impetus that eventually resulted in the American ski industry. We were in on the early part of everything around 1930 and had our own Swiss ski instructor here. He took the guests up on Cannon Mountain every day. In those days you herringboned up the side of the mountain because there was no ski lift as there is now."

LOVETT'S BY LAFAYETTE BROOK, Profile Rd., Franconia, N.H. 03580; 603-823-7761. A 32-room country inn in New Hampshire's White Mountains. Modified American plan omits lunch, although box lunches are available. Breakfast and dinner served by reservation to travelers. Open daily between June 29 and Oct. 8 and Dec. 26 and April 1. Two swimming pools, xc skiing, badminton, lawn sports on grounds. Golf, tennis, alpine skiing, trout fishing, hiking nearby. No pets. Mr. and Mrs. Charles J. Lovett, Jr., Innkeepers.

Directions: 2½ mi. south of Franconia on N.H. 18 business loop, at junction of N.H. 141 and I-93 South Franconia exit. 2¾ mi. north of junction of U.S. 3 and 18.

SPALDING INN CLUB
Whitefield, New Hampshire

Many years ago the White Mountains in New Hampshire had numerous summer resorts where "mother and children" might come up early in the season and where "father" joined them for the last four weeks or so. These resorts were wonderful, gay places where everything that was needed for a long complete vacation was either on the grounds or nearby. The lure of the mountains drew people in great numbers from Boston and New York.

Now, with few exceptions, all of these family-run resorts have disappeared, but not the Spalding Inn Club which is thriving under second and third-generation owners and innkeepers. Many of the amenities of earlier times are still preserved. For example, gentlemen

wouldn't think of going into dinner without a jacket and tie, and the inn is a focal point for the sports of lawn bowling and tennis, with several tournaments scheduled from mid-June to mid-September including the U.S. National Singles and Doubles Lawn Bowling Championships.

The Spalding Inn Club is an excellent example of entertainment and hospitality that can be provided for a family with many different preferences. For example, on the inn grounds there are four clay tennis courts, a swimming pool, a nine-hole par-3 golf course, two championship lawn bowling greens, and shuffleboard. Five golf courses are within fifteen minutes of the inn and plenty of trout fishing and boating, and enticing back roads are nearby. The

Appalachian Trail system for mountain climbing is a short walk from the inn.

There is also a well-blended balance of vigorous outdoor activity and quiet times including an extensive library, a card room, and a challenging collection of jigsaw puzzles. Groves of maples, birches, and oak trees native to northern New Hampshire are on the inn grounds and there are over 400 acres of lawns, gardens and orchards.

There are real country inn touches everywhere. The broad porch is ideal for rocking, and the main living room has a fireplace with a low ceiling, lots of books and magazines, baskets of apples, a barometer for tomorrow's weather, a jar of sour balls, and great arrangements of flowers.

Those country-inn touches also include the traditional hearty menu items so satisfying after a day of outdoor activities in the White Mountains. Among other offerings are delicious clam chowder, oyster stew, boiled scrod, poached salmon, pork chops, roast duckling, roast tenderloin, and sweetbreads. Children love the Indian pudding. All of the pies, including hot mince, the breads, and rolls are made in the bakery of the inn.

I am just as pleased and proud as I can be that Ted and Topsy Spalding continue to keep their standards high and that this delightful, elegant, resort-inn continues to offer its unique White Mountain hospitality.

SPALDING INN CLUB, Mountain View Road, Whitefield, N.H. 03598; 603-837-2572. A 70-room resort-inn in the center of New Hampshire's White Mountains. American plan only from late May to mid-October when breakfast, lunch, and dinner are served daily to travelers. Heated pool, tennis courts, 9-hole par-3 golf course, 18-hole putting green, two championship lawn bowling greens, and shuffleboard on grounds. Also guest privileges at 5 nearby golf clubs. Trout fishing, boating, summer theater, and backroading nearby. Ted and Topsy Spalding, Innkeepers.

Directions: From New York take Merritt Pkwy. to I-91; I-91 to Wells River, Vt. Woodsville, N.H. exit; then Rte. 302 to Littleton, then Rte. 116 thru Whitefield to Mtn. View Rd. intersection—3 miles north of village. From Boston take I-93 north thru Franconia Notch to Littleton exit; then Rte. 116 thru Whitefield to Mtn. View Rd. intersection—3 miles north of village. From Montreal take Auto Route 10 to Magog; then Auto Route 55 and I-91 to St. Johnsbury, Vt.; then Rte. 18 to Littleton, N.H. and Rte. 116 as above. The inn is situated 1 mi. west on Mountain View Rd.

PHILBROOK FARM INN
Shelburne, New Hampshire

Zooming across western Maine into New Hampshire on Route 2, I caught a glimpse of Philbrook Farm Inn tucked away underneath the mountains on the north side. The warm sun of late September caught the sparkle of many early turning leaves as well as the white clapboards of the house. I remember this was almost the same time and the same sensation I had had a few years ago when I first turned off the road to discover what for many people is a truly unusual New Hampshire country inn experience.

The Philbrook Farm Inn *is* New Hampshire. There is New Hampshire to be seen everywhere: New Hampshire prints, paintings, and photographs—some of them really irreplaceable. There are tints of old prints, hooked rugs, and many, many books about New Hampshire, in fact a whole library of books on the White Mountains alone. Some have been written by former guests.

Once again I followed the road over the railroad crossing and then traversed the rumbling planks of the single-lane bridge over the river. I followed the road and pulled up underneath the old apple trees in front of the inn and hoped that I would be in time to have at least a bowl of soup or some dessert from the Sunday lunch.

The garden was at its most gorgeous peak; I've never seen the flowers in more impressive bloom and the cornfield across the road had silken tassels. This is certainly one of the most gentle and pleasant times to visit the Philbrook Farm Inn, but there are other seasons, too.

Wintertime is waking up in the morning to snowstorms, and brilliant sunshine, seeing white-capped Mt. Washington over the hills in the distance, and also looking at the cross-country ski wax thermometer which gives advice on the correct wax for the day. The fields, which in summertime have Herefords standing knee-deep in the lush grass, are filled with snow.

The wealth of outdoor activity in all seasons encourages the kind of appetites that most people never knew they had. Consequently, food is on everybody's mind at least three times a day. "It is all homemade with no mixes," said Connie Leger, the innkeeper, along with her sister Nancy. "There is one main dish each night, and the dinner usually consists of a homemade soup, some type of pot roast, pork roast, or roast lamb. The vegetables are all fresh and we try to stay away from fried foods. Most of the guests enjoy roasts, because these days they are not served as much at home. All of the desserts are homemade. There's pie, ice cream, and pudding.

"For lunches, we serve salads, chowder, hot rolls, hash,

macaroni and cheese, and things like that. Breakfast is a real big farm-style breakfast. On Sunday morning we have New England fish balls and cornbread."

Besides farmhouse lodgings in the three main buildings, some of which have private baths, in the summertime guests enjoy several different cottages, some with housekeeping arrangements and their own fireplace. These too enjoy a view of the meadows, river, and the mountains beyond.

Well, I missed the lunch, but was honored to be invited to sit in the kitchen with Maxine and Tilly and enjoy a bowl of good chicken soup near the ten-burner woodburning range which was built before the turn of the century. As Nancy pointed out, "We do almost all of our cooking and baking on this range, and only use the electric stove in case of emergency."

PHILBROOK FARM INN, North Rd., Shelburne, N.H. 03581; 603-466-3831. A 20-room country inn in the White Mountains of northeastern N.H., 6 mi. from Gorham and just west of the Maine/N.H. line. American, mod. American, and European plans available. Open May 1 to Oct. 31; Dec. 26 to April 1. Closed Thanksgiving, Christmas. Shuffleboard, horseshoes, badminton, ping-pong, croquet, pool, hiking trails, xc skiing, snowshoeing trails on grounds. Swimming, golf, hiking, backroading, bird watching nearby. Pets allowed only during summer season in cottages. No credit cards. Nancy C. Philbrook and Constance P. Leger, Innkeepers.

Directions: The inn is just off U.S. Rte. 2 in Shelburne. Look for inn direction sign and turn at North Rd., cross R.R. tracks and river, turn right at crossroad, and the inn is at the end of road.

STAFFORD'S IN THE FIELD
Chocorua, New Hampshire

The first sight that caught my eye was the family of ducks. Two good-sized adults and at least ten baby ducklings were waddling their way across the parking lot down toward the new tennis court which was in its final stages of construction. I tried as unobtrusively as possible to get a closer view of the duck family, but they would

have none of it, and kept moving farther away into the high grass with mama and papa duck carefully herding the little ones out of harm's way.

The muted tan colors of the main building had a fresh look, with the gay accents of window boxes and a summer garden of black-eyed Susans and other seasonal flowers. The big old red barn, which I have admired since my first visit in 1971, was still intact and I'm sure was being put to some intriguing uses this summer.

Next to the kitchen door a small table, shaded by a bright blue umbrella, had a sign saying, "Bakery." Another small sign indicated that cookies, sandwiches, and other things would be available for guests for noontime forays into the countryside. I found Ramona Stafford and had a nice chat with her while she was doing the morning muffins. On the wooden table were the necessities and trappings of baking: a large bowl of eggs, a blender, a box of oats, a brush with melted butter, five or six recipe books, and on the shelf all kinds of tempting flavorings, in addition to a contraption for weighing and measuring the ingredients.

In the 1972 edition of *Country Inns and Back Roads* I pointed out that this was an inn of many faces. It sits at the end of the road at the top of a small hill with broad meadows on three sides and a beautiful woods behind. There is an apple orchard, stone walls, a series of small cottages, and that famous barn. A great many of the winter guests are fond of cross-country skiing and there are trails all around the inn.

Still another face of this old inn is seen in summer when the New Hampshire mountains offer many diversions including water sports like canoeing, sailing, fishing, and swimming. It's possible to find a place of unusual peace and contentment by disappearing into the woods surrounding the inn. For the more vigorous climber, Mt. Chocorua offers a worthy challenge.

Today, as in 1972, still another side of Stafford's in the Field is Ramona's gourmet cooking. I hasten to point out that "gourmet" is a word I never use lightly, but my original conversation with her convinced me that she was not merely a good cook but a dedicated searcher for true expression in the culinary art. Breads and pastries are home-baked and there is a very generous selection of Russian, French, Italian, and German dishes with à knowledgeable use of herbs and spices. One of my favorite dishes is the spare ribs cooked in maple syrup.

All of this accumulated knowledge, experimentation, and years of preparing inn meals has finally culminated in the *Stafford's-in-the-Field Cookbook.* "It has been a family project," declared Ramona. "Fred and our daughter Momo worked side by side with me, and even the boys made significant contributions."

Having watched Ramona turning out those muffins, my mouth was watering for them. I can report that I ate three hot from the oven and deliciously buttered; with the fourth I tried something new: cutting it up in several slices and pouring some delicious hot maple syrup over it.

Mmmm, terrific!

STAFFORD'S IN THE FIELD, Chocorua, N.H. 03817; 603-323-7766. An 8-room resort-inn with 5 cottages, 17 mi. south of North Conway. Modified American plan at inn omits lunch. European plan in cottages. Some rooms in inn with shared baths. Meals served to guests only. Closed Apr. and May, Nov. and Dec. Bicycles, square dancing, tennis, and xc skiing on the grounds. Golf, swimming, hiking, riding, tennis, and fishing nearby. No pets. The Stafford Family, Innkeepers.

Directions: Follow N.H. Rte. 16 north to Chocorua Village, then turn left onto Rte. 113 and travel 1 mi. west to inn. Or, from Rte. 93 take Exit 23 and travel east on Rtes. 104 and 25 to Rte. 16. Proceed north on Rte. 16 to Chocorua Village, turn left onto Rte. 113 and travel 1 mi. west to inn.

ROCKHOUSE MOUNTAIN FARM
Eaton Center, New Hampshire

Rockhouse Mountain Farm really has a great story. It is a family-run farm-inn that for more than thirty years has been a way of life for John and Libby Edge, and their now-grown son Johnny, and daughter Betsi who is married to Bill Ela.

It is not only family-run, but definitely oriented for family vacations. Just imagine taking young children to a place where there are riding horses, cows, ducks, geese, chickens, pigs, piglets, ponies, pheasants, guinea hens—all with their own names!

What about the chance to help with farm chores like haying, milking, and grooming the horses? How about the opportunity to learn not only how to canoe, but where the best blueberries are located on Foss Mountain. Think of a barn filled with hay, with swings and tunnels, and chances for playing hide-and-seek on rainy days.

There are also sailboats, rowboats, and canoes at the Rockhouse private beach, located on Crystal Lake. Then think about fresh rolls or bread every day, fresh vegetables, special desserts, and all that anyone can eat, prepared daily by Betsi.

After I had seen the lodging rooms, dining rooms, parlors and the 200-year-old barn and met all of the animals, including the eighteen little ducklings (eighteen? a new record!) belonging to Pearl, the Muscovy duck, and also a few of the twenty little piglets belonging to Buttercup and Sweetpea, Johnny's prized sows, and surveyed the beautiful vegetable garden, Johnny summed up the spirit of RMF this way, "We have tried to create an inn for families because we believe the family was the basis of society, business, and religion in colonial times, and should be the basis of our life today. Families that can vacation together and spend leisure hours together have a chance to grow together and understand one another.

"We have tried to make available to our guests the simple way of life. They can enjoy things like running through the fields and chasing our dogs, cantering along a country road as the sun rises over the hills or sliding down the waterfalls of Swift River.

"I think Dad and Mother have always seen in our place the opportunity for a 'refresher' period—a chance to exchange everyday concerns over coffee at breakfast, to enjoy the quietness of dinner by candlelight, and to exercise the body with things like tennis and golf.

"You would have to stay with us for at least a year to see all there is to do in this part of New Hampshire, and to do all there is to do at Rockhouse."

Libby Edge reminded me of the pleasant tradition that has been going on for some years at the inn. "When our first guest departed thirty years ago one of us grabbed an old school bell and rang it as a farewell. We have been doing it ever since. One bell has grown to a variety of nine, and all the guests join the Edges lined up on the front driveway as the cars of guests roll away from Rockhouse. It has gathered more sentiment as the years have gone by and everyone anticipates the royal sendoff."

RMF is informal, rustic, and gregarious. The happiest guests are those willing to lend a hand with the chores, "do" the dozens of White Mountains things together, and sit around the table talking long after it has been cleared. Long may it prosper.

ROCKHOUSE MOUNTAIN FARM INN, Eaton Center, N.H. 03832; 603-447-2880. A complete resort in the foothills of the White Mountains (6 mi. south of Conway), combining a modern 18-room country inn with life on a 350-acre farm. Some rooms with private bath. Mod. American plan. Open from June 15th through October. Own saddle horses, milk cows, and other farm animals; haying, hiking, shuffleboard; private beach on Crystal Lake with swimming, rowboats, sailboats, and canoes—canoe trips planned; stream and lake fishing; tennis and golf nearby. No credit cards. The Edge Family, Innkeepers.

Directions: From I-93, take Exit 23 to Rte. 104 to Meredith. Take Rte. 25 to Rte. 16, and proceed north to Conway. Follow Rte. 153, 6 mi. south from Conway to Eaton Center.

THE CAPTAIN LORD MANSION
Kennebunkport, Maine

Bev Davis and Rick Litchfield, the personable owners of the Captain Lord Mansion, were filling me in on a few of the intriguing historical details of the building and the town. "During the war of 1812, the British threatened to burn the port if shipbuilding and trade didn't cease. Captain Nathaniel Lord answered the needs of idle carpenters and sailors by engaging them to build this mansion using timbers intended for ships.

"Naturally, as the Lord mansion progressed through several generations of descendents, it acquired all of the trappings and legends that such a building might accumulate. We even have ghosts. One is Sally Buckland, whose portrait hangs in the front sitting room. She has the kind of eyes that actually follow you around, and you can even feel them looking at you when your back is turned.

"In addition to the cupola, the original structure claims one of the few three-story, unsupported elliptical staircases in Maine. Each window is considerably enhanced by hand-sewn draperies, and each displays its blown glass and original double Indian shutters. The beautiful floors with their original pine boards are a handsome complement to the remainder of the furnishings, most of which are antiques of such great history and pedigree that we have conducted tours for all of our houseguests."

The Captain Lord Mansion is an opportunity to be transported into an elegant era of the nineteenth century. It is a mansion of over thirty-five rooms of many descriptions. Most of the bathrooms have marble sinks. Some have light fixtures that are real silver.

Bev and Rick have made significant improvements in the quality and diversification of the hospitality presented to their guests. There are Posturepedic mattresses, thick carpets, color-coordinated linens, and lovely works of art. Fluffy comforters, handmade quilts, or 100% wool blankets provide extra warmth against those chilly Maine nights. In order to accommodate those who prefer oversized beds, there are three rooms with queen-sized and three rooms with king-sized beds.

Breakfast is served in the warm and inviting kitchen where Rick and assistant manager Nancy Blanchard bustle around serving pumpkin, zucchini, and cranberry bread, various types of coffee cakes and cinnamon rolls, as well as soft-boiled eggs, juice, and coffee or tea. Bev usually appears around 10 A.M. with the new members of the innkeeping family, Dana who is 2 years old and Stacia who is over a year. Many returning guests always comment about how "the children have grown."

As expected Rick has acquired a great deal of knowledge about the house and its history, including the legends, and also about the entire Kennebunkport area. Many guests enjoy going up into the cupola which provides such a wonderful view of the many historic houses of Kennebunkport.

"I've never met Captain Nathaniel Lord," said Rick, "nor, for that matter, any members of the Lord family, but fortunately, so much of his way of life has been preserved in this building for more than a hundred and fifty years that I feel I have a very strong tie with him. I've studied the history of the family and love to tell it to our guests."

Bev had the last word: "It's like acquiring a whole new set of ancestors."

THE CAPTAIN LORD MANSION, Box 527, Kennebunkport, Me. 04046; 207-967-3141. A 16-bedroom inn located in a mansion in a seacoast village. Lodgings include breakfast. No other meals served. Open year-round. Near the Rachel Carson Wildlife Refuge, the Seashore Trolley Museum, The Brick Store Museum, and lobster boat tours. Bicycles, hiking, xc skiing, deep sea fishing, golf, indoor swimming, and tennis nearby. No children under 12. No pets. No credit cards. Bev Davis and Rick Litchfield, Innkeepers.

Directions: Take Exit 3 (Kennebunk) from the Maine Turnpike. Take left on Rte. 35 and follow signs through Kennebunk to Kennebunkport. Take left at traffic light at Sunoco station. Go over drawbridge and take first right onto Ocean Ave., then take fourth left after Texaco. The mansion is on the second block on left. Park behind building and take brick walk to office.

THE OLD FORT INN
Kennebunkport, Maine

Shana Aldrich and I were seated by the Old Fort Inn swimming pool on a warm August afternoon. I must say she looked very fetching in her bathing suit. We were discussing how it felt to live in a place where it is like being on a vacation much of the time.

"Oh, I like it very much," she said. "I can play tennis, go swimming, and go to the beach. I always have a good suntan." Shana will be six years old in 1983.

Meanwhile, we were joined by her father, David, who is the innkeeper along with her mother. "I see that you've been getting the first-class treatment from our hostess," he said with a twinkle in his eye. "She's one of our greatest assets."

The Old Fort Inn is a very special kind of country inn. The main building of a hotel that had been on the property at one time was torn down and the handsome stone carriage house was converted into twelve large bedrooms that have fully-equipped kitchen facilities and include daily maid service. The rooms are large enough that guests can stay for longer periods without feeling cramped. They have electric heat. Guests gather at the lodge, located in a converted barn built around 1880. It has a big fireplace that serves as a meeting point on spring and fall evenings, and its open deck next to the swimming pool makes it a very comfortable place in which guests may gather in the warmer weather. The furnishings complement this handsome, rustic room with its huge beams and weathered pine wallboards. The antique shop has also been enlarged.

David took up where Shana left off. "We've done a number of things since your last visit. Our guests really appreciate the washer

and dryer that is now available. We've also installed a TV in all the rooms because we have many guests who come here for long stays and we found that they were bringing their own sets.

"By the time you visit us next summer we will have completely redecorated all twelve of our rooms. We went to many auctions and found some beautiful antique beds, furniture, and accessories. Some of the rooms have hand-done stencils and others have been papered with country wallpaper. On each table the guest will find cloth placemats and napkins and, judging by the comments, I think we're achieving our goal of the 'natural' look."

We were joined at poolside by Sheila who came with large welcome pitchers of real lemonade. Two of the guests at the inn strolled by on the way to the tennis courts. "We've always had a great many visitors from Canada," Sheila commented. "We're not too far from Montreal or Quebec City and there are times here during the summer when we are almost evenly divided between Canadians and Americans."

Our conversation turned to the fact that it is so very pleasant here in Kennebunkport during May or October. "I'm so glad that we installed a cover on our heated swimming pool, so now it's possible to swim earlier and later in both seasons. Fall and spring are the times when it is wonderfully quiet. As you know, midsummer in Kennebunkport is rather hectic."

OLD FORT INN, Old Fort Ave., Kennebunkport, Me. 04046; 207-967-5353. A 12-room resort-inn within walking distance of the ocean in a historic Maine town. Includes a continental breakfast, and a full kitchen is provided with each apartment. Daily maid service. Fireplace Lodge. Open from May 1 to Oct. 31. Heated pool, tennis court, shuffleboard on grounds. Bicycles, golf, salt-water swimming and boating nearby. Not comfortable for children under 7. No pets. Sheila and David Aldrich, Innkeepers.

Directions: Take Exit 3 (Kennebunk) from the Maine Turnpike. Take left on Route 35 and follow signs through Kennebunk to Kennebunkport. Take left at traffic light at Sunoco station. Go over drawbridge and take first right on Ocean Ave. Take Ocean Ave. to the Colony Hotel; turn left in front of the Colony, go to the Y in the road, go right ¼ mi. on left.

THE BRADLEY INN
Pemaquid Point, New Harbor, Maine

I reached out and put my hands on the firm stone base of the Pemaquid Point Lighthouse. It radiated a wonderful warmth borrowed from the brilliant September sun, so I sat down and rested against it, attempting to draw into myself some of its strength and nobility. It was my lighthouse.

Immediately in front of me, this selfsame sun created momentary jewels where the Atlantic gently lapped against the striated rocks that stretched out toward Spain. Overhead sea birds wheeled and turned and talked to each other incessantly. I closed my eyes and my thoughts drifted back to my arrival at the Bradley Inn, which is just a short pleasant walk from my lighthouse.

Early the previous evening I had taken I-95 to coastal Route 1 and continued on through Brunswick, Bath, and Wiscasset. Following Ed Ek's directions I turned off on Business Rte. 1 at Damariscotta, turned right at the top of the hill at the white church, and followed Rte. 130 fourteen miles to Pemaquid Point and the Bradley Inn.

The first greeting came from a toy poodle who barked a welcome. This was followed with an introduction to Ed and Louine Ek and Grandma, who is a definite part of the innkeeping team. We passed underneath the blue awnings of the entranceway, through a screened-in outdoor summer dining area, into a sitting room that looked very much like what I would expect to find in a Maine farmhouse.

I paused for a moment to read the blackboard that listed the menu offerings for my Sunday night visit—prime ribs of beef, leg of lamb, veal piccata, scallops cooked in white wine, a seafood casserole, Maine lobster, and several different desserts, including the famous Bradley Inn pie, for which there is now a recipe in the *Country Inns and Back Roads Cookbook.*

The Eks and Grandma are very natural, likable people for whom the Bradley Inn has become not only a way of life, but has perhaps taken on higher meanings. Ed and Louine fled the corporate life and the environs of New Jersey to seek something with greater meaning and the opportunity to be of helpful service to more people. Louine is completely in charge of the cooking, and Ed is the host and man-of-all-work.

A visit to this country inn on the rocky coast of Maine is in many respects a step backward in time. The bedrooms all share bathrooms and conveniences "down the hall." Much of the furniture came from Ed's and Louine's former home and besides decorator sheets and pillowcases in bright colors, these moderately sized rooms have firm mattresses.

246

The old-fashioned dining room provides meals not only for guests, but many people from the immediate area who consider the Bradley Inn "their inn."

All the friends of Louine and Ed who have been much concerned about Ed's fall from a scaffolding last summer, resulting in a long hospital stay, will be happy to know that I saw both of them at a *CIBR* meeting at the Quechee Inn in Vermont last November. This was really the first time the two of them were able to be away together, and Ed now walks without a cane about 90% of the time. Lots of our readers sent notes and cards, and I know the Eks are both very grateful.

THE BRADLEY INN, Rte. 130, Pemaquid Point, New Harbor, Me. 04554; 207-677-2105. A 12-room country inn (no private baths) located near the Pemaquid Lighthouse on Maine's rocky coast, 15 mi. from Damariscotta. Many cultural, historic, recreation facilities nearby. Rooms are available year-round. Continental breakfast included in room rate. Open daily to the public for dinner from mid-June to mid-Oct.; on weekends only Oct. to Jan., March to June. Restaurant is closed Christmas Eve, Christmas Day, Jan., Feb. Tennis, swimming, golf, canoeing, backroading, woodland walks, xc skiing all available nearby. No pets. Edwin and Louine Ek and Grandma, Innkeepers.

Directions: From South: Maine I-95 to Brunswick/Bath coastal Rte. 1 Exit. Follow Rte. 1 through Brunswick, Bath, and Wiscasset. Exit business Rte. 1 at Damariscotta. Turn right at top of hill (white church), follow Rte. 130, 14 mi. to Pemaquid Pt. From North: Rte. 1; exit at business Rte. 1, Damariscotta. Turn left at white church onto Rte. 130. Follow 130, 14 mi. to Pemaquid Pt.

BLACK POINT INN
Prouts Neck, Maine

Under a brilliant Maine August sun, on my last trip to the Black Point Inn, I set out after breakfast to walk the Prouts Neck path. The usual course is to follow the path directly from the front of the inn. However, this time I decided to walk counter-clockwise and wound my way up through the beautiful trees and cottages that make up the private residential area of the community. Most of these are built of brown, weathered shingles with white trim, the same design as the inn. Some of the same families have been summering here for generations.

Following Norm Dugas's directions, I cut through to the ocean at a point where I could see the Winslow Homer Studio, and then started walking in the marshlands and thickets beside the sea. Eventually, the path came out on the rocks and led to the sandy beach favored by inn guests who like chilly salt water.

The path came out on a ledge above the sea, and I stretched out on a warm rock and began to muse about the conversation I had had at dinner the night before when Norm had mentioned the fact that Prouts Neck was first settled about 1630, and in 1690, the trouble with the French and Indians caused the colonists to leave it for twelve years.

"It became popular as a summer resort in the middle of the 19th century," he pointed out. "In 1886 there were a half dozen summer cottages. One of them was occupied by Charles Savage Homer whose son, Winslow, became one of America's most well-known artists. He must have gotten his inspiration for some of those great paintings of the Maine coast from just walking on the rocks and the beaches here."

It was now about twelve noon and I could hear the tuning-up of the small orchestra that plays for both the poolside buffets at noon and for dancing after dinner. I had worked up quite an appetite on my walk and I was anxious to see what the specialty of the buffet would be on this day.

The Black Point Inn is one of the few remaining American plan hotels that flourished in New England for about 100 years. It has quiet dignity, personal service, attention to details, ocean bathing, excellent tennis courts, a golf course, exceptional food, and an unpretentious elegance. Men wear coats for dinner and many of the ladies enjoy wearing their gay, summer dresses. Dressing up is part of the fun. That is the way it has been ever since I have been visiting this inn which, like the Spalding Inn in Whitefield, New Hampshire, provides one of the last few remaining intimate resort-inn experiences.

Besides the new terrace dining room overlooking the rose

garden, one of the more recent additions at the inn is a sailboat which periodically takes guests on two- or three-hour sailing excursions.

Rooms are more readily available at the Black Point during the months of June and July. August is always a full month; however, in early July the weather has been exceptional for the last few years and it's possible to call and make a reservation a day ahead.

The "social season" runs from the last weekend in June to Labor Day, and before and after this period services are somewhat curtailed because there are group meetings at the inn. Norm Dugas makes the point that the inn is happy to take transient guests in late September or October; however, there are motorcoach tours at that time and the dining room can become rather noisy.

BLACK POINT INN, Prouts Neck, Me. 04070; 207-883-4311. An 80-room luxury resort-inn on Rte. 207, 10 mi. south of Portland. American plan. Breakfast, lunch, and dinner served to travelers. Open May 20 to Oct. 12. Fresh water whirlpool, heated salt water pool, bicycles, sailing, dancing, golf, tennis, and ocean bathing all within a few steps. No pets. Normand H. Dugas, Innkeeper.

Directions: From Maine Tpke., take Exit 7. Turn right at sign marked Scarborough and Old Orchard Beach. At second set of lights turn left on Rte. 207. Follow 4.3 miles to Prouts Neck.

THE CLAREMONT HOTEL AND COTTAGES
Southwest Harbor, Maine

The tide was out but the fleet was in as I walked down the broad lawn once again to the Boat House at the Claremont, and saw that the new volleyball net had been erected and a croquet game was already in progress, as the championships at Claremont were being held over the coming weekend.

Meanwhile on the waters of Somes Sound, there were at least eight or nine beautiful sailboats moored, their white masts sharply in contrast to the green hills on the other side. Oddly enough, my previous visits to the Claremont always seemed to be when the tide was in. This time, the bare rocks and the shore life they supported made a very interesting and striking scene.

Innkeeper Jay Madeira and I were seated on the lawn of the Claremont which has been a resort inn for almost a hundred years. It is the oldest continuously operating hotel on the island. In recent years, the McCue family has added attractive cottages which are nestled in the trees with a view of the water. "There have been more visitors from Europe," he said, "particularly from England. Many people fly to Bangor which is fifty miles away, or to Bar Harbor, which is eleven, and we pick them up. Many of our guests are coming in the early or late season, and we've adjusted our schedule for people who might enjoy Mount Desert Island when almost no one but year-round residents are here."

The Claremont opened in the summer of 1884 and has known only three owners in all of its years, which in itself is most unusual. Successive generations have been returning ever since the inn opened, although the Claremont has become more and more a place for vacationing families and honeymooners. Its designation to the National Register of Historic Places reads: "A reminder of Maine's early summer resort period of the 1870s and '80s . . . of a prosperous, relaxed and seasonal way of life."

There are twenty-two rooms in the three-story main building with additional rooms in the Phillips House, the Clark House, and other cottages.

One of the reasons for its continuing popularity is the extensive menu prepared by chef Billie McIntire, who is now in her eighth year at Claremont and has received well-deserved national recognition for her talents. Besides the lobster, scallops, steak, and tournedos, the seafood crepes have been popular. The desserts are fabulous. Many a resolve goes out the window when guests see something being served at the next table.

Ever since my first visit here, I've been struck by the wide variety of entertainment and recreation that the Claremont guests can enjoy. For example, the location on Mount Desert Island puts all of the wonderful attractions of the area within a very convenient distance.

I'm not sure I mentioned it before, however, the Claremont Hotel is one of the very few country inns that I have visited where croquet is such an important activity. There has been an on going croquet tournament held each year in late August that occasionally gets national attention because some of the supreme devotées of the wicket and stake are entries. The hotel is now making their own professional mallets.

The Claremont approaches its 100th year with great anticipation, still preserving some of the best features of the past.

THE CLAREMONT HOTEL AND COTTAGES, Southwest Harbor, Me. 04679; 207-244-5036. A 22-room rambling summer hotel with rooms also in two adjacent guest houses; on Somes Sound, Mt. Desert Island, 24 mi. south of Ellsworth. All rooms with private baths except 2 with shared baths. Hotel and dining room open mid-June thru mid-Sept. Breakfast and dinner served to guests and the public. Lunch also served during Aug. Guest-house rooms and housekeeping cottages available May thru Oct. Hotel and Phillips House rooms available only on Mod. Amer. plan during the season. Off-season, all rooms available either EP or MAP while hotel is open. Tennis, rowboats, croquet, badminton, dock and deepwater moorings on grounds. Fresh-water swimming, golf, bicycles, riding, boating, and sailing rental nearby. No credit cards. Personal checks accepted. The McCue Family, Owners; John Madeira, Jr., Manager.

Directions: From Maine Tpke., exit at Augusta and proceed east on Rte. 3 to US #1. At Ellsworth, pick up Rte. 3 again and follow Rte. 102 on Mt. Desert Island to Southwest Harbor. Follow inn signs approaching and in Southwest Harbor.

Every road to our island, to us, is a back road. Two in particular are special to me:

1) A 6.5 mile route on Pressy Village Road just beyond the inn on Route 15 will allow you to view white Maine farmhouses (one reminiscent of Wyeth's "Christina's World") and small coves with the Camden Hills in the distance across Penobscot Bay. Sylvester's Cove includes the Deer Isle Yacht Club (a euphemism), handsome sailboats and lobster boats. The traveler views tall pines and an ever-changing array of wild flowers. Each week different combinations of color are dominant and one appreciates the overall sensation of the quiet beauty of rocky land, blue waters, and rolling hills which are characteristic of Deer Isle.

2) As you leave Stonington proper on Route 15 North, instead of turning left out of town, one can continue straight past an old Mobil Oil station on the right. About a half-mile up a hill you can look over Stonington harbor, perhaps spotting one of the windjammers sailing through the Deer Isle Thoroughfare. If you continue on your left you will see a pond several acres in size that is literally clogged with pink, white, and yellow water lilies. Some are wild while others are domestic. They were started in the '30s and were allowed to multiply. This is Ame's Pond. The best time to see the lilies is between 11 A.M. and 2 P.M. The sight brings to mind Monet's "Water Lilies" and is memorable.

George and Elli Pavloff
Pilgrim's Inn
Deer Isle, Maine

Route 35 is representative of one of the most delightful tour byways in this area, regardless of season. From Naples village, Route 35 winds its way, keeping in close touch with the eastern shoreline of Long Lake, for approximately twelve miles to the village

of Harrison. The alert motorist can view both lake and the White Mountains in New Hampshire without ever leaving his vehicle. Besides, there are magnificent homes, working farms, and woods galore along this trail. From Harrison the motorist would jog over a mile to the storybook picturesque hamlet of North Bridgton, home of one of the oldest boys' preparatory schools in the nation. Campus, class buildings, dorms, and chapel—all wood frame and painted pristine white—are set above a huge rolling lawn. The Academy dominates the village which is also completely clothed in white—homes, church, firehouse, and post office. By the way, Bridgton Academy is my alma mater.

Here the motorist picks up Route 37, sister byway of Route 35, and wends his way through woodlands and lakes to the picture-perfect village of Waterford which, we are advised, is listed on the National Historic Register in its entirety. "High tea" served daily (except Tuesdays) at the Artemus Ward House in Waterford Common is a must before the "Backroader" returns to Naples and his Charmwoods base.

We suggest on the homeward trip that for the sake of variety the motorist take companion Route 35 back to Harrison and then on to Naples. The entire drive, with time out for tea in Waterford, can be conducted in leisurely fashion in an hour, more or less. The route is practically devoid of commercial establishments and is strictly for those who desire to commune with nature.

Bill and Marilyn Lewis
Charmwoods
Naples, Maine

Increasing numbers of guests driving east from New Hampshire, wind up on Route 2 in Maine. The fun starts when they head north through Mexico and Rumford up Route 17. The Swift River courses along Route 17 for approximately 43 miles, and at two points, Houghton and Byron, many visitors stop and pan for gold. A small shovel or trowel and wash basin is all the equipment they need.

Farther along, ten miles south of Rangeley at a turn-out, there's a spectacular view that encompasses many of the mountains and lakes of Maine, New Hampshire, and Vermont.

Our favorite road ends in Oquossoc, where a short right turn leads you into Rangeley and the Country Club Inn.

Bob and Sue Crory
Country Club Inn
Rangeley, Maine

CHARMWOODS
On Long Lake, Naples, Maine

Charmwoods is a unique type of inn. Set in an area of great natural beauty and maintained by conscientious hosts, the inn provides a perfect setting for an escape to the countryside.

Once a private lakefront estate, Charmwoods radiates all the flavor and ambience of the Maine woods but is a mere 2½-hour drive from downtown Boston.

As hosts, Marilyn and Bill Lewis make for a perfect combination. Marilyn is attractive and vivacious, and delights in giving her guests personal attention so as to ensure them the most pleasurable of vacations.

Bill, a former editor at the *Boston Globe* and *Boston Herald,* has unusual interests which Charmwoods guests find to be a pleasant diversion. For example, he often entertains with his 1890 Thomas A. Edison phonograph, drawing from a collection of about 500 cylindrical recordings. The newest acquisition is an antique player-piano, complete with rolls of the old favorites. Evenings it is the center of attraction for guests addicted to singalongs with a keen nostalgia for this lusty entertainment of yesteryear.

Marilyn's penchant for decorating is particularly evident in all the spacious bedrooms with their selection of handsome coordinated sheets, blankets, towels, and other accessories in distinctive colors. The master suite boasts a sunken Roman-style bathtub. Every suite enjoys a view of the lake.

The focus of activity at Charmwoods is frequently the commodious and gracious living room with its massive fieldstone fireplace and panoramic view of lake and mountains. Everything about this room encourages friendly discussions with a free exchange of information and ideas. The striking undersea photographs are provided by the Lewis's son, Jonathan.

Within fifteen minutes after my arrival Bill and Marilyn had introduced me to their guests and we were immediately on a first-name basis—chatting as would old friends. Several guests were regulars at Charmwoods, having returned for second or third visits.

Adjoining the living room and sharing center stage during much of the year is a broad deck with an unobstructed view of Long Lake. It is equally ideal for sunny breakfasts or for chatting under the stars.

A path leads down a few steps to the shoreline of this delightfully clear lake where a rowboat and canoe are docked in the boathouse. Swimming from the white sandy beach or private sundeck is ideal, and a trim cabana provides numerous amenities, including telephone service.

The village of Naples, a short stroll down the road, offers guests some interesting upcountry diversions, not the least of which is a seaplane flight providing an excellent overview of the entire resort area. The *Songo River Queen,* an old-fashioned paddleboat, and the U.S. Mailboats run excursion trips across this ten-mile lake. There is plenty of backroading and quite a few antique shops in the immediate area.

During my visit at Charmwoods nearly all the guests clutched tennis rackets, and the all-weather court saw plenty of play. There's a lakeside golf course and riding stables just a few minutes away.

Visiting Charmwoods is like being a guest at a houseparty for friends.

CHARMWOODS, Naples, Me. 04055; 207-693-6798 (winter 617-469-9673). Four bedrooms, all with private baths, plus guest cottage. Located on the west shore of Long Lake, approx. ½ hr. from Main Tpke. Open from May 30 weekend into Oct. Breakfast is the only meal served (to houseguests only). Tennis, swimming, boating, canoeing, shuffleboard, and horseshoes on grounds; horseback riding, golf, and para-sailing nearby. Summer playhouse just down the road. Not suitable for children under 12. No pets. No credit cards. Marilyn and Bill Lewis, Innkeepers.

Directions: From Boston: follow Rte. 1 north to I-95 to Exit 8 (Portland-Westbrook). Turn right and follow Riverside St. 1 mi. to Rte. 302. Turn left (west) to Naples, which is about 30 mi. ahead. Charmwoods is just beyond the village on the right with an unobtrusive sign. From North Conway, N.H.: follow Rte. 302 through Bridgton. Charmwoods sign and driveway off Rte. 302 just before Naples village.

DOCKSIDE GUEST QUARTERS
York, Maine

"If you'll just cast off, Norman, we'll head out through the harbor and into the Atlantic!"

This was going to be a real treat for me because David Lusty was taking his mother Lois and me, along with several inn guests, on a pleasant excursion that would provide all of us with some exceptional views of York harbor and some of the beautiful homes that border it.

It was an outstanding morning in late September. The sun was sparkling on the water and we were for a short time convoyed by a group of ducklings, a part of the regular harbor contingent of mallards, while the gulls swept overhead. The white pines, firs, and native spruces which remain green throughout the year were intermixed with crimsons and oranges, as well as with the rusty greens of the hickory, sumac, and beech trees.

I've always tried to arrange to visit this part of lower Maine in late September or during the early days of October because the combination of the fall colors and the waterside atmosphere make it such an enjoyable experience.

The Dockside Guest Quarters includes the original New England homestead of the 1880s, called the Maine House, and other multiunit cottage buildings of a contemporary design, each with its own porch and water view. Some have a casual studio feeling.

The innkeepers are David and Harriette Lusty. David is a real "State of Maine" man, complete with a wonderful down-east accent. They met in college and David lured Harriette to Dockside with an offer of a summer chambermaid's job. The rest is history.

As we headed out of the river, David pointed to a large orange mark on the shoreline cliff. "We have now crossed into the Atlantic Ocean," he said. "It's against the law to fish for lobsters in the York

River, but it is OK to put the lobster pots down out here," he said, indicating the dozens and dozens of bobbing markers.

He cut off the motor and pointed out a number of beautiful homes along the shoreline. "Incidentally, we have a Cliff Walk in York Harbor similar to the Marginal Way in Ogunquit," he said.

Late September and early October days in York can be spent in many different ways. There are a number of sandy beaches and swimming can be excellent when the sun is highest at midday and early afternoon. Other times it's great fun to wander along these stretches of beach and have them almost entirely to oneself. Golf and tennis are available at the golf club, the marina has rental sailboats and outboards, and guests can also visit Strawberry Banke, a Colonial restoration in nearby Portsmouth.

A few years ago David and Harriette added the Dockside Dining Room, managed by Steve and Sue Roeder, where luncheon and dinner are served, with a great many seafood specialities. One of the features of the menu is roast duckling à la Hickory Stick, which originated at the Hickory Stick Farm in Laconia, New Hampshire. Incidentally, since my last visit, John Powers, the chef, and Joanne Lees, who runs the gift shop at Dockside, were married on board the excursion steamer which plies the waters of Lake Winnipesaukee. "The wedding party took the entire ship," said David.

DOCKSIDE GUEST QUARTERS, P.O. Box 205, Harris Island Rd., York, Me. 03909; 207-363-2868. An 18-room waterside country inn 10 mi. from Portsmouth, N.H. Some studio suites in newer multi-unit cottages. York Village is a National Historic District. American plan available. Continental breakfast served to houseguests only. Dockside Dining Room serves lunch and dinner to travelers daily except Mondays. Open from Memorial Day weekend in May through Columbus Day. Lawn games, shuffleboard and badminton, fishing, sailing, and boating from premises. Golf, tennis, and swimming nearby; safe and picturesque paths and roadways for walks, bicycling, and jogging. Credit cards are not welcome for amounts over fifty dollars. Personal checks accepted for payment of food and lodgings incurred by registered guests. David and Harriette Lusty, Innkeepers.

Directions: From U.S. 1 or I-95, take the last exit before the northbound toll gate at York to Rte. 1A. Follow 1A thru center of old York Village, take Rte. 103 (a side street off Rte. 1A leading to the harbor), and watch for signs to the inn.

THE COUNTRY CLUB INN
Rangeley, Maine

Rangeley, Maine, is one of those places in the world that has a special kind of charisma. There are few locations that offer such beauty and grandeur in all seasons. The combination of wide skies, vast stretches of mountain woodland, and the placid aspect of Rangeley Lake have been drawing people to this part of western Maine long before the roads were as passable and numerous as they are today.

Innkeeper Bob Crory of the Country Club Inn, who is something of a phrase-maker, says, "The dramatic lake and mountain scenery surrounding us will tranquilize even the most jangled nerves."

He and I were sitting on the deck of the inn which, along with the lounge, the dining room, and many of the accommodations, enjoys a mind-boggling panoramic view.

"There's a funny thing about all of this," said Bob speculatively, "I've been a 'big' hotel man all my life, but even when Sue and I were managing Sebasco Lodge we always wanted to have our own small, cozy, resort inn, and we found it here. It was built by millionaire sportsmen in the 1920s and was enlarged in recent years.

"It's very handy to have an eighteen-hole par-seventy golf course a short nine-iron shot from our front door, and it's also very convenient to have the excellent fishing for square-tailed trout and landlocked salmon in all of the Rangeley lakes that are nearby."

He excused himself for a moment and Sue Cory, who is a most attractive blonde, took his place. "I see Bob's been extolling our virtues," she said with a smile. "You know, he's so enthusiastic and we've all been so happy and our guests have been so pleased with what we've done here that it's really been a wonderful experience." She shivered a little as the sun had now gone down and suggested that we go inside for a cup of tea in front of the fireplace.

The cathedral-ceilinged living room has heavy beams, wood paneling, many, many different types of comfortable sofas, armchairs, and rocking chairs. There were several jigsaw puzzles in various states of completion, a huge shelf of books, and a great moosehead over one of the two fireplaces.

"We have lots of programs going on here, including nature slide talks, barbershop quartets, bingo, movies, sing-a-longs, astronomy slide talks, and then we go out on the terrace on a clear night and try to find the stars we've been talking about.

"We have occasional dinner dances and theme parties such as luaus and Oktoberfests. We're just a short distance from Lakewood where there is one of the oldest summer theaters in Maine."

As we sat chatting for a few moments I happened to remark to Sue that I was looking for a phrase that might possibly best describe the furnishings and decor of the Country Club Inn.

"That's easy," said Bob, taking in everything in one grand gesture of his arm. "We're posh-rustic!"

THE COUNTRY CLUB INN, Rangeley, Maine 04970; 207-864-3831. A 25-room resort-inn on Rangeley Lake in Maine's beautiful western mountain-lakes country, 45 mi. from Farmington. European, modified American plans. Open mid-May to mid-Oct. Breakfast, lunch, dinner served to travelers. Near many cultural, historic, and recreational attractions. Swimming pool and lake swimming, horseshoes, bocci, and 18-hole golf course on grounds. Fishing, saddle horses, water skiing, canoeing, tennis nearby. Bob and Sue Crory, Innkeepers.

Directions: From Maine Tpke.: take Auburn Exit 12 and follow Rte. 4 to Rangeley. From Vt. and N.H.: take I-91 to St. Johnsbury; east on Rte. 2 to Gorham, and Rte. 16 north to Rangeley.

GOOSE COVE LODGE
Deer Isle, Maine

I couldn't believe it. Once again, almost a year later, to the day, I was trotting behind Elli Pavloff doing my best not to appear out of breath and feeling a little bit like either Lewis or Clark as they followed the Indian maiden through the wilds of the Northwest. Last year she had taken me to *all* of the accommodations at Goose Cove Lodge—the cabins and the cottages—and pointed out that almost every lodging room has a fireplace, and that they were all originally built so that each and every one affords a gorgeous view of Goose Cove.

Today, we were on one of the many nature walks that starts from the lodge and plunges into the woods, coming out on the rocky shore. After a few minutes of scrambling along behind her, I came out to a formation of wonderful pink granite rocks overlooking Penobscot Bay, and Elli pointed across to North Haven Island and beyond to the famous mountain at Camden where Edna St. Vincent Millay found such inspiration. She indicated a little spit of land to the north that was the town of Castine. In front of us were dozens of lobster pots bobbing on the relatively serene water.

We sat on the rocks for a moment and Elli said, "Goose Cove appeals to so many different kinds of people. We have honeymooners, senior citizens, and middle-aged folks like you and me who are beginning to creak a little. But we also have young families. It is a combination of the really spectacular beauty of the place, its privacy, and the fellowship of the gatherings in lodge, that combine to make everything a unique experience. I think the simplicity of the cottages brings the out-of-doors and nature closer to the guests. I guess I'm rhapsodizing, but this is one of the very special places with a magic all its own, and there aren't many places that are still unspoiled. We love Goose Cove. I know I'm going to miss it even while we're in France this winter, but I'll be looking forward to next spring and summer's innkeeping adventures."

We walked on farther and crossed the sandbar to Barred Island, a nature conservancy, which is accessible only at low tide. "One of our expert birdwatcher-guests drew up a list in July of over 100 different birds spotted on the lodge grounds," she said. "Several people have seen a bobcat, and baby foxes and deer may appear in September. It's quite common to see jack rabbits and other furred or quilled creatures."

Goose Cove Lodge is on the modified American plan and all guests take breakfast and dinner in the dining room. Box lunches or sandwiches which can be eaten on the beach or on the trails are cheerfully prepared by the dining room staff. Everyone gathers at the end of the day in the lodge before dinner for some of Elli's superb hors d'oeuvres and this is where the beautiful new friendships are made.

"We have various kinds of after-dinner entertainment," she commented. "We have at least two movies a week, music that might be anything from a guitar to a string quartet, at least one slide show, a jazz pianist from Baltimore is a regular, and on other occasions George and our daughter Elena might do two or three violin pieces. Their 'Twinkle, Twinkle Little Star' is noted for its delicate sentiment."

The Athena of innkeepers stood up and began striding up the beach. "The fall is lovely here," she remarked. "I wish I could preserve some of it for the summer folk to see. There's clear blue sky, blue water, dark green pines, orange leaves—a symphony of color."

GOOSE COVE LODGE, Sunset, Deer Isle, Me. 04683; 207-348-2508. A 22-room (60 people) resort-inn on beautiful Penobscot Bay approx. 1 hr. from Rte. 1 at Bucksport. Open May 1 to Oct. 15. Modified American plan June 18 to Sept. 10. Meals served to houseguests only. Swimming, boating, canoeing, hiking, and bird-watching all available at the inn. Other outdoor sports, including backroading, golf, tennis, etc., nearby. Especially adaptable for children of all ages. Elli and George Pavloff, Innkeepers.

Directions: From Bucksport, drive 4 mi. north on Rte. 1 and turn right at Rte. 15 down the Blue Hill Peninsula to Deer Isle Village. Turn right in village at sign to Sunset, Maine. Proceed 3 mi., turn right at Goose Cove Lodge sign. Follow dirt road 1½ mi. to inn.

HARTWELL HOUSE
Ogunquit, Maine

The story of my first visit to this inn begins with a sumptuous lunch at the Whistling Oyster overlooking Perkins Cove in Ogunquit. I was lamenting to John Parella that we seemed to have gone back to "square one" as far as being able to recommend an accommodation in Ogunquit.

Many years ago when I first included the Whistling Oyster, John recommended that I visit the Island House, which at that time was located just a few steps beyond the "Oyster," and for many years the combination worked very well. Then, unfortunately the Island House went out of business, and again we were faced with the original problem.

"Wait a minute!" he exclaimed, "I think I have just the place for you to see. It's called the Hartwell House, run by Trisha and Jim

Hartwell, and it's a beautiful, elegant, sophisticated small inn, actually within walking distance of where we are right now."

My first glimpse of the Hartwell House on the Shore Road leading back to the center of Ogunquit was most favorable. It was a two-story pleasantly designed building fronted with many Moorish arches. There were some gardens in the front and what appeared to be some considerable grassy acreage to the rear.

The unusually large, and attractively decorated front porch area had beautiful summer furniture with lighthearted slipcovers. There were several groups of comfortable chairs and sofas, stacks of books and magazines, and many varieties of flowers. Four houseguests were playing bridge. It had the kind of atmosphere that invited me to sit down and feel at home.

Trisha Hartwell suggested that this would be a good time for us to see the accommodations at Hartwell House since many of the guests were having dinner at the Whistling Oyster, so I embarked on a rather happy journey through a group of attractively furnished rooms, some with four-poster beds, with many antiques and beautiful bedspreads. The rooms in the back of the inn also had balconies overlooking the rear lawn.

"We're planning on making some conservative additions, including tennis courts and a gazebo," explained Trisha. "Nothing that will interfere with the very pleasant country house atmosphere. I imagine it will be a couple of years before it's all completed. Our lawn leads down to the river and our guests presently enjoy sitting quietly under the trees."

There are nine accommodations at Hartwell House including two efficiency apartments and two studios. All have private baths. These have full-sized kitchens, if the guests desire. At present there are no meals offered because Trisha is very enthusiastic about some of the nearby restaurants that serve delicious breakfasts.

Hartwell House is within walking distance of the beach, Perkins Cove, churches, and the Marginal Way. It's also on the minibus route that serves the town.

So once again I'm happy to be able to recommend lodging accommodations in Ogunquit in keeping with the elegance and tone of the Whistling Oyster, which does not have lodgings but serves both lunch and dinner. I'm certain that our readers will find the Hartwell House a very pleasant experience.

HARTWELL HOUSE, 116 Shore Road, Ogunquit, Maine 03907; 207-646-7210. A 9-room inn providing a very compatible atmosphere for a limited number of guests (4 rooms may be rented as a complete apartment). No meals offered. Open April to Nov. The ocean, Perkins Cove, the Marginal Way, Ogunquit Playhouse all within walking distance. Fishing, golf, swimming, bicycles, sailing, nearby. Shared tennis and swimming pool privileges. Not suitable for children under 14. No pets. Trisha and Jim Hartwell, Innkeepers.

Directions: Follow I-95 north through New Hampshire into Maine; take last exit before Maine toll booth; north on Rte. 1, 7 mi. to center of Ogunquit. Turn right on Shore Road approx. ¾ of mi. Hartwell House on right.

GREY ROCK INN
Northeast Harbor, Maine

"I just love honeymooners!" Janet Millet was moving deftly about in the living room at Grey Rock, laying places for the continental breakfast. The snowy napery was a fitting complement to the elegant breakfast china, and I was struck by the fact that the sitting room had now, indeed, become a bright breakfast room with a view through the trees of some of the boats on Northeast Harbor.

Carefully placing the plates, fresh breakfast rolls and breads, she continued, "I just love it when honeymooners call up to make reservations, and when possible we try to put them into the Tree House where we have a minimum stay of four nights. I think it's ideal for honeymoon couples. For one thing it is a few steps away from the main house here at Grey Rock, and it's a very cozy, rustic cottage with beamed ceilings and a Franklin stove which is sometimes used in late spring and fall. There is a small kitchen over there as well, and maybe the new bride can practice a little before starting in earnest." This last was said with a slight smile.

"Many of our honeymooners in the past years have come back for anniversaries. I find that they invariably prefer the more elegant atmosphere here in the main house."

"Elegant" is an excellent word to describe Grey Rock and almost immediately new arrivals are struck with Janet's unusual collection of wicker pieces which are rare art forms. For example, there is a tea table on wheels, a chaise lounge, three or four wicker table lamps, a wicker floor lamp, wicker love seats, a wicker desk, a wicker plant stand for two plants, and wing-backed chairs in wicker. These are all in the main sitting room and another smaller adjacent parlor.

These wicker pieces blend beautifully with the unusual collection of oriental memorabilia that Janet has gathered over the years, making this house somewhat reminiscent of a New England house of a century ago when sea captains brought back the wonderful treasure of the Orient on their clipper ships. Particularly impressive are the collection of fans and the exquisite framed oriental paintings on silk. As part of the harmonious whole, fresh flowers complete the picture.

Many beautiful and informative books with full-color illustrations on things both British and American are piled on the coffee table and again contribute to this wonderful "at home" feeling. Janet, as I have said many times, originally came from England and she brings with her the innate sophistication that comes from someone who has lived for many years among beautiful things.

Although the Tree House is certainly an ideal honeymoon hideaway, all of the lodging rooms at Grey Rock have a very romantic atmosphere. A special care has been taken by Janet to furnish them with harmonizing quilts and curtains. The beds are even turned down at night!

Grey Rock literally sits on a rocky ledge above the remainder of the town of Northeast Harbor well within its own forested area where trails lead into the woods. There is no amusement or recreation on the grounds for smaller children. The entire kaleidoscope of the wonderful natural attractions of Mt. Desert Island are literally at the front door.

GREY ROCK INN, Harborside Rd., Northeast Harbor, Me. 04662; 207-276-9360. A 12-room village inn in the town of Northeast Harbor, Me., adjacent to Acadia National Park and all of the attractions of this unusual region. European plan. Continental breakfast served to houseguests only. No other meals served. Small cottage available for minimum 4-night stay. Season from early spring to Nov. 1. Children 14 yrs. and older preferred. No pets. No credit cards. No smoking in bedrooms. Janet Millet, Innkeeper.

Directions: Located on the right-hand side of Rte. 198 approaching the town of Northeast Harbor. Note sign for inn. Do not try to make a right-hand turn at this point, but proceed about one block, turn around and approach the inn on the left up the steep hill.

HOMEWOOD INN
Yarmouth, Maine

The Homewood Inn, operated for a number of years by the Webster family, is on the shores of Casco Bay with a view of some of the 365 Calendar Islands. Many of the single and double cottages, which make up most of the inn complex, have fireplaces and are set among the juniper, cedar, maple, and Norway pine trees. There are a multitude of flowers including roses, phlox, snapdragons, marigolds, and petunias and dozens of other flowering plants and bushes.

Guests are frequently delighted to discover that they are sharing their waterside environment with many varieties of land and shore birds.

In the 1982 edition, it gave me great joy to share with you the account of the wedding of Fred and Colleen Webster's daughter, Julie, and Andrew Frank. Constant readers will be glad to know that Julie and Andy are very happy, and I saw them last fall at the Quechee Inn where they represented the Homewood at a *CIBR* inn-keepers' meeting. Julie will be back at the Homewood again during the summer of 1983.

Julie personally made all the jams and jellies at the inn and has decided to start her own business called "JF Foodstuffs." She has a teriffic grape-thyme jelly, which is a wonderful condiment for lamb, roast beef, and chicken; a great apple-ginger preserve; and also brandied cranberries. Colleen tells me that Julie's peach butter is a delight. These are all available at the inn shop.

On one of my recent trips, Fred, Colleen, and I walked around the grounds to the edge of the seawall to look at all the boats. "We have many families with children and everyone seems to enjoy being next to the water," Colleen said. The property also has a meadow and hayfield, and it is possible to walk quite deep into the fields and get a feeling of being close to the land.

"These sixteen acres are now partly utilized in two ways," she said. "Three thousand white pines have been planted out there and a local farmer has planted many acres with corn, tomatoes, beans, cucumbers, squash, and peppers. We feel good about this as we don't want to extend the building and do like to see the land utilized. We are also planning to plant Christmas trees this fall.

"We've had some auctions here this summer, all of which have been very successful. There are excellent offerings with lots of primitive and 19th-century art and Victoriana."

I'll be back visiting the Homewood during 1983 and am looking forward to a night at one of the rooms in the Maine House. Then I'll be ready for another breakfast with all the Websters and more blueberry pancakes, and further adventures of Ted and Doris Gillette, who are the denizens of the gift shop.

HOMEWOOD INN, Drinkwater Point, P.O.Box 196, Yarmouth, Me. 04096; 207-846-3351. A 46-room waterside inn in Casco Bay 20 min. north of Portland. European plan. Breakfast and dinner served to travelers daily except Mondays when a steak or lobster cookout at night is available (by advance reservation). Open June 8 through October 11. (Some rooms and cottages with kitchenettes available from mid-May and after mid-October.) Bicycles (incl. tandems), pool, tennis, croquet court, boating, hiking, salt water swimming on grounds. Golf, riding, fishing, state parks, theater nearby. Fred, Colleen, and Julie Webster Frank, Ted and Doris Gillette, Innkeepers.

Directions: From the south, take Exit 9 from Maine Tpke. (I-95) to Rte. 1-N, or Exit 17 from I-295 to Rte. 1-N, and follow signs to inn. From north (Brunswick area) from I-95, take "Yarmouth, Rte. 1" exit and follow signs to the inn.

"European Plan" means that rates for rooms and meals are separate. "American Plan" means that meals are included in the cost of the room. "Modified American Plan" means that breakfast and dinner are included in the cost of the room. The rates at some inns include a continental breakfast with the lodging.

We'll start on Maine Street, Brunswick, and glance at the large old homes on the left as we approach Bowdoin College from the center of town. Continue east on Maine Street 1½ miles and bear right on Maquoit Road to the head of Maquoit Bay (2 mi.). We can park here and walk along the shore. Back on Maquoit Road, we come to Bunganuc Road (½ mi.) and turn left to follow a winding country road past old farms and homes.

At the stop sign (1 mi.) bear left. After passing an antique shop on the left, we go down the hill to a very quaint tidal inlet at Bunganuc Landing. Have your camera ready!

We'll continue parallel to Maquoit Bay (a well-known duck habitat) as we enter Freeport and turn left at the sign to Flying Point Road (3 mi.). After three miles of winding road, we can park at the end of the peninsula before the "Road Ends" sign and walk the lane between the summer cottages. At the end, we'll see a tiny island which can be reached at low tide.

We return on Flying Point Road to Burnett Road (2 mi.). Turn left and follow the dirt road through open country (we can catch a glimpse of water on our left) past the headquarters of the Wolf's Neck Farm (famous for organic beef). Cross a narrow wooden bridge over a tidal inlet and make a sharp left by the yellow house onto Wolf's Neck Road (1½ mi.).

Now for a wonderful drive on a dirt road past the cattle barn and ancient salt box house to the new state park. Here we find picnic areas and paths through the pines to the water. Or, we can continue on through the forest to the dead-end sign and enjoy the pastoral setting of grazing cattle. As we head back up the road, we see the Castle Tower peeking across the South Freeport Harbor.

Returning on Wolf's Neck Road, we turn left three miles later on Flying Point Road and enter the outskirts of Freeport. At South Street (2 mi.) by the Civil War Monument, turn left. This road becomes South Freeport Road and we pass Porter's Landing, a haven for lobster boats. At the stop sign, turn left on Main Street and we reach the South Freeport harbor where we can have a delicious lobster roll on the dock by the marina. We'll see tiny "Pound of Tea" island offshore. We think South Freeport has the prettiest harbor on the coast and we'll get a good vantage point by turning left at the top of the hill on Harraseeket Road. Surrounded by old colonial homes and with the water on our left, we'll have a pleasant short drive (or walk) to the Castle Tower, which is all that's left of a turn-of-the-century hotel.

Back again to Main Street, turn left, and make another left on the South Freeport Road. After 1½ miles, turn left on Staples Point Road for a visit to Winslow Park (2½ mi.). Have a swim in Casco

Bay or hike along the shore. Let's not miss the duck decoy shop at the entrance to the park.

As we return from Winslow Park, take a left at South Freeport Road. At the stop sign (2 mi.) cross U.S. 1 North and enter U.S. 1 South (which becomes 295). Exit at Yarmouth and we are on Route 1 again.

The Homewood Inn
Falmouth, Maine

On the western side of Mount Desert Island, between Bass Harbor and Tremont, turn off Route 102 on to a road leading to Bernard, Maine. It is approximately 3/4 of a mile down to the end of the little peninsula of land, overlooking a typical work harbor, with lobster boats lying at anchor or moving to and fro hauling traps. Fishing piers line the harbor. Black's Lobster Pound is near the end of the road with fresh lobster available, custom picked, steamed, and ready to eat at the picnic tables provided. There are two antique shops on the way, one specializing in glassware and small antique items.

John Madeira, Jr.
The Claremont
Southwest Harbor, Maine

THE PENTAGOET INN
Castine, Maine

September in Castine. The remarkably preserved elm trees were now showing signs that fall was definitely on the way, and the bright yellow paint of the Pentagoet Inn, now accented by the green awning over the front porch, seemed to have a special autumnal glow. All of the clichés about the wine of the September air were in full use today.

I stood in the middle of the village street looking straight down to the harbor where a maple tree hanging over the road near the water's edge had early streaks of red and yellow foretelling its spectacular color to come. Out in the harbor one of the famous Windjammers rode easily on the passive waters and on the far side of the bay the low, tree-covered hills gave a feeling of snug security.

Natalie Fulton Saunders, the proprietress and innkeeper of the Pentagoet for these last few years, came skipping gaily down the front steps towards me. "Can it be that our little village of Castine is so quiet that you feel you can set up shop in the middle of the road?" I avoided the question neatly by suggesting that her usually steely-eyed gaze was a bit bluer than I remembered on my last visit.

"Oh, yes," she responded. "I think it is our nearness to the water. Many people have commented that my grey eyes are turning more blue." She took me by the right arm, as one might direct a

misbehaving child, and said, "Come inside for breakfast. Your bran muffins that I've been baking since 6:00 A.M. are piping hot."

We walked across the front porch past many guests who were

enjoying a morning breakfast, and I joined a large table in the main dining room. There were several people that I had met on a previous trip, including Jean de Raat from the Water Witch, a store specializing in imported batik clothing, just across the street.

Natalie's music box was sending out melodious strains in the background. "I've had it for a year now," she said. "It's Austrian. I bought it from an antique dealer and I really love it. We play it on the porch and it attracts people from all over."

The Pentagoet is a small, Victorian-style inn at the end of a peninsula on the unspoiled coast of Penobscot Bay.

My lodging room had a washbowl and a shared bath. In fact there were two baths within just a few steps of the door. The rather austere white walls were relieved by some colorful prints. The double bed had a comfortable mattress and there was an old-fashioned table with a lamp beside it. A chest of drawers, a comfortable chair, and two braided rugs completed the furnishings. Other bedrooms are similarly furnished and all of them have a wealth of books, magazines, and fesh flowers in season.

The living room has a very friendly arrangement of comfortable furniture, and classical music is usually playing in the background. I have enjoyed many a lively discussion in this setting.

The single-entrée dinners are not only tasty, but fun. I've met quite a few of the local townspeople, as well as staff members from the Maine Maritime Academy, on my many visits.

The Pentagoet Inn—which I've heard referred to as "Natalie's Pentagon"—is a delightful experience, and Castine's surprising history and the marvelous backroading in the east Penobscot Bay region, where trees, birds, flowers, and marine life abound, provide an ideal setting.

I'd like to stay longer to see if my grey eyes turn blue, too.

THE PENTAGOET INN, Castine, Maine 04421; 207-326-8616. A 14-room inn in a seacoast village on the Penobscot Peninsula, 36 mi. from Bangor. Some rooms with shared baths. Closed Jan., Feb. (March). Breakfast and a single-entrée, prix-fixe dinner are served. Tennis, swimming, backroading, village strolling, craft shops, chamber music concerts, Bar Harbor, and Blue Hill nearby. Clean, leashed pets permitted. Natalie Saunders, Innkeeper.

Directions: From the south, follow I-95 to Brunswick and use Rte. 1 exit. Follow Rte. 1 to a point 3 mi. past Bucksport. Turn right on Rte. 175 to Rte. 166 to Castine.

PILGRIM'S INN
Deer Isle, Maine

Travelers really have to be looking for Deer Isle and Pilgrim's Inn. It's thirty miles down from coastal Route 1 which runs between Bucksport and Ellsworth. The way leads through the Blue Hill Peninsula, across Eggemoggin Reach on the high suspension bridge to Little Deer, along the snaking causeway to Deer Isle, and then a few miles more to the village.

Spoken of locally as "The Harbor," the village of Deer Isle is one block long at its business center, and Pilgrim's Inn stands at the far end of this block. The inn is a four-storied gambrel-roofed great house which has overlooked the Long Harbor on the front and the millpond in the rear since 1793.

Dud Hendrick, who, with his wife Jean, is the innkeeper, was telling me about the original builder, Squire Ignatius Haskell. "His second wife was homesick for Massachusetts so he imported a master carpenter and builder from Newburyport to build a house in the north shore tradition. I've heard that it was modeled after Howe's Tavern in South Sudbury, which later became Longfellow's Wayside Inn. Much of the work was done on the mainland, including the magnificent carvings and paneling, and then floated across from Camden to Deer Isle."

"What I think is unusual is that the building has remained almost completely unchanged," said Jean, as she joined us. "It has the classical Colonial feature of two large rooms plus a kitchen on the ground floor. One is our Common Room and the other has been known as the Tap Room. Both have very large fireplaces and low ceilings. Food during earlier times was cooked over one of the fireplaces and then carried upstairs to the formal dining room. We still use the dining room during the early spring and late fall, but during the summer dinners are served in the old barn out in back."

The twelve guest bedrooms are mostly quite large and little changed from the Colonial and Federalist days of Squire Haskell. There are richly hued pine floorboards, a woodstove, a queen-sized bed, old wooden furniture, and an unusual selection of books and magazines in each bedroom.

About six o'clock in the evening every day, the Common Room becomes the center of attraction and conversation for everyone. Dud and Jean make certain that all the guests are well introduced and feel comfortable, and by the time dinner is served everyone feels like old friends.

There might be entertainment during dinner because there are many gifted musicians in the area. On my last visit there were two guitar-playing singers who offered pleasant folk songs in many

languages and, as one comment in the guest book relates, "The best thing we're taking away with us is memories of some warm, lovely people who made our stay such a pleasure . . . see you next year."

"Doing nothing pleasantly" is at the top of the list of activities in the inn's brochure. "This is not the place for anyone in a hurry," says Jean. "Guests paddle on the mill pond, bicycle around the island, go clamming, visit Stonington Harbor with its daily lobster and fish catch, take the mailboat excursion to nearby islands, and especially visit the local silversmiths, weavers, potters, and photographers in their studios and galleries."

Taken in whole or in parts, the Pilgrim's Inn and Deer Isle is a most unusual experience.

PILGRIM'S INN, Deer Isle, Me. 04627; 207-348-6615. A 12-room inn, some with shared baths, in a remote island village on the Blue Hill Peninsula on the Maine coast. Modified American plan, May 15 to Nov. 1, includes a hearty breakfast and a creative dinner. In season outside dinner reservations accepted. A 4-day minimum reservation is requested in August. Bicycles, badminton, ping-pong, regulation horseshoes, croquet, and a rowboat for the millpond on the grounds. The Deer Isle area is replete with all types of cultural and recreational advantages including golf, fishing, sailing, hiking, and browsing. Dud and Jean Hendrick, Innkeepers.

Directions: From Boston, take I-95 to Brunswick exit. Take coastal Rte. 1 north past Bucksport. Turn right on Rte. 15 which travels to Deer Isle down the Blue Hill Peninsula. At the village, turn right on Main Street (Sunset Rd.) and proceed one block to the inn on the left side of the street, opposite the harbor.

THE WHISTLING OYSTER
Ogunquit, Maine

It is most gratifying for me to realize how many years I've been visiting The Whistling Oyster restaurant on Perkins Cove in Ogunquit, Maine; I've been sharing my lunches and dinners with readers of *CIBR* since the late 1960s.

I am most fortunate to have known Mr. John Parella during all these years, and he and I often recall the early days when he was still on the faculty of the Music School at Temple University in Philadelphia, and was a commuting innkeeper and voice instructor.

On this particular visit, John and I once again were looking out over the waters of Perkins Cove where the lobster boats were coming in under the drawbridge and many smaller boats darted among the moored pleasure craft.

John was as enthusiastic as ever about chef Michael Allen. "He came to us directly from the Henri IV restaurant in Cambridge, and his credentials are tremendous. His awards include International Food and Wine Society's Certificate of Excellence; Confrerie des Chevaliers du Tastevin's Award of Excellence; and Boston Magazine's 'Best French Restaurant.' He studied French cuisine, both classic and nouvelle, with Madeleine Kamman, and he has received top reviews from the *Boston Globe* and the *Boston Herald American.*"

Meanwhile, the waiter had served our lunch and this time I forsook my usual order of crabmeat Snug Harbor for an order of eggs Benedict which looked almost too good to eat. Our conversation swung around to the best times to visit Maine. "Oh, to me June and September are just wonderful," John said. "It's considerably less crowded and there's more elbow room and more fun. By the way," he said, "have you ever walked the Marginal Way? You know if you really want to feel close and intimate with the sea, this is *the* thing to do for visitors in Ogunquit. The path works its way along the rocky shore and it's a wonderful experience with the movement of the waves and the swooping of gulls overhead."

I would like to share a letter I received from Rick and Bev Litchfield at the nearby Captain Lord's Mansion in Kennebunkport. It says in part, "The Whistling Oyster was closed in January when we were making plans for our wedding a few years ago, so we went to another restaurant. Forty-eight hours before we were to arrive, the restaurant could not meet our needs. At 9:30 in the evening we called John and asked if there was any way he could accommodate thirty people for our wedding party and dinner. He called back after consulting the chef, and the plans were all confirmed that evening.

"Our dinner was superb. John and his maitre d' served us personally and nothing could have been more perfect. We're so happy and will always feel a warm glow towards John Parella and the Whistling Oyster."

When I reminded John of that incident, he gave his staff credit. "Actually," he said, "I think it's one of the reasons we decided to remain open in the wintertime and got into a program of international dinners."

One further note: the parking lot for The Whistling Oyster is not the parking lot immediately across from the restaurant itself. Go another fifty yards or so farther, turn left, and follow the road about 100 yards to the Whistling Oyster parking sign.

THE WHISTLING OYSTER, Perkins Cove, Ogunquit, Me. 03907; 207-646-9521. A waterfront restaurant in Perkins Cove at Ogunquit. No lodgings. Lunch and dinner served daily. Open throughout the year. Reservations advisable. Nearby CIBR overnight lodgings can be found at The Hartwell House, Ogunquit (207-646-7210). John Parella, Innkeeper.

Directions: From the south, take the York exit from I-95. Turn north on Rte. 1 to Bourne Lane. Turn right on Shore Rd. for about 1 mi. to Perkins Cove turnoff.

I do not include lodging rates in the descriptions, for the very nature of an inn means that there are lodgings of various sizes, with and without baths, in and out of season, and with plain and fancy decoration. Travelers should call ahead and inquire about the availability and rates of the many different types of rooms.

SQUIRE TARBOX INN
Westport Island, Maine

I was driving north up the coast of Maine on U.S. Route 1. I passed through Bath and started looking for Route 144, which turns off the main road on the right and leads to Westport Island. I remembered that if I passed the Wiscasset Information Booth I had gone too far. Sure enough, there was the sign, so I turned right and followed the blacktop road through the countryside and over the bridge. There were about six more twisty-turny miles, and then once again I saw a familiar shape that is the Squire Tarbox Inn.

I found everything literally in apple-pie order, because on that particular day there were three apple pies fresh out of the oven, and Anne McInvale invited me to have a bite with a piece of delicious cheese.

I carried the apple pie along with a glass of cold milk out to the freshly painted deck with the new wooden tables and gay umbrellas in a sheltered nook between two of the buildings. Elsie White pointed with pride to a screened-in gazebo decorated with pots of geraniums.

The Squire Tarbox is a very quiet inn in a section of Maine that is sufficiently off the beaten track to be unspoiled and natural. The bedrooms are very cozy in a real "upcountry" manner, and there is plenty of opportunity to sit around in front of the fireplaces in the sitting and dining rooms and enjoy conversation.

Guests can go blueberrying or raspberry picking, walk down the pine-needled path to Squam Creek, and swim or fish in Montsweag Bay, nearby.

"What's for dinner tonight, Anne?" I asked.

"Well, first of all, you know we only serve dinner to our house-guests and we get spectacular fresh native seafood and have always made it a focal point of our menu. Tonight we're having poached North Atlantic salmon served with a dilled sour cream sauce topped

with our own feathery fresh dill. The lusciousness of this dish is definitely one which begins with the eye. The rich salmon color with the delicacy of the sauce and the dill is a visual delight. Another addition this year was halibut steaks served with *maitre d' hotel* butter."

"Our meals always feature the seasonal bounty of our garden," chimed in Elsie. "We're especially fond of our black-seeded Simpson lettuce, but I think the favorite of our guests is our juicy red ripe tomatoes served with either our own special vinaigrette or with our homemade basil mayonnaise."

"We had a wonderful spring for fiddlehead ferns, so in addition to our own garden vegetables, we often featured lovely little fiddleheads with their special, delicate flavor."

I'll have to add to this recitation of delightful culinary treats the fact that the chocolate-butterscotch pie topped with whipped cream is simply indescribable. One guest labeled it, "the ultimate chocolate experience."

If reading this description about the Squire Tarbox *sounds* irresistible, believe me, it *is*.

THE SQUIRE TARBOX INN, Westport Island, R.D. #2, Box 2160, Wiscasset, Me. 04578; 207-882-7693. An 8-room restored Colonial home on Rte. 144 in Westport, 10 mi. from Wiscasset. Six rooms with shared baths; two with private bath. All lodgings include continental breakfast. European plan. Dinners served to house-guests only. Open from Memorial Day to mid-Oct. Golf, tennis, pool, sailing, exploring, walking nearby. No pets. Anne McInvale and Elsie White, Innkeepers.

Directions: From Maine Tpke. take Exit 9. Follow Rtes. 95 and 1 to Rte. 144, 8 mi. north of Bath. Follow Rte. 144 to Wiscasset-Westport Bridge. Inn is located 6 mi. south of bridge on Westport Island.

"European Plan" means that rates for rooms and meals are separate. "American Plan" means that meals are included in the cost of the room. "Modified American Plan" means that breakfast and dinner are included in the cost of the room. The rates at some inns include a continental breakfast with the lodging.

THE WATERFORD INNE
East Waterford, Maine

"We're such a tiny inn," said Barbara Vanderzanden as she set down the tray with some teacups, "that we personally speak to *every* guest who stays with us. As you see everybody is drawn together in our living room and oftentimes we spend the entire evening with our guests chatting or playing bridge. Because we are small our guests get to know one another, too. Many nights they are all seated together at the dinner table and we can hear them exchanging addresses for future visits. Recently two couples got together to make reservations for the next *CIBR* inn to be visited the following evening. Two couples met here in the summer last year and returned to spend New Year's Eve."

At The Waterford Inne, located in the little-known Oxford Hills area of western Maine, "small and tidy" is beautiful. The original house was built in 1825 and has five upstairs bedrooms that step out of the 19th century. These were augmented by four additional rooms created in a wing leading to a very large barn. A recent addition to the building by Barbara and her mother Rosalie has provided greater convenience for the kitchen chores, and also for Barbara and Rosalie's own personal space. Jan Lindstrom's new sketch of the inn shows how well it balances off the remainder of the house.

Innkeeping responsibilities are divided between this mother-daughter team, both of whom had been schoolteachers from Oradel, New Jersey. "Mother is the real creative force in the kitchen," said Barbara, as we settled down in the main living room with its warm barnboards and views of the hills in two directions. "She's developed some wonderful recipes and does all the cooking. I do the serving and the two of us pitch right in and take care of all the other chores in the house.

"We serve a fixed-price dinner every evening for both house-guests and visitors. We do all our own baking and in season use only fresh vegetables from our garden. Often there's less than an hour between picking and eating!

"Cross-country skiing is very popular here," Rosalie continued. "We have some trails leading from our own property into the woods and beyond. People also bring their own snowshoes. In warmer weather, there are dozens of diversions."

Rosalie excused herself to run into the kitchen and Barbara went out to greet some new guests, leaving me the opportunity to contemplate the many books and periodicals. There was also a whole shelf filled with such parlor games as backgammon, checkers, and chess. The coffee table carved out of natural wood was also a cribbage board, and in one corner an old buggy seat was piled high with magazines.

Rosalie returned with a letter in her hand, saying, "Here's a letter from one of our guests that I thought you'd find interesting." The letter read in part, "After our visit with you I feel as if we've been friends for years—something very rare indeed in this hectic and sometimes uncaring world that we live in."

THE WATERFORD INNE, Box 49, East Waterford, Maine 04233; 207-583-4037. A 9-room farmhouse-inn in the Oxford Hills section of southwest Maine, 8 mi. from Norway and South Paris. Closed March and April. Breakfast and dinner served to travelers by reservation. European plan. Within a short distance of many recreational, scenic, and cultural attractions in Maine and the White Mountains of New Hampshire. Cross-country skiing and badminton on grounds. Lake swimming, golf, rock hunting, downhill skiing, hiking, canoeing nearby. No credit cards. Alcoholic beverages not served. Well-behaved pets welcome; however, advance notification is required and a fee is charged. Rosalie and Barbara Vanderzanden, Innkeepers.

Directions: From Maine Turnpike: use Exit 11, follow Rte. 26 north approximately 28 mi. into Norway, then on Rte. 118 west for 8 mi. to Rte. 37 south (left turn). Go ½ mi., turn right at Springer's General Store, up the hill ½ mi. From Conway, New Hampshire: Rte. 16 to Rte. 302 east to Fryeburg, Me. Take Rte. 5 out of Fryeburg to Rte. 35 south, thence to Rte. 118, which is a left fork (with Rte. 35 going right). Continue on Rte. 118 east, past Papoose Pond camping area, then watch for right turn onto Rte. 37. Go ½ mi. to Springer's General Store. Take immediate right turn, ½ mi. up hill.

WHITEHALL INN
Camden, Maine

I'd like to share some portions of a letter I received from a reader who lives in Billerica, Massachusetts. She is telling about her visit to the Whitehall Inn:

"The inn was humming with activity when I arrived—parking places were few and far between, but I squeezed my mid-sized car between a lamp post and an Audi with Illinois license plates. This was obviously a popular place for guests and natives alike. Even so, as busy as they were, they managed to find an empty table for me where I sat and drank in my surroundings. The lights were low, Mozart filled the air, the candles glimmered behind cut-glass holders which in turn reflected the light a hundred times over. Flowers leaned gently on the rims of their vases and all of these things made for a softly elegant, quietly enjoyable evening. The meal and service were both excellent. I left the dining room with a nicely full, nicely relaxed feeling.

"To my delight, Camden had already begun to change from its green summer uniform to its gold and red autumn wardrobe. Sitting atop Mt. Battie, camera slung over one shoulder, binoculars over the other, I didn't know which to reach for first as the sun broke through the morning haze scattering light over the bay below setting it a-shimmering like a basketful of precious gems. A Windjammer sailed gracefully into view, its many sails filled with enough wind to carry it smoothly and serenely to the harbor. Such peace, such tranquility, such perfection—all here this day in Camden, Maine.

"I ventured forth into Camden State Park and later walked

around the village finding many new and exciting things in the shops.

"Later back at the inn I struck up the acquaintance of some

other guests and noted a couple playing checkers in one corner of the lobby. I reached for one of the many worn leatherbound books and chose a Dickens novel, the pages of which were yellowed with age and dog-eared from obvious constant use.

"Mr. Dewing inquired after my day's activities and was interested in hearing how I had bided my time in a town he obviously loves a great deal.

"Next morning I was invited to eat breakfast with my new friends and we had a lovely conversation over blueberry griddle cakes, spicy sausages, and cold, fresh orange juice."

Thank you very much. On my most recent visit to the Whitehall I arrived at 7:45 A.M. on a busy August morning, and for any readers who wonder what proprietors do at that hour even in a sizable inn, let me say that I found Ed at the front desk checking people out and giving last-minute directions and advice, and his wife Jean and daughter Heidi in the kitchen cooking lots and lots of tempting, inviting-looking sausages and scrambled eggs. Chip Dewing and his bride of six months, Kathy, were also on morning shift. Come to think of it, I never did see Jonathan, the other son. For any of you who are considering going into the country-inn business this is a clue to how early and how hard innkeepers work.

WHITEHALL INN, Camden, Me. 04843; 207-236-3391. A 38-room village inn in a Maine seacoast town, 75 mi. from Portland. Modified American plan omits lunch. Breakfast and dinner served daily to travelers. Open, May 25 to Oct. 15. Tennis, bicycles, shuffleboard, harbor cruises on grounds. Golf, hiking, swimming, fishing, day sailing nearby. No pets. Jean and Ed Dewing, Innkeepers.

Directions: From Maine Tpke. take Exit 9 to coastal Rte. 95. Proceed on 95 to Rte. 1 at Brunswick. Follow Rte. 1 to Rte. 90 at Warren, to Rte. 1 in Camden. Inn is located on Rte. 1, ¼ mi. north of Camden.

"European Plan" means that rates for rooms and meals are separate. "American Plan" means that meals are included in the cost of the room. "Modified American Plan" means that breakfast and dinner are included in the cost of the room. The rates at some inns include a continental breakfast with the lodging.

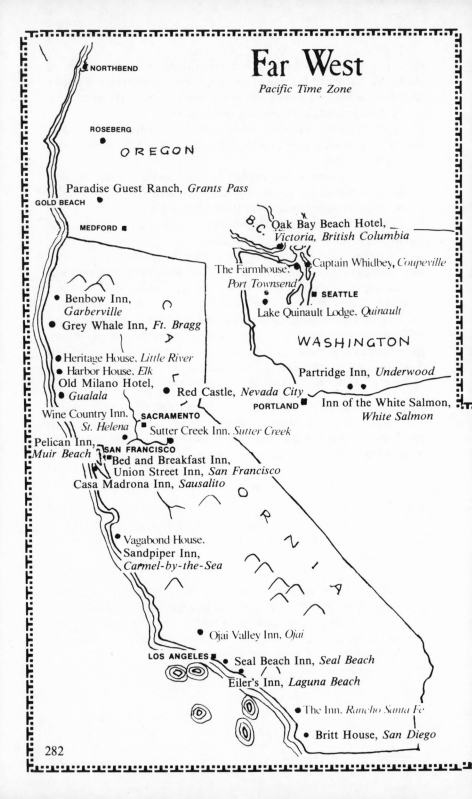

Far West

Pacific Time Zone

NORTHBEND

ROSEBERG

O R E G O N

Paradise Guest Ranch, *Grants Pass*

GOLD BEACH

MEDFORD

B.C. Oak Bay Beach Hotel,
Victoria, British Columbia

The Farmhouse, Captain Whidbey, *Coupeville*
Port Townsend

SEATTLE

Benbow Inn,
Garberville Lake Quinault Lodge, *Quinault*

Grey Whale Inn, *Ft. Bragg*

W A S H I N G T O N

Heritage House, *Little River*

Harbor House, *Elk* Partridge Inn, *Underwood*

Old Milano Hotel,
Gualala Red Castle, *Nevada City*

PORTLAND Inn of the White Salmon,
White Salmon

Wine Country Inn, SACRAMENTO
St. Helena Sutter Creek Inn, *Sutter Creek*

Pelican Inn, SAN FRANCISCO
Muir Beach Bed and Breakfast Inn,
Union Street Inn, *San Francisco*

Casa Madrona Inn, *Sausalito*

O R N I A

Vagabond House,
Sandpiper Inn,
Carmel-by-the-Sea

Ojai Valley Inn, *Ojai*

LOS ANGELES Seal Beach Inn, *Seal Beach*

Eiler's Inn, *Laguna Beach*

The Inn, *Rancho Santa Fe*

Britt House, *San Diego*

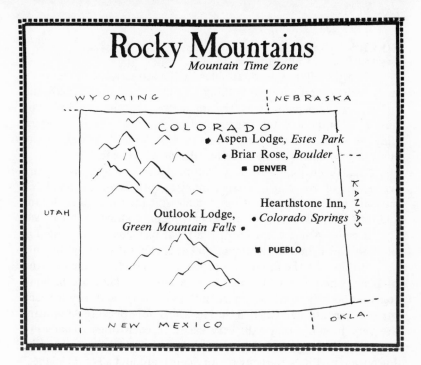

Rocky Mountains
Mountain Time Zone

WYOMING   NEBRASKA

C O L O R A D O

● Aspen Lodge, *Estes Park*
● Briar Rose, *Boulder*
■ DENVER

UTAH

KANSAS

Outlook Lodge,
Green Mountain Falls ●

Hearthstone Inn,
● *Colorado Springs*

■ PUEBLO

NEW MEXICO   OKLA.

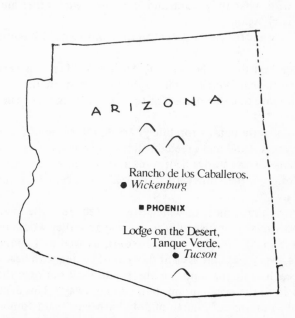

A R I Z O N A

Rancho de los Caballeros,
● *Wickenburg*

■ PHOENIX

Lodge on the Desert,
Tanque Verde,
● *Tucson*

EILER'S INN
Laguna Beach, California

Gently sheltered on three sides by the attractive, colorful two-story gallery, and with the tinkling fountain, the baby's breath, the rubber tree and palm trees, the impatiens, the philodendron, the humming birds, and the fish pool, I could have been in northern Italy, or southern France or Spain. But, indeed, I was in the courtyard of Eiler's Inn at Laguna Beach, California.

I had been joined by Kay Trepp, Annette Wirtz, and Jonna Iversen, all of whom are directly connected with the operation of this intimate bed-and-breakfast inn, which is at the same time elegant and rather sophisticated. We were enjoying the continental breakfast.

Because Annette is a European I was particularly interested in pinning down some of the things that appealed to her about the inn.

"I think it's the family atmosphere," she replied. "It's the kind of place where everyone talks to one another. They are brought together here by the atmosphere in this courtyard and they see each other at breakfast and also in the late afternoon. Because Americans are very friendly, they talk very easily to each other. That's not normally the way with Europeans, but the place is really quite European, isn't it, with the two-story courtyard and all of the plants."

Jonna also chimed in. "One of the most rewarding things about being here is that we have so many guests who return. I think we provide them with what they want and they meet each other and then all come back again."

I asked Kay what the best off-season time was to be in Laguna Beach.

"I think the best time is November, April, and May. It is very crowded here in the summertime, but in the fall and springtime we have people who love to come back. The town is quiet, and it's easier to shop and dine."

Eiler's Inn is aptly named for Eiler Larsen, the colorful Dane who for many years stood and greeted residents and visitors as they entered the village. It has twelve bedrooms and one suite. The focus of the basic design is the courtyard. "It's really the center of our world," said Kay.

The lodging rooms, most of which are entered from the open galleries are individually furnished in such a way that they would be equally at home in Maine, Ohio, or Missouri, as well as Laguna Beach. There is a very pleasant deck at the rear of the inn with beach chairs and a beach umbrella, and the guests can look out over the roofs of the town to the ocean, about half a block away. "This deck is where we have our annual Fourth of July barbecue," said Jonna.

Laguna Beach, which is a pleasant drive south of Los Angeles, is one of the most sought-after vacation spots in southern California. Besides the beach, which certainly is the big attraction in all seasons, the atmosphere could best be described as a charming art-and-shopping village with the Festival of the Arts held every year, as well as a Pageant of the Masters. One of Eiler's enjoyable features is the opportunity it offers to step inside its two-story New Orleans facade into the quiet and peaceful courtyard and leave some of the cares of the world behind.

Eiler Larsen, the tradition that you nurtured and preserved for so many years is being continued in Laguna Beach, California, at an inn that bears your name.

EILER'S INN, 741 South Coast Highway, Laguna Beach, Ca. 92651; 714-494-3004. A 13-room bed-and-breakfast inn (every room with a private bath) within a short drive of Los Angeles. Open every day. The beach is a half-block away and many recreational opportunities including tennis and golf are nearby. No pets. Kay Trepp, Jonna Iversen, and Annette Wirtz, Innkeepers.

Directions: Leave 405 Freeway or 5 Freeway to the 133 Freeway (Laguna Canyon Road) and proceed to end at Main Beach. Turn left on Coast Highway, the inn is 4 blocks south on the ocean side of the highway near Cleo St. in the middle of the block. It is possible to park briefly and then get directions for the inn parking spaces at the rear.

UNION STREET INN
San Francisco, California

"We are Edwardian, not Victorian."

Helen Stewart and I were having breakfast seated in the sunny garden at the rear of the Union Street Inn. The fragrance of lilacs, camellias, and violets filled the air, and an occasional hummingbird darted from blossom to blossom. Some guests were enjoying breakfast on the spacious deck overlooking the garden, and there was the unmistakable aroma of fresh coffee and croissants. In this quiet retreat it was difficult to realize that we were in the heart of one of San Francisco's most attractive shopping and entertaining areas.

"I say Edwardian," Helen continued, "because we're rather proud of the fact that in a city that has so much Victoriana, we are a bit different. The Edwardians, already into the 20th century, were less ostentatious than their elders. Their ornamentation was tempered by a new conservatism, and we like to feel that many of our decorations and furnishings are understatements."

Helen is a former San Francisco schoolteacher who found herself involved in a mid-life career change. She restored and remodeled this handsome turn-of-the-century building, using tones and textures that are not only in the period, but also increase the feeling of hospitality.

The five bedrooms have such intriguing names as Wildrose, Holly, Golden Gate, and English Garden. Two have private bath-

rooms, and the others have running water in the rooms and share two bathrooms.

Two of the bedrooms have queen-sized beds with canopies, two have gleaming brass beds; all have really impressive, carefully chosen antiques. The brochure of the inn explains the different color schemes for each room. "If reservations are made sufficiently in advance, and the guests can anticipate a mood, these can all be coordinated." Helen made this comment with the faint suggestion of a twinkle.

My room had one of the queen-sized beds with very pleasant dark green wallpaper and matching draperies, which were very helpful in keeping the sun from intruding too early. The walls were adorned with two of the well-known Degas prints of ballet dancers. I thought they were quite appropriate, remembering King Edward's fondness for pretty women.

One end of the room had been turned into an alcove containing a rather elegantly decorated wash basin with mirrors and generous, fluffy towels. A very handsome antique mahogany dressing table had a three-way oval mirror. This is typical of the appointments of the other bedrooms and I found many welcome living plants in all of the bedrooms.

"How far are you from Fisherman's Wharf," I asked, helping myself to another tasty croissant. "Oh, we're just minutes away," she said. "Our guests walk to Ghirardelli Square, The Cannery, and Pier 39. It's possible to take streetcars and cable cars to almost every point of interest in San Francisco."

Since that first visit on a sunny morning when we were joined by Charles Felix of the Pelican Inn at Muir Beach just a few miles north of San Francisco *(CIBR)*, Helen has converted the old carriage house at the bottom of the garden into a very fetching accommodation. It has a large bay window overlooking the garden and its own jacuzzi. It's a perfect romantic hideaway for people who want to be alone.

UNION STREET INN, 2229 Union St., San Francisco, Ca. 94123; 415-346-0424. A 5-room bed-and-breakfast inn; 3 rooms share 2 baths. Convenient to all of the San Francisco attractions including the cable car line. Breakfast only meal served. Open every day except Christmas and New Year's. Unable to accommodate children under 12. No pets. Helen Stewart, Innkeeper.

Directions: Take the Van Ness exit from Rte. 101 to Union St.; turn left. The inn is between Fillmore and Steiner on the left side of the street.

THE BED AND BREAKFAST INN
San Francisco, California

Good, bad, or indifferent, every bed-and-breakfast inn or bed-and-breakfast home on the West Coast owes a debt of gratitude to The Bed and Breakfast Inn in San Francisco. For quite a few years it was the only one of its kind, and now I understand that there are over forty in that city alone. It's a pity they did not all borrow the high standards and admirable objectives, as well as the idea, of The Bed and Breakfast Inn.

It was a wonderfully warm morning in mid-September. The sun shone down from a completely cloudless sky, and happy San Franciscans moved briskly up and down the many hills of the city

pursuing the day's occupations—the kind of a day in which I knew everything would go right, and it did.

I had walked a few blocks on Union Street, then turned on Charlton Court, and I was standing in front of one of San Francisco's Victorian houses, painted light green; wooden stairs ascended the front of the building to the very top floor. There were beautiful golden marigolds in boxes and pots placed around the porches and a birdhouse with a very chipper occupant. The sign said, "The Bed and Breakfast Inn."

The reception room apparently was used as one of the breakfast areas. It had a very light and airy feeling, enhanced by white wicker furniture, many flower arrangements, and light touches everywhere. The enticing aroma of fresh coffee filled the room, and some guests were just finishing delicious-looking croissants.

There followed in delightful order my first meeting with Marily Kavanaugh and her husband, Bob; a tour of all of rooms in the inn and a leisurely chat on the garden deck.

First the lodging rooms: some of them are named after various parts of London. There's Covent Garden, Chelsea, Green Park, and Kensington Garden. Other rooms are called The Library, Autumn Sun, The Willows, Mandalay, and The Celebration. A new accommodation, "The Mayfair Flat," has been created in the Kavanaughs' former duplex apartment on the top floor. It has a spiral staircase to a bedroom loft, a double tub, a kitchen, and a view of the Golden Gate Bridge.

Each room provides an entirely different experience. For example, many have completely different sets of sheets, pillowcases, and towels. There are all varieties of beds, including traditional shiny brass bedsteads. There are flowers everywhere, thermos jugs of ice-water, many books, baskets of fruit, an electric clock with an alarm, down pillows and gorgeous coverlets and spreads. Five of the bedrooms have their own bathrooms, and the others share. Four rooms have the garden view. I saw old-fashioned British ceiling fans in some of the rooms.

The location of the Bed and Breakfast is another virtue. Charlton Court is a little dead end street off Union, between Buchanan and Laguna. It's within easy walking distance of Fisherman's Wharf. In fact, San Francisco is such a "walking place" that it's convenient to everything. The nicest part of it is that when people get tired of walking, they can always take the cable cars!

THE BED AND BREAKFAST INN, Four Charlton Court, San Francisco, Ca. 94123; 415-921-9784. A 9-room European-style pension in the Union Street district of San Francisco. Convenient to all of the Bay area recreational, cultural, and gustatory attractions. Continental breakfast is the only meal offered. Open daily year-round. Not comfortable for small children. No pets. No credit cards. Robert and Marily Kavanaugh, Innkeepers.

Directions: Take the Van Ness Exit from Route 101 and proceed to Union Street. Charlton Court is a small courtyard street halfway between Laguna and Buchanan, off Union.

So often my guests are tired and tense from driving. Their first night here, I often suggest a walk to one of the nearby restaurants or Balboa Park, but for the adventurous ones I have my special walk which goes over a trestle bridge and a suspension bridge and passes many grand old homes from the turn of the century up to the 20s.

Head north on Fourth to Quince. Go west (left) on Quince over the trestle bridge. Turn right on Second and walk to Spruce. Walk west (left) to Front and cross a very bouncy suspension bridge. Turn right on Curlew and right on Thorn (at this corner there is a mansion that boasts, "On this spot in 18___ absolutely nothing happened"). Left on Brant, right up Upas, left on Albatross and right on Walnut (at this corner there is a lovely Victorian home that belonged to San Diego's leading art patrons, the Timkems. You will have just passed four Irving Gill houses, all of which are San Diego Historic sites, too). Go left on Front, right on Brooks, right on Third and left on Walnut. Come back "home" by turning right on First, Third, or Fourth. This walk takes about a half-hour and passes some of our nicest homes.

Daun Martin
Britt House
San Diego, California

"Ranchos Los Alamitos"—from Bettenhausen's Seal Beach Inn, go up 5th Street, two blocks north to Pacific Coast Highway, go north on Pacific Coast Highway about one mile to Westminster Avenue. Right on Westminster (just after the Market Place on a Lake Shopping area). At the first stoplight on Westminster, go left on Studebaker. You will cross the Los Angeles River and not long after crossing the Freeway, you will come to a small street— Anaheim Street. Go left to its dead end (a short distance). On the left will be a small guardhouse. Tell the guard at the gate of Bixby Knolls Estates that you are here to see the Ranchos Los Alamitos, open Wed. thru Sun., 1 to 5:00 P.M. Up a hill, past gracious homes, one suddenly comes on the Rancho, a lovely historic preserve. The Rancho sits on several acres of lovely tree-shaded grounds. Docents guide the public through the house and private garden area. This is the oldest house in the Los Angeles area and the history goes back to the 1500s when this was a Spanish land grant. It later became Mexico, then part of California, and last of all part of the Union.

Marjorie and Jack Bettenhausen
The Old Seal Beach Inn
Seal Beach, California

A favorite walk or drive with a picnic: take Union Street three blocks to Fillmore. Turn right on Fillmore and go to Chestnut. Go left on Chestnut, which is the heart of the Marina shopping district and is like turning the clock back to the 30s. There, you will find everything you could need or want for a picnic—cheese, wine, cold chicken, and even Mrs. Field's chocolate chip cookies (to die for!). Continue on Chestnut five or six blocks to signs reading "Palace of Fine Arts," turn right, and in two blocks you enter the park where you can sit on a bench by the small lake. Later, walk through the fascinating do-it-yourself museum, The Exploritorium.

Robert and Marily Kavanaugh
The Bed and Breakfast Inn
San Francisco, California

HARBOR HOUSE
Elk, California

The Harbor House was built in 1916 by a lumber company as an executive residence. The construction is entirely of redwood taken from nearby forests. Four of the five rooms of the inn have fireplaces and there are four additional cottages on the south side, all with private baths. The hand-carved and hand-fitted redwood ceiling and walls in the livng room were coated with hot beeswax in 1916, which has preserved the quality and color of the wood for over sixty years.

Innkeeper Patricia Corcoran and I strolled around the outside of the inn and I admired the unusual number of brilliantly colored flowers, including fuchsia, old-fashioned geraniums, and nasturtiums. A source of great pride for Patricia is the rapidly growing kitchen garden where many of the menu items can be freshly picked every day.

From the front of the inn there is a winding path and steps which lead down the bluff to the caverns in the rocks along the seashore below. Patricia pointed out the Victorian benches that have now been added at intervals. Many guests welcome the opportunity to "sit a spell."

"We've discovered that many of our guests are coming in what used to be called the 'off season!' For one thing, the Pacific waves crashing on the rocks are very spectacular in January, February, and March. It never gets very cold. Another awesome sight is the whales on their way south early in December until late February, when they go north again. We also have many sea otters."

Guests enjoy ocean wading, abalone and shell hunting, fishing, hiking, biking, and some beautiful backroading along the coast and in the forest. There are also many opportunities to sit in front of the big living room fireplace for an evening of guitar-playing and poetry reading.

Once again, I peeked into the room I had occupied on my previous trip, which has the four-poster bed, an old-fashioned cast iron stove, and a collection of watercolors. It has an unobstructed view of the massive rock formations with their tunnels which extend out into the blue Pacific.

Passing by the open kitchen window, I detected the intriguing aroma of freshly baked bread and rolls. "We make homemade soups like broccoli and mushroom," Patricia said, "and two of the most popular desserts are mocha-toffee pie and the Bavarian layered dessert." The recipe for that delectable mocha-toffee pie is in the new *CIBR Cookbook*.

Under Patricia Corcoran the Harbor House, which I first visited in 1976, has now earned a reputation as one of the most successful and sought-after inns in northern California. It is one of the rapidly growing number of inns with women innkeepers. I'm very proud of them all.

HARBOR HOUSE BY THE SEA, 5600 S. Hwy. #1, Box 369, Elk, Ca. 95432; 707-877-3203. A seaside inn with 5 rooms in the inn and 4 cottages, 16 mi. south of Mendocino, overlooking the Pacific. Modified American plan omits lunch. Breakfast and dinner to houseguests served daily. Open year-round. Ocean wading, abalone and shell hunting, fishing, and hiking on grounds. Biking, boating, deep-sea fishing, golf, and canoeing nearby. No credit cards. Unsuitable for children or pets. Patricia Corcoran, Innkeeper.

Directions: Take Rte. 128 from I-101 to Coast. Turn south on Hwy. #1, 6 mi. to Harbor House.

"European Plan" means that rates for rooms and meals are separate. "American Plan" means that meals are included in the cost of the room. "Modified American Plan" means that breakfast and dinner are included in the cost of the room. The rates at some inns include a continental breakfast with the lodging.

HERITAGE HOUSE
Little River, California

"To Don and Hazel Dennen, the deans of northern California innkeeping!"

We all rose as one, glasses raised high, and Don Dennen, the innkeeper of Heritage House, modestly raised his hand acknowledging the well-deserved compliments from other innkeepers who had gathered here for a day of good conversation and exchange of ideas and a lovely dinner at this truly original inn on the spectacular northern California coast.

"It doesn't seem possible that it was 1949 when Hazel and I came through here, saw the location and remembered that the farmhouse was built in 1877 by my grandfather, John Dennen. We decided to open a quiet country inn. Actually the arrangements were made within an hour. In just a few months, we built the first guest cottages."

"Well, I'm certainly glad you did," said Jane Way of the Sutter Creek Inn. "I'm sure you remember the day I came up here and you encouraged me to open my inn over in the gold country."

Patricia Corcoran from nearby Harbor House in Elk, chimed in, "I don't think we could have made it if it hadn't been for Don and Hazel. They were tremendously encouraging."

Jim Smith from the Wine Country Inn in St. Helena said, "I know that my mother and father came here many times to talk to the Dennens about innkeeping. This is my first visit, but I've never seen anything quite like it."

That particular comment, "I've never seen anything quite like it," is typical of the compliments that I receive in great numbers from readers who visit Heritage House. Here's an excerpt from a lady who had been using *CIBR* to tour California: "We drove to Heritage House which is just a lovely dream. The chicken tarragon and corned beef with ginger glaze was incredible. We stayed in one of the little cottages you mentioned back in the 1971 edition, because it was on a point overlooking both the inlet and the ocean. We set our alarm so we would be sure to see the sunrise."

"Oh, I believe I remember them," said Hazel Dennen, her eyes lighting up with a nice smile. "They sent us a long letter and said they were going to write you."

The Heritage House is about a three-hour drive up the coast from San Francisco. Although there are a few guests' rooms in the main building, most of the accommodations are in the cottages tucked unobtrusively into the landscape with an unobstructed view of the ocean. They have names inspired by early-day buildings of the area. For example, "Scott's Opera House" was the center of

entertainment on the coast with traveling minstrel shows and, later, a hand-cranked moving picture operation. It was moved to its present location overlooking the ocean. Other cottages are named "Country Store," "Bonnet Shop," "Ice Cream Parlor," "Barber Pole," "Stable," and the like. Most of the furnishings have come from the area.

"We never advertise," said Don. "All of our guests come to us because some former guest has recommended us. Frankly, we like it that way, because the place attracts the kind of people we like and many of them have become warm friends. We keep our atmosphere informal and relaxed. We don't arrange any games or activities, because we feel our guests would prefer not to be regimented. There are numerous walks along the beaches and through the forest, and we can provide our guests with ample information about circle tours along the coast and into the great redwoods."

He smiled, pulled on his earlobe, then with a twinkle in his eye said, "I can honestly say, I have never known a guest to be bored."

HERITAGE HOUSE, Little River, Ca. 95456; 707-937-5885. An elegant oceanside inn with 52 accommodations on Coast Highway #1, 144 mi. north of San Francisco, 6 mi. south of Mendocino. Modified American plan omits lunch. Breakfast and dinner served to travelers daily by reservation. Open from February through November. No pets. No credit cards. No amusements or special facilities for children. Don Dennen, Innkeeper.

Directions: From San Francisco (a 3-hr. drive); follow Rte. 101 to Cloverdale then Rte. 128 to Coast Highway #1. Inn is 5 mi. north of this junction on Hwy. #1.

BENBOW INN
Garberville, California

I first visited the Benbow Inn in 1973 and was immediately intrigued not only with its location in the glorious redwood country of northern California, but also with its design, which shows definite influences of the Art Deco of the early 1920s. There are also some touches of an English Tudor manor house found in the half-timbers, carved dark wood paneling, solid oak furniture, bookcases, hardwood floors, a truly massive fireplace in the main living room and handsome oriental rugs.

Eleanor Roosevelt visited here, Herbert Hoover fished the Eel River outside the door, and John Barrymore was an overnight guest.

The owners-innkeepers of the Benbow are Patsy and Chuck Watts, whom I first met many years ago when they owned the Vagabond House in Carmel, California. The one outstanding quality that each of them has in such marvelous quantities is enthusiasm, and all of the improvements and additions to this truly unusual northern California inn have been undertaken with great joy and love.

"Ever since day one," said Chuck Watts, "we have been very

happy and have had a really tremendous time. It's a continuing challenge and we've gotten a great deal accomplished, but I like the idea that the future is big with plans."

"We feel that we are a destination resort-inn, able to accommodate and provide amusement and diversion for all our guests of any age," chimed in Patsy. "We have acquired some fabulous antique pieces, most particularly a magnificent carved buffet for the dining room. We have added a beautiful carved mantel for the fireplace in the lobby and have installed an antique mantel and a fireplace in the cocktail lounge.

"We will be having our wine tasting in November and this has now become a semi-annual affair with about fifteen of the boutique California wineries represented."

The Benbow is, indeed, a destination resort-inn—in addition to swimming, it now offers tennis on two new tennis courts nearby, a good golf course within walking distance, hiking, and magnificent backroading. By the way, it's very accessible by public transportation since the Route 101 buses stop almost at the front door.

At Christmastime there's a twelve-foot tree with teddy bears playing drums hanging from every branch. Under the tree there are Patsy's very special antique, oversized toys. An antique sleigh is on the front porch filled with presents and wreaths. Holly and masses of decorations are all over the inn.

On Christmas Day there is a special two-seating Christmas dinner and everyone has a wonderful time.

Incidentally, in the fall and all through the holidays, English tea and scones are served in the lobby. Chuck's mother, Marie, is the tea lady.

The Benbow also has a film library with over 75 classic films. These are shown every evening. On my last visit I cheered and wept a little at James Cagney's great portrayal of George M. Cohan in *Yankee Doodle Dandy.*

Patsy, Chuck, and Muffin (their gorgeous Afghan hound, the most photographed canine in northern California) are having a wonderful time greeting guests, sharing their enthusiasm, and providing their own bubbling brand of warmth and hospitality. In short, they're model innkeepers. I'm glad they and the Benbow Inn found each other.

BENBOW INN, 445 Lake Benbow Drive, Garberville, Ca. 95440; 707-923-2124. A 70-room English Tudor inn in the redwood country of northern California. On Rte. 101 near the Benbow State Park. European plan. Breakfast, lunch, and dinner served to travelers daily. Open March 26 to Nov. 28; Re-open Dec. 17 for holiday season. Swimming on grounds; golf, tennis adjacent. Hiking, magnificent backroading, and tennis nearby. Chuck, Patsy, and Muffin Watts, Innkeepers.

Directions: From San Francisco follow Rte. 101 north 200 mi. and exit at Benbow.

BRITT HOUSE
San Diego, California

January 12, 1980, I received a very spritely letter from Daun Martin, innkeeper at Britt House along with her husband Robert Hostick, as follows:

"Last February my husband and I acquired a lovely white Victorian home which is a historic site. From February to November we sanded, scraped, and peeled wallpaper and paint. We opened November 10, 1979 (five minutes before our first open house we were still painting and planting).

"We now have eight large bedrooms, each decorated differently with antiques, wallpapers reminiscent of the Victorian era, fresh flowers and plants, and original drawings by my husband. We have four bathrooms, one with a sauna and one with two tubs and bubble bath. There is a large parlor with a basket of books for guests to choose from and a grand piano for them to play. We have no televisions or telephones in the rooms.

"Each morning I prepare breakfast for the guests, which they may have in their rooms, in the dining room, or in the parlor. This is such a romantic place that most guests opt for their rooms. I make breads fresh-out-of-the-oven daily and we squeeze fresh orange juice, and include a hardcooked egg. We also grind Viennese coffee each morning and filter it into a thermal pot, garnished with a cinnamon stick. We do a new yeast bread each day and never the same bread twice during the week."

In November of 1981 I discovered that that letter was very explicit and truthful as far as it went, but it didn't go far enough. For example, Britt House itself is a Victorian delight, one of the few in San Diego. There are two striking features: one is a tower which could grace an inn on the banks of the Rhine, and the other is a truly magnificent, massive stained glass window on the west side of the house. The Victorian staircase permits a close examination of the many intricate designs and figures in the window.

Daun and Robert are a perfect team to extend hospitality to guests of this bed-and-breakfast inn. He is a freelance artist and designer and there are many examples of his work throughout the inn, which blend beautifully with the rich woods and elaborate designs. Daun's warmth and good sense of humor came through for me during a long conversation I had with her in the kitchen while she was preparing breakfast. "We're delighted with everything," she said. "It's nice being so close to Balboa Park. I'm so pleased when our guests discover what a wonderful experience they can enjoy here in San Digeo."

There are dozens of extra touches to be found in every room and parlor in the house. There are one-of-a-kind antiques, such as platform rockers, wicker trunks containing extra patchwork quilts, and each room has a basket of towels. I understand that Robert and Daun are collecting photographs of their grandfathers and grand- mothers with which to adorn the walls. Each of the rooms has a distinctive name, such as Governor's Room, Ibis Room, and Summer House Room.

BRITT HOUSE, 406 Maple St., San Diego, Ca. 92103; 714-234- 2926. A 9 (8½)-room bed-and-breakfast inn with shared baths located just a short distance from Balboa Park with its world- famous zoo, Museum of Art, Man and Natural History, Reuben H. Fleet Space Theater, and the beaches, desert country, and Mexico (13 mi.). Breakfast only meal served (special dinners can be arranged with advance notice). Open all year. Sauna on grounds; jogging, biking, skating, bicycles nearby. No pets. Not particularly suitable for young children. Daun Martin and Robert Hostick, Innkeepers.

Directions: Take Airport-Sassafrass turnoff coming south on Hwy. 5. Proceed on Kettner. Turn left on Laurel; left on Third; right on Nutmeg; right on Fourth St., and come down one block to the corner of Fourth and Maple.

OJAI VALLEY INN
Ojai, California

I well remember my first trip to the Ojai Valley Inn. It was in the late '60s, in February, when the sun was shining brightly on the beautiful mountain-ringed valley. My telephone call back to the Berkshires disclosed that there were at least fourteen inches of fresh snow on the ground and it was still snowing!

The only decision I had to make was whether to play golf or tennis or go horseback riding. What a shame to miss all the snow-shoveling and traffic tie-ups!

This is a place where sports and the weather get together. Innkeeper Bill Briggs explained to me that the mountains provide a year-long shelter from fog, smog, or dampness. "Temperatures are moderate, from 70 to 90 degrees in summer," he explained, "and from 60 to 85 degrees in winter. You know, we are 1000 feet up so the air is quite dry."

These factors make it perfect for sports enthusiasts since golf, tennis, riding and swimming can be enjoyed year-round. The Club has its own 6800 yard par 70 golf course with a natural rolling terrain that is beautifully maintained. Ray Reitzel is still the tennis pro, and each time I have visited he's managed to scare up a game of singles or to fit me into some doubles.

I might add that none of these attractions has changed in over ten years, and the inn is even getting larger! What has pleased me most is the fact that I've received so many letters from readers who enjoy the somewhat posh four-sport facilities. It's larger than the average inn in this book.

On my most recent visit, I had enough time to go horseback riding in the mountains. The inn has its own stable, and there are hundreds of miles of trails through the valley and into the adjoining ranch country.

I also enjoy having lunch out on the terrace. It is really a delightful experience. I pointed out to Bill that the beautiful tree in the middle of the terrace was missing. "Yes," he said, "we hated to take it down, but it had finally reached the point where it had to go. However, we've replaced it with some new young trees that will soon be as beautiful as our old friend. In fact the birds are beginning to nest in them already."

Birds, flowers, beautiful sunshine and clean fresh air abound here. Bill explained that the word Ojai, which is pronounced "O-hi," is the Indian word for "the nest." I wasn't surprised when I realized that it actually nestles in the vast amphitheatre of Sierra Madre mountains, about fourteen miles from the shores of the Pacific. "It's

really quite different from the rest of California," Bill said. "Many of our visitors love it so much they come back and buy some land."

At the Ojai Valley Inn gentlemen are requested to wear jackets and ties to dinner, and ladies usually wear dresses or pants suits in the evening. When I commented on this to Bill, he said, "Our guests tell us that they prefer it this way."

OJAI VALLEY INN & COUNTRY CLUB, Ojai, Ca. 93023; 805-646-5511. A 113-room resort-inn with its own championship golf course, 12 mi. northeast of Ventura on U.S. 33. American plan. Breakfast, lunch, and dinner served to travelers daily. Open year-round. Tennis, riding, heated pool, golf, and bicycles on the grounds. No pets. Bill Briggs, Innkeeper.

Directions: From the Ventura Freeway, exit at Hwy. 33.

I do not include lodging rates in the descriptions, for the very nature of an inn means that there are lodgings of various sizes, with and without baths, in and out of season, and with plain and fancy decoration. Travelers should call ahead and inquire about the availability and rates of the many different types of rooms.

CASA MADRONA HOTEL
Sausalito, California

"This," said Debra Boyer, giving her long Victorian skirt a special twirl, "is the Bordello Room!" She ushered me into a lodging room resplendent with red-flocked wallpaper and a red velvet quilt on the bed, both of which were delightfully accented with lace. It has a very pleasant view of the bay and a uniquely shaped lamp. There's a little corner sink with rose buds. "Of course it's all done in fun," she said. "However, at one time rumor has it that our lovely Casa Madrona of today was indeed a bordello. I think there's

something rather charming and naughty about that, don't you?"

The house was converted to an inn in 1910 and for over fifty years managed to endure a colorful history, ranging from a bordello to a beatnik crash pad in the Fifties. In 1976, John Mays, a local commenced extensive renovations that included everything from redecorating and refurnishing each room to shoring up the foundation.

Through Mays' efforts, the elegant Victorian atmosphere has been preserved and augmented by conveniences like small refrigerators in most of the rooms and cottages and continental breakfast served on the veranda overlooking the truly magnificent harbor.

We continued our tour of the five rooms on the first floor, all comfortable, light and airy—some with crisp white wicker and others with a French country air in more golden tones. There are eight rooms on the second floor, many with striking views of the harbor. One in particular in natural redwood trim and floors, with exposed brick and a nautical lighting theme, appealed to me very much. The three cottages, adjacent to the hotel on the hillside, have all the charm of the hotel rooms and boast a breakfast served in bed.

A French restaurant on the hotel ground floor offers a romantic candlelit dining room with a sweeping harbor view. Specialties include pigeons de Berville, veau St. Amour, and some very fascinating desserts including peach flambe and cherries jubilee.

Of course, Debra and I ended up on the veranda overlooking the harbor and she observed that Sausalito is a well-known artists' community with several art galleries nearby as well as other shops. "It's a wonderful shopping area," she said, "and there is a ferry service just a half-block away that takes you to downtown San Francisco. It's the best of both worlds."

Since my most recent visit, 16 new bedrooms have been planned to be opened in spring 1983. The rooms all with their own private decks overlooking the bay and most with fireplaces are situated on the hillside below the old hotel.

CASA MADRONA HOTEL, 156 Bulkley Avenue, Sausalito, Calif. 94965; 415-332-0502. A 29-room (plus three cottages) Victorian-style, 97-year-old mansion situated on a hillside with a splendid view of Sausalito harbor and San Francisco Bay. Located ten minutes north of the Golden Gate Bridge and San Francisco. Open year-round. Room tariff includes a continental breakfast as well as wine and cheese in the evening. Dining room open six evenings a week. No recreation on grounds, but the entire San Francisco Bay area, Napa wine country, and nearby beaches are convenient. No pets. John Mays, Innkeeper; Debra Boyer, Manager.

Directions: From San Francisco, take Rte. 101 north and exit at Alexander Ave., which winds its way to the main street of Sausalito. Turn left at Princess Ave. and go up the hill. It veers to the right, turning into Bulkley Ave. Go two more blocks, watch carefully for signs of Casa Madrona on the right. It is a very narrow drive; as you approach, keep to the left on the upper driveway to the hotel. Park and go to check-in desk for further instructions.

THE OLD MILANO HOTEL
Gualala, California

The kitchen could very easily have been in Philbrook Farm Inn in Shelburne, New Hampshire. The old faithful woodstove was sending out a glow that pervaded the adjacent rooms and a marvelous aroma of good things to eat drifted around my head like nimbus clouds. Old-fashioned country adornments and a collection of different types of jars, bottles, and pitchers lined counters and shelves.

However, this is the point at which the resemblance to upper New Hampshire ended. For the benefit of eastern readers, country inns in California *are* different. Don't mistake my meaning, they're just as warm and friendly and accommodating as those found elsewhere, but they *do* have their own flair and style.

The Old Milano Hotel is a good case in point. It's jampacked with all types of really outstanding furniture of various ages and genres. For example, there are Tiffany (not Tiffany-type) lamps, real Morris chairs, great white-painted cast iron beds, sleigh beds, thick comforters, high-back chairs, settees, and hassocks without number; not one, but *two* living rooms, telephones left over from the 1920s, and hundreds and hundreds of books. There are twelve lodging rooms, all with some view of the Pacific which is just a few steps away.

In addition to all of this wonderful nostalgia, rose water and herbal bouquet, the Old Milano has things that can only be found in California.

For example, one of the bedrooms has a huge bed used in the film *Wuthering Heights*. In fact, it's the bed in which Merle Oberon dies.

There are also accommodations in a turn-of-the-century, honest-to-gosh railroad caboose. It has a double bed and is decorated with some colorful railroad posters and memorabilia. There is a chunk stove in one corner, and bunks for kids. A little sign warns: "Do not flush the toilet while the train is in operation."

Perhaps the most 'California' of all things is the outdoor hot tubs. These are kept at 102° which means that even in the coldest weather one can soak in them for twenty minutes, get out, sit in the cold air for a few minutes, stagger into bed, and sleep for about twelve hours.

After a rather auspicious beginning in 1905, the hotel fell upon hard times, but was rescued and revived by Theadora and Bruce McBroom. He is a superb photographer and she is a costume designer for films. They are augmented and assisted by Judith Fisher, who is a sort of all-inclusive innkeeper, an individual who seems to be born to the position. She cheerfully makes dining arrangements at various nearby restaurants for all guests, plans day trips up and down the coast and back again to the hinterland, and as I discovered during my stay, was able to keep guests happy and contented even though the electricity was off for 24 hours because of a bad coastal storm.

That in itself was a most interesting evening because she set candles out in the large, comfortable living room and the atmosphere couldn't have been more romantic.

In the morning, it was breakfast as usual consisting of home baked breads served with sweet butter, a selection of coffee blends or tea, and a fresh fruit dish.

Does the Old Milano Hotel sound like a lot of fun? There's no doubt about it.

THE OLD MILANO HOTEL, Highway #1, Gualala, Ca. 95445; 707-884-3256. A 9-room bed-and-breakfast inn (some lodgings without private bath) on cliffs at the edge of the Pacific Ocean, about 3 hrs. north of San Francisco. Open April through November (also winter weekends). Hot tubs on grounds. Sunbathing on the grassy cliffs. Tennis, swimming, golf, bicycles nearby. Continental breakfast only meal served. Not suitable for children. No pets. Theadora and Bruce McBroom, Owners; Judith Fisher, Innkeeper.

Directions: From San Francisco, take Hwy. 101 to Santa Rosa, follow Russian River Rd. (Hwy. 116) west to Jenner and north on Hwy. 1 to hotel. From Eureka take Hwy. 101 south to Willits, Hwy. 20 west to Fort Bragg and Hwy. 1 south to Gualala.

THE GREY WHALE INN
Fort Bragg, California

Ever since the first edition of this book in 1966, I have visited inns that were formerly gristmills, poorhouses, majestic mansions, carriage houses, stagecoach taverns, farmhouses, and log cabins. However, the Grey Whale is the first inn that began life as a hospital!

"The inn was built in 1915," explained John Bailey who, with his wife Colette, acquired it in 1978. "It was the Redwood Coast Hospital before it was transformed into an inn in 1974."

John, Colette, and I were browsing through the thirteen guest rooms, eleven of which have private baths. Its early life as a hospital creates a distinct advantage for present-day inn guests, because the rooms are quite large, with many generous windows.

The Grey Whale features an unusual variety of textures and colors, ranging from the marvelous weather-beaten exterior boards to the brilliant colors of the interior carpeting and the wide selection of original contemporary paintings. The lodging rooms have comforters with matching pillow covers, bright decorator sheets, and one has a working fireplace.

Each contains a folder which describes all of the sights and attractions of Fort Bragg and the Mendocino Coast, including the redwood forest, art galleries, the Botanical Gardens, the beautiful Pacific Ocean beaches, the Skunk Railroad, and a brief summary of some of the restaurants. (The Grey Whale offers bed and breakfast.)

When we passed through the second-floor dining room, Colette explained that she bakes all the breads and coffee cakes that are served on the continental breakfast. "These can be enjoyed right here, or the tray may be taken to the bedroom. Many guests like to eat breakfast in bed," she said.

Colette received two blue ribbons at the Mendocino County Fair and Apple Show—her apricot-prune coffee cake and the lemon-yogurt bread were winners, and St. Timothy's coffee cake won a third prize. John said, "Competition was keen, but no match for the specialties that we serve our guests at the Grey Whale Inn."

Motorists passing through Fort Bragg on Highway #1 just can't miss the Grey Whale, because it stands at the north end of town surrounded by a large grass and turf area with some very colorful plantings of marguerite, California poppies, amaryllis, African daisies, and geraniums.

"Whale watching is one of our great pastimes," said John. "The whale watch starts in mid-December and from then on through March there are programs planned at various points along the coast."

It was from John that I learned of the many activities and attractions in this section of northern California. "We have theater, craft shows, scuba diving, fishing, hiking, and many museums," he reported. "We appeal to the art buff, the whale watcher, the beachcomber, and anyone who wants to have some unhurried hours away from pressures."

Whether the traveler is headed north or south along the Mendocino Coast, or bent on staying a few days, the Grey Whale provides a unique country inn experience.

THE GREY WHALE INN, 615 No. Main St., Fort Bragg, Ca. 95437; 707-964-0640. A 13-room inn located on Hwy. #1 at the north end of Fort Bragg. Continental breakfast included in room rates. (Only meal served.) Open every day in the year. Many natural, historic, and recreational attractions within a short distance. Available by Greyhound Bus and Skunk Train. Beachcombing, scuba diving, fishing, and hiking nearby. John and Colette Bailey, Innkeepers.

Directions: From the south, follow Hwy. 101 to Cloverdale, take Rte. 128 west to Hwy. #1, and follow north to Fort Bragg. Alternate route: Exit Hwy. 101 at Willits, then west on Rte. 20 to Fort Bragg. Driving time from San Francisco, 4 hrs. Another alternate: Hwy. 1 along the coast. Driving time from San Francisco: 6 hrs.

THE OLD SEAL BEACH INN
Seal Beach, California

As I observed in an earlier edition, the first time I was introduced to Marjorie Bettenhausen, I knew that she was lit from within, someone who looked upon the challenges of this life as the opportunity to progress.

Marjorie, with the tremendous aid and support from her husband Jack, and her children — Robin, 18, Christian, 15, and Baron, 8 — has taken a complex of buildings originally built as a motel in 1924, and created a French Mediterranean inn with flowers, trees, and decorations that are typical of those that I have seen in southern France. Here are a few of the interesting innovations that have changed a frog into a prince.

The French Mediterranean appearance is enhanced by the truly extraordinary gardens. All of the lodging rooms are named after flowers including fuchsia, gardenia, and camellia. The full-time gardener keeps the flowers blooming even in the winter with the aid of the mild year-round weather in this part of California. There are rare vines, climbing vines, flowering bushes, sweet-smelling bushes, deciduous trees, evergreen pear trees, and a wonderful variety of a cascading willowy tree that looks like a weeping willow, but really isn't. It stays green all year.

On my second visit I found that lush plantings and antique newell posts are now beside each lodging room door, and in the rooms lovely burgundy, rust, and peach comforters and dust ruffles set off the wrought-iron headboards. The bridal chamber with its very own veranda at the poolside and the little tearoom has been completed as well.

There is a diversified assortment of accommodations among the 22 lodging rooms that have been converted from their motel origins. They range from four very small rooms known as "petite bedrooms," to those of a medium size and even one penthouse suite. One has John Barrymore's four-poster bed.

The entrance to the inn from the street is through a three-sided square around which the lodgings are situated and this is indeed a flower-filled courtyard, lit by street lamps that were rescued from the scrap pile at nearby Long Beach. There is a red English telephone booth in one corner, and a kiosk (that would be quite at home in Nice) has notices of all the nearby attractions. The entrance to the reception area is through a tiny door over which is a blue canopy with the legend "concierge" on it. The scene lacks only a smart-looking *gendarme* to make it the set for *American in Paris*.

The preoccupation with things French is aromatically continued with freshly baked croissants served every morning accompanied by steaming hot coffee and fresh juice. These can be enjoyed in the tea room, or at poolside, or in the little salon, a room jampacked with books, magazines, and an atmosphere that draws guests together.

The Old Seal Beach Inn is quite close to such attractions as Disneyland, the Queen Mary, Knott's Berry Farm, Universal Studios, and the Lion Country Safari.

Marjorie states the new long-range objectives of the inn: "We have a goal to give our inn the aura of a place to be loved . . . where there is asthetic, material, and spiritual enjoyment, so that people will sense that they are really, truly cared about. We all feel that this is indeed a wonderful opportunity."

Marjorie, you've certainly made the most of it.

THE OLD SEAL BEACH INN (Bettenhausen's), 212—5th St., Seal Beach, Ca. 90740; 213-493-2416 or 213-430-3915. A 22-room village inn located in a quiet residential area of an attractive town, 300 yds. from beach. Near Disneyland, Knotts Berry Farm, Lion Country Safari. Catalina Island 20 mi. offshore, and California mountains and lakes 2 hrs. away. Long Beach Playhouse, Long Beach Music Center nearby. Breakfast only meal served. Open all year. Swimming pool on grounds. Tennis, beach, biking, skating, golf nearby. No pets. Marjorie and Jack Bettenhausen, Innkeepers.

Directions: From Los Angeles Airport take Hwy. 405 Freeway south to Seal Beach Blvd. exit. Turn left toward the beach, right on the Pacific Coast Hwy., left on 5th St. in Seal Beach, which is the first stop light after main street. Inn is on the left, 2 blocks toward the beach on 5th St.

RED CASTLE INN
Nevada City, California

"We are, I believe, one of the prime examples of Gothic Revival architecture in California." Jerry Ames, Chris Dickman, and I were seated in the pleasant garden of the Red Castle Inn high above Nevada City, discussing the history and other fascinating features of the inn. Chris, who is extremely knowledgeable about such things, asserted that, as far as he knows, the Red Castle is one of two examples of genuine Gothic Revival design on the West Coast, and this should not be confused with "Carpenter Gothic," which is quite common. "It's particularly identifiable by the arched windows on the top floor and the double brick walls. The house has never been altered since it was built in 1860 by Judge John Williams, a mine owner and civic leader who, with his family, crossed the plains in 1849.

"In near-ruins, the house was restored by James W. Scharr in 1963. I think it stands today as a proud reminder of the part that the 'Argonauts' played in the heritage of California. It's a registered point of historical interest and recognized as such by the Daughters of the Golden West."

The house tour included one fascinating feature after another.

On that particularly warm day, I was delightfully impressed by the fact that the temperature inside the house was at least twenty degrees cooler than it was outdoors. Jerry said that was because of the double brick walls. I saw all eight bedrooms, five of which have private baths, and all are furnished with very handsome antiques.

Each one has its own individuality. "By the time we bought it, the house had been through several different careers," commented Chris. "Fortunately, it has never been altered, which is wonderful because some of these old buildings have been butchered over the years." Chris proved to be rather adamant on the subject of preservation, undoubtedly because of his background in interior design.

We started from the very top floor and worked our way down, and it was on the small balcony way up in the treetops that I learned about one of the early inhabitants, Judge William's son and his penchant for playing the cornet from this vantage point. I believe it had something to do with communicating with the ladies of the town. There's a photograph of him in the hallway sporting a very fierce mustache.

Throughout the house there are wonderful collections of wall hangings and such decorative pieces as beautiful fans and theatrical masks from all over the world, including a Japanese "No" mask made about 1870 and signed by the actors. I've never seen an inn with a collection of masks before. Much interesting reading is available with a wide selection of magazines and books.

We tarried for awhile in the main living room where I felt the sense of buoyancy that fresh flowers give to a room. On an antique desk there was an old-fashioned brass telephone with a separate earpiece, as well as stereoscopic photographs and a special viewer. Fascinating bric-a-brac filled almost every corner. "We've tried to keep everything as authentically 'period' as possible," Jerry said.

In Nevada City, California, where gold strikes were a way of life a hundred years ago, I found one of my own: the Red Castle Inn.

RED CASTLE INN, 109 Prospect St., Nevada City, Ca. 95959; 916-265-5135. An 8-room inn located on a hill overlooking one of the great gold rush communities in the foothills of the Sierra Nevada Mountains. Approximately 2800-ft. altitude. Lodgings include continental breakfast (the only meal served). Open year-round. There are numerous historic, cultural, and recreational attractions, all within a very short distance. No recreation on grounds. Hiking, golf, xc skiing nearby. No diversions for small children. German and Spanish are spoken. Jerry Ames and Chris Dickman, Innkeepers.

Directions: Nevada City is on Rte. 49, the Gold Rush Highway. Eastbound: When arriving in town, take Broad St. turnoff. Turn right, and then right again up the hill to the Exxon station. Take a hard left into Prospect St. Westbound: Take Coyote St. turnoff. Turn left down the hill, and left on Broad St., right on Sacramento; up the hill to the Exxon station and a hard left into Prospect.

THE PELICAN INN
Muir Beach, California

In the haunting moonlit scene, fragrant with the scent of honey-suckle and jasmine, the white, half-timbered building set amongst the trees might well have been in Shropshire or Surrey. In reality it was in Muir Beach, California, just twenty minutes from the Golden Gate Bridge. This was the Pelican Inn.

Before I reached for the knob of the heavy wooden door it was thrown open, and there stood the archetype of all British innkeepers, Charles Felix. In accents unmistakably nurtured in English public schools and further strengthened by service in the RAF, he welcomed me to the Pelican Inn and invited me to take a place by the great Inglenook fireplace and join in the Sunday night festivities.

"Let me get you something from the pub," he said. And so began what was for me a most pleasurable evening.

Charles Felix is, as he proudly announces, "the son of a publican." He cuts a most impressive figure in fawn-colored trousers, tweed coat, and suede shoes. His distinctive white hair and mustache are further accentuated by a rich California tan.

We sat for quite awhile in the low-ceilinged room with its heavy exposed posts and beams, and beautiful old tables, hutches, side-boards and the like. Charles explained that they had been sent over from England and many of them were almost 200 years old.

The Inglenook fireplace is really based on Count Rumford's formula. There is another Rumford fireplace in Cobb's Cove on Cape Cod.

The patrons were seated around long wooden tables and making the most of the last few hours of freedom before the weekend would be over. The Sunday night menu included navy bean soup, roast loin of pork, shrimp scampi, lasagna, shepherd's pie, bangers (another word for large, very good English sausages), and many desserts.

"After a long search my wife Brenda and I found this location a number of years ago, and set out to create an authentic English-style inn," he said. He nodded appreciatively as one of the celebrants ran up a most respectable score at the dart game.

The leaded glass windows came from England; the pressed tin lamps were made of Cornish tin in New England; old bricks and beams were scavenged from destroyed buildings in San Rafael and Sausalito.

"Actually," he said, "we are surrounded by the Golden Gate National Recreational Area and have miles of hiking and riding trails. The beach is just down at the bottom of the road.

There followed a tour of the Tudor-style lodging rooms with

the heavy exposed beams and white plaster walls typical of several traditional British inns. Hogarth prints and English countryside scenes adorned the walls. There were half-tester beds, and a profusion of fresh flowers. The morning paper and a hearty English breakfast are part of the tariff. Hanging over one of the beds was a stone with a hole in it to prevent rickets in case of pregnancy. Witches and the little folk are all kept at bay which, as Charles says, "makes the Pelican a haven from the evil eye."

A discreet card is found in each room with the legend, "It is humbly requested that your breakfast be consumed between 8:15 and 10:00 a.m. since the management is intimidated by a ferocious cook who commences luncheon preparations at that time. It is further requested that your departure be completed by noon to allow the harried chambermaid to attend to the rooms."

Incidentally, afternoon tea with India tea and wafer-thin sandwiches, cakes, and other things British and Empire is served by the fire.

It was indeed a lovely evening at the Pelican Inn and for anyone planning a first-time trip to Britain, a visit here is bound to put one right in the mood.

THE PELICAN INN, Muir Beach, Ca. 94965; 415-383-6000. A 6-room English inn on the northern California coast, 8 mi. from the Golden Gate Bridge. Breakfast, lunch, and dinner served daily. Swimming, tennis, backroading, walking, and all San Francisco attractions nearby. Price of lodgings includes breakfast. Charles Felix, Innkeeper.

Directions: From Golden Gate Bridge follow Rte. 101 north to Mill Valley exit, turn left at traffic lights and follow Hwy. #1 to Muir Beach.

SUTTER CREEK INN
Sutter Creek, California

The gate in the white picket fence was unlatched so I stepped through, closed it, walked up the narrow path and started to knock on the double front door. A note caught my eye directing me to the back door. I circled the house past the flower beds and fir trees and knocked on the back door. Still no answer. Edging inside, I saw a beautiful big kitchen and large old fireplace with andirons in the shape of black owls. A long country Chippendale pine table was set with ten rabbit-eared chairs in place.

I heard a light step on the back porch and in came innkeeper Jane Way with an apron full of tomatoes. "Oh, hello Berkshire Traveller, would you like a nice ripe tomato? They're wonderful with salt on them."

And so back in 1967 began my first visit to the Sutter Creek Inn, which is as neat a bit of old New Hampshire as you'll find west of New Hampshire. The house was built over 100 years ago by people who were homesick for the Granite State.

"I took a guess on the kind of a room that I thought you would like," she said. "We have many with fireplaces, some have canopied fussy and frilly beds, and others are tailored and simple. However, I decided that you would enjoy the Washroom, which is just off the back porch and up the steps. The Oriental cook lived there for many years." (Since that time I have stayed at about every room in the inn.)

She finished washing the tomatoes and, laying them out on the table, suggested that we would both enjoy a glass of iced tea under the grape arbor.

"We serve breakfast here every mild morning at nine sharp. It's

with the compliments of the inn." Jane also pointed out that other meals are not served at the inn.

"You see, there are so many fascinating things to do that our guests really prefer to spend the day roaming about. We have some unusual Serbian boarding houses nearby that serve simple food. We generally direct our guests to one of them."

Breakfasts are really great fun; the food is hearty and the talk is lively. Guests frequently decide to join forces for the day in exploring the mother lode countryside.

That's the way it has been for years now at the Sutter Creek Inn, deep in the mother lode country. Fireplaces blaze in cold weather and there are warm, lazy summer days to be spent in hammocks or out exploring this fascinating gold rush country. Sutter Creek, Jackson, Volcano, Murphy's, Angel's Camp, and Sonora are all part of the great living legend of gold in California and they're all on or near Route 49 which runs along the foothills of the Sierras.

Because the inn is rather intimate in nature, children are not encouraged as guests. Reservations in advance are almost always necessary and there's a two-day minimum stay on weekends, whether Friday and Saturday, or Saturday and Sunday.

"Once in a while," Jane explained, "we do have last-minute cancellations."

For many of her guests, Jane Way and the Sutter Creek Inn are the "first" country inn experience. "People frequently ask me," she said, "about the essential qualities for successful country innkeeping. In fact, I've had so many inquiries that I'm now working on a book on that subject and I hope that you will write the introduction!"

I readily agreed. After all, I've been visiting the Sutter Creek Inn since 1967.

SUTTER CREEK INN, 75 Main St., Sutter Creek, Ca. 95685; 209-267-5606. A 16-room New England village inn on the main street of a historic mother lode town, 35 mi. from Sacramento. Lodgings include breakfast. No meals served to travelers. Closed all of January. No children under 10. No pets. Water skiing, riding, fishing, and boating nearby. Mrs. Jane Way, Innkeeper.

Directions: From Sacramento, travel on the Freeway (50) toward Placerville and exit at Power Inn Rd. Turn right and drive one block, note signs for Rte. 16 and Jackson. Turn left on Fulson Rd., approximately ¼ mi., follow Rte. 16 signs to right for Jackson. Rte. 16 joins Rte. 49. Turn right to Sutter Creek. From San Francisco, follow Freeway (80) to Sacramento and take previous directions or drive via Stockton to Rte. 49.

THE SANDPIPER INN
Carmel-by-the-Sea, California

"That looks very much to me like an English holly tree, is that true?" Graeme Mackenzie smiled indulgently and congratulated me upon my knowledge of horticulture. "Indeed it is," he said, "although Irene and I have been in the accommodations business all over the world for thirty years, we still treasure our British heritage. We're both from Scotland."

True to the British tradition of having flower gardens in the front of houses, The Sandpiper's terraced entry is graced with many types of begonias, camellias, and several other varieties of most colorful flowers and trees, creating the atmosphere that makes it such a joyous experience. There were potted plants and window boxes everywhere and the beautiful English holly trees are very much in harmony with the Monterey cypress trees.

Graeme also proudly pointed out the two new inn signs carved out of redwood. The words, "The Sandpiper Inn," are etched in gold leaf and underneath that it says, "A Country Inn."

We were met at the front door by Irene Mackenzie wearing beige and light brown colors that accented her beautiful red hair and California tan. "Come into the library," she said, "we're having a proper tea."

The spaciousness of this room was emphasized by a cathedral ceiling, a beautiful old stone fireplace, and a big comfortable sofa. Standing in front of the windows was a long table with many chairs around it, and this is where guests take their continental breakfast. Everything was decorated for fall with pumpkins and pine cones.

The more we chatted and the more I later saw of the Sandpiper, the more I was struck by its resemblance to an English country house hotel. Irene and Graeme are knowledgeable, educated, and articulate individuals, prepared not only to discourse on the delights of Carmel and the Monterey Peninsula, including all of the many restaurants, but also have that easy sociability that allows them to sit down with their guests and discuss anything from music and art to the most recent best seller. It's exactly the type of hospitality and ambience that make a country inn experience so pleasant.

Both of them are very much interested in outdoor sports, including golf, tennis, and racquet ball, and are happy to introduce their houseguests to some of the clubs on the peninsula in which they have memberships.

Irene is proficient in French and German, and because of her experience as an interpreter at the United Nations, is quite at home in other languages as well. I discovered that she is also a most talented artist and that some of the watercolors in the bedrooms were her work.

Accommodations at this inn are in fifteen handsomely furnished rooms and cottages all with comfortable beds and private bathrooms. Some have views of the Carmel beach and others have woodburning fireplaces. These rooms all reflect a sort of bright, British taste with eye-catching quilts, very pleasant draperies, and colorful pictures. A very unusual set of prints of old hotels and way stations of many years ago was artfully hung along the staircase wall.

Graeme told me that Carmel has rigid zoning codes and that the Sandpiper is in what is otherwise a totally residential area. "We're all very low key here," he said with a twinkle in his eye.

Guests were returning from long walks on the beach or perhaps a round of golf at one of the famous courses nearby and Irene and Graeme excused themselves, leaving me to reflect on how fortunate I was to have discovered this beautiful inn at the beach at Carmel.

THE SANDPIPER INN at-the-Beach, 2408 Bayview Ave. at Martin St., Carmel-by-the-Sea, Ca. 93923; 408-624-6433. A bed-and-breakfast inn with fifteen rooms and cottages near the Pacific Ocean, Carmel and Stuarts Cove beaches, Old Carmel Mission, Point Lobos State Park, 17-Mile Drive, and Big Spur State Park. Breakfast only meal offered. Open all year. Ten-speed bicycles available; jogging and walking on beach. Arrangements to play at nearby private golf and tennis clubs with pools and hot tub. Children over twelve welcome. Please no pets. Graeme and Irene Mackenzie, Innkeepers.

Directions: From Hwy. #1 turn right at Ocean Ave. through Carmel Village and turn left on Scenic Dr. (next to ocean), proceed to end of beach to Martin St. and turn left.

THE INN
Rancho Santa Fe, California

The town of Rancho Santa Fe, California, is one of the most attractively designed that I have ever visited. It has been well described as a "civilized planned community." The homes and estates have been created in perfect harmony with nature's generous endowment of climate and scenery. One of the dominating factors is the presence of the gigantic eucalyptus trees.

Innkeeper Dan Royce told me the story. "It's hard to imagine this place without these great trees, but back in 1906 it was nothing but an area of sand and occasional low trees and brush. At that time the Santa Fe Railroad purchased the land for the purpose of growing eucalyptus trees for railroad ties. About three million seedlings were planted, but the project failed when it was discovered that the wood was not suitable. Fortunately, the trees were left to flourish and today we have glorious shade and beauty. They provide homes for literally thousands of birds.

"The first building of The Inn was constructed in 1923 and is now a part of the main building of today's inn. Beginning in 1941 it was expanded into a quiet resort where guests could enjoy the truly beautiful surroundings.

"In 1958, my father Steve acquired the property and it's been a family operation ever since."

At this mention of Steve Royce, who was dean of southern California hotelmen for many years, I was reminded of my first visit to Rancho Santa Fe.

Steve had given me the pleasure of a tour of the entire community with its beautiful homes and orange groves. When I mentioned this to Danny, he smiled and said, "Yes, my father certainly made a great contribution to innkeeping. One thing I learned from him that will never leave me is to make a point of meeting personally every guest in The Inn during his or her stay. I think in the true definition of the word dad was a real innkeeper."

This "family" feeling is extended even further when guests learn that the stunning framed needlepoints very much in evidence through the main lobby and living rooms of the inn, have been done by Danny's mother. For example, there is one very large, extremely handsome piece showing a large eucalyptus tree. It has become the symbol of the inn and is found on all of the stationery. My favorite is a needlepoint clock on one wall of the cathedral-ceilinged living room.

Cottages are scattered among the towering trees, and there's recreation for everyone here, including the younger set. The Inn has membership in nearby private 18-hole golf courses, and there are three tennis courts and a croquet green on the grounds. The swimming pool has an outdoor terrace where luncheons and refreshments are available. Also, The Inn has a beach cottage at nearby Del Mar for use during the summer months.

Part of the pleasure of staying at The Inn is the opportunity to visit the shops in the village. They are all designed to be attractive, but unobtrusive. I stood in front of one building for three minutes without realizing that it was a supermarket!

All of this is happening today at Rancho Santa Fe because eucalyptus trees could not be used for railroad ties!

THE INN, Rancho Santa Fe, Ca. 92067; 714-756-1131. A 75-room resort-inn, 27 mi. north of San Diego Freeway #5, 5 mi. inland from Solana Beach, Del Mar. European plan. Breakfast, lunch, and dinner served to travelers daily. Open year-round. Pool, tennis, and 6-wicket croquet course on grounds. Golf and ocean nearby. Daniel Royce, Innkeeper.

Directions: From I-5, take Exit S8 and drive inland about 6 mi.

I do not include lodging rates in the descriptions, for the very nature of an inn means that there are lodgings of various sizes, with and without baths, in and out of season, and with plain and fancy decoration. Travelers should call ahead and inquire about the availability and rates of the many different types of rooms.

Spring Mountain Road is a little-known mountain road tha⋅ links St. Helena with Santa Rosa. This winding two-lane road takes off from downtown St. Helena and almost immediately passes Spring Mtn. Winery (Falcon Crest, for you TV fans), which is not open to the public except by appointment, but can be seen from the road. It then winds up through magnificent firs and redwoods to the crest of the mountain. If you look back, the view of the Napa Valley is spectacular. It then runs down into a tight little valley, following a year-round creek that offers nice picnic areas. There are no stores and few houses on this stretch of back road California-style.

Jim Smith
Wine Country Inn
Helena, California

Twelve miles from the Sutter Creek Inn is an old town with a population of 125 people. The town of Volcano used to be the largest city in California. Today, it has an old hotel that is still operating and serves the most delicious dinners for miles around. Reservations have to be made before 1 P.M. Up a few doors is a luncheon place called The Jug and Rose. It serves the most elegant sandwiches I have ever eaten. The menu is limited to several specialties, and ice cream sodas, sarsaparilla, and foreign teas are favorites, plus unusual coffees and desserts. There are a few small shops in the town, but it is crowded in the summer with tourists going to Daffodil Hill or shopping for antiques. Each small town in this county has special fairs, bakery and homemade goods for sale, church suppers and luncheons with house tours. It is a beehive of activity from early spring until winter comes. Many guests at the inn go to this small

community every time they come, getting to know the merchants and owners of the various establishments. These are people who have gone into business in a small way to earn a living and express their ideas of beauty in service to humankind; not out to set records nor expand, but to enjoy life as they find it and offer sustenance to those who pass by. If one is sensitive to these vibrations, they are easily felt and appreciated. There are far too few of these places left in our world today.

Jane Way
Sutter Creek Inn
Sutter Creek, California

A little known, but beautiful, drive near the inn is the drive to Ebey's Landing from Coupeville. You drive out of picturesque Coupeville on Engle Road. Just a mile and a half out of Coupeville, you turn right on Hill Rd. As the road comes into the trees it takes a 90° turn. The trees form a beautiful, mossy, primeval forest. As you continue just a short way, the road makes another 90° turn. At this point you look over the white cliffs of Whidbey out through the Straits of Juan de Fuca and the Pacific Ocean beyond. The view is framed by the wind-swept trees which form a natural tunnel. As you continue down the hill you come to the beautiful beach at Ebey's Landing, which has recently been acquired by the National Parks Service, a great place for a picnic.

The Stone Family
The Captain Whidbey
Coupeville, Washington

VAGABOND HOUSE
Carmel, California

Yes, this was Fourth and Dolores Street in Carmel, but where was the Vagabond House? Then I saw the discreet sign, the tasteful entryway. I smiled, remembering that on the occasion of my first visit, I had stood for at least a full minute thinking I had come to the wrong place.

I walked up the stone steps and entered an atmosphere that seemed almost magical. It was a three-sided courtyard enhanced by many trees, including mock orange, magnolia, and live oaks. There were camellias, primroses, tulips, and daffodils in great profusion, along with impatiens, rhododendrons, fuchsias, and many other varieties of flowers.

I sat down for a moment just to drink in the aromas and colors, and was immediately joined by two Siamese cats who rubbed up against my legs and purred contentedly.

"Oh, I see that Suki and Little Arthur are the first ones to greet you," said Karen Levett who, with her husband Dennis, is the innkeeper at the Vagabond House. "They are as much a part of the Vagabond House as we are," she said. "They are asked for, petted, given snacks, brought goodies, and even receive cards. I guess you might call them the 'lords of the manor.'" They were shortly joined by a very frisky little champagne-colored cocker who answered to the name of Charlie.

I gave my two feline friends a scratch behind the ears, patted Charlie, and followed Karen into the lobby-living room. A small fire burned at one end and two guests were musing over several menus from the great number of restaurants in Carmel, Monterey, and Pacific Grove.

Once again I was impressed with Dennis's large collection of hunt-and-coach scenes. Karen introduced me to the other guests and they said they were going to spend the day on the golf links. "It's a part of a vacation I've looked forward to every year, because there are so many golf courses in this area," said the man.

Now the other guests from the various cottages were joining us, and soon everybody was making recommendations about what to do for the day and where to eat dinner. Many of them had cameras.

Accommodations at the Vagabond House are in twelve completely different cottage rooms or suites, many of which have their own woodburning fireplaces. The rooms are large and pleasingly furnished with early American maple furniture, quilted bedspreads, and antique clocks. Some have kitchens. Each room is supplied with its own coffeepot and fresh ground coffee for brewing, and the guests

are provided with fruit juice and Danish rolls for light breakfasts.

Later on Julie Brown, who is associated with Dennis and Karen at the Vagabond House and is well known to all guests, told me that the first family wedding was held recently when her son Henry was married in the parlor. "The garden had been carefully groomed for the happy day and we got some lovely photographs," she said proudly.

The world may be speeding by at a great rate everywhere else, but inside the little courtyard of the Vagabond House there's a special kind of sweet serenity.

VAGABOND HOUSE, Fourth & Dolores Streets, P.O. Box 2747, Carmel, Ca. 93921; 408-624-7738 or 408-624-7403. A 12-room village inn serving continental breakfast to houseguests only. No other meals served. Open every day of the year. Bike renting, golf, natural beauty nearby, enchanting shops. Not ideal for children. Attended, leashed pets allowed. Dennis and Karen Levett, Jewell Brown, Innkeepers.

Directions: Turn off Hwy. 1 onto Ocean Avenue; turn right from Ocean Avenue onto Dolores, continue 2½ blocks. Parking provided for guests.

THE WINE COUNTRY INN
St. Helena, California

The story of this inn goes back a few years when Ned and Marge Smith visited me in Stockbridge, Massachusetts, and we talked about the ideals and objectives of innkeeping. They live in St. Helena, in the beautiful Napa Valley, where Ned is a prominent real estate broker. They were looking for the qualities that they most admired in country inns because they were interested in having an inn of their own.

After visiting about fifteen New England inns they returned to California and began to give form to their ideas. A perfect site was found and the Smith family, all of them, began to work on building their inn.

In June of 1975 I called them to say that I was planning to come to California in late August. "Wonderful," said Marge. "We'll be open by that time for certain." The day arrived and I drove down

from Elk on the coast and approached St. Helena from the north on Rte. 128. At the outskirts of St. Helena, following directions, I turned down Lodi Lane and in about thirty seconds I saw a spanking new sign, "The Wine Country Inn."

After our reunion, we set off on a complete tour of every nook and cranny of the new inn. Ned explained that the building was carefully designed to fit the site which overlooks the upper part of the Napa valley in full view of Glass Mountain.

"We tried to arrange for every room to have a view. So some have intimate balconies and others have patios leading to the lawn. The natural wild mustard, lupines, poppies, and live oak trees have been blended with plantings of oleanders, petunias, and Chinese pistachios to accent the scenery."

Today, as then, each room is individually decorated with country antique furnishings refinished and reconstructed by members of the family. Many of the rooms have fireplaces, canopied beds, tufted bedspreads, and handmade quilts. There are no televisions or radios, but a generous supply of magazines and books, and big, comfortable, fluffy pillows encourage the lost art of reading.

To top everything off there is a generous continental breakfast served every day with fresh California fruit and muffins or delicious caramel pecan rolls served warm.

There are two pieces of recent news that I find very exciting. For one thing, Marge and Ned's son Jim is now the innkeeper of The Wine Country Inn. I met him at the time of my first visit in 1975 when the entire family was involved in putting the finishing touches on the inn just prior to opening. Since that time, he has attended the Hotel and Restaurant Management School at City College in San Francisco and also was employed on the staff of The Bed-and-Breakfast Inn in San Francisco.

A great many of us had the opportunity to see Jim and his staff (including younger brother Jeff) in action in November, 1981, when we held a two-night meeting of innkeepers at The Wine Country Inn. Everything ran smoothly, and believe me, it's not an easy job to play host to a group of more than forty innkeepers who are bent on having a productive business meeting and at the same time making the most of a few days of vacation!

The Wine Country Inn is a real thrill for me since I was in on it when it was a gleam in the Smiths' eyes. The care and consideration that have gone into the designing and the result prove that a country inn doesn't necessarily have to be old to be legendary.

It's the spirit that matters.

THE WINE COUNTRY INN, 1152 Lodi Lane, St. Helena, Ca. 94574; 707-963-7077. A 25-room country inn in the Napa Wine Valley of California, about 70 mi. from San Francisco. Continental breakfast served to houseguests, no other meals served. Open daily except December 22-27. This inn is within driving distance of a great many wineries and also the Robert Louis Stevenson Museum. Golf and tennis nearby. No children; no pets. Jim Smith, Innkeeper.

Directions: From San Francisco take the Oakland Bay Bridge to Hwy. 80. Travel north to the Napa cutoff. Stay on Hwy. 29 through the town of St. Helena, go 1¾ mi. north to Lodi Lane, then turn east ¼ mi. to inn.

PARADISE GUEST RANCH
Grants Pass, Oregon

I was down at the empty corral very early in the morning with Ollie Raymond. "Let's have some fun," he said, reaching in his pocket for a small whistle. He blew three long blasts and said, "Now just wait a minute."

In a very short time I could hear the horses coming from the upland pastures, and then they hove into sight, manes flying and hooves pounding on the soft dirt. They headed right into the stalls and began eating their breakfast.

"We don't feed them a lot because we have open pastures," he explained. "Most of the time our guests are up long before breakfast getting acquainted with their mounts. Some of them want to learn more about their horses, and we show them how to brush them down, how to handle and saddle them. Then everybody goes to breakfast, after which we have our first trail ride."

Paradise Guest Ranch is a picturebook ranch with white fences, green meadows, neat barns, and extremely high-quality livestock. It is located in the beautiful Rogue River Valley of southern Oregon.

Mattie and Ollie have been here for fourteen years and they are the kind of people who seem to gather up all of their guests and make them feel very wanted and much at home. It is a wonderful place to bring children, which is another reason it appeals to me.

There is a lot more than horseback riding. For one thing there is an all-day raft trip on the Rogue River in the ranch's own boat which is carefully supervised. It is a wonderful outdoor activity. There's also fishing, swimming, soaking in the hot tubs, tennis, horseshoes, volleyball, and boating on many of the small lakes that surround the ranch property.

After a staggering breakfast, Mattie and I sat out on the porch. "We think of guests as friends," she said. "Over 90% of them have returned several times. Some of our guests prefer to stay right here on the property, in and out of the kitchen and dining room, and perhaps read books or just sit under the trees and look out over the lake and the grasslands. Oh, here comes Ollie and Turbo."

Sure enough, around the corner on the tractor came Ollie and on his head was a white pigeon flapping its wings. Noticing the amazed look on my face, Mattie explained, "Turbo really rules the roost around here in more ways than one. He is very tame and after awhile he will come and feed from our guests' hands and even ride on their shoulders and heads. Everybody takes photographs of Turbo.

Once again, here was a ranch-inn that was a family affair, because two of the Raymond children, now adults, are right on the property. Their daughter Elise is married to Allen, who is the foreman of the spread. Their son Bradley also works here.

During the summertime guests are on the full American plan, including three meals a day. During the winter the inn offers bed and breakfast.

Accommodations are in sophisticated-rustic quarters that are quite appropriate for the entire atmosphere.

Ollie came up on the porch steps. "Would you like to go for a surrey ride?" he asked. "We have some guests coming in at the local airport and this is the way we usually pick them up."

I accepted with alacrity and so off we set, passing by the big barn where there is all kinds of indoor rainy-day activity for guests of all ages, and headed out into the country. "Are you having a good time?" he asked, his bronzed face breaking into a grin under the ten-gallon hat.

Was I ever!

PARADISE GUEST RANCH, 7000 Monument Drive, Grants Pass, Oregon 97526; 503-479-4333. A splendid 6-bedroom ranch-inn nestled in the beautiful mountains of the Rogue River Valley. Open year-round. Full Amer. plan in summer; bed-and-breakfast available remainder of year. Horseback riding and instruction, trail rides, heated swimming pool, tennis courts, fishing, surrey rides, hayrides, cattle roundup, square dancing, recreational barn and children-watching available on grounds. Spectacular Rogue River raft trips and all-day horseback riding nearby. Mattie and Ollie Raymond, Innkeepers.

Directions: From the Bay Area follow Rte. 101 north to Crescent City and then Rte. 199 to Grants Pass; turn north on Rte. 5 and exit at Merlin. Go under Rte. 5, turn right on Monument Mountain Drive for 2½ miles. Ranch is on left.

CAPTAIN WHIDBEY INN
Coupeville, Washington

"Coming about," John Stone swung the rudder hard over and the boom moved to the starboard side of our trim sailboat; I fumbled for a moment or two with the jib as we set out on a new tack.

The morning was the kind that inspires poetry. The blue waters of Penn Cove in front of the Captain Whidbey Inn were ruffled by a slight breeze. Overhead there were just enough white clouds to accent the tremendous expanse of azure skies. To the east, the Cascades, dominated by Mt. Baker at more than 10,000 feet, were glistening in the sunshine. On the western side, the Olympics, with Mt. Olympus at almost 8,000 feet, also had a white blanket. It was early June and Captain Whidbey Island, already blessed with dozens of varieties of spring flowers, was basking in the warm sunshine. John Stone, the innkeeper of Captain Whidbey Inn, and I were taking advantage of the opportunity to do a little sailing.

"I'm sorry that Mother and Dad are not here this weekend," he said, "but they are enjoying a good holiday."

"Mother and Dad" in this case were Steve and Shirlie Stone who purchased the Captain Whidbey Inn a number of years ago and made it into as fetching a piece of New England as you can find west of Cape Cod. It is an old-fashioned inn and the New England touches come quite naturally, because Steve Stone is a native of Nantucket Island and a good example of the old saying "you can take the boy out of Nantucket but you can't take Nantucket out of the boy"; the tweedy look, the unmistakable accent, and the corncob pipe are all there.

The exterior of the inn is, however, pure northwest, built in 1907 of the distinctly regional madrona logs. The interior remains just about the same as it has always been, with highly polished log walls decorated with antiques and bric-a-brac.

The natural center of the inn is the living room with a very big fireplace made out of round stones. Here everybody, houseguests and dinner guests alike, sit around talking and leafing through the dozens of magazines. There is a fire almost every evening, because as John says, "It really does draw people together."

Some of the lodging rooms are upstairs in the main house. It is here that a relaxing area with comfortable chairs has been set aside especially for houseguests, with floor-to-ceiling shelves jampacked with books.

In recent years an additional number of rustic lodgings called Lagoon Rooms were built in the woods across the road from the main house. They overlook their own private lake.

Observing John as he expertly maneuvered the sailboat on a new tack, I couldn't help but remember what a young lad he seemed about ten years ago when I first met him on Nantucket Island. He was visiting some members of his family, and came to a *CIBR* inn-keepers' meeting we were holding at the Jared Coffin House. Today John is not only the innkeeper at the Captain Whidbey Inn, but is happily married to Mendy, and has two sons—Andrew, who is almost four, and Ian, going on two. Mendy is in charge of the gift shop at the inn and has added a number of local craft items. Earlier she proudly told me that her scrimshaw artist won first place in the International Scrimshaw Show at Mystic Seaport, Connecticut.

"We're having a good time," he said, "but I've got to return to the inn to help my brother Geoff. We're putting out an extra number of lunches today. Tell me, how does baked Dungeness crabmeat sound to you?"

It sounded just fine.

THE CAPTAIN WHIDBEY INN, Rte. 1, Box 32, Coupeville, Wash. 98239; 206-678-4097. A 25-room country inn, 50 mi. north of Seattle, 3 mi. north of Coupeville. European plan. Four cottages with private bath; 12 rooms with private bath. Breakfast, lunch, and dinner served daily to travelers. Open year-round. Boating and fishing on grounds. Golf nearby. Pets allowed in cottages only. The Stone Family, Innkeepers.

Directions: Whidbey Island is reached year-round from the south by the Columbia Beach-Mukilteo Ferry, and during the summer and on weekends by the Port Townsend-Keystone Ferry. From the north (Vancouver, B.C. and Bellingham), take the Deception Pass Bridge to Whidbey Island.

LAKE QUINAULT LODGE
Quinault, Washington

"A rain forest?" I asked. "I always associated the term with the Amazon River." Marge Lesley smiled and said, "Even though we're within a very short distance of snowcapped mountains, here in the Quinault rain forest, the temperature runs between 40 and 70 degrees year around and we have an annual rainfall of between 110 and 160 inches. These conditions produce the ideal growing environment of a greenhouse and there's a wide variety of plants from 300-foot centuries-old Douglas firs, to tiny mosses and delicate ferns."

Marge and I were driving up Route 101 which leads from Aberdeen to Port Angeles on the extreme western coast of Washington. Great stretches of the road are cut between avenues of majestic trees, and it reminded me of northern California and the redwood country.

We were going to visit Marge and Larry Lesley's Kalaloch Lodge, which overlooks the beautiful Pacific Ocean in the Olympic National Park.

"The two places are quite different," she said. "The Lake Quinault Lodge overlooks the placid waters of the lake and is surrounded by mountains with great fir forests. Our guests spend the days walking or driving in the woods.

"Kalaloch, on the other hand, is by the ocean and there people enjoy beachcombing, clamming, and fishing. At Kalaloch, we have hotel, motel, and cabin accommodations, whereas Lake Quinault Lodge is more like a traditional country inn."

I nodded in agreement, remembering that late the previous afternoon I had walked through the big front door of the Lodge into a most welcome living room with a fire crackling in the fireplace. There was a fresh supply of wood stacked up on either side of the massive chimney. On one side of the room great glass doors provided a view of the spacious lawns of the Lodge which lead down to the lake. I could see some children playing croquet.

There was a chess game going on in front of the fireplace, and other guests were reading magazines and taking a few moments of respite after what I presume was a busy, pleasant day in the forests.

Fran Still, at the reception desk, gave me a warm greeting and assured me that I had time for a quick swim in the indoor pool before dinner. "Marge and Larry will join you a little later on," she said.

She pointed out that the Lesleys have been adding considerably to their collection of Indian objects, including wall hangings, rugs, and similar crafts. "We're all very proud of the Indian heritage of this section, and the Lesleys have really gone out of their way to preserve as many as possible of the old things and the old ways."

Most of the bedrooms at the Lodge are very colorful and comfortable, ranging from rustic to modern. Many have individual fireplaces, Tiffany-style lamps, and panoramic views of the lakes and the mountains.

One thing that always impresses me about this place is the number of ways devoted to keeping children happily occupied. Besides some lakeside playground equipment such as swings and slides, there is a fully equipped game room in the basement with all kinds of electronic games and pinball machines, ping-pong, and billiards.

Naturally, one of the things that keeps all guests occupied for part of every day is eating. Marge spoke at length on this subject: "We're primarily known for seafood and steak. Our principal seafood dish is lobster. Everybody loves the salmon, too—either poached or grilled—which is caught fresh nearby."

LAKE QUINAULT LODGE, Southshore Rd., Quinault, Wash. 98575; 206-288-2571. A 55-room resort-inn in the Olympic National Forest of the State of Washington, about 40 mi. from Aberdeen. European plan. Breakfast, lunch, and dinner served daily to travelers. Open every day of the year. Indoor swimming pool, chipping green on grounds. Hiking, mountain climbing, fishing, nature walks nearby. Fee for pets; must be attended. Marge and Larry Lesley, Innkeepers.

Directions: Use Quinault exit from Rte. 101. Proceed 2 mi. on south shore of Lake Quinault to inn.

CONWAY'S FARMHOUSE
Port Townsend, Washington

My life is considerably enriched not only for my visits to Dorothy and John Ashby Conway at their restaurant located in Port Townsend on the Straits of Juan de Fuca, but for the lively and entertaining correspondence I have enjoyed with them over the years. Their yearly newsletter (available on request) also has flashes of John's literary *hors d'oeuvres,* sometimes as spicy as his Greek and Hungarian dishes.

His most recent letter starts off with the joyous news that the BRIDGE IS OPEN and still floating after four years' closing! (He is referring to the Hood Canal floating bridge between Kitsap and the Olympic Peninsula which was partially destroyed during a windstorm.) For what seems to have been an interminable period of time, patrons of Conway's Farmhouse Restaurant had to use a temporary ferry route. Now we can all return to the regular route—the Edmonds-Kingston ferry and then Route 104 over the Hood Canal Bridge to Route 101 north.

John has endured this painful experience with good humor, and apparently the regular devotées of the Farmhouse have endured the journey because it seems to be more popular than ever.

Here's another bit of news from his newsletter: "We have often joked about having a story on page one of the *Wall Street Journal,* and believe it or not we landed right in the middle of the coveted page, featured in a story about garlic. It called our roast beef the 'Saturday Night Special,' and it brought a flood of letters and telephone calls from all over the country. I gave information gladly, happy to do anything to raise the level of knowledge about food in this country. It is the first time in anyone's recollection that a restaurant has been so honored. What matter that the recipe was misquoted? We hope they are more accurate with their stocks and bonds than they are with their recipes."

Conway's Farmhouse is a genuine gourmet restaurant and John and Dorothy have a couple of ground rules that I would like to explain: There is one set menu each month and reservations are imperative. (I hope that all of our readers will telephone in advance.) Please do not drop in on the Farmhouse.

Here are the monthly specialties: February - Mandarin food from North China; March - a German menu; April - classic Greek food; May - curry and sambales from northern India.

In June, July, and August, there's a summer schedule for Thursday, Friday, Saturday, and Sunday. Thursday's entrée is marinated leg of lamb; Friday's is seafood; Saturday's is usually roast beef; and Sunday the entrée is fowl served in a Persian style with pomegranate syrup from Damascus.

September, the inn is open weekends, including Friday, with an Italian menu. In October, it's Hungarian; November is classic Japanese, and the inn is closed in December and January.

I was pleased when Conway's Farmhouse received the prestigious *Travel-Holiday* award again. They were the fourth recipients in the five northwestern states. John says it's the equivalent of the "Ph.D." in the restaurant business.

Remember: one menu at a time, limited seating means reservations in advance, and *please* telephone if your plans change. Guests are asked not to bring young children. The food is too sophisticated for them, and as John says, "an unhappy or unruly child can discommode an entire dining room." Short shorts are out, but campers are invited, and it is suggested that they wear their best camping clothes.

CONWAY'S FARMHOUSE, North Beach, Port Townsend, Wash. 98368; 206-385-1411. A unique gourmet country restaurant, 50 mi. from Seattle. Meals by reservation only. Dinner served Thursdays through Sundays in June, July, and August; dinner served Fridays, Saturdays, and Sundays from September through May. Closed months of December and January. Dorothy and John Ashby Conway, Innkeepers.

Directions: From Seattle take Edmonds-Kingston Ferry and follow Rte. 104 over Hood Canal Floating Bridge to Rte. 101 N. Exit at Port Townsend and make inquiries for Conway's Farmhouse before driving into town.

THE PARTRIDGE
Underwood, Washington

For two years before my first visit to The Partridge in 1977 I had a lively correspondence with Nora McNab. Her letters described the view of the Columbia River from the dining room windows, the pear and apple orchards surrounding this country restaurant, and how

her Columbia River Salmon was purchased in season right out of the Indians' nets. Because hers was a small country restaurant, she explained, it was open by reservation beginning at five p.m. on weekdays and at noon on Sundays.

On January 8, 1980, I had a letter from Nora which said in part, "I'm enclosing a clipping about my husband-to-be. He is a very good and sincere man, as well as being a great deal of fun. He was born in Oklahoma and at one time worked for the Matson cruise ship lines."

The next letter had clippings showing Jacque and Nora on the day of their wedding, which was held at The Partridge. I must say the bridal couple looked extremely pleased with themselves.

The most recent letter was a sort of update: "We've done some rather elegant things which have been fun. For instance we had a moonlight dinner party ending with a fantastic view of the moon over the river, and Jacque served some of his flaming desserts. He enjoys dressing in one of his tuxedos any evening or Sunday to meet our guests and show them to the reception room for a cup of Washington apple cider, chilled in summer, warm-spiced in winter. I think that we've added a new dimension to our little inn without destroying the homely, friendly atmosphere.

"We no longer have any lodging rooms available for our guests, but refer them to the Inn of the White Salmon, which is just five miles distant — they have lovely rooms and breakfast, but no dinners.

Dinners are served in what Nora calls "farm style." It includes the best-of-the-season foods, with nearly all of the fruits and vegetables grown locally. There are two or three entrées on each table, always including the specialty—partridge (cornish game hen)—surrounded by bowls and platters of vegetables, bread dressing, German potato cakes, pickles, and relishes. Dinner features warm bread and pear butter made from Partridge Inn orchard pears. Fresh pies are made each day—rhubarb, strawberry, blackberry, wild huckleberry, pumpkin, and mince, along with ever-popular apple, banana cream, and pecan. When people make reservations for a birthday they can sometimes be served their favorite variety of pie, and Jacque carries it to the table with a lighted candle, singing, "Happy Birthday."

Visits to the Columbia River Valley can ideally combine having dinner at the Partridge Inn and remaining overnight at the Inn of the White Salmon, which would make a most pleasant holiday.

Incidentally, many friends of Jacque and Nora will be glad to know that for the past two winters they have been at the Albermarle Hotel in St. Petersburg, Florida *(CIBR)*, where Jacque can be found presiding over the dining room while Nora is supervising in the kitchen.

Nora's cookbook, *Fifty Years of Cooking*, has been a very pleasant success. Many dinner guests at the Partridge Inn purchase a copy because they would like to know how Nora performs that culinary magic.

THE PARTRIDGE, Box 100, Underwood, Wash. 98651; 509-493-2381. A country restaurant with an excellent view of the Columbia River Gorge, located 60 mi. east of Portland, Ore. or Vancouver, Wash. Dinners by reservation beginning at 5 p.m. weekdays and noon on Sundays. No lodging rooms. Hiking trails and camping, logging flume and falls nearby. Pears and apples for sale most of the year. No credit cards. Jacque and Nora Moyse, Innkeepers.

Directions: On Washington Hwy. 14, 60 miles east of Ft. Vancouver turn left onto Cook-Underwood Rd. at the confluence of the Columbia and White Salmon Rivers. (This road has 2 ends, do not turn off at Cook.) Follow yellow line up the hill for 2 mi. When the Columbia River is on the left begin to look for inn sign on the right. Coming from the Oregon side along Interstate 84N, 60 mi. east of Portland cross the interstate bridge at the town of Hood River. Turn left and drive 2 mi. to Cook-Underwood Rd. directly after crossing the White Salmon River. Follow directions up the hill as above. From coastal region take any highway leading to Portland, Ore., then pick up 84N going east.

INN OF THE WHITE SALMON
White Salmon, Washington

I had never before seen such a "continental" breakfast—three or four different varieties of juices, fruits, breads, and special breakfast goodies, including some positively scrumptious sticky buns. There was all the tea, coffee, and cocoa that one could imagine and other guests were "oohing and ahing" as soon as they entered the breakfast room. The entire array took up three large tables. Even as I was making a choice, Loretta Hopper brought in another pan of special breakfast breads. There are at least 37 varieties!

To make this entire breakfast scene even more unique, there was a continuous, large-screen showing of spectacular color slides of scenes along the Columbia River Gorge, the ski areas, the orchards, Mt. Hood, Mt. Adams, and Mt. St. Helens. It was one of the most interesting and novel ways of presenting the story of recreational and scenic advantages I've ever seen. I stayed an extra long time at breakfast and not one slide was repeated.

Loretta and Bill Hopper are the innkeepers of the Inn of the White Salmon. For forty years it had been a rather ordinary hotel located in a quiet town halfway up the hill with occasional views of the Columbia River. However, the Hoppers saw the possibility of converting it into a very special place. Since Bill is a captain and pilot with Continental Airlines, he and Loretta have had a great deal of world travel.

"Loretta and I had visited Europe and many German inns and guest houses and realized the old hotel could be redecorated to fit into the 'Rhineland' theme which has been adopted by both the town of Bingen on the banks of the Columbia River and White Salmon in the hills above."

At the time of my visit the inn was in a state of transition. Many impressive changes had taken place since the Hoppers took it over in 1978. The entrance is through beveled glass doors into a small reception area where a brass-decorated cash register, an elaborately framed mirror, a real old-style guest register, and old-fashioned wallpaper immediately take the guest backward in time.

Several lodging rooms have been completely redecorated and refurnished in a warm and accommodating country-inn style with good beds, pastel sheets, wool blankets, fluffy comforters, and extra large towels in the bathrooms. Books and magazines can be found in every room and there are old-fashioned hand mirrors, hair-brushes, and pincushions on the bureau tops. Second-floor rooms have a bird's-eye view of the Columbia River Valley and the mountains beyond.

Breakfast is the only meal served; for dinner, guests are frequently referred to The Partridge in nearby Underwood.

Loretta explained that the Rhineland theme would be carried out with staff members wearing dirndls.

With all of this very pleasant nostalgia there is an interesting modern touch—the inn boasts outdoor hot tubs located in the rear. There are also plans for a conventional swimming pool. "We provide our houseguests with terrycloth bathrobes," Loretta said.

Bill Hopper recently informed me that the White Salmon can now make arrangements for its guests to have the fun of a river-rafting trip on the mighty Columbia River. The inn is also the headquarters for backpack trips as well.

Back to the breakfast scene. I was on my third hot sticky bun when I asked Loretta what the cost of the breakfast would be. "There's no charge at all," she said, her black eyes laughing merrily. "It's included in the cost of the room!"

INN OF THE WHITE SALMON, Box 1446, White Salmon, Wash. 98672; 509-493-2335. A 21-room village inn 60 mi. east of Portland, Oregon. Near the Columbia River Gorge, Mt. Adams, Mt. Hood, Mt. St. Helens. Breakfast only meal served. Open all year. Hot tubs, swimming pool (planned) on grounds. River-raft and backpack trips arranged. Golf, steelhead and salmon fishing, hiking, skiing, berry picking, backroading nearby. No pets. Loretta and Bill Hopper, Innkeepers.

Directions: From Portland: follow I-84 east to Hood River, Ore., take White Salmon exit, cross toll bridge over Columbia River. Follow large green signs to White Salmon; inn is 4 mi. from Hood River, Ore., on west side of town.

OAK BAY BEACH HOTEL
Victoria, British Columbia

My host, during my first visit at the Oak Bay Beach Hotel in Victoria, was Kevin Walker who already had several years' experience in the inn business. "I think it's wonderful," he said. "I just can't imagine being involved in anything else. I have worked in almost every department, but I guess because my father is the owner, I've had to work that much harder."

Kevin and I were enjoying high tea in the beamed, low-ceilinged living room overlooking the Straits of Juan de Fuca. A fire crackled in the fireplace.

"We're the only seaside hotel in the area," he said. "Very often we can see killer whales, seals, and salmon.

"Right in front of us are the Straits of Haro with the United States-Canadian border running right at mid-channel." He pointed toward a small island, "That is Discovery Island named for Captain Vancouver's ship, and those are the San Juan Islands across the Strait. Mount Baker is to the east and it's more than 10,000 feet high. You ought to see it when the sun catches the snow-clad peaks and glaciers in the early morning or evening. We are a combination of water and mountains."

Even while we were watching, a cruise ship glided through the Straits, disdainfully ignoring a stubby tugboat towing one of British Columbia's most abundant resources: logs.

Kevin and I had just finished a tour of the hotel lodgings. Each room has a character of its own. For example, there's a group on the third floor with names like "Georgian Suite" and "Samuel Pepys" room. "These accommodations are inspired by English history and literature," he explained. "In fact, most of the antique furnishings were acquired in England."

Still another very handsome room was called "Prince Albert." One suite overlooked the Oak Bay Marina.

"English" is indeed the word to describe the Oak Bay Beach Hotel. I've often observed that Victoria was the most English of all Canadian cities, and this inn in many ways resembles several inns and country houses I have visited in England. One that comes to mind is the Mermaid in Rye, which also has the handsome Tudor-style half-timbers.

There were other reminders of England here at this British Columbia inn. One was a public room with a water view known as

"The Snug." Kevin explained that this was the Canadian equivalent of the Englishman's "local." "Some people have been coming here for a long time as you can see from their names on the mugs hanging there. It's an English tradition."

There's been some very interesting news since my last visit. For one thing, Kevin, my host, was married recently, and he writes, "My new bride is my old high-school sweetheart. She is the marketing director for the Victoria Attractions Association, and we are thrilled with the new life ahead of us."

The chef at Oak Bay Beach, Don Bottcher, was the recipient of a prize in a culinary contest for his Veal Prince Charles — veal tenderloin and peach halves with Camembert and bleu cheeses melted on top. It is now featured regularly on the menu of the inn.

OAK BAY BEACH HOTEL, 1175 Beach Drive, Victoria, B.C. V8S 2N2; 604-598-4556. A 48-room seaside inn located in one of the quiet suburbs of Victoria. A short distance from the spectacular scenery and recreational resources of British Columbia. European plan. Breakfast, lunch, and dinner served to travelers. Open every day in the year. Swimming on grounds. Golf, tennis, fishing, sailing, and Butchart Gardens nearby. No pets. Bruce R. Walker, Innkeeper.

Directions: Take Johnson St. or Fort St. from downtown Victoria east to Oak Bay Ave., which leads into Newport Ave. Turn left into Windsor Ave. to Beach Dr. Turn right and continue to 1175 Beach Dr. If arriving by air at Victoria Airport, I suggest you take public transportation to the center of the city and then take a taxi to the hotel.

THE LODGE ON THE DESERT
Tucson, Arizona

The slanting rays of the western sun, providing spectacular backlighting for the great banks of clouds that seemed to skim the jagged peaks of the Santa Catalina Mountains, streamed through the casement window and lit up the interior of my spacious studio bedroom at the Lodge on the Desert.

Even though the afternoon temperature in September reached 85°, I knew that later that evening I would want a fire in my fireplace to ease the chill of the cool desert night.

My bedroom was really most impressive, with three windows on two sides and a patio facing north. The two double beds had rich bedspreads that complemented the orange curtains, and an armful of freshly picked flowers lent an air of gaiety to the dark tones of the carved wooden tables and chests. The full-sized closet reminded me that many people come here to spend weeks at a time, enjoying the benefits of a friendly climate in both summer and winter, plus the many opportunities for outdoor recreation, as well as the pursuit of the arts.

Tucson is one of the most sophisticated cities in the Southwest with many fine homes and good shops in the downtown area. The University of Arizona is an active cultural center with a continuing program of music, drama, and art and craft exhibitions.

"My father built the Lodge on the Desert outside Tucson in 1936," explained Schuyler Lininger, the *patron grande* of this resort inn. "Now the city has grown up around us; fortunately, we have no tall buildings to disrupt our guests' view of the mountains, and yet we are set apart by the hedges around the property. However, many of our guests find nearness to the center of things in the city most desirable, even though it seems we are way out in the country."

Here in the Southwest desert during the outdoor weather everybody gathers around the swimming pool, and here is where many conversations and lasting friendships start.

For cooler days, the Lodge has a very spacious and inviting living room with lots of books which guests are free to take to their rooms, a chess game, a jigsaw puzzle, and many opportunities just to sit and relax.

The lodging rooms of the inn have been designed after the manner of Pueblo Indian farmhouses, the beige adobe color frequently relieved by very colorful Mexican tiles.

Although the dining room features many dishes of the Southwest, I found there were also such favorites as Chateaubriande for two, roast rack of lamb, and several veal dishes. Schuyler explained that he and Helen have gone to great lengths to bring milk-fed Wisconsin veal to the table in different versions. Incidentally, one of the most popular features of the inn is breakfast served on the guest room patios in the beautiful early morning sunshine.

I believe another guest succinctly summed up my feelings about the Lodge on the Desert while we were both taking advantage of that bright September sun to get a few more degrees of tan.

"What I like about it here," she said, "is the really endless variety of things that are going on in Tucson—the Art Center, the many different theaters, the new museum, the exhibition of Indian arts, the opera company, the ballet, the Tucson Symphony, the golf courses, the racetrack and all kinds of sports events—it's so *civilized!*"

THE LODGE ON THE DESERT, 306 N. Alvernon Way, Tucson, Ariz. 85733; 602-325-3366. A 35-room luxury inn within the city limits. Near several historic, cultural, and recreational attractions. American and European plans available in winter; European plan in summer. Continental breakfast included in European plan. Breakfast, lunch, and dinner served to travelers every day of the year Attended, leashed pets allowed. Swimming pool and lawn games on grounds. Tennis and golf nearby. Schuyler and Helen Lininger, Innkeepers.

Directions: Take Speedway exit from I-10. Travel about 5 mi. east to Alvernon Way, turn right (south) onto Alvernon (¾ mi.). Lodge is on left side between 5th St. and Broadway.

RANCHO DE LOS CABALLEROS
Wickenburg, Arizona

Knee High and I were doing just fine. The reason we were doing just fine was because I was letting Knee High have his (her?) own way, even though earlier, Ed, our wrangler, had put us all in a semicircle and explained that the horses at Los Caballeros were all extremely well trained and broken properly.

"You have to let them know you're the boss," he said, while actually *rolling* a cigarette. "Buford Giles, our boss, the head wrangler, has the best string of dude horses I've ever worked with."

This was the late-afternoon cookout ride at Los Caballeros and we were all strung out on the ascending trail of the high desert back of the ranch, headed toward Vulture Peak where rumor has it that a prospector named Wickenburg discovered by accident (is there any other way?) the richest gold mine in Arizona. None of our party was a really experienced rider, and in my case the last outing had been at Los Caballeros about four years before. There's something frightening and yet deliciously expectant about riding a horse, and it is surprising how even the most timid people soon discover they have a knack for it.

As we walked along with Knee High picking the way among the rocks and small hummocks I thought about the many times I have visited Los Caballeros. This time, however, was rather special because I'd been picked up by my good friend Larry Hyde with the ranch car at the Phoenix Airport (a service supplied to guests). Larry, with his wife Molly, and children, Toby and Phoebe, had made the great decision to leave upper New York State, where he had been an innkeeper, and to join Rusty Gant and the staff at Los Caballeros.

After a very pleasant dinner in the ranch dining room I spent a comfortable evening in front of the fireplace in the main lounge catching up on some of my reading.

The next morning after a sun-drenched breakfast in the dining room overlooking the swimming pool, Larry and I took a golf-cart tour of the eighteen holes of the Los Caballeros golf course. Because of the extensive watering system the fairways are marvellously green—they are like a handful of emeralds tossed out on a beige carpet.

In the afternoon I had my first chance at skeet shooting with twelve other guests. Gene, our instructor, not only was a past master at encouraging us to learn how to hit the clay targets, but he also possessed a wonderful sense of humor. I actually managed to hit six out of twenty-five.

Rancho de los Caballeros is an elegant ranch-inn. Many of the lodging rooms and suites are built around a carefully planned cactus garden and oversized putting green. They are decorated in Arizona desert colors with harmonizing hues of tan, yellow, and brown. Each "casita" has a private patio and many of them have fireplaces. A program of planned activities for younger people is one of the reasons this ranch experience is so popular with families.

Well, we arrived at the rendezvous point for our cookout, and the steaks never tasted so good, and the joshing and good-natured kidding were exhilarating in themselves. Some of the guests told me that when they arrived they were appalled to find that there were no television sets or telephones in the rooms. "I was really surprised at first, but now I can see I wouldn't want it any other way," said one gentleman from Alabama. "You really don't need or want them."

Los Caballeros is an Arizona resort-inn that has adapted to the broadening desires of the American vacationer. It's a place where people of all ages and sensibilities can come together and have a great time.

RANCHO DE LOS CABALLEROS, Wickenburg, Ariz. 85358; 602-684-5484. A luxury 62-room ranch-resort, 60 mi. from Phoenix in the sunny dry desert. American plan. Breakfast, lunch, dinner served to travelers daily. Open from mid-October to early May. Swimming pool, horseback riding, hiking, skeet shooting, putting green, tennis, and golf on grounds. Special children's program. No pets, no credit cards. Dallas C. Gant, Jr., Innkeeper.

Directions: Rtes. 60, 89, and 93 lead to Wickenburg. Ranch is 2 mi. west of town on Rte. 60 and 2 mi. south on Vulture Mine Road.

As you know, southern Arizona has a great many back roads which are interesting trails to wander. Going down the back road through Sonoita and Patagonia to Nogales is certainly a different way to travel, and on the northwest side of Tucson, there is the old Picture Rock road. This goes into the Avra Valley and takes you by some old Indian drawings.

Another interesting back road is going north toward Oracle Junction toward Oracle and into Peppersauce Canyon on the back side of the Catalina Mountains. The Canyon has a great picnic area and it is an interesting drive over a road that is not well maintained.

These are a few of the fascinating back roads that surround Tucson and environs, and of course there are quite a few ghost towns that are easily accessible.

Schuyler and Helen Lininger
The Lodge on the Desert
Tucson, Arizona

I would suggest that the trip on Route 89 from Wickenburg to Congress, then on a dirt road to Hillside, then on to Kirkland and Prescott and back to Wickenburg on Rte. 89 is a treat, and will provide the traveler with a real insight into Arizona ranching, and the different kinds of Arizona landscapes that exist within thirty to forty miles of the ranch. The dirt road section is very easy and is in fact better than some paved roads.

Rusty Gant
Rancho de los Caballeros
Wickenberg, Arizona

All roads from the Lodge lead into the mountains. A favorite begins and ends (a loop drive) at our back door. The guests often take a lunch (either packed by me or themselves, as our guests are welcome to use our newly renovated country kitchen at any time). They then drive or hike to our falls which are unspoiled and beautiful. There isn't even a picnic table to ruin the view. You perch on a boulder or spread a blanket on the ground, listen to the roar of the falls, and enjoy your lunch.

The road to Cripple Creek, one of our most famous attractions, carries too much traffic to be called a back road. However, there are two gravel roads that take off from Cripple Creek that are unknown by the average traveler. Phantom Canyon road is a little-traveled road to the Royal Gorge through some of the most spectacular scenery in the Rocky Mountains.

Another road winds back to Highway 24 through our practically unknown fossil beds. A couple of miles from the visitor's center at the

Fossil Monument is a wonderful restaurant in an old, plush, private railroad car called, of course, "The Fossil Inn."

There are other back roads such as Eleven-Mile Canyon and Tarryall Creek, roads that lead to uncrowded fishing streams teeming with trout.

Impy Ahern
Outlook Lodge
Green Mountain Falls,
Colorado

TANQUE VERDE
Tucson, Arizona

"This is now the third time I have been to this ranch and I have talked to Herr Cote and am making reservations to return for the fourth time next March."

Guests returning to Tanque Verde for the fourth and fifth times are not particularly unusual, but this guest happened to be from Nuremburg, Germany. He explained that he stayed two days the first time, five days on the second visit, a week on the third, and in the spring was coming back for three weeks. "My wife and I, we just love it, and each time we bring some more friends, also."

We were in the cottonwood grove enjoying the weekly steak roast, which is one of the many opportunities that guests have to get together during their vacations at this historic guest ranch. In the background, I could hear a man playing a guitar, his pleasant voice lamenting the loss of his sweetheart to a man on the black horse who "carried her away." The big fire around which many guests were seated, gave off its friendly warm light and there was the compelling aroma of grilled steaks, succulent ranch beans, and coffee.

I talked with Crystal Puschak, a tour leader for a group of Europeans who were stopping at Tanque Verde on a swing through the West. "This is about the sixth time that I have visited here," she said. "It is by far one of our most popular stops. For one thing, my German and Swiss groups are thrilled to see the unusual desert country and the spectacular sunsets and scenery. They get into desert horseback riding immediately, and they particularly enjoy the breakfast rides and watching the sun come up. It's such a thrill to ride up through the desert to the mountains knowing there is a delicious breakfast of flapjacks, bacon, and hot coffee waiting."

Actually, in the many years that I have been coming to Tanque Verde, this was the first time that I've visited during the summer, and I was surprised at the number of guests from Europe. When I mentioned this to innkeeper Bob Cote, he said, "During July and August we have so many guests speaking so many different languages we could almost advertise it as a good place for children to get some tutoring in French and German. The small tour groups from Europe seem to come mostly in the summertime. During the winter we have a continual stream of Americans and Canadians with their children. Children especially take to ranch life, and it's a fact of life that kids and horses get along like two peas in a pod."

Tanque Verde has a one-hundred-year-old history of one of Arizona's pioneer guest cattle ranches, and even has stories about Indian raids. It is set back in a sunny circle of mountains about a thirty-minute drive from downtown Tucson and the airport. The predominant activity has always been horseback riding in the desert. However in recent years, four tennis courts, a complete indoor health spa, a fully automated exercise room, and an indoor swimming pool have been added for guests' enjoyment.

Accommodations are in almost luxurious individual *casitas*, all of which have their own Spanish-style corner fireplaces.

Everyone eats at long tables in the vaulted dining room, and there's nothing like the desert air to encourage big appetites.

My new German friend summed up his and my feelings about Tanque Verde very well. "It has what we Germans call *gemütlichkeit!*"

TANQUE VERDE RANCH, Box 66, Rte. 8, Tucson, Ariz. 85710; 602-296-6275. A 65-room ranch-inn, 10 mi. from Tucson. American plan. Breakfast, lunch, and dinner served to travelers by reservation. Open year-round. Riding, indoor and outdoor pool, tennis, sauna, exercise room, and whirlpool bath on grounds. Robert and Dee Dee Cote, Innkeepers.

Directions: From U.S. 10, exit at Speedway Blvd. and travel east to dead end.

"European Plan" means that rates for rooms and meals are separate. "American Plan" means that meals are included in the cost of the room. "Modified American Plan" means that breakfast and dinner are included in the cost of the room. The rates at some inns include a continental breakfast with the lodging.

BRIAR ROSE BED & BREAKFAST
Boulder, Colorado

"We are the first bed-and-breakfast inn in Boulder."

Emily Hunter and I were enjoying a cup of afternoon tea in the main living room of Briar Rose and she was telling me about how much fun she and her associate Tessa Penick had had and the perseverance they had exercised in putting the inn into operation.

"Well, for one thing Tessa refers to our little Queen Anne house as being 'English country.' That means it's a little more elaborate than an English cottage. We searched Boulder for almost a year before we found this beautiful home. It was almost as we both had visualized it. Tessa grew up in London, so she felt quite at home here."

After touring the bedrooms, the sunporch, the garden, and admiring the beautiful tulip tree on the lawn, I was quite prepared to agree. The building has beautiful rose-colored brick to the second floor and fancy shingles above. I've seen many cottages just like this in the English countryside.

Almost all of the furnishings are Regency Victorian and there are many splendid additional touches, such as roses in several rooms, including bathrooms. The furniture is most appropriate for the setting. I was happily impressed with baskets of fruit on the nightstands and beautiful down comforters on the beds.

There are seven bedrooms, five of which have their own private patios. Two have private baths. Some extensive renovation and redecorating was being done in two bedrooms in the garden area at the time of my visit.

The innkeepers at Briar Rose have gone a step beyond bed-and-breakfast by providing their guests with the evening meal upon request. "Although we do have several excellent restaurants in Boulder," Emily explained, as she passed me another one of the teatime pastries, "there are times when our guests, many of whom have flown in from the East, just prefer to have a quiet dinner here. We have single-entrée evening meals that include a salad and a simple sweet for dessert. We are not a public restaurant, but we like to accommodate our guests."

Breakfast at Briar Rose is more than the usual continental fare with fresh warm croissants, pastries, European-style yogurt, fresh orange juice, and market-blend coffee.

This was my first trip to Boulder, and with Emily's help I began to realize what attracted so many people to this beautiful 5,400-foot-high city that is close to the 14,000-foot peaks of the Continental Divide.

"We have an ideal climate with four distinct and wonderful

seasons," she commented. "There are over 300 sunny days a year. There are many things for visitors to enjoy, both recreational and artistic. Of course, the mountains offer everything, including climbing, hiking, and cross-country skiing. Some people say that the powder snow offers the best downhill skiing in the world. Biking is also popular here.

"The Boulder Philharmonic recently celebrated its 25th season and there is also a chamber orchestra and many cultural events at the University of Colorado, including theater and dance. They sponsor the Shakespeare Festival Under the Stars.

"We have chamber music concerts here at Briar Rose; in fact, we're having one this Sunday and I hope that you can stay over and join us."

Sitting in Emily's quiet, reserved English sitting room having a cup of tea, I reflected that Briar Rose was indeed a place where West greets East.

BRIAR ROSE BED & BREAKFAST, 2151 Arapahoe Ave., Boulder, Colo. 80302; 303-442-3007. A 7-bedroom inn located in a quiet section of a pleasant, conservative Colorado city, approx. 1 hr. from Denver. Some bedrooms with shared baths. Open all year. Breakfast included in lodging rate. Evening meal available upon request. Afternoon tea served. Convenient for all of the many recreational, cultural, and historic attractions nearby. Limousine service available to and from Denver airport. Emily Hunter, Innkeeper.

Directions: From Denver follow I-25 north and Rte. 36 to Boulder. Turn left on Arapahoe Ave. Briar Rose is on the right about a half-block from 22nd st.

ASPEN LODGE
Estes Park, Colorado

Pointing out the great Rocky Mountain peaks visible from the Aspen Lodge, Bill Adams said, "We are at 9,100 feet, and those are the Twin Sisters there at 11,428 feet—over there is Long's Peak at 14,256 feet; Mt. Meaker is 13,900 feet and Battle Mountain is over 12,000 feet." It was a relatively warm 30-degree morning on November 10th and about two inches of new snow blanketed the landscape.

I had driven up from the airport in Denver the previous evening, and with no difficulty found my way to Estes Park and the Aspen Lodge, even though it was well past sundown. As I was parking my car the front door of the main lodge had opened and a powerful, masculine voice called out, "Welcome, Norman, we waited dinner for you." This was my introduction to Bill Adams, who for years was a sales engineer, and now with his wife Peg, his sons Jon and Jay, and daughter Suzanna, has made a rousing success out of the Aspen Lodge Guest Ranch.

He ushered me into the large dining room with its vaulted ceiling and raised fireplace and on into the kitchen where I was invited to have dinner with the family. This was really off-season, and Peg explained that, of course, the guests all took their three meals in the dining room. "Except for when we put up a boxed lunch for them," she added, her eyes twinkling.

"Twinkling" is a wonderful word to describe the atmosphere at Aspen Lodge. There is a spirit of good fun and personal hospitality that pervades the atmosphere. I'll explain that later, but first let me introduce the cast of characters at Aspen Lodge.

I've already mentioned Bill and his attractive wife, Peg. Jon, who is 23 years old, is the cook, and even though it is a big kitchen and a lot of responsibility, Peg and Bill assured me that he is superb. "He is going to make a wonderful husband to somebody someday," said Peg admiringly. Another son Patrick is very much on the premises during the summer. The Adams' daughter Suzanna is married; however, she is here at the Lodge in the summertime and her husband is the head wrangler.

In addition to the main building of the Lodge, which has the dining room and a very large living room with windows overlooking the impressive mountain scenery, individual cabins are built along the side of the hill and all have an extremely comfortable and cozy atmosphere.

The feature that I found most attractive about Aspen Lodge is the fact that it is such a great experience for families. There are shared activities for everybody to enjoy, including horseback riding, all kinds of trail rides, hiking, fishing, and outdoor games right on the grounds.

A children's counselor takes charge of the young people three days a week. "The first thing we do with children is to familiarize them with everything here on the property," explained Bill. "They are taken to the lake, the stable, and the swimming pool, and we introduce them to the pigs, chickens, goats, and sheep."

On Sunday evenings after everyone has checked in there is a "hootenanny," which is really the staff show. That's the time when the guests and staff all gather and introduce themselves to each other.

Evenings are filled with slide shows, nature talks, bingo, square dancing, and movies. I would be remiss not to mention Jon's great meals which include steak and lobster, prime rib, and Rock Cornish game hen.

I've been looking for a guest ranch in Colorado that I could recommend to my readers. I finally found one that twinkles.

ASPEN LODGE AND GUEST RANCH, Long's Peak Rte. (Rte. 7), Estes Park, Colorado 80517; 303-586-4241. A Rocky Mountain resort inn. Accommodations in main lodge and adjacent cottages. Full American plan (3 meals). Open June 5 to Sept. 3: June 5 thru July 9, 3-night minimum with arrival and departure any day of week. July 10 thru Aug. 20, one-week minimum with arrival and departure on Sun. Aug. 21 thru Sept. 3, 3-night minimum with arrival and departure any day of week. Horseback riding, nature trails, fishing, volleyball, basketball, shuffleboard, heated pool, ping-pong, children's playground, library on grounds. Hiking, backroading, and many other diversions nearby. No credit cards. No pets. The Adams Family, Innkeepers.

Directions: From Denver take I-25 north; turn west on Rte. 66, and follow Hwy. 7 to Aspen Lodge. Public bus transportation from Denver to Estes Park where pick-up service to Lodge can be arranged.

HEARTHSTONE INN
Colorado Springs, Colorado

The title of the book was *From the Kitchen of the Hearthstone Inn*. I had just received it through the mail and before turning to the many enticing recipes—breakfast entrees, breads, luncheon and dinner suggestions, soups, salads and vegetables, desserts and cookies, and a special section on Christmas and other festivities—I was reading the preface.

It contained not only a little of the history of Colorado Springs, but also the history of the Hearthstone Inn, and a great deal in particular about the inspiration and innkeeping philosophy of its two owner/innkeepers, Dot Williams and Ruth Williams.

Here's some of what they say about the inn: " . . . it is a large, stately home, quite visible with its manicured lawns, iron fence, and Victorian colors of lilac, plum, bittersweet, and tan. There are 26 guest rooms each one with its own distinct flavor and color combination, antique furniture, and name. As you get to know the inn you will also get to know the view of Pike's Peak from the side porch, the squirrel who will take food from your hand, or, in winter, the warmth of the fireplaces in the dining room and parlor and the smell of fresh bread baking which makes you feel as if you just walked into your mother's kitchen."

The preface continues, "During the restoration of the house, friends who held down regular 8 to 5 jobs would help out after work until the early hours of the morning; our postman welded a gate latch for us, our lawyer wallpapered on weekends; friends from Michigan who owned an inn called periodically with words of encouragement; and we cannot forget the bank that sent us, for our opening, two dozen red roses, and, we are sure, a silent prayer or two.

I leafed through the cookbook and discovered to my delight that the dividers between the sections were actually drawings of the rooms at the inn, including the several newly added bedrooms in the house next door, which during 1982 was redecorated and refurnished in complete harmony with the original building.

I visited the Hearthstone recently and this new addition—which incidentally has been artfully joined to the main building by moving the carriage house, thus creating a sitting room link—came as a complete surprise. Dot and Ruth had never given me any inkling about their plans and both of them were delighted with my amazement.

We also had a breakfast meeting along with Impy Ahern of Outlook Lodge and Emily Hunter whose inn, The Briar Rose, is new to *CIBR* in 1983.

Naturally, Dot and Ruth took all of us on a tour of the inn with its beautiful, carefully researched wallpaper, curtains, bedspreads, and furniture. The elaborate walnut, cherry, and oak beds, marble-top dressers, and ornate sofas came from all over the Midwest and were restored and refinished by hand. Green plants abound and the brass lighting fixtures from another era sparkle.

A great deal of the talk was about the new Pike's Peak ski area which will bring many enthusiastic skiers to Colorado Springs for many winters to come.

THE HEARTHSTONE INN, 506 N. Cascade Ave., Colorado Springs, Co. 80903; 303-473-4413. A 26-room bed-and-breakfast inn within sight of Pike's Peak, located in the residential section of Colorado Springs. A full breakfast is included in the price of the room; only meal served. Open every day all year. Convenient to spectacular Colorado mountain scenery as well as the Air Force Academy, Garden of the Gods, Cave of the Winds, the McAllister House Museum, Fine Arts Center, and Broadmoor Resort. Golf, tennis, swimming, hiking, backroading, and Pike's Peak ski area nearby. Check innkeepers for pet policy. Dorothy Williams and Ruth Williams, Innkeepers.

Directions: From I-25 (the major North/South Hwy.) use Exit 143 (Uintah St.) travel east (opposite direction from mountains) to third stop light (Cascade Ave.). Turn right for 7 blocks. The inn will be on the right at the corner of St. Vrain and Cascade. A big Victorian house, tan with lilac trim.

OUTLOOK LODGE
Green Mountain Falls, Colorado

Sometimes letters from our readers pick up the spirit of an inn better than anything I could say. For instance here is one from a reader in New York City; let's join her as she describes Outlook Lodge:

"We felt we were in an inn in the truest sense of the word . . . that is, a place that serves not just as a residence, but as a warm, inviting gathering place where guests get to know one another and enrich each others' visits.

"In the morning, drawn by Impy Ahern's delicious homemade breads and muffins and a good hot cup of coffee, we sat around the dining room tables, eagerly sharing ideas for places to visit in the Colorado Springs and Pike's Peak area. In the afternoon, some of

us would sit on the porch overlooking the green hills, discussing the day's experiences, and at night those who were not out sightseeing felt free to lounge around the dining and living rooms, playing cards, talking, and joking.

"It was fascinating getting to know people from Kansas, Texas, and Wisconsin, as well as other Easterners. Many of us exchanged names and addresses for the future.

"The atmosphere at Outlook Lodge was very special—even those who were initially shy, relaxed and made themselves at home. This warmth and cordiality I believe had most to do with the proprietress Impy Ahern. She showed a genuine interest in each of her guests and her friendliness and enthusiasm filled the air.

"Thank you for recommending Outlook Lodge. It was a wonderful home base for our travels and made our visit a memorable one."

I think that letter has caught the true essence of Impy and Outlook Lodge. However, since essence alone isn't enough, let me say that this is a country Victorian inn with twelve lodging rooms located literally on the lower slopes of Pike's Peak. It's only eight miles from Colorado Springs, but worlds apart in a great many other ways. The village is located at an altitude of almost 8,000 feet and the inn is located next to the historic "Church in the Wildwood."

Lodgings include a complimentary continental breakfast featuring homemade breads. There are kitchen facilities for guests who would care to prepare an occasional meal at the inn themselves.

As the letter hints, everything is geared towards family enjoyment and in addition to sing-alongs, often with Impy leading the way, the dining room becomes a guest playroom and there are lots of games that can amuse children of all ages.

Besides all of the nostalgia and the really homelike feeling, the Outlook Lodge is also very convenient to an awesome collection of sightseeing opportunities during all seasons of the year. Those that come readily to my mind are Pike's Peak, the Cog Railway which runs to the top, the old gold-mining town of Cripple Creek, and the Air Force Academy. Energetic guests can go horseback riding or hiking; enjoy tennis, swimming, or other vigorous pursuits. The back roads have magnificent pine-scented views of the impressive mountain scenery.

It's worth noting that Outlook Lodge may be open for a few days during the winter in the future to accommodate skiers who are visiting the new Pike's Peak Ski Area. Better check ahead to make sure.

OUTLOOK LODGE, 6975 Howard, Green Mountain Falls, Colo. 80819; 303-684-2303. A 12-room rustic lodge on the slopes of Pike's baths) on the slopes of Pike's Peak, 8 mi. from Colorado Springs. European plan. All lodgings include continental breakfast. No other meals served. Open from June 1st through Labor Day weekend. Immediately adjacent to all the copious mountain recreational activities as well as the U.S. Air Force Academy; Colorado Springs Fine Arts Center; Cripple Creek Gold Camp. Tennis, swimming, horseback riding, hiking, backroading, all nearby. Impy Ahern, Innkeeper.

Directions: Green Mountain Falls is 8 mi. west of Colorado Springs on U.S. 24. Outlook Lodge is located next to the historic Church in the Wildwood.

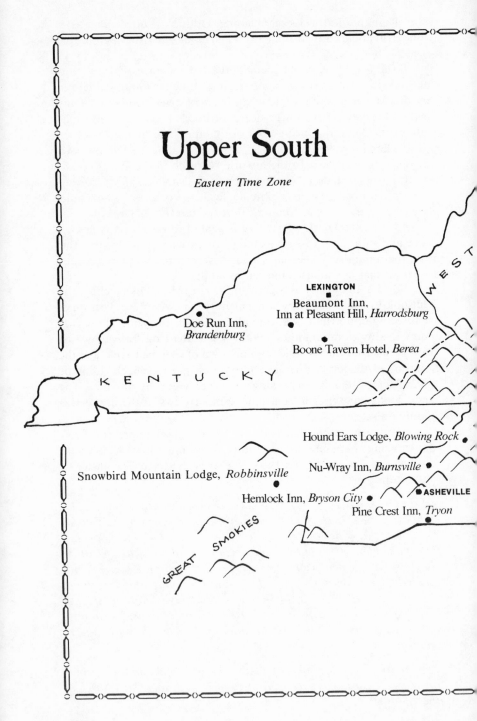

Upper South

Eastern Time Zone

LEXINGTON

Beaumont Inn,
Inn at Pleasant Hill, *Harrodsburg*

Doe Run Inn,
Brandenburg

Boone Tavern Hotel, *Berea*

K E N T U C K Y

WEST

Hound Ears Lodge, *Blowing Rock*

Snowbird Mountain Lodge, *Robbinsville*

Nu-Wray Inn, *Burnsville*

ASHEVILLE

Hemlock Inn, *Bryson City*

Pine Crest Inn, *Tryon*

GREAT SMOKIES

Country Inn, *Berkeley Springs*

M A R Y L A N D

WASHINGTON

Red Fox Tavern, *Middleburg*
Wayside Inn, *Middletown*

Maryland Inn, *Annapolis*

Old Club Restaurant, *Alexandria*

Robert Morris Inn, *Oxford*

V I R G I N I A

Graves Mountain Lodge, *Syria*
Prospect Hill, *Trevelians*

CHARLOTTESVILLE

General Lewis Inn, *Lewisburg*

Alexander-Withrow House, *Lexington*

Gristmill Square, *Warm Springs*
Meadow Lane Lodge, *Warm Springs*

verside Inn,
nce Springs

V I R G I N I A

RALEIGH

N O R T H

C A R O L I N A

ROBERT MORRIS INN
Oxford, Maryland

I've always been a great admirer of novelist James Michener. I must say that I've particularly admired the tremendous amount of research that has gone into all of his books, and the way he involves his readers with the facts and background of his subjects.

That's why this most recent letter from Wendy Gibson at the Robert Morris Inn . . . well, let me quote from it, as I believe this will illustrate my point: "James Michener has just completed a personal seven-year study on the Maryland crabcake. The Robert Morris Inn was given the highest rating of any restaurant on the Eastern Shore. On Michener's scale of 1 to 10, we received a rating of 9.2. We were especially proud to be recognized, as Ken has steadily striven for years to achieve the best crabcake. Michener particularly likes seeing the lumps of crabmeat sticking out of the sides of our crabcakes."

Since the early days of the 18th century, the Robert Morris Inn has undergone many owners and vicissitudes; however, fortunately, it has been in the capable hands of Ken and Wendy Gibson for the last thirteen years. I appeared on the scene shortly after their acquisition.

In addition to lodgings in the main building, guests are accommodated in the Robert Morris Lodge, located a short distance away on a point of land overlooking the bay. In the 1982 edition I spoke extensively of how the Lodge has been redecorated and refurnished. An old carriage house has also been turned into two attractive waterfront lodgings.

Since that first visit so many years ago I've watched Ken and Wendy's two sons, Kent, 11, and Ben, 9, grow up in the inn. Last year I noted that they had gone into the business of supplying plastic bags of corn to guests and visitors for the purpose of feeding the wild ducks and swans that are always congregating next to the ferry slip adjacent to the inn. I understand that it's turned out to be a very growing business; so much so, in fact, that they opened their own checking account this year.

I mention the ferry slip because this is one of the ways to reach Oxford. The ferry plies between Bellevue and Oxford and was the way I arrived in Oxford eleven years ago. It provides a beautiful view of the boatyard and the street that runs alongside the river on the Oxford side. When the ferry is filled up or when the captain feels he has waited long enough, he departs for the opposite shore. There's a little signal arrangement on each bank to tell the captain that cars are waiting.

The inn's location in the Chesapeake Bay area means that there is considerable emphasis on seafood at lunch and dinner. Besides the aforementioned crabcakes there are many other delicious offerings from the sea, including shrimp, oysters, and several kinds of fish. Breakfast includes scrapple as well as home fries, omelettes, and luscious blueberry pancakes.

Readers wishing accommodations in the high summer season, should reserve by March or April, even for midweek stays. The inn does not take reservations for the new year until after January 10th, but they start receiving telephone calls in January for August and September.

Mr. Michener, I would have been happy to tell you about Robert Morris crabcakes years ago. In fact, I did.

ROBERT MORRIS INN, Oxford, Md. 21654; 301-226-5111. A 35-room waterside inn in a secluded colonial community on the Tred Avon. 10 mi. from Easton, Md. European plan. 15 rooms with private baths; 20 rooms with shared baths; 4 rooms with private porches overlooking the Tred Avon. Breakfast, lunch, and dinner served to travelers daily. Open year-round except Christmas. Tennis, golf, sailing, swimming, and bicycles nearby. No pets. Kenneth and Wendy Gibson, Innkeepers.

Directions: From Delaware Memorial Bridge, follow Rte. 13 south to Rte. 301 and proceed south to Rte. 50, then east on Rte. 50 to Easton. From Chesapeake Bay Bridge, follow Rte. 50-301 to Rte. 50 and proceed east to Easton. From Chesapeake Bay Bridge Tunnel, follow Rte. 13 north to Rte. 50 and proceed west to Easton. From Easton, follow Rte. 322 to Rte. 333 to Oxford and inn.

MARYLAND INN
Annapolis, Maryland

This time I was approaching Annapolis from the south and east, coming along U.S. 50 over the thrilling expanse of the Bay Bridge which now has two suspended roadways over the Chesapeake. There were a number of freighters in the shadowy mist making their way up through the bay, and several sailboats were running before the wind.

I turned off at the sign for the Naval Academy and followed Maryland Route 450 continuing on between the Naval Academy and St. John's College and then, using the steeple of St. Ann's Church as a heaven-pointing guide, made a right turn and came into Church Circle and the Maryland Inn. The discreet sign at the front door indicated that Ethel Ennis was appearing in the King of France Tavern and one of my old favorites, Charlie Byrd, would be the next attraction in the jazz series.

I couldn't help but think that Thomas Hyde, who built the original inn and advertised it as "an elegant brick house in the dry and healthy part of the city . . . one of the finest houses in the State for a House of Entertainment," would be quite pleased with the many different aspects of the Maryland Inn today.

The entertainment is continuing at the King of France Tavern where hundreds of the world's finest jazz musicians have been presented for the past ten years. In addition, the sounds of bluegrass are heard on Tuesday evenings, and on Mondays the entire tavern is transformed for formal dining by candlelight and the stage is occupied by entertainers with guitars, flute, and voice. The menu features Maine lobster, flown in fresh that very morning.

I'm certain that the lodging rooms far exceed any of Mr. Hyde's wildest dreams. I have been visiting the Maryland Inn since the late 1960s and I've seen all of the rooms undergo an impressive restoration of both furnishings and decor, which includes having each bed turned down at night, with wrapped chocolate mints on the pillows.

The modern equivalent of Ordinary-Keeper Hyde is Paul Pearson who explains that the Maryland Inn is part of a concept called "The Historic Inns of Annapolis," consisting of four buildings including the Maryland Inn. When all of the houses have been restored, over a hundred lodging rooms will be added to the present 44 at the inn. These fine old buildings that have stood empty and forlorn for many years will now play an even more significant contemporary role.

The jewel of this project is the Paca House, the home of the signer of the Declaration of Independence. It is now available for select conference groups.

Over a cup of tea in the Treaty of Paris dining room I asked innkeeper Peg Bednarski, a dear friend of many years, about the menus of the restaurants in the inn. "Well, as you know we're located right on Chesapeake Bay so we have eight to ten fish offerings every day including red snapper, grouper, trout, swordfish, mako shark, cohoe salmon, pompano, monkfish, flounder, and rockfish. We musn't forget the famous crab bisque, the popovers, and corn-sticks." I agreed with that as I took another delicious bite of a cornstick.

MARYLAND INN, Church Circle, Annapolis, Md. 21401; 301-263-2641. A 44-room 18th-century village inn in a history-laden town, 20 mi. from Baltimore and Washington, D.C. Near U.S. Naval Academy and Chesapeake Bay. European plan. Breakfast, lunch, and dinner served to travelers daily. Jazz Club, music nightly except Mondays in the King of France Tavern. Tours arranged to historic and scenic points of interest. Tennis and sailing school available. Paul Pearson, Proprietor; Peg Bednarsky, Innkeeper.

Directions: From Baltimore, take Rte. 2 south to first directional turnoff "Washington/Annapolis." From Washington, take Rte. 50 east to Exit "Annapolis Naval Academy, Rowe Blvd."

RIVERSIDE INN
Pence Springs, West Virginia

I was enjoying a special lunch by reservation on the screened porch of the Riverside Inn, and this was made all the more enjoyable because my luncheon companions were Kelley and Ashby Berkeley, the innkeepers.

Through the open door I could see the low ceilings and rugged, massive fireplace at the far end of the main dining room. The beautiful oak tables were set off by the pewter underplates and pistol-handled knives at each place setting. The walls are made of logs with white plastering in between.

It is in this impressive log building that Ashby, who grew up in the Greenbrier River Valley, and Kelley have created an inn with an atmosphere akin to early 17th-century Jamestown, Virginia. The Riverside Inn has the intimacy of a Colonial roadside tavern where travel-weary guests once refreshed themselves with the tablefare of their hosts.

Today's tablefare features fruit-stuffed duckling for two, Colonial meat pies, mountain rainbow trout, fresh seafood pie in a cheese pastry, roast lamb, beef, and pork—all served with local fresh vegetables. The famous scalded English slaw, a hot cabbage salad with bacon-vinegar dressing, dates to the Jamestown era, and one of the favorites for dessert is rum bread pudding.

The English mulled cider served warm before each meal is made from fresh cider pressed especially at the nearby Morgan Orchard.

Ashby had an anecdote about the Riverside Inn. "We had a couple who made a longtime reservation for our cottage, and we always warn everybody that it is just a simple little fishing camp—nothing fancy. No television, just a lot of outdoor activities—hiking, and so forth. This couple came in, had dinner, checked into the cottage, and seemed to like it very much. About eight o'clock that evening it was misty and raining, and I walked over to ask them if everything was all right—did they need more blankets or firewood. They said everything was fine and everybody was happy, but 'what do you do about the noise?!'

"I began to imagine all of the worst things possible, but I still couldn't hear any noise. I said, 'Listen!' Everybody got very quiet and we were listening, when I realized it was the tree frogs and the crickets that were making the noise. They said, 'Can't you do anything about it?' I said, 'No, there isn't anything we can do about it.'"

Incidentally, Ashby explained that they have only token lodgings and are always booked in advance. They suggest to all of their dinner guests that they make reservations at the General Lewis Inn in nearby Lewisburg (also in *CIBR*) because it is only 35 minutes away.

That afternoon, as I was returning to Lewisburg, Kelley and Ashby walked out to the car with me. "On a day like this it is easy to see why West Virginia has been named 'Little Switzerland,'" said Kelley. "It is also easy to see why Ashby and I remain here. Maybe it's a little off the beaten track; however, I've yet to talk to anyone who has not said it was worth it and who does not intend to return—sometime!"

RIVERSIDE INN, Rte. 3 Pence Springs, W. Va. 24962; 304-445-7469. A country restaurant 12 mi. from Hinton, W. Va., located in the beautiful West Va. mountains on the Greenbrier River on Rte. 3 between Hinton and Alderson. 12 mi. from Lake Bluestone. Limited lodgings. Dinner served 5 to 9 P.M. Mon. thu Sat. from May 31 to Labor Day; open Wed. thru Sat., April 15 to May 31 and Labor Day to Oct. 31; open Fri. and Sat., Nov., Dec. Closed Christmas and Jan. to April 15. Lunch served by special reservation only. Skiing, boating, hiking, swimming, spelunking, white water canoeing nearby. O. Ashby and Kelley Berkley, Innkeepers.

Directions: From the east, take Alta exit off I-64, follow Rte. 12S to Alderson then Rte. 3-W 8 mi. to Pence Springs. From the west, from W. Va. Tpke. follow Rte. 3 from Beckley through Hinton to Pence Springs. The inn is located in Pence Springs on Rte. 3 between Hinton and Alderson.

THE COUNTRY INN
Berkeley Springs, West Virginia

I was back at the Country Inn in Berkeley Springs, West Virginia, with two of my most favorite people—Adele and Jack Barker. I have visited with them many times since my first visit in 1972, during my travels in this part of the country with my son Keith, and I have seen many very interesting changes and improvements. This time we were discussing what I'm sure is the most spectacular innovation of all—the redesigning and redecorating of the dining room featuring a glass wall that actually creates the impression of being in a garden.

"Of course the garden room has been here for about three years," Adele said, "It was one of the projects started by Jack and our innkeeper, Bill North, a few years ago. They created a wonderful, luxurious garden feeling with different types of plants and decorations, but last year we decided to open up the wall of the dining room and let it all become part of a whole." The translucent roof brings the outdoors in, and strings of tiny white lights complete the bright, airy quality of the room with its many hanging plants. There's a dance floor, too.

Still another recent change is the completion of the "Gallery." One of the large main-floor rooms has been lined with over 100 framed pictures and posters and lit with soft-track lighting. The furniture has been arranged in conversation groups in the center of the room, so that the result is a combination art gallery and lobby for sitting, reading, playing cards, conversation and, of course, enjoying the art. The room is warm and colorful.

Of brick and Colonial design, the inn has a spacious lobby, a very gracious Colonial dining room, and bright, comfortable bedrooms with color TV. It is located in the center of the small town of Berkeley Springs and adjoins the town park and village green.

The nation's oldest health spa is adjacent to the Country Inn, and over the years I have remarked that among the early patrons was George Washington, along with many other notable people connected with the growth of our country. It is possible to enjoy a Roman or a Turkish bath followed by a relaxing massage, and the cost is surprisingly reasonable.

The menu is an extension of the homey atmosphere, with such popular offerings as country ham, smothered chicken, salmon soup, duckling with orange sauce, and homemade hot breads.

Jack and Adele Barker are just the kind of people who should be keeping a country inn. Now with Bill North, who is a Cornell Hotel School graduate, they all bring a genuine concern for guests' comfort, a wealth of experience, generous amounts of intellectual curiosity and practicality, and the good sense that it takes to run a very demanding business.

This section of West Virginia, which is identified as the Potomac Highlands, offers boating and fishing, as well as many, many antique shops and excellent backroading in every season. "Our guests come here in the winter to enjoy the quiet and peacefulness of a get-away weekend," Adele remarked. "We're just a little ol' country town with very friendly people in our shops and stores."

THE COUNTRY INN, Berkeley Springs, West Va. 25411; 304-258-2210. A 37-room resort inn on Rte. 522, 34 mi. from Winchester, Va. and 100 mi. from Washington, D.C., or Baltimore, Md. Berkeley Springs Spa adjoins inn. European plan. Most rooms with private baths. Breakfast, lunch, dinner served to travelers. Open every day of the year. Hunting, fishing, hiking, canoeing, antiquing, championship golf nearby. Jack and Adele Barker, Innkeepers; Bill North, General Manager.

Directions: Take I-70 to Hancock, Md. Inn is 6 mi. south on Rte. 522.

I do not include lodging rates in the descriptions, for the very nature of an inn means that there are lodgings of various sizes, with and without baths, in and out of season, and with plain and fancy decoration. Travelers should call ahead and inquire about the availability and rates of the many different types of rooms.

GENERAL LEWIS INN
Lewisburg, West Virginia

I had just returned from a walking tour of Lewisburg with its 19th-century residences and generous sprinkling of historic markers. I paused for just a moment at the bottom of the crescent-shaped drive that leads to the inn to read a marker which said, "Confederate troops under General Henry Heth on May 23, 1862, were repulsed by Colonel George Crook's Brigade."

As I settled into one of the rocking chairs on the long, shaded veranda, Mary Hock Morgan came out and joined me. "Well, what do you think of our little town?" she asked. I readily admitted that, as always, I was still completely captivated by Lewisburg.

"It was established in 1782 and is the third oldest town in the state," she said proudly. "It was named for General Andrew Lewis, who defeated the Indians at the first battle in the American Revolution in 1774.

"The old part of the inn where the dining room is located was built in 1798 as a private dwelling. Later on, additions were made and in 1929 it was taken over by my mother and father as an inn. It took them many years to collect all of these antiques including the four-poster canopy bed you are going to sleep in tonight. Incidentally, most of the rooms have their own bathrooms and those that do not have sinks in each bedroom."

The General Lewis Inn is like a permanent flashback to old West Virginia. It is furnished almost entirely in antiques. There is a sizable collection of old kitchen utensils, spinning wheels, churns, and other tools used many years ago, as well as an unusual collection of chinaware and old prints. The parlor has a friendly fireplace flanked by some of the many different types of rocking chairs that are scattered throughout the inn. The atmosphere is made even more cozy by the low-beamed ceilings.

The inn is surrounded by broad lawns, and in the rear there are fragrant flower gardens, tall swaying trees, and even a small rock garden.

The menu has many things that I associate with country cooking—pork chops, apple butter, pan-fried chicken, and West Virginia ham, to name a few.

Dusk had fallen while we were talking, and the gaslights which illuminate the tree-lined streets began to dot the late twilight. Our talk turned to some of the famous golf courses here in the Greenbrier area, and we discussed some circle tours of the mountains that would include the fabulous scenery and a generous glimpse of rural West Virginia.

Small wonder that some call it "almost heaven."

GENERAL LEWIS INN, Lewisburg, W. Va. 24901; 304-645-2600. An antique-laden 30-room village inn on Rte. 60, 90 mi. from Roanoke, Va. European plan. (Modified American plan only during W. Va. State Fair.) Breakfast, lunch, and dinner served daily. Dining room closed Christmas Day. Famous golf courses nearby. Mary Hock Morgan, Proprietor.

Directions: Take Lewisburg exit from I-64. Follow Rte. 219 south to first traffic light. Turn left on Rte. 60, two blocks to inn.

I do not include lodging rates in the descriptions, for the very nature of an inn means that there are lodgings of various sizes, with and without baths, in and out of season, and with plain and fancy decoration. Travelers should call ahead and inquire about the availability and rates of the many different types of rooms.

"European Plan" means that rates for rooms and meals are separate. "American Plan" means that meals are included in the cost of the room. "Modified American Plan" means that breakfast and dinner are included in the cost of the room. The rates at some inns include a continental breakfast with the lodging.

A trip to an Appalachian coal mine is a diversion from the Lewisburg area scenery. Most of the trip is along easy roads (easy for those tired of the slow mountain switchbacks), which provide continuously changing views of the broad and peaceful Greenbriar and New rivers. A trip into the Beckley Exhibition Coal Mine is well worth the $4.00 admission, but there are also some surprises along the way.

From Lewisburg take WV219 north to I-64 west. Go seven miles (first exit) and exit on WV12 south. Go south about eleven miles into Alderson and pick up WV3 to Beckley. One-way time is about 1 hour and 45 minutes. The first fifty miles are leisurely, and after Alderson you might want to park at one of the many points along the Greenbriar River. Take a picnic and some fishing gear, if you are inclined.

The Riverside Inn (CIBR) is about fifty minutes from Lewisburg and is known as one of the most unique and finest in the area. It's on the left by the river and clearly marked, but you might want to plan your trip for a dinner at the Riverside on the return trip. Be sure you make reservations first. Use that sweater you planned for the coal mine here, too. The river cools the area so much that a large fire in the fireplace is not unusual in the summer.

Farther down the road, you climb a mountain (not too far up). Slow down near the top and look to the left for a bigger-than-life (or is it?) memorial of John Henry. You should stop and muse over this man. Was he real or legend? Look over the cliff and see the rails run arrow-straight into the mountain, into the Big Bend Tunnel. Was it far below the ground here that Big John wielded his 10-lb. hammer to drill holes for blasting charges? Did he take on the new-fangled steam drill and beat it, and did he die in the town of Talcott below? Perhaps. Perhaps not. But there is no more powerful image of the strength of man's will in the face of a machined world.

The road now descends back to river level, and before long you cross a bridge and the New River can be seen on the right in glimpses between touristy trailer camps, fast-food shops, and fishing-gear

stores. Then you start a long and slow climb back into the mountains. The scenery is nondescript and doesn't improve as you near Beckley, which is after all a coal-mining town. It is interesting only if you've never seen a coal-mining town. It is interesting only if you've never seen a coal-mining town, but take heart because you are not far from the Exhibition Coal Mine.

Getting to the mine in Beckley is a little tricky. Exit on WV16/WV3 Business just after Grandview and before entering Beckley. This is also Fayette Avenue (or Street?). You still have a way to go into town and just after passing what seems to be near the center of town, there is a small sign on an insignificant street on the left. The sign simply says, "MINE." The street is Price Street, but in July, 1982, the sign was knocked down. Turn left on Price and, at the top of the hill, there is a park. Turn right and go all the way around the park. The mine entrance is obvious after you go around the park.

General Lewis Inn
Lewisburg, West Virginia

OLD CLUB RESTAURANT
Alexandria, Virginia

"The food must be good," I thought, "because the natives eat here."

In this case, the "natives" whose cars were in the Old Club's parking lot, were the business people of Alexandria and nearby Washington. I learned this from looking at the license plates of the cars in the parking lot.

I stopped long enough to look at the very well-kept grounds — particularly the English walnut tree and the black walnut tree that are said to have been given to General Washington by the Marquis de Lafayette. Although we were just a few squares from downtown Alexandria, the white fence and high hedges provided an attractive cushion against the urban intrusions. I particularly liked the terrace with lush grass growing between flagstones.

A few years ago I stopped here with my son, Keith, and we both enjoyed the Virginia country ham served over cornbread and covered with maple syrup. This time, however, I resisted this in favor of Allegheny mountain trout, which was boned and stuffed with mushrooms and rice. A good tartar sauce was the topper. I might have ordered chicken Laura Lee, which is a chicken breast on hickory ham with a mushroom sauce. Both of these are really something!

The oldest part of this Colonial house was built by George Washington and his friends as a private club. The little brick building on the north is said to have been young Washington's office while he was surveying this area. There are dozens of little stories connected with this place, including the fact that during the War of 1812 when the enemy was at the gates of Alexandria, all the good furniture was buried in the vegetable garden.

When Keith visited with me, it was for him, as it is for so many people from the north, the first time that he had ever experienced real Southern food. One of the things that he simply couldn't resist was the peanut soup which is a feature of this historic restaurant. I am very fond of it myself and have found that a cup is the perfect amount. After lunch, I drove down the George Washington Parkway and parked at a convenient distance enabling me to spend part of the afternoon at the Washington Monument and the Lincoln Memorial. They are both just a few pleasant moments from Alexandria.

Many guests visiting "DC" (as the city of Washington is known in the area) for the first time are impressed with the beautiful and well-preserved Colonial and Federalist buildings in Alexandria. To me they are reminiscent of those in Charleston, South Carolina; Providence, Rhode Island; and Nantucket, Massachusetts. I found a booklet at the Old Club with an extensive walking tour of Alexandria that included 27 locations just minutes away.

OLD CLUB RESTAURANT, 555 So. Washington St., Alexandria, Va. 22314; 703-549-4555. Just across the river from Washington, D.C. in one of the country's best preserved Colonial cities. No lodgings. Lunch and dinner served daily except Mondays and Christmas. Convenient to Christ Church, Robert E. Lee House, Gadsby's Tavern, Old Apothecary Shop, and Potomac River. Mt. Vernon and Gunston Hall nearby. Lee Palmer, Innkeeper.

Directions: North and southbound traffic on 495 take Exit #1 North to Rte. 1. Turn right on Franklin St. and left on Washington St., 1 block to inn. (Mount Vernon Memorial Hwy. is Washington St. in the city.)

RED FOX TAVERN
Middleburg, Virginia

There are not many country inns in North America that have remained in the same building more than 200 years. However, the Red Fox Tavern in Middleburg, Virginia, which started as a simple way station when the road to the west was known as "Ashby's Gap Turnpike," has passed the midway point of its third century, and is an integral part of American history.

Joseph Chinn was the first proprietor and the inn became known as Chinn's Ordinary. His first cousin was George Washington, who was engaged by Lord Fairfax to survey the area around the tavern, which in turn became known as Chinn's Crossroads.

It's probably true that soldiers from both the American and British lines stopped at this local tavern during the war for American Independence.

In 1812, Chinn's Ordinary became the Beveridge House and was enlarged to 35 rooms. It was the political, social, and economic focal point of Middleburg, which was already an important grain and farming area.

During the War Between the States, Confederate General J.E.B. Stuart needed lodgings for the night and chose the large rooms above the tavern. It was in these rooms that Colonel John Mosby and his Raiders had a celebrated meeting with Stuart, and it was downstairs in the tavern where many of the wounded received care.

The inn became known as the Middleburg Inn around 1877, and was changed to the Red Fox Tavern in 1937, no doubt to recognize one of the most famous four-footed residents in this part of the country, for Middleburg had already gained a reputation as one of the nation's foremost areas for thoroughbred horse breeding and fox hunting.

There are seven tastefully decorated lodging rooms; six are in the main building, some with sitting areas and 18th-century, documented wallpapers and paint colors. Each room is furnished with period antiques and has canopied beds and working fireplaces. There is a two-bedroom suite in an ancient stone building a few doors away.

On the second floor of the tavern there is a very comfortable pine-paneled lounge with two fireplaces, deep leather couches and chairs, and a warm feeling that draws everyone close together.

The main entrance leads directly into one of the two low-ceilinged dining rooms where the thirty-inch-thick walls are appropriately decorated with fox-hunting regalia. Cheery fires are always lit during the chilly months. A secluded terrace at the rear of the inn underneath the trees has an intimate outdoor feeling and is very popular during the spring, summer, and fall months.

The menu includes fresh crab-cake platter, crisp duck, steak au poivre, and beef Wellington.

It was at the Night Fox, a small bistro located behind the main building, that I discovered the skill of playing darts has reached a new dimension. Not only are there friendly games each evening, but frequent tournaments are held.

Just a short distance away from the main inn, an 18th-century historic building has now been completely renovated, furnished, and decorated in the Colonial manner similar to the Red Fox Inn. The several new bedrooms were sorely needed because of the growing popularity of Mr. Joseph Chinn's Ordinary, and I am sure that he would be particularly gratified to know that travelers to Middleburg are still received with gracious Virginia hospitality.

RED FOX TAVERN, Middleburg, Va. 22117; 703-687-6301. A 13-bedroom historic village inn near the Blue Ridge Mountains, approximately 40 miles from Washington, D.C. Near Manassas Battlefield, Oatlands, and Oak Hill (President Monroe's White House). European plan. Breakfast, lunch, and dinner served to travelers. Open every day of the year. Spectator sports such as polo and steeplechasing available nearby. No activities available for small children. Consult innkeeper for policy on pets. The Reuter Family, Innkeepers.

Directions: Leave the Washington D.C. Beltway (495) at Rte. 66 West, to Rte. 50. Follow Rte. 50 West for 22 miles to Middleburg.

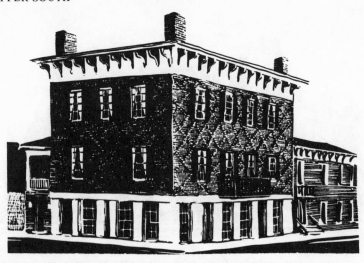

THE ALEXANDER-WITHROW HOUSE
Lexington, Virginia

I first saw the Alexander-Withrow House on a beautiful sunny June afternoon in 1974 and was immediately impressed with its unusual design. I was amazed to learn that such a sophisticated structure had been built in 1789, just two years after the founding of the town. It has four corner chimneys, a most elaborate brickwork design which is known as "diapering," and a handsome Italianate roof. According to an article by Royster Lyle, Jr., published in the *Journal of The Roanoke Valley Historical Society,* the house was described as "occupying a conspicuous place in the village and was a most respected and pleasant abode. Its apartments seem spacious and airy. The prospect of the surrounding hills and majestic mountains was beautiful and grand."

Today this historic house, which is now included in the National Register for Historic Places, is an exquisite guest house. Its restoration and preservation was the first chapter in a very extensive program in the town of Lexington.

The innkeeper is Beth Thompson, who also maintains a very busy bookstore on the first floor. The owners are Mr. and Mrs. Peter Meredith.

There are seven rooms or suites all furnished with period antiques, and although television is not emphasized, there are sets— usually kept in closets—available to be plugged into the cable system.

Each of the suites has its own sitting room, bedroom, and small refreshment area.

Since our last edition the big news is the opening of a historic house built as a residence in 1809, "The McCampbell Inn," right across the street from the A-W House. There are double porches along one side and the back, affording guests a place to relax in rocking chairs and view this lovely little town.

By the summer of 1983, the A-W House will have a total of 23 beautiful rooms or suites furnished with antiques and with the little touches that make a country inn.

There are no meals served at the A-W House; however, guests can walk around the corner to a pastry shop and have their morning meal there or take it back to the inn to be enjoyed in the very pleasant courtyard or in their rooms.

Beth has suggestions for area restaurants that serve lunch and dinner and makes sure that her guests are well-supplied with information about Lexington, including the famous walking tour.

A few years ago Ladybird Johnson, the widow of President Lyndon B. Johnson, paid a short visit to the area and was a guest at the A-W House.

Lexington is one of the most interesting but off-the-beaten-path areas in the northeast. Besides the campuses of Virginia Military Institute and Washington and Lee University, it contains much memorabilia connected with Stonewall Jackson. Both Jackson and Robert E. Lee are buried in Lexington. The surrounding countryside is replete with some very impressive southwest Virginia scenery, including Natural Bridge, which is a towering limestone structure 215 feet high; the Blue Ridge Parkway, which winds along the peaks of the Blue Ridge; Goshen Pass, a breathtaking mountain gorge; and Cyrus McCormick's farm and workshop, where he invented the mechanized reaper.

Visitors to the Blue Ridge Mountains of southwest Virginia and the town of Lexington will find the Alexander-Withrow House a most accommodating and appropriate inn to enjoy.

THE ALEXANDER-WITHROW HOUSE, 3 West Washington St., Lexington, Va. 24450; 703-463-2044. Two historic houses offering 23 elegant suites and bedrooms. Lodgings only. No meals served. Advance reservations recommended. Open year-round. Within walking distance of Virginia Military Institute, Washington and Lee University, and the George C. Marshall Research Library. Natural Bridge. Blue Ridge Parkway nearby. Golf, hiking, Appalachian Trail, canoeing also available. No pets. Mr. and Mrs. Peter Meredith and Sons, Owners; Beth Thompson, Innkeeper.

Directions: Take any Lexington exit from I-64 or I-81. Follow signs into Lexington. The Alexander-Withrow House is on North Main at the corner of Main and Washington Streets.

Boy, are we loaded with back roads here in Virginia. Our Route 613 wasn't on any maps until I wrote to the state—since nobody knew where Trevilians or Route 613 was at the state travel office! It is an old road dating to the early 1730s and was only paved in 1960. It was known as the Carolina Road and was replaced by the James Madison Highway (Rte. 15—one mile east of us) in the early 1800s. That is a country road going from Canada to the Carolinas and passes through some famous places like Harrisburg, Pennsylvania; Leesberg, Virginia; Appamattox; and into the Carolinas. One mile to the north is Route 640, known as the Mountain Road, and this was the "low road" dating back to the 1720s (passing over streams, etc., so horses and mules could be watered) from Williamsburg to the Shenandoah Valley over the Blue Ridge. That is still not paved and is ideal for meandering. A jogger's paradise!

We frequently send guests on two circuitous routes. One, Route 22, goes past Castle Hill, the home of Dr. Thomas Walker, Jefferson's guardian, and then north on Route 231 to Gordonsville. It continues west on Route 33 to a vineyard and winery at Barboursville, then to Charlottesville on Route 20 all the way, passing horses and cattle grazing in open pastures with white fences and beautiful estates overlooking all. Another drive is Route 33 west to Gordonsville, then north on Route 231 to Madison, and continuing along the east side of Shenandoah National Park, north to Sperryville. Then up to Skyline Drive for an hour, looking south over the Shenandoah Valley, and then east on Route 33 back to Prospect Hill.

Bill and Mireille Sheehan
Prospect Hill
Trevilians, Virginia

Meadow Lane Lodge is located on a back road; one of the country's most beautiful and also one of the most historic. So historic, it has been named by the Virginia legislature as the "Charles Lewis and Andrew Lewis Memorial Highway." Those two gentlemen were two of the more famous colonists and Indian fighters, and were the heroes of the Battle of Point Pleasant in 1774, now known

to be the opening battle of the Revolutionay War. Route 39, the official number for this fascinating road, runs from Lexington, Virginia, to the West Virginia line, passing through Goshen Pass, crossing the Cow Pasture and Jackson Rivers, headwater streams of the James River, and traversing the Allegheny Mountains as it winds its way west. The site of Fort Dinwiddie, one of George Washington's chain of forts during the French and Indian War period, is located just off Route 39 (a state historical sign marks the spot) on Meadow Lane Lodge property.

Philip and Catherine Hirsh
Meadow Lane Lodge
Warm Springs, Virginia

This eight-mile drive to Lake Moomaw from the inn is one of our very favorites.

Drive west on Route 39 about one mile. Turn left on Route 687. Down this road is the tiny village of Bacova. This entire town was purchased by one man in the 1960s. He restored each home and revitalized the town's only industry—a guild that uses a fiberglass and silk-screen process to craft mail boxes, ice buckets, and gift items.

Continue on Route 687 through the town to open meadows ringed by hills and mountains. After one mile, turn right on Route 603. This narrow two-lane gravel road gives instant shade from trees arching and touching overhead. On the left are laurel, maple trees, and boulders. To the right is the beautiful Jackson River. Stop and fish for trout (parts of the river are posted) or find a huge flat rock for a picnic. At the end of this 3½ mile stretch are open picnic areas at the base of Lake Moomow—a 9-by-2-mile man-made lake headed by Gathright Dam. You can continue down the road along the lake to the visitors' center and the dam and return by way of Covington or return on the same road—just as nice the second time by.

Jack and Janice McWilliams
Gristmill Square
Warm Springs, Virginia

GRISTMILL SQUARE
Warm Springs, Virginia

I've known Jack and Janice McWilliams, the innkeepers at Gristmill Square, for a great many years, having met them for the first time in the mid-60s when they were the owners of the Bromley House Inn in Peru, Vermont, one of the first inns to be included in the early editions of *CIBR*.

Now, after many intervening years they have returned to innkeeping at Gristmill Square, a delightful cluster of preserved and restored buildings built around three sides of an open square, in a tiny village in the southwest Virginia highlands. Dominating the square is a waterwheel next to a clear mountain stream.

The inn rooms have been cleverly integrated into the second floors of a country store, an art gallery, and other shops. Some of them are furnished in antiques and old prints while others are done in a more contemporary style.

The Waterwheel Restaurant has been artfully fashioned from the very romantic old-fashioned grain mill which has been on the same site since 1771. The heavenly aroma of the grain, the beige patina of the walls, and the geometric patterns created by the beams and posts make a most unusual setting for a candlelight dinner.

The menu features boneless Monterey mountain trout, barbecued baby spareribs in a special sauce, several veal specialties, and sautéed chicken "Simon Kenton" (name of an early settler) cooked in mushrooms and a tarragon cream sauce. I was particularly captivated with a special dessert called "Little Mountain," a concoction of rum-flavored ice cream and summer fruits topped with meringue and toasted almonds. Another hard-to-resist-sweet is frozen Amaretto soufflé.

Jack and Janice have also provided additional amenities for guests who will enjoy longer stays. Across the road from the Square is the Bath and Tennis Club with a swimming pool, and tennis courts that are playable for many months of the year.

"Guests are within a short drive of the famous Cascades and Lower Cascades golf courses," Jack commented as we were enjoying a morning stroll. "There is golf here for players of all abilities.

"We have horseback and carriage riding just over the hill, trout fishing, downhill and cross-country skiing, and some of the most beautiful backroading and hill-walking that can be found anywhere."

With the addition of the Miller House right next door to Gristmill Square, several new attractive country-inn bedrooms are now available to inn guests. The restoration was very successful, retaining the original handsome wainscoting and the original woodwork. Brass fixtures and pedestal sinks add a pleasant touch,

and the furniture was imported from Cornwall, England.

One of the nice touches here is the continental breakfast for inn guests which is prepared in the inn kitchen and delivered to each of the separate lodging rooms at the time requested. It's a very good McWilliams touch.

GRISTMILL SQUARE, P.O. Box 359, Warm Springs, Va. 24484; 703-839-2231. An unusual restoration which includes a restaurant, accommodations, and many resort attractions in a small country town in the Allegheny Mountains 19 mi. north of Covington. European plan. Restaurant open for dinner daily Tuesday-Sunday, and for Sunday lunch. Lunch served May 1 to November 1, Tuesday-Sunday. Restaurant closed Mondays. Many types of accommodations available. Suggest telephoning for details. Children welcome. Three tennis courts, swimming pool on grounds. Golf at nearby Cascades or Lower Cascades. Skiing at Snowshoe, West Va., a little over an hour away. Skating, riding, hiking, fishing, hunting, antiquing, and backroading nearby. Jack and Janice McWilliams, Innkeepers.

Directions: From Staunton, Va. follow Rte. 254 to Buffalo Gap; Rte. 42 to Millboro Spring; Rte. 39 to Warm Springs. From Lexington, take Rte. 39 to Warm Springs. From Roanoke, take Rte. 220 to Warm Springs. From Lewisburg, W. Va. take I-64 to Covington; Rte. 220 north to Warm Springs. From northern W. Va. travel south to Rte. 39 east to Warm Springs. The inn is on Rte. 645. From Rte. 220 going north, turn left on Rte. 645 in Warm Springs. From Rte. 39W turn left on Rte. 692 and left again on Rte. 645 at Warm Springs.

WAYSIDE INN
Middletown, Virginia

Christmas celebrations at *CIBR* inns can be most unusual. For example, at the Wayside Inn a Christmas tree located in the center hallway is decorated with many years' accumulation of hand-crafted ornaments. They are all donated by local townspeople, houseguests, and area residents from as far as a hundred miles away. These ornaments were created as a result of a "Christmas Tree Ornament-Making Contest" held every year, which is now a unique and cherished tradition at the inn.

Each December new ornaments are entered for judging and they are prominently displayed at the front desk for all to see. The prior years' ornaments are on the tree for display. This wonderful tradition has become a focal point for all of the guests during the holiday season, along with complimentary afternoon tea, strolling carolers, and outstanding Colonial holiday decorations.

The Wayside Inn dates from at least 1797. It is correctly referred to as a historic restoration. It was carefully restored to its present form after 1960 when Leo Bernstein, a lawyer and banker from nearby Washington, happened to drive through the main street in Middletown and recognized the inn's tremendous possibilities. The inn is an antique lover's paradise. Its rooms are packed with a mind-boggling collection of tables, chests, paintings and *objets d'art*.

In earlier days the Wayside Inn served as a way station where fresh teams of horses waited to harness up to arriving stagecoaches traveling the Shenandoah Valley Turnpike. Soldiers from both the North and South frequented the inn, then known as Wilkinson's Tavern, seeking refuge, comfort, and friendship during the War Between the States.

The menu includes some very old country recipes, such as spoon bread and peanut soup, country-fresh vegetables, Virginia country ham with red-eye gravy, and both smothered and pan-fried chicken. Homemade bread and real whipped butter accompany every dinner. Young people wearing period costumes serve these tempting dishes. One of the favorite desserts is German chocolate cake which is always brought to the table warm, as are the fruit pies and breads. Saturday night dinners are made special by a strolling balladeer in Colonial garb who moves about from table to table. This entertainment continues after dinner in the Rose Garden Patio Lounge.

Guest rooms at the Wayside Inn are decorated in many different styles because of Leo's passion for collecting. He has an eye out for antiques of any kind, hence, each lodging room is quite apt to be a potpourri of anything from Byzantine to Victorian pieces.

Patrons at the inn have always had a wealth of diversions at their disposal, including the Wayside Theater which has extended its season through December. Dinner is served starting at five p.m. on show nights, to provide guests enough time to walk the one-and-a-half blocks to the theater.

Guests are also invited to visit Wayside Wonderland, a two-hundred-and-fifty-acre recreational park with natural woodlands offering swimming at Half Moon Beach, hiking, fishing, boating, and a tour of Crystal Caverns.

Today the Wayside Inn is many different things. It has history, regional offerings on the menu, an opportunity to spend an extended vacation enjoying all of the attractions in the Shenandoah Valley, and it is a haven for collectors of all kinds.

WAYSIDE INN, Middletown, Va. 22645; 703-869-1797. A 21-room country inn in the Shenandoah Valley, about 1½ hrs. from Washington, D.C. European plan; breakfast, lunch, and dinner served Monday through Saturday. Sunday: breakfast and dinner. Open every day of the year. Professional Equity Theater, Belle Grove, Cedar Creek Battlefield, Blue Ridge Parkway, Crystal Caverns, Hotel Strasburg, Washington's Headquarters, Wayside Antique Warehouse, and Strasburg Antique Emporium nearby. Convenient to Apple Blossom Festival. Marjorie Alcarese, Innkeeper.

Directions: Take Exit 77 from I-81 to Rte. 11. Follow signs to inn.

PROSPECT HILL
Trevilians, Virginia

"Actually all of this really started because a log cabin burned down!" Bill Sheehan, the innkeeper of Prospect Hill, and I were strolling about the impressive grounds and talking about the history of this plantation-cum-inn. "The Roger Thompson family owned it in 1732 and converted a barn on the property into their home after their log cabin burned.

"In 1840 a man named William Overton purchased the property and bought up other shares and quarters and increased it all to 1,576 acres. He enlarged the original house by adding the two wings and the spiral staircase.

"The next chapter is a bit sad because after the War Between the States, the Overton's son William returned to find everything in a completely run-down condition and of course the slaves were gone. It took quite an adjustment and, among other things, they began to "take in" guests from the city and in 1880 additional bedrooms were added to the manor house and the slave quarters were enlarged to accommodate guests."

Accommodations are in the main house as well as in three of the outbuildings, including Uncle Guy's House which has rooms both upstairs and down, the Overseer's cottage which has a suite, and The Boys' Cabin. It is to this building that Bill addressed himself more specifically. "The first half is early 18th century, having been built in the early 1730s as a cabin for the boys in Roger Thompson's family, and was later used as a slave cabin and spinner's cottage. As you see," he went on, "it's quite small inside, only twelve feet square. To the original fireplace, log walls, and pine flooring, we have added a new addition to the rear wall and call it '20th century Californian' because it has a very modern bath with a deck for morning coffee complete with a whirlpool soaking tub."

When I mentioned the enticing aromas from the kitchen, Bill said, "I ring the bell at dinnertime and the guests join together in the dining room where we serve either a four- or a five-course meal which is prepared jointly by Mireille and myself. But because Mireille is French, and I am a student of French cuisine it's usually something rather continental in nature.

"Each day here begins with a full country breakfast served in bed or at a table in the guests' room. It can be just about anything that inspires me because I'm the breakfast cook.

"We really are a family operation," he continued. "Our son and daughter, Mike and Nancy, are here when Longwood College is not in session, and Melvin, the young man who started with us five years ago, has blossomed into our manager and handles a great deal of the maintenance and office work. He is invaluable.

"These have been great formative years for us. Our recent major project was the renovation of the Boys' Cabin, and as you know we've made great strides with the grounds since your first visit here a number of years ago. I think we've revived a long-forgotten way of life, many aspects of which deserve to be preserved."

PROSPECT HILL, Route 613, Trevilians, Va. 23170; 703-967-0844. A 7-room country inn on a historic plantation 15 mi. east of Charlottesville, Va.; 90 mi. southwest of Washington, D.C. Bed and breakfast-in-bed Sun. thru Tues. Mod. American plan with full

breakfast-in-bed and full dinner Wed. thru Sat. Dinner served Wed. thru Sat. by reservation. Dining room closed Sun., Mon., and Tues. Breakfast always served to houseguests. Accommodations in manor house and restored slave quarters. Swimming pool. Near Monticello, Ashlawn (Pres. Monroe's home), Univ. of Virginia, Castle Hill, and Skyline Drive. Children welcome. No pets. Bill and Mireille Sheehan, Innkeepers.

Directions: From Washington, D.C.: Beltway to I-66 west to Warrenton. Follow Rte. 29 south to Culpeper, then Rte. 15 south thru Orange and Gordonsville to Zion Crossroads. Turn left on Rte. 250 east 1 mi. to Rte. 613. Turn left 3 mi. to inn on left. From Charlottesville or Richmond: take I-64 to Exit 27; Rte. 15 south ½ mile to Zion Crossroads; turn left on Rte. 250 east 1 mi. to Rte. 613. Turn left 3 mi. to inn on left.

MEADOW LANE LODGE
Warm Springs, Virginia

When Phil and Cathy Hirsh sold Gristmill Square they didn't go very far way. They moved permanently to an estate comprising approximately 1,600 acres of woods, fields, and streams located in a peaceful valley about ten minutes from the center of Warm Springs. The property has been in Philip Hirsh's family for many years and he spent many of his summers there as a boy.

Besides the main building of the lodge where there are two suites and two double bedrooms, with private baths, there is also Craig's Cottage which has two suites with accommodations for two or four. The new wing has a high-ceilinged bedroom with a large picture window looking over meadows and mountains, a big brick fireplace across the corner opposite the beds, and a fully equipped bathroom.

A full breakfast is prepared by Phil. He's already made his mark as a morning chef and specializes in all kinds of egg dishes, delicious pancakes, and french toast. Breakfast is served in a most attractive sunroom with a view of the farmlands.

A note from Cathy Hirsh says in part, "Yesterday Phip (pet name) and I took a couple of hours off and with two of the dogs went up into the woods to walk around the horse exercise track which was hewn out of the forest by Phip's father. We saw lady-slippers in bloom and lots of trillium and dwarf iris. Then we drove along the Jackson river to the trout ponds and the spring where the wild azalea and dogwood are flowering, and the watercress is a great patch of vivid green. The river is one of Virginia's designated scenic rivers and two miles of it are on the farm.

"Many of our guests who are animal lovers enjoy the barnyard and bucolic pastures where the sheep and goats graze and gambol.

Chickens, guinea fowl, ducks, geese, and turkeys inhabit the old horse stalls in the large stable. Cats and kittens mingle, as do farm dogs. We do not permit guests to bring their pets to the farm, as we already have many animals.

"On cool spring and fall mornings and evenings the two fireplaces in the living room of the lodge burn cheerily. The upstairs rooms have screened-in porches with delightful views and breezes. Our large front porch has comfortable wicker furniture for relaxing and chatting with other inn guests.

"Trout fishing is one of the big attractions here. We have available to our prospective guests a special folder about the limits and varieties."

Besides all of the wonderful walks and rides in the mountains, as well as the tennis court at the lodge, guests also have the advantage of being close to the famous Cascades and lower Cascades golf courses—another diversion that Phil calls, "creative loafing."

In addition to the accommodations at the Meadow Lane Lodge, the Francisco Cottage, located in the center of the village of Warm Springs, has been restored and furnished in the manner of the log house originally erected on this site, circa 1820. It offers luxurious accommodations, including living room, porch, bedroom, kitchen, bath, and amenities and a beautiful view of the hillsides. A minimum stay at the Francisco cottage is for three nights; on weekends a minimum stay at the Lodge is for two nights.

MEADOW LANE LODGE, Star Route A, Box 110, Warm Springs, Va. 24484; 703-839-5959. Meadow Lane Lodge is a portion of a large estate where guests are accommodated in the main building as well as in a comfortable outbuilding. Additional lodgings are in a historic building in the village of Warm Springs. There are seven lodging rooms in all. Open March 20 to Jan. 2. A full breakfast, the only meal served. Dinners are available at the Water Wheel Restaurant 10 minutes away. Ideal for children because of typical animals and poultry. Tennis courts and excellent fishing on grounds. Also, miles of hiking and walking trails. Golf, riding, skeet and trap shooting, swimming pool nearby. Philip and Cathy Hirsh, Innkeepers; Hella Armstrong, Manager.

Directions: From Staunton, Va., follow Rte. 254 west to Buffalo Gap; Rte. 42 south to Millboro Spring; Rte. 39 west to Warm Springs. From Lexington, take Rte. 39 west. From Roanoke, take Rte. 220 north to Warm Springs and Rte. 39 west to Meadow Lane Lodge. From Lewisburg, W. Va., take I-64 to Covington; Rte. 220 north to Warm Springs. Lodge is on Rte. 39, four miles west of Warm Springs.

GRAVES' MOUNTAIN LODGE
Syria, Virginia

It was a noisy, happy breakfast table. A group of hungry innkeepers, who had stayed up well toward midnight talking shop, exchanging ideas, and telling inn stories, were now gathered to continue more of the same and enjoy the superb country breakfast offered every morning at Graves' Mountain Lodge. The occasion was a regional meeting of innkeepers from *CIBR,* this time from West Virginia, Virginia, Pennsylvania, and North Carolina. We were being hosted at this most unique inn at the end of the road in Syria, Virginia, on the edge of the Blue Ridge Mountains.

Spread out before us was a great valley filled with cattle, sheep, farmland, and acres and acres of peach and apple trees which would burst into bloom in just a few more days. A point was made that this panorama resembled both New England in one respect and the English Lake Country in another. However, Rachel Graves, her

merry eyes laughing, said, "I don't think it resembles any of those. I think it resembles Virginia."

As were the other guests at the inn that morning, we were all seated around a long table and there was much passing of bacon, eggs, sausage, coffee, cereal, pitchers of milk, apple butter, two kinds of rolls fresh from the oven that very minute, and gallons of apple juice. Even though these innkeepers were certainly acquainted with what a delight a real Southern breakfast can be, many of them shook their heads in wonderment at the marvelous country tastes and variety of goodies.

Following breakfast we took a short tour of some of the sleeping accommodations at GML. Bill Sheehan from nearby Prospect Hill was particularly taken with Pete's House, a cozy four-room cottage with two double beds and a bunk bed downstairs, and four single beds upstairs. There's a fireplace and air conditioning, and also electric heat.

I've always been particularly partial to the old Farm House, part of which is built of logs. Most of the rooms there have half-baths, but for those that don't, there's always the short walk on the porch to the wash house.

Besides these rustic lodgings, GML also has many other tastefully furnished motel-type bedrooms located near the crest of the hill and enjoying the view of the Blue Ridge Mountains.

This is an excellent place for a family vacation because there is much to do on the grounds, including swimming, tennis, horseback riding, hiking, fishing, rock hunting, and many points of interest nearby for backroading.

In addition, guests enjoy touring the apple and peach cannery that is also part of GML.

"Apples are very important to us here," said Jim Graves, whose family has owned this property for many generations. "We have the Apple Harvest Festival on two weekends in October when people can have lunch at our picnic grounds while watching us make the cider and apple butter the way my daddy and his daddy did. It's really very exciting to see so many people having such a wonderful time."

I did have the opportunity to once again take a walk along the nature trail. It's about a half-mile long and there are little tags on the trees and wildflowers and bushes that help to identify them. At the top there is a carved board showing the various mountains and buildings that are visible across the valley. This was created last year and has been very popular with GML guests.

GRAVES' MOUNTAIN LODGE, Syria, Va. 22743; 703-923-4231. A 38-room secluded resort-inn on Rte. 670, off Rte. 321, 10 mi. north of Madison, Va. 38 mi. N.W. of Charlottesville, Va. American plan. Rustic lodgings including 11 cottages and cabins and two modern motel units. Breakfast, lunch, dinner served to travelers by reservation only. Closed Dec. 1 to late March. Swimming, tennis, horseback riding, hunting, fishing, a special nature walk, rock hunting, and hiking on grounds. Golf nearby. Jim and Rachel Graves, Innkeepers.

Directions: Coming south from Wash. D.C., take I-66 to Gainsville. Follow Rte. 29 south to Madison, turn right onto Rte. 231 West, go 7 mi. to Banco, turn left onto Rte. 670 and follow 670 for 4½ mi. to lodge.

Berea College Campus

BOONE TAVERN HOTEL
Berea, Kentucky

From time to time during the past few years I have shared with you some of the letters I have received from Clare and Lucy DeeDee who live in Grand Rapids, Michigan, and who have been dear friends for many years. They have also recommended country inns in out-of-the-way places that I have then visited and included in subsequent editions.

This time as I was headed for the Boone Tavern in Berea, Kentucky, I reread the letter I received from them telling of their adventures in visiting this place for the first time. Here are a few excerpts:

"On our way home from Florida we had the pleasure of stopping at Boone Tavern for a night and just had to tell you that being here is like an oasis in the desert. Not that Kentucky is a desert, it is one of the most beautiful places we have ever visited. We were driving north on the Interstate, and decided to stop off in Berea and found that they had a charming room available for us. We dressed for dinner as gentlemen are expected to wear coats, and then just plain relaxed. It was beautiful. In other words, 'we love this place.' We bought some beautiful pottery here and the food is delicious. Clare had extra helpings of the spoon bread."

I couldn't help but remember my own first trip to the Boone Tavern in 1968. It was a very damp day at the end of two weeks of rain, and when I arrived I was delighted to find a fire in the sitting room fireplace and Dick Hougen, then the innkeeper, greeting me with a broad smile and a friendly welcome.

Now, many such trips later, stepping out of the bright August sunshine into the comparative coolness of the inn, I felt the welcome from Curtis Reppert and Cecil Connor was every bit as enthusiastic as Dick's had been in 1968.

First order of the day was the touring of several of the newly redecorated lodging rooms, and I found them both attractive and spotless. Most of the furniture has been made in the college wood-working shop and as always, about ninety percent of the staff is a part of the student work program or enrolled in the hotel management course.

"Many of our first-time guests stop here because it is on the main road to and from Florida," said Curtis. "But they return year after year for other reasons." One of these reasons, I couldn't help but reflect, is the food at the inn. For example, for lunch I enjoyed chicken served in a bird's nest. In this case the "bird's nest" was a basket of shredded potatoes with a little spot of cinnamon-berry jelly to add spice.

Also on the menu were several other of Dick Hougen's highly original dishes which are still being used at the inn. These include southern fried chicken with hush puppies, roast leg of lamb in a caper gravy, and minced chicken patty with a supreme sauce and served with fresh cranberry relish at all seasons of the year.

For dessert I had the Jefferson Davis pie which is also in one of the Boone Tavern cookbooks. In addition there was banana cream pie, cherry cobbler à la mode, and several others. The evening meal has the same basic menu as the one offered at lunch, except that there are some additional first courses. Incidentally, anyone intending to have lunch or dinner should phone ahead for reservations.

BOONE TAVERN HOTEL, Berea, Ky. 40403; 606-986-9341. A 60-room village inn in a unique college community on I-75, 40 mi. south of Lexington, Ky. European plan. Breakfast, lunch, dinner served daily to travelers by sittings only. Dinner and Sunday noon, coats required for men, dresses or pant suits for ladies. Open every day of the year. All campus activities open to guests; campus tours twice daily except Saturdays and Sundays. Tennis on grounds. Golf, pool, bicycles nearby. Berea is on Eastern Time. Curtis Reppert and Cecil M. Connor, Innkeepers.

Directions: Take Berea exit from I-75. One mi. north to hotel.

DOE RUN INN
Brandenburg, Kentucky

America has had many frontiers since the landings in Jamestown and on Cape Cod, but there is certainly no more colorful frontier than western Kentucky when it was fought over by Indians and settlers during Daniel Boone's time.

I was talking to Innkeeper Lucille Brown about the considerable Daniel Boone tradition at the Doe Run Inn. "Well, Daniel Boone was never here because it was built in 1816. However, his brother Squire Boone discovered the property in 1778 and was the original landowner. Patrick Henry, who was the Governor of Virginia at the time, signed the original deed. Incidentally, it was known as 'Little York, Virginia.'"

Pioneer America lives at the Doe Run Inn. I'm sure that it has changed very little in 165 years. The building with the huge, four-foot-thick limestone blocks on the outer walls was made to repel Indian attacks. The tremendous front door could withstand almost any attempt to break in, and the huge fireplace still sends warmth radiating through the room.

Interestingly, the property has changed hands relatively few times and has remained virtually intact over the years. There has

been no intrusion in the natural environment which takes in 1,000 acres. There are many walks and trails through the woods.

"One of the early innkeepers was my great-grandfather, 'Wash Coleman,'" explained Lucille Brown with a note of pride in her voice. "Of course, Curtis and I ran the inn for many, many years until he passed away last year. We are continuing on as I know he would like us to and I've always had some wonderful people helping me out."

The building was originally a woolen mill and then a gristmill.

An old record shows a payment made to Abraham Lincoln's father who worked as a stonemason on the building.

Lodging rooms are most unusual. Many have antique beds, tables, and chairs that would be at home in a museum. Just a few have private baths. The lodging rooms are much the same as they have been for the last fifty years, and there has been very little "modernization." As Lucille says, "There's very little we can do with this old building. The folks who like us always have a good time, but sometimes they expect more than we have."

The food is real "Kentucky." Hot homemade biscuits, vegetables served southern style, Kentucky-fried ham, and fried chicken and gravy. The old-fashioned lemon pie tops the desserts.

Thanksgiving Day is always special with many foods that were offered at the first Thanksgiving, such as turkey, chicken, turnips, sweet potatoes, and fried pies!

DOE RUN INN, Rte. 2, Brandenburg, Ky. 40108; 502-422-9982. A 17-room country inn reminiscent of the backwoods on Rte. 448, 4 mi. south of Brandenburg, 38 mi. south of Louisville. Near Fort Knox. European plan. 5 rooms with private bath; 12 rooms with shared baths. Breakfast, lunch, and dinner served to travelers daily. Closed Christmas Eve and Christmas Day. Hiking, fishing, and swimming nearby. Lucille Brown, Innkeeper.

Directions: From Louisville take 64W through Indiana to 135 S. Cross the toll bridge to Kentucky and follow 1051 to the dead end. Turn right on 448 and follow signs to Doe Run Inn.

I do not include lodging rates in the descriptions, for the very nature of an inn means that there are lodgings of various sizes, with and without baths, in and out of season, and with plain and fancy decoration. Travelers should call ahead and inquire about the availability and rates of the many different types of rooms.

"European Plan" means that rates for rooms and meals are separate. "American Plan" means that meals are included in the cost of the room. "Modified American Plan" means that breakfast and dinner are included in the cost of the room. The rates at some inns include a continental breakfast with the lodging.

THE BEAUMONT INN
Harrodsburg, Kentucky

Helen Dedman and I had found a quiet corner at the Beaumont Inn and she was enthusiastically telling me about some of the highlights at the inn during the past year. "We generally open early in March with a gala opening weekend that includes a Friday afternoon tea, Bingo in the parlor, and a Saturday social hour. There is always some kind of entertainment. By March 21st, the first day of spring, the bluegrass, spring flowers, and early shrubs, warmed by our Kentucky sunshine, are gorgeous.

"The Keeneland Track opens early in April. During the last week in April the Red Mile Night Harness Racing Track is open with trotters and pacers."

Helen continued, "Kentucky Derby weekend is one of our most exciting times and we can pack box lunches for our guests who are going to Churchill Downs. The races are always on view in our TV lounge that afternoon. Our guests have been going to the Derby for as long as anybody can remember."

"As long as anybody can remember" covers a lot of territory here at the Beaumont Inn which is now on the National Register of Historic Places. The truly handsome brick building with the six supporting Ionic columns was built in 1845 as a school for young ladies. Later, it became known as Daughters' College, and still later as Beaumont College. In 1916, it was purchased by Mr. and Mrs. Glave Goddard and converted into the Beaumont Inn.

The ownership and management passed from Mrs. Goddard to

her daughter, Mrs. Dedman, and then to Mrs. Dedman's two sons. Today, Bud Dedman is the owner-manager and his son, Chuck, is following tradition and becomes the fourth generation trained in the innkeeper's art.

Samuel Dixon Dedman, Helen and Chuck's first child, could be the fifth-generation innkeeper at the Beaumont Inn and, as this book goes to press, still another potential innkeeper is expected!

The inn, as befits its previous academic history, is set in a campuslike atmosphere surrounded by maples, dogwood, walnut, and catalpa trees. One of the catalpa trees in the front has been used literally for generations by families and guests for appropriate photographs.

The decorations and furniture in all the parlors and lodging rooms reflect American history. The hallways on the main floor have several cabinets with beautiful old china and silverware. The sitting rooms have elegant fireplaces and wallpaper decorated with roses.

One might expect that with so many venerable pieces in such an impressive old building there would be an attempt to preserve the inn as a kind of museum. "Not a bit of it," explains Chuck Dedman. "There were five children in our family and this was our home. Mother and dad taught us respect for old things, but we were expected to enjoy them. We want our guests to feel the same way."

The restoration of Bell Cottage now has added two more lodging rooms to the Beaumont Inn. Mary Elizabeth Dedman, Chuck's mother, did all the decorating and each of the suites contains bedroom, sitting room, and bath, beautifully furnished in antiques and reproductions.

Mrs. Dedman also supervised an enlarged, revised edition of the Beaumont Inn Cookbook which includes several dishes served at the inn never before available to the guests. The first Beaumont Inn cookbook was written by her grandmother in 1931.

BEAUMONT INN, Harrodsburg, Ky. 40330; 606-734-3381. A 29-room country inn in the heart of Kentucky's historic bluegrass country. European plan. Lunch and dinner served to travelers; all three meals to houseguests. Open every day from March 1 through November 30. Tennis, swimming pool, shuffleboard on grounds. Golf courses and a wide range of recreational and historic attractions nearby. No pets. The Dedman Family, Innkeepers.

Directions: From Louisville: Exit 48 from east I-64. Go south on Ky. 151, to U.S. 127 south to Harrodsburg. From Lexington: U.S. 60 west, then west on Bluegrass Parkway to U.S. 127. From Nashville: Exit I-65 to Bluegrass Parkway near Elizabethtown, Ky., then east to U.S. 127.

THE INN AT PLEASANT HILL
Shakertown, Kentucky

The Inn at Pleasant Hill is located in a restored Shaker community in one of the most beautiful sections of central Kentucky. Although the word "Shaker" is becoming more and more familiar to us, perhaps a word of explanation would be helpful.

The Shakers were members of a religious sect, the United Society of Believers in Christ's Second Appearing. They were actually an offshoot of the Quakers. The founder was Mother Ann Lee who brought her ideas to America late in the 18th century. After many trials and tribulations, the Shakers began to prosper.

They held some advanced social ideas. They were hospitable to visitors and took in orphans and unwanted children. One of their fundamental beliefs was in hard work and austere discipline that sought perfection. This sense of perfection is extended into the design of their furniture, and many people learn about Shakers for the first time as a result of being attracted by the beauty and simplicity of the functional Shaker designs.

The Shakers lived in communal dedication to their religious beliefs of celibacy, public confession of sins which culminated in the frenetic dances which gave them the name of Shakers, renunciation of worldliness, and common ownership of property.

There were five "families" at Pleasant Hill which was established in 1805. By 1820 it was a prosperous colony of five hundred persons. "Family" had a particular meaning since the Shakers did not believe in marriage. Men and women, they maintained, could live more happily as brothers and sisters helping one another, but living personally apart.

The Civil War plus 19th-century industrialism and worldliness seeped into Pleasant Hill, and the celibacy rules prevented the natural increase in their numbers. In 1910 they were dissolved.

The inn is located in the Trustees House, one of twenty-five or more buildings clustered along the single country road. To construct buildings of enduring strength, some with walls three or four feet thick, the Shakers quarried limestone from the river bluffs and hauled granite slabs a mile uphill from the river. Most of the buildings are of deep red brick or limestone.

The restaurant is on the first floor of the Trustees House, and the lodging rooms on the second and third floors are reached by two marvelous twin-spiraled staircases that are unmatched for craftsmanship. There are many additional bedrooms on the second floor of restored Shaker shops.

The experience of sleeping in a Shaker room is most refreshing. In my room were two single beds, each with its own trundle bed underneath. The Shaker rockers were classic and the extra chairs were hung by pegs on the walls.

Many of the tasty dishes served in the dining room are prepared from Shaker recipes. The young men and women on the staff all wear replicas of simple Shaker garb. Much of the produce has been raised on the fields of the restored community.

Fran Kramer of Pittsford, New York, wrote me about her visit to Shakertown: "It was a privilege to be there. From the moment we entered until we left, we were impressed by the outstanding hospitality. We stayed above the Cooper Shop in an immaculate room. Dinner that evening was outstanding—the fresh applesauce with marshmallows was zesty, the appetizer bowl including pickled okra was a delight, and the Shaker lemon pie was superb. The buffet breakfast kept us 'not hungry' for the next 24 hours."

It is to the credit of the incorporators of Pleasant Hill that they have managed to accomplish such a great deal in such a short time, although there are still many other buildings to be restored and reconstructed.

INN AT PLEASANT HILL, Shakertown, Ky., P.O. address: Rte. 4, Harrodsburg, Ky. 40330; 606-734-5411. A 63-room country inn in a restored Shaker village on Rte. 68, 7 mi. northeast of Harrodsburg, 25 mi. southwest of Lexington. European plan. Breakfast, lunch, dinner served daily to travelers. Open year-round. Suggest contacting inn about winter schedule. Closed Christmas Eve and Christmas Day. Ann Voris, Innkeeper.

Directions: From Lexington take Rte. 68 south toward Harrodsburg. From Louisville, take I-64 to Lawrenceburg and Graeffenburg exit (not numbered). Follow Rte. 127 south to Harrodsburg and Rte. 68 northeast to Shakertown.

HOUND EARS LODGE
Blowing Rock, North Carolina

The balcony of my room at Hound Ears seemed to rest almost in the top branches of an oak tree. By now the sun was directly overhead casting a dappled pattern on the floor of the porch. In the distance, Grandfather Mountain was shimmering and to my left, perched on various levels of the lower mountains, were the attractively designed homes of the Hound Ears community.

Below, in the foreground, were some young people walking to the swimming pool, which I intended to visit shortly. However, dominating the valley floor, with many of the trees and greens visible from my vantage point, was the Hound Ears golf course.

Perhaps it was this picture of verdant greens and fairways punctuated by clear, white, menacing sand traps that momentarily made it difficult to realize that there had been eight or nine inches of snow here last Christmas and that the other face of Hound Ears, the winter visage, is one that includes spectacular skiing, roaring fireplaces, and the exhilaration of pure winter air.

After a cool night's sleep, I strolled across the flower-lined walk to the main lodge for breakfast, and was on the first leg of the Hound Ears tour.

As I moved from the accommodations in the main lodge to the chalets, and from the swimming pool to several of the private homes of native stone and wood, I found excellent taste everywhere.

The furnishings, appointments, interiors, and exteriors were carefully harmonized. For example, my room was done in complementary shades of brown with yellow sheets on my bed. All of the buildings were set among rhododendrons and evergreens, and in many places huge handsome boulders were allowed to remain where they rested. The road was built around them, curving and twisting and climbing.

The *CIBR* inns in North Carolina represent a very interesting mix, expressing five different and individual approaches to personal accommodations. Hound Ears is a luxurious, modified-American-plan resort-inn and the rates reflect the additional services and elegance. In the more than twelve years I have been revisiting Hound Ears I've always found a very gratifying number of *CIBR* guests who enjoy the same things that I do at this resort-inn.

The whole concept of Hound Ears which, by the way, is named for a rock formation on the mountain behind the lodge, is the inspiration of the Robbins brothers, all of whom were born and raised in this part of North Carolina. They saw the marvelous possibilities in making a resort-inn to which were added skiing and golf facilities.

Other resort-inns with extensive golf facilities in *CIBR* include Rancho de los Caballeros, The Inn at Rancho Santa Fe, the Ojai Valley Inn, and the Country Club Inn.

HOUND EARS LODGE and CLUB, P.O. Box 188, Blowing Rock, N.C. 28605; 704-963-4321. A luxurious 25-room resort-inn on Rte. 105, 6 mi. from Boone. Near natural attractions. American plan. Meals served to houseguests only. Open year-round. 18-hole golf course, swimming, skiing, and tennis on grounds. David Blust, Innkeeper.

Directions: From Winston-Salem, follow Rte. 421 west to Boone, then travel south on Rte. 105 to inn. From Asheville, follow Rtes. I-40 east to Marion then Rte. 221 north to Linville and Rte. 105 north to inn. From Bristol, Va., and I-81, follow Rte. 58 east to Damascus, Va., then Rte. 91 to Mountain City, Tenn. and Rte. 421 to Boone, and Rte. 104 south to inn (5 miles).

HEMLOCK INN
Bryson City, North Carolina

In each lodging room at the Hemlock Inn there is a reprint of a portion of Pete Johnston's article in the New York Times of January 16, 1972 about country inns. Pete points out that country inns are not for everyone, including travelers in a hurry, or those who demand speedy service, or those who crave sophisticated entertainment and who must have a television set and telephone in their room. They are for travelers who seek simple comfort, hospitality, quiet, and tranquility. I know for a fact that Pete at that time had not visited the Hemlock Inn. If he had, it would have typified what he had in mind.

On the other hand, *I* have had the good fortune to visit the Hemlock Inn many times, and once again it was so much fun sitting between Ella Jo and John Shell and being introduced to the other people at the Lazy Susan tables. Many of them were regular September guests because that's the month with a touch of autumn. Each succeeding morning the trees that were formerly green turn a little more yellow and red. The September air, so clean and cool. These are the beautiful days before the color has totally changed, although the Great Smokies are almost free of travelers.

"I always come to the Hemlock Inn in September," said one lady from Palm Beach. "We think it's the best time of year because it's still possible to take a raft trip and the water is still warm enough." Rafting, birdwatching, walking . . . these are some of the things that we talked about at the dinner table and meanwhile everybody kept helping themselves to extra portions of things they liked best. I lost count of all of the different dishes on the table. There were many different kinds of relishes, vegetables, and meats, and it was surprising how quickly the contents of the dishes diminished because almost everybody had spent the day outdoors and had mountainous appetites.

After dinner a lot of us wandered out and sat in the rocking chairs to watch the constantly changing and shifting hues of the mountains as they turned into dark blue silhouettes that finally melted into the darkening sky. I recognized accents from Georgia, North Carolina, New Jersey, and even New England, as there was an exchange of the day's activities, and promises and plans to be

Ella Jo and I had lots of things to catch up on. For one thing, by the time this edition goes to press her daughter Lainey will have become Mrs. Morris White. "We're just going to have a wonderful time at the wedding," Ella Jo exclaimed.

"Of course, our other big news is that our new cookbook, *Recipes From Our Front Porch,* which, as you know, we have been working on for years, is now in print. We've included some scenes of the Smoky Mountain area and some of John's table blessings. We will have them at the inn as well as at Lainey's gift shop, the Teddy Bear Cupboard, in Hendersonville, North Carolina."

Ella Jo said that Margaret and Arthur Stupka had been there earlier in the summer for wildflower walks and talks. "So many of our guests are interested in hiking and nature and their advice and hints are invaluable."

John joined us in the rocker on my left. "What is your favorite season here?" I asked.

"Wildflower time—the last week in April and the first two in May. I think it is every bit as spectacular as the late fall."

No, there are no television sets or room telephones in Hemlock Inn. There is lots of comfort, hospitality, tranquility, laughter, and one more important ingredient . . . . love.

HEMLOCK INN, Bryson City, N.C. 28713; 704-488-2885. A 25-room Smoky Mountain inn 4 mi. from Bryson City and 60 mi. from Asheville. Near Fontana Village, Cherokee, and Pisgah National Forest. Modified American plan omits lunch. Breakfast and dinner served to travelers by reservation only. Sunday dinner served at noontime. Open from end of April to Nov. 1. Shuffleboard, skittles, ping-pong, hiking trails on grounds. Tubing, rafting, and tennis nearby. No pets. No credit cards. Ella Jo and John Shell, Innkeepers.

Directions: Located 1 mi. off Rte. 19 between Cherokee and Bryson City, N.C. Take paved road to top of mountain.

"Winding Stairs"—a 64-mile round trip from Hemlock Inn—three to four hours, depending how long your picnic lasts and how many times you stop to look and to "smell the flowers."

From the inn, go one mile to Highway 19 and turn right. Stay on 19 thru Bryson City. Bear left at second traffic light in Bryson City and pass shopping center on right.

One mile on left is Blue Jean factory outlet. Stay on Highway 19 toward Murphy, at the intersection of 19 and 28. On the right side of the highway, you will see flagstone for sale all along the way. Sixteen miles from the beginning point is where the Applachian Trail crosses Highway 19 at Wesser Creek Road. One mile from here is the Nantahala Outdoor Center (white-water rafting on the Nantahala River). At this point, you enter the Nantahala Gorge. There will be a swinging bridge and a rock quarry on the right. One mile farther is Ferebee Memorial Park, a beautiful picnic area by the river—ideal for the lunch the inn has packed for you to take along. Just past this park on the right side of the highway a sign will read "Roadside Table 1/4 Mile," and on the left, "Nantahala National Forest Boundary." You turn left on an unpaved road (unmarked) at this point.

This road is Winding Stairs. It is marked "single lane road with turnouts" and that is just what it means! There is a beautiful old elm tree with moss and fern hanging from the limbs just before you get to the old bridge. You must observe this natural beauty. At this point, you have been 24 miles.

You cross two bridges over the Nantahala River—watch for rafters going under the bridge. On Winding Stairs, you will see a waterfall, the beautiful vista of the surrounding mountains, and the flora is great. (Be sure and take along a wildflower book to identify the wildflowers as you ride along at 10-15 miles per hour, it's just like walking in the woods.)

At the top of the mountain, you come to a beautiful small lake called Queen's Creek Lake. You are now near the little settlement of Briartown. Stay left and do not turn on "Dead End"—at this point the pavement begins. Three miles down the road is Nantahala High School on left. Just past the school, you will stop at an intersection. Turn right. A few miles on the right will be a gorgeous waterfall. The Nantahala River will be on one side as you ride along. The Nantahala Power Plant will be on the left just before you get back to Highway 19. Launchings of white-water rafts are made at this intersection. The name of the road you have just left is Wayah Road.

On the way back to the inn, stay on 19-A past Bryson City exit and you will miss the town. If you look over to the left just above the white two-story farmhouse, you will see the inn nestled among *the mountains of the Great Smokies. The vista is beautiful! Your exit is Hyatt Creek Road. Turn right at stop sign. After two miles turn left on old Highway 19. Another two miles and look for our sign on the dairy farmyard. Turn right one mile . . . you've made it back!!*

John and Ella Jo Shell
Hemlock Inn
Bryson City, North Carolina

The old U.S. 176, which used to be the main road from Spartanburg, South Carolina to Asheville, North Carolina, was replaced by Interstate-26 a few years ago. This scenic Route 176 is now enjoying a renaissance with the addition of several new mountain craft and antique shops where casual unharried travelers may spend their time.

Route 176 is bordered by the Pacolet River from Saluda to Tryon (a distance of eight miles), and includes Pearson Falls where 1200 varieties of wild flowers bloom in the spring. As one of our guests put it, "This is where Camelot meets the Pacolet." Many of our guests enjoy this short trip while visiting the inn; especially those who are shopping for the unusual, or enjoy hiking.

Bob and Fran Hull
Pine Crest Inn
Tryon, North Carolina

NU-WRAY INN
Burnsville, North Carolina

There was a noise—an insistent, urging, cajoling clang of a bell. I awakened from a sound sleep in my somewhat austere bedroom on the third floor of the Nu-Wray Inn and realized that Rush Wray, the innkeeper, was informing all of his houseguests that it was eight o'clock, and exactly thirty minutes before breakfast.

About 29½ minutes later I stumbled down the stairway into the main living room where I found the other houseguests seated on the

various Carolina antique furnishings that Rush has scattered around informally, all shaking their heads and saying the same thing:

"I don't know how he does it. This is the only place I've ever stayed where they wake you up with a bell." In just a few moments the bell rang once again, this time with our host standing in the hallway at the entrance to the dining room.

Upon that signal we all ventured forth like a group of hungry hippopotami, to be greeted in the main dining room by the most magnificent sight that I could imagine at that hour of the morning— great long tables with white tablecloths covered with platters of scrambled eggs, steaming pancakes, warm syrup, country ham, grits, applesauce, hot biscuits, apple butter, great compotes of honey, and tubs of fresh country butter.

Rush introduced all of the newcomers, and we sat down to pass the food, talk, laugh, and eat.

What a fantastic way to start the day in the North Carolina mountains!

There are two meals a day served at the Nu-wray; the other is dinner. It is at six-thirty and reservations are necessary. There is just one sitting, and if you are not there when the bell rings, you've missed it. Smoking is not permitted in the dining room.

At the Nu-Wray there are old-fashioned door keys, and every guest returns his to the old-fashioned key rack in the lobby. There is a big fireplace at one end, and many, many antiques, including rockers. There is an old Regina, like the one at the Botsford Inn in Farmington, Michigan, which is an old-fashioned music box that has metal discs. On the second floor they have a most charming drawing room furnished with family antiques.

Burnsville is located 3000 feet above sea level in the North Carolina mountains just a few miles from the highest peak in the East, Mount Mitchell. The Parkway Playhouse Summer Theatre, which has been operating for thirty years, offers a new play every week during July and August, and the Burnsville Painting Classes, a fine art school which has been operating for thirty-one years, is also in session during those months. "Music in the Mountains" presents lovely concerts every Sunday night during the summer. The area is rich in beautiful drives and walks, and is ideal for photographs, botany, bird watching and backroading.

THE NU-WRAY INN, Burnsville, N.C. 28714; 704-682-2329. A 35-room village inn on town square on Rte. 19E, 38 mi. north of Asheville. A few miles from Mt. Mitchell. Modified American plan omits lunch and Sunday night supper. Breakfast and dinner served every weekday to travelers. Noon dinner served on Sundays only. Open daily May to Dec. 1. Golf, swimming, hiking, and skiing nearby. Howard and Betty Souders, Innkeepers.

Directions: From Asheville, go north on Rte. 19-23 for 18 miles, then continue on 19. Five miles from Burnsville, 19 becomes 19E. From the north via Bristol or Johnson City, Tenn., take Rte. 19-23 to Unicoi. Turn left on 107 to N.C. State Line. Take 226 and turn right on Rte. 197 at Red Hill to Burnsville.

"European Plan" means that rates for rooms and meals are separate. "American Plan" means that meals are included in the cost of the room. "Modified American Plan" means that breakfast and dinner are included in the cost of the room. The rates at some inns include a continental breakfast with the lodging.

PINE CREST INN
Tryon, North Carolina

Oh boy, what a morning! The sun was burning off the light fog that was rising over the beautiful North Carolina mountains, and the day bade fair to be as ideal as the last half-dozen or so—cool nights and warm sunshine.

I had chosen an ideal time, the first of October, to spend a few days at the Pine Crest Inn and I was enjoying every moment of it. After playing eighteen holes at the Red Fox Country Club the previous afternoon, innkeeper Bob Hull and I had strolled about the grounds looking at some of the very unique cottages that are a part of the inn complex. Many of them have views of the mountains and almost all of them have their own fireplaces. As always, I was impressed with the way that he and Fran had tastefully adapted the rooms taking advantage of the attractive Carolina furniture that is handmade locally.

Bob explained that because many inn guests come for longer stays, quite a few of the lodging rooms also have sitting room areas. The atmosphere in all of them is a type of rustic sophistication with massive beams overhead and log wall construction. Oddly enough, one of them has a shower with six shower heads, the water shoots out from the side as well as overhead. One cottage served as a hideaway for F. Scott Fitzgerald in the '20s.

Tryon is in the foothills of the Blue Ridge Mountains near Asheville. Many artists and writers have moved there during recent years, finding inspiration in the scenery where nature has been so generous. Because of its advantageous location and an unusual thermal condition created by the encircling mountains providing

protection from the north winds, Tryon is an ideal place to spend a longer vacation in early spring and late autumn. Many guests return to the Pine Crest year after year and make arrangements to meet each other on future trips.

Spring in this part of the world rivals fall because of the beautiful blossoms of the dogwood, rhododendron, camellias, and azaleas, and the fourteen varieties of ubiquitous holly and ivy.

The Pine Crest serves both lunch and dinner, and each meal is carefully supervised by Fran Hull. She also bakes the bread and makes the desserts. For lunch the previous day I had savored turkey pancakes, and in the evening the main dish was broiled ribeye steak with broccoli in hollandaise sauce. Other evenings the main dish might be roast leg of lamb, fried chicken, veal, or pork chops. Sunday night the buffet features shrimp, a cheese tray, and finger sandwiches, as well as roast turkey, baked ham, roast beef, fresh fruit salad, and the like.

"Everything about the area and the Pine Crest encourages people to come here for longer stays," Bob remarked. "Besides the many golf courses, the tennis, and the beautiful mountain scenery, we also have the Sidney Lanier Library in the village and many excellent art galleries, native craft workshops, and theatricals."

Bob summed it up saying, "We like to do things our own way. We like jackets and ties on gentlemen for dinner, although ties can be eliminated in the warm weather. We think it is important to have the morning paper at your table at breakfast, a delivery of ice to your room in the late afternoon, and the fireplaces in the lodging rooms are relaid after breakfast."

PINE CREST INN, P.O. Box 1030, Tryon, N.C. 28782; 704-859-9135. A 34-room resort-inn midway between Asheville, N.C. and Greenville/Spartanburg, S.C. Breakfast, lunch, and dinner served daily by reservation to travelers. Coats required for gentlemen at dinner. Open Mar. 15 to Dec. 31. Golf, tennis, and swimming at nearby country clubs. Reservations required at all times. Attended leashed pets allowed. Robert and Fran Hull, Innkeepers.

Directions: From Asheville, take I-26 to Tryon exit, then 108 to Tryon. Go through town. Do not cross railroad tracks but bear left to Pine Crest Lane. The inn is at the end of the lane. From Spartanburg/Greenville take I-85 north to I-26. Exit at Columbus, N.C. Take Rte. 108 toward Tryon—go through town. Do not cross railroad tracks but bear left to Pine Crest Lane. The inn is at the end of the lane.

SNOWBIRD MOUNTAIN LODGE
Robbinsville, North Carolina

Bob Rhudy handed me a card that listed 314 birds of the Middle Atlantic states. "I've been able to identify about 70 of these," he said, "but I'm still in the learning stage. Some of our guests can go as high as 110. We are really a focal point for people who love birds."

Bob and I were sitting where everyone sits at Snowbird Mountain Lodge — on the terrace that almost hangs over Lake Santeetlah, at least a thousand feet below. Gazing over the railing we could see a tiny automobile on the thin, winding sliver of road climbing the adjacent mountain. Directly in front of us, almost close enough to touch, were at least fifteen majestic peaks with heights from 4,000 to 5,000 feet. Connie, Bob's wife, joined us and the talk turned to the changing colors of the leaves and flowers with each of the seasons.

"In the springtime," Connie informed me, "the trailing arbutus, all of the violets, and the laurel and dogwood are indescribably beautiful. We go into midsummer with the crimson bee-balm, cardinal flowers, Turk's cap, Carolina lilies, and the rhododendron, which reaches its peak bloom about the 4th of July.

"What can we say about fall? Can you imagine all of these trees in full color in October?"

The Rhudys, along with their two children Bobby and Becky, moved to this gorgeous part of the world from Maryland a few years ago.

"We haven't made very many changes in the Lodge," Bob commented. "We remodeled the cottage and several of the rooms to increase our capacity to 22 bedrooms. We seem to attract a lot of people who seem to enjoy hiking our trails — as well as those in Joyce Kilmer Forest — and want to spend their whole day out-of-doors. have extended our season a little bit at both ends."

Connie announced that lunch was ready and I noticed that quite a few people whom I had met at breakfast were missing. Bob explained that box lunches are provided in lieu of lunch at the Lodge if guests prefer.

It didn't take the Rhudys long to discover that every one of their guests would return to the inn at the end of the day with a ravenous appetite. Connie pointed out that entrée changes are arranged to accommodate the guests who stay for a longer period of time. The evening menu includes mountain trout, roast beef, fresh ham, and steaks.

After dinner that evening we all gathered in the beautiful high-vaulted living room in front of the big fireplace. It was easy to slip into conversation because most of the guests were talking about the day's hiking, and comparing notes about flowers and birds.

Bob sat down at the piano and somebody brought out a guitar, and we had a regular sing along going.

After a few years' absence, we are delighted to welcome Snowbird Mountain Lodge in the Great Smokies of North Carolina back to the pages of *CIBR*. It is a lovely experience.

SNOWBIRD MOUNTAIN LODGE, Joyce Kilmer Forest Rd., Robbinsville, N.C. 28771; 704-479-3433. A 22-bedroom inn on top of the Great Smokies, 12 mi. from Robbinsville. American plan (room and 3 meals). Open from end of April to early November. Lunch and dinner served to travelers by reservation only. Shuffleboard, table tennis, archery, croquet, horseshoes, badminton on grounds. Swimming, fishing, hiking, backroading nearby. For nature lovers. Not suitable for children under 12. No pets. The Rhudy Family, Innkeepers.

Directions: The inn is located at the western tip of North Carolina, 10 mi. west of Robbinsville. Approaching from the northeast or south take U.S. 19 and 129; from the northwest take U.S. 129.

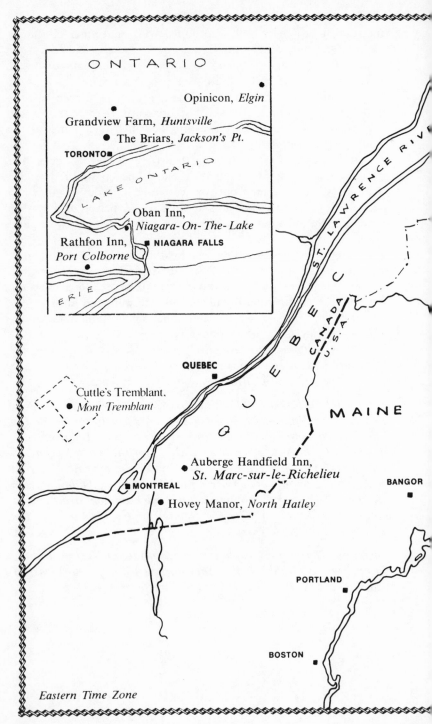

ONTARIO

Opinicon, *Elgin*

Grandview Farm, *Huntsville*
● The Briars, *Jackson's Pt.*

TORONTO■

LAKE ONTARIO

Oban Inn,
Niagara- On- The- Lake

Rathfon Inn, ■ NIAGARA FALLS
Port Colborne

ERIE

ST. LAWRENCE RIVER

QUEBEC

CANADA
U.S.A.

QUEBEC■

MAINE

Cuttle's Tremblant,
● *Mont Tremblant*

Auberge Handfield Inn,
St. Marc-sur-le- Richelieu

BANGOR ■

■ MONTREAL
● Hovey Manor, *North Hatley*

PORTLAND ■

BOSTON ■

Eastern Time Zone

408

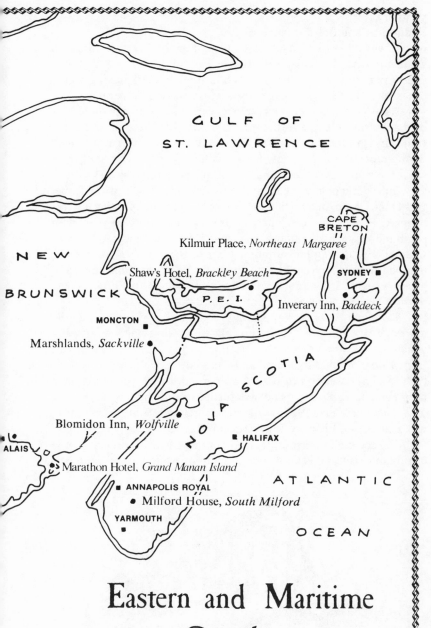

GULF OF
ST. LAWRENCE

NEW

BRUNSWICK

CAPE
BRETON

Kilmuir Place, *Northeast Margaree*

Shaw's Hotel, *Brackley Beach*

SYDNEY ■

P. E. I.

Inverary Inn, *Baddeck*

MONCTON ■

Marshlands, *Sackville* ●

NOVA SCOTIA

Blomidon Inn, *Wolfville*

HALIFAX ■

ALAIS

Marathon Hotel, *Grand Manan Island*

ATLANTIC

■ ANNAPOLIS ROYAL

● Milford House, *South Milford*

YARMOUTH ■

OCEAN

Eastern and Maritime
Canada

Atlantic Time Zone

409

INVERARY INN
Baddeck, Cape Breton, Nova Scotia

It was good to be back at Baddeck and the Inverary Inn once again for what I could guess was at least my tenth visit. It was a sunshiny morning, and the sounds of schoolchildren playing on the other side of the high hedge were a most pleasant experience.

As usual, I was up for an early morning walk down to the shores of Lake Bras d'Or, another practice that has become almost a tradition with me. Besides being a wonderful way to greet the Nova Scotia morning, it also provides me with the opportunity to observe what the MacAulay family has accomplished since my last visit.

Indeed, there have been many changes since I first visited Isobel and Danny MacAulay when they just contemplated purchasing this property. There has been a particular surge during recent years with the building of a swimming pool which is very handy for warm-weather dips during midsummer. Next to the pool is a complex of new bedrooms which enables the Inverary to accommodate the many guests who find it almost a necessity to include this little village in their visit to Nova Scotia and Cape Breton.

This time two new happenings were in prospect: One was the marriage of their son Scott the following November (something which has become a fact at this printing). I had a long telephone call from Isobel at Christmastime and she told me it was the "event of the year." She went on to say, "Oh, Norman I wish you could have been here. Terri, Scott's bride, was just beautiful and it was a perfect day. They were married in our little church here and the reception was held at the Inverary Inn, naturally."

The second important development that was almost completed during my visit and is now very much in operation is the establish-

ment of a waterside seafood restaurant among the pine trees on the shores of one of the bays of the lake. Scott took me on a tour of it and explained that lobsters, fresh fish chowder, and other Nova Scotia seafood would be offered particularly to the guests of the inn, although it is also a public restaurant. I was most impressed by the attractive view of the boatyard and some of the fishing boats and sailboats that could easily be seen while enjoying one of those delicious Nova Scotia lobsters.

Scott remained on the site to continue his work and I walked back up the hill to the main entrance. Stepping inside the living room, I received a cheery greeting from the lady at the desk and we both agreed that the Cape Breton sunshine was never more brilliant. There was a low fire in the familiar stone fireplace and I recalled with pleasure the cup of tea I took before retiring the previous night, sitting and talking about travel with many guests of the inn. We were also treated to a short concert by a young woman piper, complete with kilt and tam-o'-shanter, who frequently entertains the guests at dinner.

The Inverary Inn has several types of accommodations; some are in the main house and others are in adjoining outbuildings and cottages. The newer lodging rooms are principally used to accommodate bus tours.

The menu includes many hearty offerings including several authentic Scottish dishes.

The Inverary, which had such modest beginnings during my first visits, has now become one of the most popular travel objectives in Nova Scotia — a well-deserved reputation.

INVERARY INN, Box 190, Baddeck, Cape Breton, N.S. Canada 902-295-2674. A 40-room village inn on the Cabot Trail, 52 mi. from Sydney, N.S. On the shores of Lake Bras d' Or. European plan. Some rooms with shared bath. Breakfast and dinner served to travelers daily. Open from May 15 to Nov. 1. Bicycles and children's playground on grounds. Boating and small golf course nearby. Isobel MacAulay, Innkeeper.

Directions: Follow Trans-Canada Hwy. to Canso Causeway to Baddeck.

BLOMIDON INN
Wolfville, Nova Scotia

Many times I am asked how inns come to be selected for *Country Inns and Back Roads*. The Blomidon Inn is a good case in point and it begins with a letter I received in January, 1982, from Gale Hastings who, with her husband Peter, is the keeper of this handsome Victorian inn located in the university town of Wolfville in central Nova Scotia.

The letter reads in part: "Please allow me to tell you a little about ourselves and our inn. We purchased the Blomidon in the fall of 1980 and immediately began work. We would come from Mahone Bay to Blomidon each weekend to scrape, sand, paint, and wallpaper. During the week Peter would refinish furniture while I made curtains and quilts. We opened July 10, 1981, with eleven guest rooms, nine with private baths.

"Blomidon was built in 1877 by Captain Rufus Burgess, a descendant of New England planters, and it was one of the grandest houses in the Annapolis valley. Much of the fine mahogany and walnut featured in the woodwork was brought as ballast on his ships as they returned from more temperate climes. Captain Burgess imported two Italian craftsmen who fashioned the lovely cornices and dadoes.

"The inn has working fireplaces and all of our rooms are furnished with mahogany low-poster beds and quilts. We are situated on two acres of terraced lawns that are shaded by huge elms, maples, and chestnuts. Although we are in town, we are flanked by about 25 acres of family woodland that is marvelous for walking. From our veranda we can see the Minas Basin and the North Mountain.

"We are situated in perhaps the best backroading area of the province. Given our Maritime geography, we basically have one road that rings the province, with several side trails. In the valley, however, we have a strong agricultural heritage as well as a Maritime history and hence Wolfville is surrounded by countless beautiful trails that lead to delightful small farming and fishing communities. The diversity of the Annapolis valley is wonderful, ranging from the gentleness of the Minas Basin dikes to the ruggedness of the Bay of Fundy cliffs."

After a letter like that I was literally drooling to see the Blomidon Inn and along with several other innkeepers from the Maritime provinces, paid a visit in September, 1982, and we all agreed unanimously it was an exceptional experience. Both the Reads from the Marshlands Inn and Isobel MacAulay from the Inverary Inn told me that they had had several recommendations from their guests who had stopped at Blomidon.

Our *CIBR* innkeepers roamed the entire house, including all the bedrooms, sitting rooms, dining room, and hallways, and each came back with glowing endorsements. There was high praise, not only for the furnishing, but also for the decorations and wall hangings, some of which are drawings of costumes used at the Stratford Ontario Shakespeare Festival.

Gale Hastings does the cooking which she typifies as being sophisticated country cooking. "The menu is simple; we avoid the so-called trends," she said. "It changes fairly regularly, but we always have a roast because I think country inns should have one, and we frequently have our stand-by chicken breasts which I prepare in many different ways. We always have a sorbet before the main course to clear the palate."

We welcome the Blomidon to the pages of *Country Inns and Back Roads* and, incidentally, it's about four hours from the Bar Harbor-Yarmouth ferry and if you arrive a little later than dinner they'll always set out a tray.

BLOMIDON INN, 127 Main St., P.O. Box 839, Wolfville, N.S., Canada, BOP 1XO; 902-542-9326. An 11-room Victorian mansion on Main St. in Wolfville. Continental breakfast included in room rates. Full breakfast available. Licensed dining room serving travelers daily. Nine rooms with private bath. Closed during Christmas season. Golf, xc skiing, hiking, tennis, swimming nearby. Close to Provincial and Federal parks and museums. Gale and Peter Hastings, Innkeepers.

Directions: Take either Exit 10 or 11 from Hwy. 101 and proceed to the eastern end of Wolfville. Located on Main Street.

KILMUIR PLACE
Northeast Margaree, Cape Breton, Nova Scotia
Here are some excerpts from a most recent letter from Isabel

Taylor who has a tiny country inn on the Cabot Trail on Cape Breton, in Nova Scotia.

"Good morning, 'Mr. Norman': You've been neglected recently. The number one reason—I was having the chaise reupholstered and couldn't write in any other corner. The number two reason—I had to stir myself and work a little more in the kitchen so there is not as much leisure. Number three—the garden grew so well it kept me busy picking vegetables and flowers.

"We have had a good summer, many calls from *CIBR* friends and a lot of young people and that is interesting. I like to see young folk coming this way, as you sort of feel they'll be back.

"Our friend, Isobel MacAulay from the Inverary Inn, gives us a call on the phone every so often. She has been busy as a beaver herself.

"The blueberry muffins are in demand, and I see a lot of birds gathering outside my kitchen window. They are ready to depart south. All look plump and ready to stand the long journey to warmer climates. The hummingbirds are gone, but the warblers are still here, soon to be on their way also."

Kilmuir Place can accommodate six comfortably. The inn operates on the American plan serving breakfast and dinner to houseguests only. It's necessary to have firm reservations. The home is filled with treasures and other dear things collected over the years. In the dining room, the beautiful mahogany set and silver are outstanding.

On a visit in June, before the season really got underway, I had lobster caught fresh from the Gulf of St. Lawrence and I did something that I've never done—I understand it's an old Cape Breton thing—I sprinkled some vinegar on the lobster. It was delicious.

414

All of the rooms were taken at that time and the guests were doing some of the fabulous salmon fishing, playing cards, or just sitting and rocking on the porch.

At Kilmuir Place they know how to live.

KILMUIR PLACE, Northeast Margaree, Cape Breton, N.S., Canada BOE 2HO; 902-248-2877. A 5-room country inn on Rte. 19, 28 mi. from Baddeck. Some rooms with shared baths. Modified American plan. Breakfast and dinner served to houseguests only. Open from June to mid-October. Salmon fishing in the Margaree River, touring the Cabot Trail and both fresh water and salt water swimming nearby. Not suitable for children under 12. Mrs. Ross Taylor, Guy and Nancy Parry, Innkeepers.

Directions: After crossing Canso Causeway to Cape Breton, follow either Rte. 19 (coast road to Inverness) and turn right on Cabot Trail at Margaree Forks, or follow Rte. 105 and turn left on Cabot Trail at Nyanza.

Nova Scotia is the land of Longfellow's Evangeline; *Acadie, the land of the Acadians. These French people settled there in 1605 and founded Port Royal (now Annapolis Royal), but in 1621 Sir William Alexander was granted the peninsula and adjoining islands by the English crown, and trouble followed. In 1710 the British captured Port Royal, and by 1713 France had given up all claim to the peninsula, but not to Cape Breton Island, off its tip. In 1745 American soldiers and British ships besieged and captured Louisburg, and in 1755 the British loaded the Acadians aboard ships and took them off to the French colony of Louisiana. British land and sea forces under General Jeffrey Amherst had to recapture Louisburg all over again in 1758. This time, by the terms of the Treaty of Paris, France ceded Cape Breton Island to England.*

The best back road in Nova Scotia is the Cabot Trail which winds around the top of the province next to the Gulf of St. Lawrence, through the great forests, and back down to Lake Bras d'Or. It takes in the Cape Breton Highlands National Park. It can be traversed in one day, but it's more satisfying to stay at one of our country inns and go clockwise the first day, and counterclockwise the second day.

MILFORD HOUSE
South Milford, Nova Scotia

The time was 7:30 A.M. I awakened to the sound of the lake water lapping against the shore, and I looked outside the window of my cabin to see an errant canoeist drifting by in the middle of the lake. I bounded out of bed, in and out of the shower, and dressed rapidly so as not to miss a single moment of my time at this "almost-wilderness" resort inn in southern Nova Scotia.

My accommodations, like all the others, were in a tidy rustic cabin where there were two bedrooms and a large combination sitting and dining room with windows looking out at still another view of the lake.

There were fresh flowers in my cabin and although the furnishings were very plain, everything was absolutely spic and span. Each of the cabins has its own facilities, including plenty of hot water.

It was breakfast time, so I walked down to the end of the lane and hurried up the woods road, and who should I see but Cathy Hirsch from Meadow Lane Farm in Virginia striding toward me on a morning walk.

(Cathy and Philip Hirsch were suprise visitors at a meeting of Nova Scotia *CIBR* innkeepers being held at the Milford House.)

"Oh, I think it is so wonderful here," she said. "We left the windows open and just loved listening to the loons. Philip and I are going to stay on and take a canoe trip."

We continued together to the main lodge and joined the other innkeepers for a hearty breakfast of bacon, eggs, pancakes, home-made muffins, and coffee.

For a number of years, even before my first visit in 1973, the Milford House has been expertly managed by Margaret and Bud

Miller and their daughter Wendy. It was Wendy who gave me my first tour and about whom I have written continuously over the years. Now she is a young lady who has had considerable experience in the field of geology.

Milford House guests take their breakfasts and dinners at the main lodge where there are vegetables from the garden, roasts, fresh fish, blueberries, raspberries and ample homebaked breads and pastries.

This time I took delight in the unusual number and varieties of books that are available. These have been treasured by guests for many, many years. Some of the titles that caught my eye were *Green Dolphin Street, Below the Salt* by Thomas Costain, *Clea* by Lawrence Durell, *Park* by John Cheever, and many others.

Our meeting, which included all of the Nova Scotia inns in *CIBR* as well as the two in New Brunswick and one in Prince Edward Island, was really very delightful. We exchanged many useful ideas and were particularly entranced with Bud Miller's great ability as a storyteller. Bud explained that one of the reasons why many guests return each year is that there is a wonderful feeling of actually being in a totally natural, quiet place. "We arrange canoe trips, hikes, and excursions. Bird watchers love us."

True to the Milford House tradition, as some of the members of our party departed, those who remained stood on the front porch waving their napkins. It is always one of the sweetest moments.

MILFORD HOUSE, South Milford, R.R. #4, Annapolis Royal, N.S., Canada, B0S 1A0; 902-532-2617. A rustic resort-inn with 27 cabins on 600 acres of woodlands and lakes, 90 mi. from Yarmouth, N.S., near Kejimkujik National Park. Modified American plan. Breakfast and dinner served daily with picnic lunches available. Open from June 15 to Sept. 15; fall and winter by special reservation. Tennis, fishing, croquet, canoeing, birdwatching, and swimming on grounds. Deep-sea fishing and golf nearby. Warren and Margaret Miller, Innkeepers.

Directions: From Yarmouth follow Rte. 1 to traffic lights in Annapolis Royal. Turn right and continue on Rte. 8, 15 mi. to inn. The Blue Nose Ferry from Bar Harbor to Yarmouth N.S., arrives in time for guests to make dinner at the Milford House.

This drive starts in the village of Bear River. Turn left at the service station and follow the road about one kilometer to the head of the river. Continue straight towards the hydro tower, and at the sign of the Bear River Indian Reservation take the lower right-hand road following along the river. At first the riverbed is very rocky with massive outcroppings containing examples of fossils. These rocks are remnants of the action of the glaciers. We shall follow the west branch of the river until the river widens and, farther along, there is a lovely quiet pool in the upper river where one can stop, take pictures, watch for water movement of fish, muskrat, or beaver, or listen for bird songs.

At approximately five kilometers from the beginning, we come to an intersection in the road and at the centre is a neat farmstead; at this point take the left-hand road and continue through the forest leaving the river for about four more kilometers to the fire tower. There is a sign here that says, "Visitors Welcome—Climb at Your Own Risk." I am sure the view from this sixty-foot tower is spectacular, inasmuch as from the ground you can already see a large lake in the distance.

Leaving the fire tower, on the road, we soon catch sight of this lake in the distance and it is indeed a beautiful lake. Along the six-kilometer road to the lake we can see where old farmsteads had once been beside the open fields, and old apple trees once grew there. We finally come right to the shores of the lake—there is nothing remaining here of the once-prosperous community, and in the field above the lake, the Boy Scouts come every spring to plant trees and camp out. It is interesting to read of the history of this once-thriving community which has completely disappeared.

In the early 1900s this was the site of a unique industrial venture. By the side of the lake, a large sawmill was built, powered by one of the first steam units in western Nova Scotia. A clothespin factory was part of the complex. Because of the distance from Bear River village, a number of workers were housed in permanent lodges containing dormitories. There were also quarters for families and a small school and community social hall.

In the spring, logs were yarded in the lake and sent on their tumultuous journey down the river. Logrolling was a favorite sport on the lake and continued to be a feature of all carnivals in Bear River for a number of years. In the winter, it would be a sight to see the convoy of logging teams working out of here and bringing provisions the sixteen long kilometers we have just traveled so easily on this good gravel road.

Apart from the historical significance of this lake, it is a great

place for a picnic or a swim and, from the Milford House, a slight change of scenery and a good way to spend a few hours or a whole day.

Warren and Margaret Miller
Milford House
Annapolis Royal, Nova Scotia, Canada

One of the nicest back roads is Route 106 from New Canaan, past the reservoir, to Route 33 in Wilton and then north to Ridgefield. All along the way are beautiful old New England homes built prior to the Revolution. Ridgefield is a beautiful New England town whose main street is complete with white churches and stately homes. In Ridgefield there is Stonehedge, the Elms, and the West Lane Inn to visit.

Another interesting drive is north on Route 7 from Wilton. Antique shops and farm stands are all along the way. You can start out in the morning, make some stops and still be in northern Connecticut or even Sturbridge for lunch.

Frank C. Whitman, Jr.
The Silvermine Tavern
Norwalk, Connecticut

SHAW'S HOTEL
Brackley Beach, Prince Edward Island

I was now seeing Shaw's Hotel through the eyes of Gordon Shaw's two strapping sons, Robbie and Michael. The occasion was a very happy one because a group of Canadian Maritime innkeepers from *CIBR* were gathered for a meeting at this PEI resort inn to enjoy the lobster and the warm, pleasant hospitality as well as to exchange ideas about innovations in innkeeping.

Shaw's Hotel was a fortunate discovery for me a few years ago. I traveled to the island on the ferry from Caribou, Nova Scotia, and shared the trip with a group of young French students who lived on one of the islands in St. Lawrence Bay. As I recall, they sang during the entire trip.

The Brackley Beach area was a complete surprise, as I never expected to find such warm waters in an area that seemed so far north. Furthermore, as soon as I walked through the front gate of Shaw's and saw the old barns and the house with its red mansard roof, I knew that this was something special.

"It all started in 1860," said Robbie, "and it has been in the family ever since. We have about 75 acres of the original Shaw pioneer farm, a property which was settled in the 18th century. We've been adding accommodations, including cottages, and some of these have two, three, and four bedrooms because we have a lot of families every summer. Five of the cottages have fireplaces."

Michael joined in, "We still keep some farm animals here because it's a wonderful opportunity for city people to become familiar with them. It's only a short distance through the forest to the beach. It's one of the principal attractions for all of our guests."

"Of course, we grew up here," Robbie said, as he reached over and petted one of the playful dogs, "and so did our father. We are probably the oldest family-operated summer resort in eastern Canada."

"We open around June 15th and close around September 15th, Michael said, "and I think the first two weeks and the last two weeks are ideal times of the season. It's very warm and pleasant here in June and September is another month of beautiful weather, and since most of the young people have gone back to school, it becomes our 'quiet season.' During the height of the season we could have thirty or forty children here."

Bud Miller who is the innkeeper at the Milford House in Nova Scotia joined our little cavalcade as we walked down through the fields to the inlet. "You know, what I like about this place," he said, "is the bedrooms. They are so bright and colorful and so inviting with their flowered wallpaper. They have a wonderfully old-fashioned look, and they are just as clean as a whistle."

I thought that was a pretty good capsule description of Shaw's Hotel. "A wonderfully old-fashioned look, and as clean as a whistle."

The summertime outdoor activity, including swimming, sailing on the bay, deep-sea tuna fishing, golf, tennis, bicycling, walking, and horseback riding, contributes to very big appetites. Consequently, the cooks at Shaw's have become adept at preparing all kinds of dishes including fresh salmon, lobster, mackerel, cod, and halibut. Dinner is fun because everyone is eager for a hearty meal and the atmosphere is full of enthusiasm engendered by the day's activities.

SHAW'S HOTEL and Cottages, Brackley Beach, Prince Edward Island, Canada COA 2HO; 902-672-2022. A 24-room country hotel within walking distance of Brackley Beach, 15 mi. from Charlottetown. American plan. Some rooms with shared baths. 10 guest cottages. Breakfast and dinner served to travelers daily. Open from June 15 to Sept. 15. Pets allowed in cottages only. Tennis, golf, bicycles, riding, sailing, beach, and summer theatre nearby. No credit cards. Personal checks accepted. Gordon Shaw, Innkeeper.

Directions: Prince Edward Island is reached either by ferry from Cape Tormentine, New Brunswick (near Moncton), or Caribou, Nova Scotia. In both cases, after arriving on P.E.I. follow Rte. 1 to Charlottetown, then Rte. 15 to Brackley Beach. P.E.I. is also reached by Eastern Provincial Airways, Canadian National Railways, and Air Canada.

MARSHLANDS INN
Sackville, New Brunswick

Every year I hear from a great many people who drive across Maine into New Brunswick to reach Nova Scotia, Prince Edward Island, and Newfoundland the long way—by land.

Almost all of these letters make some reference to the Marshlands Inn, which is located just a few miles from the Nova Scotia border and the P.E.I. ferry. This is what one couple reported: "Our first stop was the Marshlands Inn. We had planned a three-week camping trip with an occasional overnight stop to get a bedroom and an adjoining bathroom, the pleasures you miss even in the best Provincial parks. Our itinerary brought us to the Marshlands Inn for a late lunch. We must admit the setting, decor, and food exceeded our expectations." (I have many letters from people who stop at the Marshlands and mention the fact that they never expected to find such a sophisticated inn so far north.)

"While paying our bill we found a copy of *Country Inns and Back Roads,* perused the table of contents, and noticed your entry regarding the Marshlands. We found that we were in complete agreement with your comments and enjoyed your personal observations. Believe it or not we never expected that such a purchase would determine the roads that we would eventually take." Incidentally, that couple also visited the Inverary Inn and the Milford House in Nova Scotia, both a single day's drive from Sackville.

My personal dilemma when visiting the Marshlands is to make a choice of entrees at dinner. The Atlantic and Miramichi salmon are very tempting, but the curried lamb with Marshlands chutney is very enjoyable, too. There are also lobsters, scallops, beefsteak and kidney pie, the famous fiddlehead greens, and many curry dishes. All the rolls, breads, ice cream and sherbets are homemade.

I am happy to say that innkeepers Herb and Alice Read continue to pursue the Marshlands tradition of leaving ginger snaps and a thermos pitcher of hot chocolate in the front parlor for guests who like a late snack.

Although the Marshlands seems like it is just a few miles from the North Pole to those of us who live below the Canadian border, it would be unusual in any setting. The china is Spode, and all the waitresses wear dark blue uniforms with white collars and aprons.

The breakfast offerings include freshly-squeezed (honest) orange juice, baked apples, fresh homemade apple sauce, stewed foxberries, (foxberries?), slow-cooked oatmeal, cracked wheat porridge, creamed salt cod, buckwheat pancakes with maple syrup . . . should I continue?

Incidentally, Marshlands is named after the Tantramar Marshes that surround the town of Sackville. Tantramar comes from the Indian word, meaning "sound of bird wings." The marshes are home to millions of migrating waterfowl. This area, now largely controlled by Ducks Unlimited and the Marsh Reclamation Board, is one of the main flyways of North America. In the spring and fall huge flights of geese and ducks may be seen coming in to rest on the marshes.

The Marshlands is not only a place where East meets West, but also a place where North meets South—then all sit down to eat!

MARSHLANDS INN, Box 1440, Sackville, N.B., Canada EOA 3CO; 506-536-0170. A 10-room village inn near Tantramar Marshes and Fundy Tides. European plan. Eight rooms with private baths. Breakfast, lunch, and dinner served to travelers daily. Closed during the Christmas season. Golf, xc skiing, curling, hiking, and swimming nearby. Herb and Alice Read, Innkeepers.

Directions: Follow Trans-Canada Highway to Sackville, then Rte. 6, 1 mi. to center of town.

I do not include lodging rates in the descriptions, for the very nature of an inn means that there are lodgings of various sizes, with and without baths, in and out of season, and with plain and fancy decoration. Travelers should call ahead and inquire about the availability and rates of the many different types of rooms.

MARATHON INN
Grand Manan Island, New Brunswick

Grand Manan is a quiet, unspoiled island of great natural beauty fifteen miles long and four miles wide—a paradise for naturalists, bird watchers, photographers, artists, divers, and rock hounds. The best way to experience the island is by walking.

As the ferry from Black's Harbour approached the wharf at North Head on Grand Manan Island, I could readily see that this was a place where men made their living from the sea. There were fishing boats, seining weirs, and weathered docks on tall stilts; a necessity because of the very high tides in the Bay of Fundy. I could see the Marathon Inn at the top of the hill—a gleaming three-story building with a mansard roof.

The owner-innkeepers of the inn are Jim and Judy Leslie, and Jim's mother, Fern. The Leslies are all Canadians. Fern is from Saskatchewan, and both Judy and Jim were brought up in Toronto.

There's no doubt that the Marathon Inn is a real family undertaking. "It's really the only way we can do it," said Jim, who is an enthusiastic individual. "Fern, my mother, is in charge of the kitchen. I try to keep all of the new projects moving both inside and out, and Judy is very busy with the housekeeping details, checking people in and out and, of course, being a mother, as well."

The first thing I did on arrival was to take a plunge in the heated swimming pool and arrange for a game of tennis. Jim joined me about an hour before dinner on the front porch overlooking the harbor.

"Our guests often like to take advantage of the chance to go deep sea fishing for herring, pollock, and haddock with the island fishermen. There are also boating trips to Gannet Rock, Machias Seal Island, and Tent Island. Children seem to have such a wonderful time here, and that is very gratifying. I think one of the reasons that Judy, Fern, adn I moved out to the island to begin with was that we thought it would be a wonderful place to raise children. We now have four.

"We have some excellent spring programs which are available to our guests at a slight additional charge," Jim said. "There are three four-day birdwatching tours in May and June conducted by Mary Majka. Also in June we have a special photographic workshop conducted by Freeman Patterson and a watercolor seminar by John Austen.

"During the fall months we have a program called 'Ocean Search' which enables our guests to learn more about the great whales off the island and also to go out on the sea in boats. Our naturalist shows slides several evenings during the week with a special emphasis on those great mammals during that time. The whales can usually be seen between August 1 and September 15."

I had a long talk with Fern regarding the inn menus. "We always have a choice of fresh fish or another meat at every evening meal," she said. "We offer our seafood chowder and another soup, and there's a choice of desserts. I make homemade buns every day and all of the desserts."

Later, I joined all of the Leslies around the kitchen table for a piece of raspberry pie. "Yes, things are going well here, but there are still a lot of challenges," said Jim. "More and more people are discovering us, but we think that Grand Manan will remain basically unspoiled."

MARATHON INN, North Head at Grand Manan, New Brunswick, Canada EOG 2MO; 506-662-81144. A 38-room resort-inn on Grand Manan Island in the Bay of Fundy, 40 mi. from St. John in New Brunswick. Modified American and European plans. Closed in winter months. Breakfast and dinner served to travelers daily. Heated swimming pool, tennis courts on grounds. Beachcombing, bird watching, swimming, fishing, hiking, diving, bicycles, golf nearby. Whale watching in season. Pets allowed on ground floor annex. Jim, Judy, and Fern Leslie, Innkeepers.

Directions: Grand Manan Island is reached by ferry from Black's Harbour which is just off Rte. 1, midway between Calais, Maine, and St. John, New Brunswick. Check inn for schedule.

HANDFIELD INN (AUBERGE HANDFIELD)
St. Marc-sur-le-Richelieu, Quebec

I will certainly never forget my first visit in late March to the Handfield Inn and the "sugaring-off party" held by innkeeper Conrad Handfield at his own maple sugar grove a few miles from the inn. The spell of winter was on the land with much snow and many cross-country skiers.

The "sugar shack" was a low-ceilinged rough building where great iron cauldrons of maple syrup were boiling down over a roaring fire. About eighty French-Canadian innkeepers and their wives were enjoying a great feast of pancakes, maple-cured ham, and eggs, all served with maple syrup. A fiddler and an accordion player accompanied while *all* were singing at the top of their lungs.

Innkeeper Handfield explained that these sugaring parties start at the beginning of March and run to the end of April and are very popular with the inn guests. "They are part of the fun of visiting Auberge Handfield at this time of year," he said.

The second time, the Richelieu River (part of the waterway which carries boats down to the St. Lawrence and to the tip of Florida) was blue and sparkling in the summer sun. The marina in front of the inn had several visiting boats, and there were people sitting around the swimming pool enjoying animated conversations in both French and English. The fields were bursting with ripening grain and I could see a number of farm animals, including sheep, goats, ducks, and geese.

I was greeted upon my arrival by Madame Huguette Handfield who enthusiastically explained all the things there were to do, both on the inn grounds and in the immediate area. She also explained that theatrical performances were given on the converted ferry boat, *l'Escale,* which is moored on the river a few hundred yards from the inn.

With her help in translating the menu, I found that among the main courses that evening were a homemade paté (quite traditional among the European restaurants), salmon from the Gaspé, duck, chicken in wine, filet mignon, and steak au Poivre.

Accommodations were in rustic rooms decorated and furnished in the old Quebec style, but with touches of modern comfort including tile bathrooms and controlled heating. My room had rough wooden walls and casement windows overlooking broad fields. Madame Handfield explained to me later that most of the inn is decorated either with antiques or furniture made by local craftsmen.

The village of St. Marc was wonderfully French and I had

animated communication with the village baker, he in French, I in English, while the aroma of his bread and rolls sent my gastronomic senses reeling. The little supermarket reminded me of similar stores I had visited in France. St. Marc stretches along the Richelieu River, and has a twin village on the opposite side called St. Charles, which is reached by ferry.

The Handfield Inn is a great many things: it is a venerable mansion that has seen a century and a half of history; an enjoyable French restaurant; a four-season resort; and perhaps best of all, it is an opportunity to visit a French-Canadian village which has remained relatively free from the invasion of developers. Its ancient stone houses remain untouched and its farms still raise good stock and poultry.

HANDFIELD INN (Auberge Handfield), St. Marc-sur-le-Richelieu (Saint Marc on the Richelieu River), Quebec, JOL 2EO, Canada; 514-584-2226. A 45-room French-Canadian country inn about 25 miles from Montreal. Different lodging plans available. Please consult with the inn in advance. Some rooms have shared baths. Breakfast, lunch, and dinner served daily to travelers. Ladies are expected to wear a skirt or dress and gentlemen, a coat at dinner. Open every day all year. No pets. All summer and winter active sports easily available. Many handcrafts, antique, and historical tours in the area. M. and Mme. Conrad Handfield, Innkeepers.

Directions: From Champlain, Victoria, or the Jacques Cartier bridges, take Hwy. 3 to Sorel, turn right at Hwy. 20. From the east end of Montreal go through the Hyppolite LaFontaine Tunnel. Rte. 20 passes through St. Julie, St. Bruno, and Beloeil. Leave Hwy. 20 at Exit 112 turning left on Rte. 223 north. Handfield is 7 miles distant.

HOVEY MANOR
North Hatley, Quebec, Canada

"I know this is going to sound funny," I said, "but it seems to me that from out here on the lake, the inn looks exactly like . . . "

"Like a replica of Mt. Vernon," said Steve Stafford. "Excuse my interrupting you, but I knew exactly what you were going to say, and many of our American guests notice the resemblance immediately.

"You see, Hovey Manor was built in 1900 by a man named Henry Atkinson who purposely made it as close to Mt. Vernon as possible. We even have a portrait of George Washington painted on glass in our dining room. It's over 150 years old."

Steve and I were taking a speedboat ride on Lake Massawippi to Ripplecove Lodge, which is also owned by the Stafford family.

"This part of Quebec has always had very strong American ties," he said. "A great many visitors from Georgia, Virginia, Maryland, and Alabama built summer homes around Lake Massawippi at the same time that Atkinson built Hovey Manor. There's a story that even in 1900 some of these Southerners continued to feel such antipathy toward the Yankees that on the train trip north every summer they would draw the blinds while passing through New England.

"We are a real year-round resort inn," Steve continued. "In the summer we have sailing, canoes, paddleboats, water skiing, fishing, and tennis here on the grounds. We've also added windsurfing and free windsurfing lessons. There are ten golf courses within a half-hour ride. Besides there's summer stock at the Piggery Theatre, and concerts at the Mt. Orford Arts Centre.

"In winter we have forty kilometers of cross-country ski trails right from our door, and downhill skiers can buy an interchangeable ticket that is valid at five mountains in our area. We've also arranged for Hovey guests to use the facilities of a nearby racquet sports and tennis complex."

Steve put his mouth close to my ear because our speedboat was really gaining momentum. "We have a regular trip each day between each inn so that guests in each place have the opportunity to visit the other," he said. "It makes a very nice change for everybody."

Our visit to Ripplecove proved to be very interesting, and I nodded to several people whom I recognized as being Hovey Manor guests. We returned to the northern end of the lake and went to the upper terrace to enjoy a cup of coffee and bask in the warm sunshine of high noon.

Although Hovey has a large a la carte menu, most of the guests take advantage of the table d'hote menu which features unusual offerings such as local pheasant in a fruit sauce, sautéed calves' sweetbreads, and fresh Gaspé salmon hollandaise.

"We serve traditional holiday feasts at Thanksgiving, Christmas, New Year's, and Easter, and the Manor is decorated accordingly. I wish you could be here for our gala party on New Year's Eve."

Children seem to enjoy themselves at Hovey Manor because the beach is safe and there is a big game room for rainy days and lots of space for everybody to enjoy themselves.

Accommodations at Hovey Manor are at the main house and also in a series of snug cottages stretched out around the shore of the lake. Many of the rooms have woodburning fireplaces.

HOVEY MANOR, North Hatley, Quebec, Canada JOB 2CO; 819-842-2421. A 29-room resort inn (8 with woodburning fireplaces) on Lake Massawippi, ½ hr. from U.S./Canada border. Modified American and European plans. Breakfast, lunch, dinner served every day. Open all year. Lighted tennis court, two beaches, sailing, canoeing, paddleboats, water skiing, windsurfing, fishing, xc skiing on grounds. Downhill skiing, horseback riding, year-round tennis, racquet sports and golf (10 courses); also many scenic and cultural attractions nearby. Happy experience for children of all ages. Pets allowed in cottages but not in Manor House. Stephen and Kathryn, and Jeffrey Stafford, Innkeepers.

Directions: Take Vermont I-91 to Vermont/Quebec border and follow Rte. 55 to No. Hatley Exit (No. 29). Follow Rte. 108E for 5 mi. to "T" junction at Lake Massawippi in North Hatley. Turn right for ¾ mi. to Hovey Manor sign and private drive on left.

There are many fine drives to be taken from Hovey Manor, and Lake Massawippi and its valley are the focus for one of the most scenic and, fortunately, one of the most convenient. A series of paved and dirt roads are available to take you right around the lake, offering a mosaic of rural farms, picturesque villages, and spectacular countryside. The total distance is only 25 miles and a morning drive is recommended to take advantage of the sun's striking the mountain ridge along the lake's west side. In autumn, this is particularly impressive.

Driving around the lake in a counterclockwise direction, the recommended stops, in order, are as follows:

1) Boutique Les Arrivants (North Hatley)—a good choice of Scottish woolens and the work of local artisans.

2) Brandt Farm (Route 143)—fresh organic asparagus (in season).

3) Du Moulin and Montrency Antiques (Ayers Cliff)—an eclectic assortment of Canadian and Victorian antiques at reasonable prices.

4) Ripplecove Inn (Ayers Cliff)—lunch on the lakeside patio.

5) Covered Bridge Park (Ayers Cliff)—a good spot for a picnic lunch.

6) Catholic Church (Katevale)—an excellent example of a rural Quebec church—very large in proportion to the tiny village.

Steve and Kathy Stafford
Hovey Manor
North Hatley, Quebec

I feel I cannot leave these comments on Canada without mentioning an outstanding radio program which originates from the Canadian Broadcasting System and is heard on many public radio stations in the U.S. at 6:30 P.M., Monday through Friday. It's called

"As It Happens," and in many instances follows an excellent PBS news program, "All Things Considered." The Canadian version is made up for the most part of direct telephone interviews with personalities that are directly connected with news events of the day. It is lively, pointed, and done with a marvelous touch of Canadian humor.

WELCOME— BIENVENUE

This is a good opportunity for me to make a few suggestions about U.S. visitors to Canada. This is a trip that I've made many times and recommended to everyone.

To begin, customs regulations permit you to bring into Canada personal baggage, recreational equipment, a two-day's food supply, and your vehicle, all duty and tax free. At the end of your visit, the non-consumable items must leave with you.

Canadian and American currency systems are similar, a dollar is 100 cents; however, at the moment the American dollar is worth thirteen to eighteen percent more than the Canadian dollar. I urge you to convert to Canadian funds at any financial institution. American bank cards and credit cards are honored in Canada. You can save money on credit-card purchases since these are billed at the U.S. dollar equivalent of the Canadian price.

Now that you're on your way, buckle up. Canadian law requires the use of safety belts in most provinces.

The French language, heritage, and culture of Quebec make it a unique place to visit. Ethnic cuisine, horse-drawn carriages, cobble streets, and great fortresses will sweep you back in time without the sacrifice of modern conveniences. There were some places in Quebec where I found no English spoken; however, if you persist, sooner or later, the problem can be solved.

On your return trip you're allowed a $300 exemption (retail value) on articles acquired in Canada under the following conditions: if they are to be used for personal use or gifts; if the articles accompany you; if you've been out of the country for at least 48 hours; and if you've not claimed the exemption within the preceding thirty days. If you are planning on bringing something exotic home, I'd suggest you check the U.S. Customs.

CUTTLE'S TREMBLANT CLUB
Mont Tremblant, Quebec, Canada

It was early morning and I was once again at Cuttle's. I bounded out of bed (as is my usual wont) to look at the thrilling panorama of lake and mountain. However, my attention was arrested by a great flock of grosbeaks feeding on the lawn and advancing toward my window. First one would dart ahead, and then another, and then a third and a fourth would jump over the first as if they were chessmen. I had a peculiar feeling that they were a delegation of some kind. They stopped just below my window and then all of a sudden flew away as a group.

Jim and Betty Cuttle, who are as active a pair of innkeepers as I have ever met, have taken advantage of the wonderful combination of lake and mountains here in the Laurentians north of Montreal to create a multi-season country inn.

It is their love of outdoor activity that has been a central factor in the inn's growing success. They themselves were ski instructors when they first came here, and even today the inn ski school, which includes videotape recordings as part of their teaching method, is an important part of the winter activity.

During earlier trips I enjoyed the skiing at Mont Tremblant — riding the ski lift with Jim and Betty — learned some fine points of sailing from Jim, and had several good sets of mixed doubles. Later, on the day of this visit, the Cuttles shared their latest enthusiasm with me.

"We started windsurfing about five years ago," Jim said. "We were in Mexico in the early spring on a holiday, liked the idea, and said let's take four or five days to learn the sport."

"Windsurfing is a combination of skiing, surfing, and sailing," explained Betty. "Now we've been holding a windsurfing regatta in front of the club for the last four years and last summer there were over 200 boards. It's unbelievable to see 200 sails of different colors."

We left the little piano lounge area where Plumber (honest, that's his name) was playing the electric keyboard and singing, and continued on to the dining room. We sat at a table beside the window that offers a truly spectacular view of Lac Tremblant and the famous skiing mountain on the other side. As dusk fell little pinpoints of light began to appear on the lakeshore and other homes on the opposite side.

"Have I told you about our Tour de Gourmet?" asked Jim. "We have combined with three other Laurentian inns, and during the summer season guests on the modified American plan can pick one or more of the other inns on a given night and enjoy dinner at one of the other three."

The dinner menu at Cuttle's has an emphasis on French cuisine, including onion soup, a cold seafood plate with fish from the Gaspé Peninsula, roast leg of veal, braised calves' sweetbreads, and boned chicken Bayonnaise. The menus are bilingual so everyone can practice his or her French or English, as the case may be.

Cuttle's is a good place to bring active, outdoor-minded young people of all ages. There is a game room for them to enjoy in the evening.

Although the word "club" is used in the name of this somewhat sophisticated resort-inn, it is, nonetheless, open to the public. Guests come in all seasons and stay from one night to three weeks. There are lots of Americans because the Canadian exchange rate is very favorable.

CUTTLE'S TREMBLANT CLUB, Mont Tremblant, Quebec, Canada JOT IZO; 819-425-2731. A 32-room resort inn on Lac Tremblant facing Mont Tremblant, the highest peak in the Laurentians. Modified American plan omits lunch. Breakfast, lunch, and dinner served daily to travelers. Open year-round. Tennis, swimming, sailing, windsurfing, boating, fishing, and xc skiing on grounds. Golf, riding, trap shooting, Alpine skiing nearby. No pets. Jim and Betty Cuttle, Innkeepers.

Directions: From Montreal, 85 mi. northwest via Laurentian Autoroute 15 to St. Jovite. Turn right on Rte. 327 north 7 mi. to Lac Tremblant. Cuttle's is on the west shore facing the mountain.

GRANDVIEW FARM
Huntsville, Ontario

Bruce Craik throttled down the speed of the motorboat so that we were barely moving through the canal between Fairy Lake and Penn Lake. "There is a blue heron that lives here," he said, "and perhaps we can catch sight of him."

The water was very still at twilight, and he nudged me to point out a beaver who was busily engaged on a half-submerged log.

We were in the twilight of a near-perfect summer day. I had made the pleasant trip from Niagara Falls, New York, and arrived at Grandview Farm just in time to see Bruce and part of a working crew load the last of the bales on the farm cart. There were horses in the meadow, and as I drove past the barn, once again the two goats, Homer and Jethro, poked their heads out of the window and eyed me with some justifiable suspicion.

I had time for a quick swim and then joined Bruce and Judy under the beautiful yellow canopy that covers the terrace in the summertime. In addition to being a resort-inn, with many activities during summer and winter, Grandview Farm Inn is also a restaurant serving three meals a day.

Lodgings are in the main house and in six other attractive cottages set among some fine old trees either on or near the lakeshore.

All the rooms are very comfortable, from the corner room with the four-poster in the inn, to the fireplace rooms in the "Tree Tops," and those in the little waterside cottage called "Puffin Hill."

Back on our odyssey through the lake, Bruce put his finger on his lips and pointed ahead. I saw a stately, graceful blue heron standing in the bulrushes along the side of the lake. "When he is frightened," Bruce whispered, "he stands up as straight as possible and that long neck blends into the background of the shore." Suddenly our friend flapped his large wings and took flight, skirting the shore. Bruce speeded up the boat to stay as close as possible, saying, "He likes to play like this and continues for quite a few minutes, I think he understands that we really mean no harm."

Those events took place during a visit a few years ago. Meanwhile, the Craik family has been very busy, and there are now all-weather tennis courts as well as platform tennis; the old barn has been enlarged and given the rather lofty name of "The Mews," and now contains three dining areas and a conference center.

Some of the assorted Craik offspring, now adults, have left the fold and are making their own lives. For example, their eldest son Ian is in the Royal Navy, and Judy and Bruce went to Trinidad to meet the *H.M.S. Fearless* and to enjoy a visit with him. A recent letter from Bruce says in part, "The period from April 6 until the

capture of Port Stanley in June, 1982, was a very trying time for all the family and for Ian's fiancée, Judith, in Liverpool.

"We managed to get away in July to witness the triumphal return of the *Fearless* and her crew from the Falklands. What a spine-tingling experience of pride and pleasure to see it slide alongside to the strains of 'Hearts of Oak' and 'Rule Brittania' with all the helicopters hovering overhead."

Ian and Judith were married on October 30, and the day after the wedding, the Craik's eldest daughter Virginia became engaged to Lt. Stephen Pyne of the Royal Navy, also. Even as I was writing this in January, the happy couple were being married in Surrey, England.

I will catch our readers up on the further adventures of the Craik family in 1984.

GRANDVIEW FARM, Huntsville, Ontario, Canada POA 1KO; 705-789-7462. A 29-room resort-inn on Fairy Lake, 142 mi. (227km) north of Toronto in a beautiful lake and mountain resort area. American and modified American plans. Breakfast, lunch, and dinner served to travelers daily. Open mid-May to mid-Oct.; Dec. 26th to Mar. 31st. Closed Christmas Eve and Christmas Day. Tennis, swimming, sailing, windsurfing, waterskiing, canoeing, xc ski trails (10km), alpine skiing close by. No pets. The Craik Family, Innkeepers.

Directions: From Niagara Falls, N.Y. (I-95): take Rainbow Bridge, Rte. 420 to Queen Elizabeth Way, north to Toronto, Rte. 427 north to Rte. 401 east to Rte. 400 north to Barrie, then Rte. 11 north to Rte. 60 (just north of Huntsville), then right for 4½ mi. (7km). Grandview Farm is on your right. Hwy. 60 is the main route to Ottawa from this part of Ontario.

435

THE OBAN INN
Niagara-on-the-Lake, Ontario

Nine o'clock of a brisk September morning—I was luxuriating in an unhurried morning bath. I felt as if I could have been in a small English hotel, and one might say I was at the first cousin of a small English hotel—the Oban Inn on the Canadian shores of Lake Ontario, just a few miles from Niagara Falls.

My room had a very pleasant secluded balcony with a view of the gay and colorful blooms that filled the interior gardens of the inn.

Niagara-on-the-Lake has a long and distinguished history, having been the site of an old Indian village and settled at the close of the American Revolution by British Empire Loyalists coming mainly from upper New York State, Connecticut, and Pennsylvania. They took up land along the Niagara River close to the shore of Lake Ontario, and were quickly followed by pioneer spirits from England, Scotland, Ireland, France, Germany, and Russia.

There are dozens of beautiful old homes lining the tree-shaded streets attesting to the prosperity of these citizens of 150 or more years ago.

Today the famous Shaw Festival attracts visitors during several middle months of the year. But there is really something during every season to delight visitors, whether it's strolling the old streets, spending the afternoon exploring the museum and small, English-style shops, or enjoying the comfort of the Oban Inn.

I pulled myself out of this reverie realizing that I would be meeting innkeeper Gary Burroughs very shortly for one of our pleasant, biannual chats.

Even though a stiff breeze was whipping the waters of Lake Ontario into white caps that glittered in the morning sun, some indefatigable golfers were already out on the links. The first hole is immediately across the road from the inn.

I walked through the Pub past the corner which contains a magnificent oil painting of George Bernard Shaw, along with some of the photographs of stars of theater and cinema who have appeared at the Shaw Festival during the past years. This room would soon be humming with the serving of an excellent bar lunch at noon.

The dining room, which overlooks the lake, was looking unusually bright this morning, mostly because Gary's mother was busy putting flowers on all of the tables. Gary himself arrived exactly on time and it was good to feel the surge of his enthusiasm.

"I love a day like today," he said. "It's really the beginning of our 'off' season, and that's when we most enjoy being innkeepers and feel that we have the time to look after our guests the way we know we should. Do you realize that over 100,000 people go through our dining room every year, and I would say that 80,000 are here during the four months of summer. It's a matter of looking after them the best we can. But the other eight months we really enjoy ourselves; there's always a fire going and a real inn atmosphere, something that is truly gratifying.

"The town is beautiful because it's a small town and we're rather conservative. For example we don't salt the roads, so the snow just packs down and stays very white. Our early 19th-century houses with their evergreens and hedges are so attractive after a snowstorm.

"We offer two kinds of off-season special inducements: A week-end package which runs from November 1st to April 1st and starts with dinner on Friday night, continuing through to a full buffet lunch on Sunday. We also have midweek winter breaks which include dinner the first night and run until after lunch on the third day. Any choice of weekdays is available."

THE OBAN INN, 160 Front St., Box 94, Niagara-on-the-Lake, Ontario LOS IJO; 416-468-2165. A 23-room village inn on a quiet street in one of Canada's historic villages approx. 12 mi. from Niagara Falls, N.Y., on the shores of Lake Ontario. Near Ft. George and Ft. Niagara, and the Shaw Festival. All plans available. Breakfast, lunch, dinner served daily to travelers. Open every day of the year. Golf, xc skiing, sailing, fishing, tennis nearby. Owner-controlled pets welcome. Gary Burroughs, Innkeeper.

Directions: Exit Hwy. 55 at St. Catharines from the Queen Elizabeth Hwy. Follow signs to Niagara-on-the-Lake.

THE OPINICON
Chaffey's Locks, Elgin, Ontario

Ever since I was a boy I've been hearing about those wonderful, almost inaccessible fishing and hunting resorts in Canada that are always situated on sylvan lakes and surrounded by primeval forests. Friends of my father would disappear a couple of times each year and return with tales of fish that practically leapt into the boat and game in Paul Bunyan dimensions. There were stories about highly voluble guides and idyllic days spent in the forest and on the water, followed by trenchermen's meals, very often including the day's catch.

In the summer of 1980 I found such a Canadian retreat with all of the virtues listed above, plus many more that make it a wonderful place for a rusticated vacation.

The Opinicon resort-inn is situated on a lovely wooded hill overlooking Opinicon Lake, and surrounded by seventeen acres of

well-groomed lawns, giant oaks, a large flower garden, and quiet spots in the woods or on the lake in which to observe nature. Accommodations are in the main building which is an old-fashioned yellow clapboard, two-storied residence with completely modernized rooms, many opening onto a porch or balcony. In the woods, set back from the lakeshore, are a series of cottages accommodating from two to eight persons each.

The cheerful dining room offers three sumptuous meals a day under the American plan, and I understand they've had the same chef for twenty years. Guests' freshly caught fish can be cooked and served at any meal, and the dining room is conducted like many old resort inns that have now disappeared. I sat at the same table and had the same waitress for all my meals. She and the other waitresses were friendly young ladies from the area.

Innkeeper Al Cross, whose Bay State accent I recognized

immediately, is from Newton, Massachusetts. His wife Janice's family has been running this resort-inn for many generations. Al is a somewhat rumpled type of man who is always on the go, greeting guests, taking care of their needs, and keeping the staff members on their toes.

With over 200 lakes in the area, the Opinicon is known for its great fishing. It appeared to me that about fifty percent of the guests in residence during my visit were interested in this sport for which boats and experienced local guides can be arranged. The inn provides basket lunches if desired.

On the other hand, a great many people enjoy the great variety of recreational activities available, including boating, lake and pool swimming, tennis, croquet, shuffleboard, horseshoes, ping-pong, volleyball, and for the occasional inclement days, a good lending library. There's also an honest-to-gosh country store, with a real soda fountain.

One of the most interesting things to do is to take the short walk to Chaffey's Locks which are a part of the Rideau Canal System. This system was opened in 1832 to connect Kingston with Ottawa, thus avoiding the rapids of the St. Lawrence. It is still a navigable waterway, and the locks, models of stone engineering construction, are operated by hand by two gatekeepers.

The Opinicon is a great place to take the entire family for a real Canadian woods holiday. Rates have been structured in such a way that it is within the financial means of the average North American family, especially when you think of hungry kids eating three meals a day.

THE OPINICON, Chaffey's Locks, RR #1, Elgin, Ontario, Canada K0G 1C0; 613-359-5233. An 18-room resort-inn on Opinicon Lake, part of the Rideau Canal System of eastern Ontario; accommodations also available in rustic cottages. Full American and modified American plan. Open early April to late November. Fishing, boating, tennis, heated swimming pool, shuffleboard, bicycles on grounds, golf course nearby. Excellent for children of all ages. No credit cards. Personal checks accepted. Albert and Janice Cross, Innkeepers.

Directions: From south: Interstate 81 to 1000 Island Bridge to Ontario Rte. 401 west. Turn off exit No. 106 at Rte. 32 (right), go north to Rte. 15, turning right (north). Follow to 2 miles beyond Elgin (bypassed). Turn left on Chaffey's Locks Road. From east: Rte. 401 west to exit No. 112 (Brockville), turn north (right) on Rte. 42, follow Rte. 42 to Crosby, turn south (left) on Rte. 15 for 2 miles and turn right on Chaffey's Locks Road.

THE BRIARS
Jackson's Point, Ontario

I'm sure that many readers share my enthusiasm for the famous *Jalna* books written by the Canadian author, Mazo de la Roche. That's why it was such a thrill for me to be standing in front of the cottage called "Birdie" at The Briars, where she was a guest during the last five summers of her life. "As a young woman, she spent vacations at Lake Simcoe," explained John Sibbald. "She also wrote extensively about the area in her autobiography."

John and I were enjoying a purposeful walk through just a few of the 200 acres of The Briars' grounds on a chilly December afternoon when the air was filled with shimmering snowflakes. John and his wife Barbara are the innkeepers of this resort-inn 45 miles north of Toronto. The land has belonged to the Sibbald family for more than a century, and as we walked through the woods to Golfer's Lane, John explained that there are actually two sections:

"There is Sibbald House," he said, "which has many guest rooms, and the Country Club, which has been a seasonal resort since 1942. There are several private cottages next to the 18-hole golf course, and also by the lake. We opened the original homestead in 1977, and we are now a year-round holiday and conference center."

We flushed a few birds out of the undergrowth as we cut through a portion of the woods, and John pointed out the five acres of garden which provide a great many of the table vegetables at the inn. Our walk continued around the ice skating rink and the tennis courts, and we tramped across the snow-covered lawns into Sibbald House to the drawing room where a cup of tea was in order. Here, in front of a crackling fire, I learned about Susan Sibbald, John's great-great-grandmother who came to this part of Ontario in 1835. "I'm sure she provided some inspiration for Mazo de la Roche," said John, as he passed the cream.

"She would be very happy with what's happened here a hundred years later. There's always been an emphasis on family holidays, and children in particular have a good time because we have an entertaining program for young people throughout the week, and this allows grownups freedom to do their own thing if they desire. We have two heated outdoor swimming pools, tennis courts, a sauna, and bathing in the lake, besides shuffleboard and badminton. The children even have their own playground.

"In the wintertime we have great cross-country skiing, snowshoeing, ice-fishing, and lots of opportunities just to curl up quietly in a corner with a good book."

Accommodations at The Briars are in the Sibbald House (where the cosily furnished bedrooms have such names as the Four-poster Room, the Petit Point Room, and the Canopy Room), as well as in seventeen additional guest cottages which are scattered about next to the golf course and along the lake. They are named after golfing expressions.

During 1982 the Leacock wing was officially opened. This provided additional rooms, most with fireplaces, a new lounge, and Great Hall for dining and meetings, as well as an indoor pool, whirlpool, sauna, and a billiards and games room.

THE BRIARS, Jackson's Point, Ontario, LOE 1LO Canada; 416-722-3271. A resort-inn on the shores of Lake Simcoe, approximately 45 miles north of Toronto. Open every day. Breakfast, lunch, and dinner served to non-residents. Summer activities include 18-hole golf course, two outdoor swimming pools, lakeshore swimming, two all-winter tennis courts, and many lawn sports. Winter sports include xc skiing, skating, tobogganing, snowmobiling, ice-fishing, and curling. There is an excellent children's program during the summer and Christmas holidays. Excellent for families in all seasons. John and Barbara Sibbald, Innkeepers.

Directions: Jackson's Point is located near Sutton, Ontario, and can be reached by Highway #48 from Toronto.

"European Plan" means that rates for rooms and meals are separate. "American Plan" means that meals are included in the cost of the room. "Modified American Plan" means that breakfast and dinner are included in the cost of the room. The rates at some inns include a continental breakfast with the lodging.

RATHFON INN
Port Colborne, Ontario, Canada

Was I ever delighted to discover the Rathfon Inn. For many years I have been traveling across Ontario, and the Rathfon provides a welcome and interesting respite on journeys between Detroit or Sarnia and Niagara Falls.

The inn is situated on a sweep of lawn jutting into the north shore of Lake Erie and is surrounded by an impressive expanse of meticulously maintained lawns, flower gardens, ornamental shrubs, and shade trees. Completely encircling the grounds is a high, four-foot-thick wall of limestone.

I entered through the large wrought-iron gates and followed a long stretch of drive lined on both sides with flowering crab apple trees and seasonal flower beds that Robertta Cash told me had tulips in the spring and marigolds in the warmer months.

This inn began its days as a family home. It was once the farm of a Mennonite from Pennsylvania. The stone farmhouse, the heart of the inn, was built in 1797 and was lived in by seven generations of the same family. The Rathfon family was among subsequent owners. For twelve years, however, the inn was unused; windows were boarded up and many of the inside fixtures were stolen. Fortunately, it was rescued in 1941, and in 1981 was purchased by Fred and Robertta Cash. They have done a tremendous amount of refurbishing and redecorating, and have added the outdoor patio swimming pool.

Every guest at the Rathfon Inn is enchanted by the presence of Lake Erie and almost every one of the tastefully decorated bedrooms enjoys an intimate view of the water. The dining room and the patios also have views of the lake. Like many other lakes of its size, Lake Erie has many moods.

The Welland Canal connecting Lake Erie and Lake Ontario is literally just a short distance away and there is almost always a parade of lakegoing vessels in sight. Part of the fun is watching them go by and speculating about their comings and goings.

Robertta Cash and I took a stroll around the inn grounds and one of the things that she pointed out to me is the fact that the inn has its own gas well (a real *CIBR* "first") located on the well-trimmed lawns. It provides hot water and heat, and I can imagine that other innkeepers of my acquaintance would love to have such an unusual feature so readily available.

The proximity to Niagara Falls raised a rather obvious question in my mind about whether or not there were many honeymooners. "Oh, yes," she responded. "Both Canadians and Americans take advantage of our proximity to the Falls, but at the same time they find the rather quiet 'get-away-from-it-all" atmosphere is much to their liking. We find them returning for their anniversaries as well."

All this walking about had aroused my appetite and so we went in to dinner, and the biggest decision I had to make that day was between rack of lamb, the veal Marsala, and the salmon hollandaise.

I'm delighted to welcome the Rathfon Inn to the small select group of *CIBR* inns in Ontario.

RATHFON INN, Box 14, Lakeshore Rd., Port Colborne, Ont., Canada L3K 5V7; 416-834-3908. A 17-bedroom inn on the shore of Lake Erie, 4 mi. west of Port Colborne. European and modified Amer. plans available. Breakfast, lunch and dinner served daily. Open year-round. Conveniently located for visiting Niagara Falls, Niagara-on-the-Lake, the Welland Canal, and other areas of historic and natural interest. Private beach, heated swimming pool on grounds. Golf, xc skiing, excellent walking, nature preserve, and backroading nearby. Fred and Robertta Cash, Innkeepers.

Directions: From Niagara Falls follow Queen Elizabeth Way south to Port Erie, continue on Rte. 3, travel west through Port Colborne to the inn. From Detroit, follow Rte. 401 to Ingersoll, turn south on Rte. 19 to Tilsonburg and east on Rte. 3 to Rathfon.

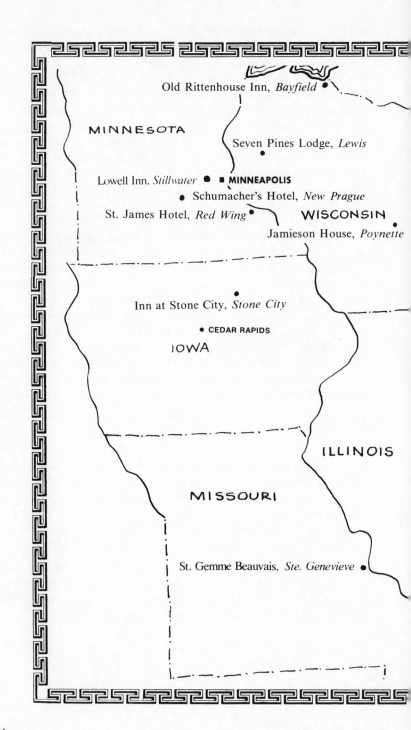

Old Rittenhouse Inn, *Bayfield*

MINNESOTA

Seven Pines Lodge, *Lewis*

Lowell Inn, *Stillwater*   ■ MINNEAPOLIS

Schumacher's Hotel, *New Prague*

St. James Hotel, *Red Wing*

WISCONSIN

Jamieson House, *Poynette*

Inn at Stone City, *Stone City*

● CEDAR RAPIDS

IOWA

ILLINOIS

MISSOURI

St. Gemme Beauvais, *Ste. Genevieve*

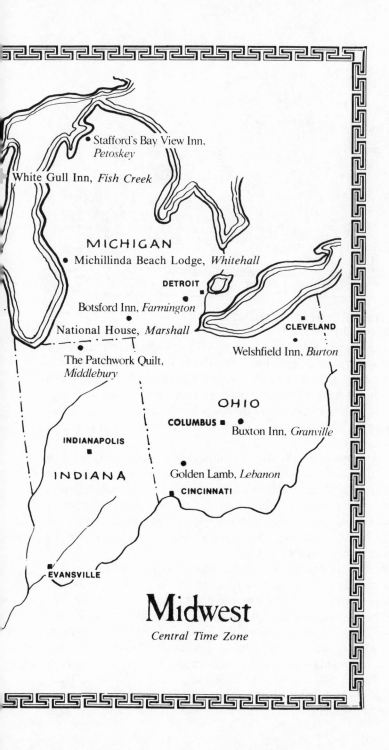

Stafford's Bay View Inn, *Petoskey*

White Gull Inn, *Fish Creek*

MICHIGAN

Michillinda Beach Lodge, *Whitehall*

DETROIT

Botsford Inn, *Farmington*

National House, *Marshall*

CLEVELAND

Welshfield Inn, *Burton*

The Patchwork Quilt, *Middlebury*

OHIO

COLUMBUS

Buxton Inn, *Granville*

INDIANAPOLIS

INDIANA

Golden Lamb, *Lebanon*

CINCINNATI

EVANSVILLE

Midwest

Central Time Zone

445

PATCHWORK QUILT COUNTRY INN
Middlebury, Indiana

Every so often Arletta Lovejoy and the staff of the Patchwork Quilt Country Inn send out newsletters to their many friends bringing us all up to date on the continuing new developments at this lovely inn set back in the cornfields of northern Indiana.

Imagine my surprise and delight when I saw a photograph of myself on the front page and a short news item about my most recent visit last fall.

I well remember the day, because it began before daylight in the pouring rain in southern Indiana and included a long trip north past Vincennes to central Illinois and then back to northern Indiana, where I arrived about two hours late for dinner. However, I found Arletta, Milton, Treva, and Herb still seated around the dinner table and I'm happy to say I didn't miss a single luscious bite of the Patchwork Quilt evening meal.

The biggest news in the many years that I have been visiting Arletta and Milton is the fact that the inn now offers bed-and-breakfast accommodations to overnight guests. There are two double bedrooms with shared bathrooms available for guests and they are available on Tuesday, Wednesday, Thursday, or Friday nights. The room rate includes a continental breakfast of hot homemade breakfast rolls or toast, homemade jam, and creamery butter. There's also fresh fruit in season, juice, and coffee or tea.

That evening I stayed in a room called the "Treetop" that has a canopy bed, a hand-painted armoire, and a turquoise velvet chair.

It is paneled in white and turquoise and has a beautiful print entitled "Shimmering" above the Franklin fireplace.

The other room known as the "Meadow" is paneled in wattled walnut hardwood and has an early-American cannonball bed with a mini-canopy made from a quilted counterpane.

Other good news shared by all of us is the fact that the Patchwork Quilt has received national recognition as first-place winner in the annual strawberry promotion contest sponsored by the California Strawberry Advisory Board. Treva Swarm's daughter Marcia assisted Arletta in the preparation of the presentation, including pictures, artwork, menus, recipes, advertising, and decorations, and I admired the engraved silver trophy awarded to the winner.

Other news was that the buttermilk-pecan chicken recipe has been included in *Bon Appetit's* new cookbook, *Favorite Restaurant Recipes*. This is the famous recipe that really thrust Arletta into national prominence a number of years ago.

The Patchwork Quilt Inn serves five-course farmstyle dinners in the large farmhouse on a 260-acre working farm that has been continuously operated by the Lovejoy family for over a hundred years. Milton and Arletta have now been joined by Treva and Herb Swarm.

Some of the main courses might include such offerings as herbed roast beef, open-hearth baked ham, burgundy steak, or the prizewinning buttermilk-pecan chicken. The desserts are positively heaven.

Now, if you reserve far enough in advance, you will be able to stay overnight at the Patchwork Quilt Country Inn.

PATCHWORK QUILT COUNTRY INN, 11748 C.R. #2, Middlebury, Ind. 46540; 219-825-2417. A working farm restaurant and bed-and-breakfast inn about 20 mi. east of Elkhart. Dinner served by reservation only. Lodging rooms available only on Tuesday, Wednesday, Thursday, and Friday evenings. Rates include continental breakfast. Closed Sunday, Monday, Thanksgiving, Christmas, and New Year's. Thresher's Lunch served Wednesdays, 11 A.M. to 2 P.M. during June, July, and August. No credit cards. Arletta Lovejoy, Innkeeper.

Directions: From east or west, exit Indiana Toll Road at Middlebury (Exit 107) and go north ¼ mi. to Country Rd. #2 and proceed west 1 mi. to inn. From Middlebury follow Indiana Rte. 13 for 8 mi. north to Country Rd. #2 and west 1 mi.

THE INN AT STONE CITY
Anamosa, Iowa

I discovered the Inn at Stone City a few years ago and in previous editions have written about innkeepers Mike and Lynette Richards and how they have projected some of their warm ideals about hospitality into the Stone City experience.

"Many of our visitors comment on the healing atmosphere of the valley, the inn, and the good companionship," Lynette told me. "Meals are served family style and we also provide a very appropriate setting for small group-learning events. Every year various seminars are scheduled on such topics as creativity, photography, wild-life, painting, and so forth."

This is Grant Wood country. The second-best-known of Mr. Wood's paintings is entitled *Stone City,* painted right here in 1930. His most famous painting is *American Gothic;* I'm sure we're all familiar with the Iowa farmer with his wife and his pitchfork.

Stone City from the very start was an expanding concept. For example, on the second weekend in June the Grant Wood Art Festival is held, and in the spring and fall, music festivals are held in conjunction with the music and art department of nearby Cornell College.

This expanded concept is illustrated in excerpts from a recent letter I had from Mike. "I'm sure you remember visiting the General Store, which was built of native stone in 1897. This project is now completed. Downstairs, the Stone Cutter's Pub is open five nights a week with friendly conversation, a roaring fire, dart games, and sometimes spontaneous music and singing. On the next floor is a concert hall that serves as a showcase for the best folk, bluegrass, and contemporary musicians in the region.

"We now have some interesting variations on country-inn hospitality, including chauffeur service in a classic car from any location in Cedar Rapids or Iowa City, gourmet candlelight dinners, a moonlight ride in a real antique surrey with a fringe on the top, along with a serenading minstrel. We are also offering a candlelight bath for two in our Jacuzzi spa, a massage by our 'masseuse in residence,' accommodation in our Lover's Suite with fresh flowers, a platter of hors d'oeuvres for a midnight snack, breakfast in bed, overnight laundry and shoe service, and a guided Stone City tour."

Each of the bedrooms in the main house is named for artistic or literary personalities who were associated with this part of Iowa— Grant Wood, John Stuart Curry, Thomas Hart Benton, and Elbert Hubbard. As Mike pointed out, "Elbert Hubbard was not from Iowa, but our idea of starting the Inn at Stone City was greatly influenced by Mr. Hubbard. There are some pieces of furniture in the inn that were done by the Roycroft Studios of Elbert Hubbard in East Aurora, New York. They have the distinctive Roycroft signature. Decorations in these individual bedrooms frequently include photographs of the personalities for which they are named."

Grant Wood . . . stone quarries . . . great, well-preserved stone buildings . . . art festivals . . . folk music concerts . . . a gathering of writers, artists, and special people who want a secluded place in which to recharge their creative batteries. All of these go to make up the experience at the Inn at Stone City—so near, yet so far away from everyday.

THE INN AT STONE CITY, Anamosa, Iowa 52205; 319-462-4733. A 6-room inn (no private baths) in a naturally attractive, scenic area 20 mi. from Cedar Rapids. This inn is in the historic district of the famed Grant Wood Art Colony of the 1930s. Breakfast, lunch, and dinner served by reservation to outside groups. Open Feb. 1 to Dec. 24. Volleyball, croquet, horseback riding on grounds. Golf, tennis, swimming, cross-country skiing, canoeing, backroading, hill and dale walking nearby. No credit cards. Michael and Lynette Richards, Innkeepers.

Directions: From I-80 exit north on Highway 1. Drive 25 mi. north to Anamosa. Go west on Main Street out of town on the "Ridge Road," 3 mi. to Stone City.

In our area, northeast Iowa is a backroader's paradise. (Iowa has more miles of well-maintained country roads than any state in the Union.) Backroading in our area has many delightful surprises, here are a few of our favorite routes.

1) Freemont Road—Starting about a half-mile from the inn you wind along a country road with woodland on either side. You come into an idyllic little valley with limestone cliffs and an old iron bridge that spans the meandering Buffalo Creek. Right at this bridge the river makes a wide bend forming a natural pool. This is the swimming hole frequented daily by our sons Michael and Ben and many of the other children of all ages in the neighborhood. The kids have hung ropes from tall oak trees for a long swing and splash into the pool! Right across the road from the swimming hole is a small "Garden of Eden," thirty acres maintained by a pleasant retired couple, Mr. and Mrs. Beam, as a bird and wildlife sanctuary. The Audubon Society's annual bird-banding for this part of Iowa takes place at this sanctuary. We helped with the banding last year and within two hours we had banded over fifty different varieties!

2) Directly across the valley from the inn, you drive past several stone houses built in the 1800s, the old stone general store, the blacksmith shop, and across the river to St. Joseph's, a beautiful stone church with fine stained glass windows. Across the road from the church are two lanes that lead back to eight stone buildings: a depot, the old quarry office, a round stone tower, the ice house, the Green mansion, a gigantic stone barn, a coach house and another blacksmith shop. These were the buildings that were used for the Grant Woods Art Colony of the 1930s—and are being restored. On these grounds are annual events such as the Grant Wood Art Festival, which takes place on the second Sunday in June and the Stone City Music Fest, which takes place on the Sunday of Labor Day weekend. These buildings are all on the National Register of Historic Places.

3) Our third back-road trip is one which we travel regularly when we shuttle overnight guests upriver for a conoe float back to Stone City on the Wapsipinicon River. This back-road trip starts as you go west on the Ridge Road. You then take a left when you see a little country schoolhouse on the south side of the road. This road meanders along next to the Wapsipinicon River to the village of Waubeek. Waubeek was settled in 1840 by Russian whalers! The whalers decided to try a new occupation; farming. Today Waubeek has a few stone buildings remaining and about fifty residents.

Michael and Lynette Richards
The Inn at Stone City
Anamosa, Iowa

For the unusual go to Irvington, Kentucky. From Doe Run Inn take Highway 448 to Bypass 1051. Turn left to Highway 79, and then another left to Irvington. There you will see Dick Frymire, the one and only "Treeologist." He forecasts the weather from a chinese elm tree.

Then you may want to go to Indiana by way of Welch Toll Bridge. Take Route 135 to Exit 92 to Leavenworth—a lovely drive through wooded hills and pretty farmland. There you can visit the Cabbage Patch antique shop, Stephenson & Co. General Store, with authentic 19th-century furnishings, and the Overlook Restaurant, with a fantastic view of the Ohio River.

If you are interested in Coca Cola, go to the Coca Cola Museum at Elizabethtown about 32 miles from Doe Run Inn on Highway 31 W. They have everything Coca Cola ever made—trays, serving machines, glasses, and hundreds of other things. I know you will enjoy the great display.

Lucille Brown
Doe Run Inn
Brandenburg, Kentucky

THE GOLDEN LAMB
Lebanon, Ohio

An antique music box tinkled merrily in the lobby of the Golden Lamb and on the table a handsome bowl was filled with punch. Decorative blue wooden interior shutters, a glowing fire in the fireplace, an old Shaker stove, flooring of intricate tile, and antique chairs and benches completed the picture.

The inn has played host to distinguished visitors from many lands, as well as many American presidents and notables. In fact, its history dates back more than 170 years.

Speaking of presidents, on this particular evening a little poster in the lobby described the favorite meal of Martin Van Buren when he stayed at the Golden Lamb.

Since this lovely old inn is a part of the heartland of America, it stands to reason that the main dishes would be representative of American cooking. For example, there is filet mignon, rainbow trout, and fried Kentucky ham steak. Other dishes offered that we think of as typically American are roast duckling with wild rice dressing, flounder, Warren County turkey, and pork tenderloin. When possible, vegetables from the Ohio countryside are used.

Rooms at the Golden Lamb would enhance a museum of early Americana. There are huge four-posters, intricately carved chests and tables, and an almost priceless collection of 19th-century prints. The rooms are named for the distinguished visitors of the past including Dickens, DeWitt Clinton, and Ulysses S. Grant.

On this visit I occupied a twin-bedded room named for Samuel Clemens. It had an old-fashioned school desk, twin maple beds, a handsome blanket chest, and a rocking chair with a rush seat. On the top floor there are antique rooms for guests' observation. Among them are a Shaker pantry with a complete description of all the kitchen items—extra chairs hang from pegs.

There is also a Shaker Retiring Room where the bed has a trundle bed beneath it. There are examples of Shaker costume hanging from pegs, and quite a few of the simple cabinets, desks, and stoves. Innkeeper Jack Reynolds commented on the relationship between the Ohio Shakers and the New Lebanon, New York, Shakers who lived just over the mountain from the Berkshires, and he suggested that I visit the Shaker Room at the Warren County Museum just a few doors away. He also mentioned the reproduction of a 19th-century village green surrounded by tiny shops and stores. "It's all in the museum," he explained.

This section of Ohio has really become quite a holiday and vacation focal point. There's the Little Miami, Ohio's scenic river with fishing, canoeing, hiking, and riding. The Glendower State Museum is a restored Greek Revival mansion; and one of the most popular places is King's Island, centered around a 33-story replica of the Eiffel Tower, where there is a variety of rides and entertainment, as well as a Jack Nicklaus golf center.

While her husband was signing the register, I heard a lady who was visiting the Golden Lamb remark, "It's like a 19th-century sampler."

THE GOLDEN LAMB INN, 27 S. Broadway, Lebanon, Ohio 45036; 513-932-5065. A historic 20-room village inn in the heart of Ohio farming country on U.S. Hwys. 63, 42, and 48. European plan. 19 rooms with private baths. Breakfast served only on Sundays. Lunch and dinner served daily except Christmas. Golf and tennis nearby. No pets. Jackson Reynolds, Innkeeper.

Directions: From I-71, exit Rte. 48 N, 3 mi. north to Lebanon. From I-75, exit Rte. 63 E, 7 mi. east to Lebanon.

I do not include lodging rates in the descriptions, for the very nature of an inn means that there are lodgings of various sizes, with and without baths, in and out of season, and with plain and fancy decoration. Travelers should call ahead and inquire about the availability and rates of the many different types of rooms.

THE BUXTON INN
Granville, Ohio

I always seem to be arriving in Granville at the height of the foliage season. Once again it was a beautiful day in mid-fall and this attractive little town, whose founders came from Granville, Massachusetts, was showing off its autumn finery.

The first thing I noticed at the Buxton Inn was a tasteful arrangement of wicker furniture on the front porch, occupied at the moment by some of the luncheon guests of the inn. The gazebo and wading pool with the fountain were now completed, and there was a new brick smokehouse and patio in evidence, as well.

A coal-black, half-grown kitten rubbed up against my legs purring contentedly. I learned later that its name is "Spirit."

The Buxton was originally built in 1812, and the Orr family, Orville and Audrey and their daughters Melanie and Amy, have recreated the atmosphere of an inn of that period, even to the point of having waitresses and hosts and hostesses dressed in carefully researched costumes of the time.

My first visit to Granville was in 1974 and ever since that first day I've been noting with great pleasure and pride the progress made by the inn and the innkeepers.

For example, Amy Orr, who was my first guide in Granville, will be finishing her junior year in high school and is on the cheerleading squad. Her sister Melanie is a sophomore at Indiana University and is very much an experienced cook. Both of these young ladies have literally grown up in the inn business.

There was some time before lunch so Audrey took me on a tour of the three newly decorated bedrooms at the inn. More are anticipated, perhaps by the time this book goes to press. As we passed through a little passageway on the second floor, I noticed a working loom and she explained that there is a weaver at the inn on Fridays, Saturdays, and Sundays. All three of the bedrooms are furnished with beautiful carved Victorian beds, marble-top dressers, and other Victorian accessories.

Audrey and Orville are very proud of the inn's reputation for excellent food and service. There are several different dining rooms. One of them has a low ceiling, and the posts and beams are painted with colors that are similar to the salmon-pink exterior hues.

We had a very lively lunch and as I had noted in other editions, the Buxton has one of the most extensive menus I have ever encountered. I asked the attractive young waitress to recite all of the luncheon desserts into my tape recorder and this is what she said:

"Fudge-walnut cake, pistachio cake served warm with ice cream, pecan pie served with whipped cream, cheesecake either plain

or with a strawberry topping, gingerbread served hot with lemon sauce, a double-dark chocolate cake with icing and served chilled with mint-chocolate ice cream, triple mousse cake served with whipped cream, raspberry or rainbow sherbert, mint-chocolate chip or vanilla ice cream."

Doesn't it just make you want to jump in the car and drive to Granville, Ohio?

THE BUXTON INN, 313 E. Broadway, Granville, Ohio 43023; 614-587-0001. A 3-room inn in a college town in central Ohio near Denison University, the Indian Mounds Museum and the Heisey Glass Museum. European plan. Lunch and dinner served daily. Closed Christmas Day. Golf, tennis, horseback riding, cultural activities nearby. No pets. Orville and Audrey Orr, Innkeepers.

Directions: Take Granville exit from I-70. Travel north 8 mi. on Rte. 37 into Granville.

I do not include lodging rates in the descriptions, for the very nature of an inn means that there are lodgings of various sizes, with and without baths, in and out of season, and with plain and fancy decoration. Travelers should call ahead and inquire about the availability and rates of the many different types of rooms.

"European Plan" means that rates for rooms and meals are separate. "American Plan" means that meals are included in the cost of the room. "Modified American Plan" means that breakfast and dinner are included in the cost of the room. The rates at some inns include a continental breakfast with the lodging.

WELSHFIELD INN
Burton, Ohio

I was standing in the kitchen at the Welshfield Inn talking with owner-chef Brian Holmes about two things very near to his heart. One was the preparation of baked and mashed potatoes, and the other was his philosophy of keeping a restaurant. The planned additions to the kitchen, which were on the drawing board during my last visit, had now become a reality and everything was moving with great efficiency.

"Norman, when I bake potatoes I believe in having the skin clean enough to eat; I like to eat the skin myself, especially because it contains so many minerals. First we scrub the potatoes thoroughly and put shortening or oil on them. We put them in the oven at about 400° to 425° and after they've been in the oven for an hour and a quarter they should be ready — I test the doneness by inserting a fine-tine fork.

"We're known far and wide for our whipped Idaho potatoes. We whip them in an electric mixer which puts more air into them and makes them much whiter. These are also made in small batches so they're fresh. One of the secrets of good food is preparing in small quantities. I learned that from an old-time restaurant man."

A raisin sauce for the baked ham was bubbling on the stove and the wonderful aroma of apple pies already in the oven filled the kitchen. There were pans with baked acorn squash, stuffed zucchini, and the makings of fresh strawberry shortcake. "Our recipe for Indian pudding came from Cape Cod," Brian said. "We took it as a compliment when one of our customers said it tasted exactly like the pudding at the Red Inn at Provincetown."

One of the waitresses dressed in an attractive early American costume complete with a white duster cap carried a tray of fresh rolls into the dining room. "That's another thing," he said, "we never use mixes — our rolls and breads are made from scratch."

We took a few minutes to walk through the many dining rooms and I even stopped to drop a coin in the famous nickelodeon. "I hope you've had a chance to visit our Country Store," he said. "It's expanding all the time and Polly is very much involved with that."

The Welshfield Inn is a country restaurant about 30 miles from Cleveland and is extremely well-known in the area as "the" place to go for Easter, Mother's Day, Thanksgiving, and Christmas. On the day of my visit a great number of families were dining at tables of eight and ten.

Brian paused long enough at the front door to bid me goodbye and he had a final thought for me:

"I'm known for being fussy and particular," he said. "I believe if you're in the restaurant business, the main thing in that business is *food*. Food preparation and serving of food is most important and Polly and I feel that nothing is too good for our customers. I'm happy to say that we seem to be able to please more people every year and a great many of them arrive with your book tucked underneath their arms. You've extended your territory since your first visit in 1972 and we're even more pleased than ever to be included."

Brian, it is *we* who are proud to have you.

WELSHFIELD INN, Rte. 422, Burton, Ohio 44021; 216-834-4164. A country restaurant on Rte. 422, 28 mi. east of Cleveland. No lodgings. Lunch and dinner served weekdays. Dinner only served on Sundays and holidays. Closed the week of July 4th and three weeks after Jan. 1. Closed Mondays except Labor Day. Near Sea World and Holden Arboretum. Brian and Polly Holmes, Innkeepers.

Directions: On U.S. 422 at intersection of Ohio 700, midway between Cleveland and Youngstown, Ohio.

I do not include lodging rates in the descriptions, for the very nature of an inn means that there are lodgings of various sizes, with and without baths, in and out of season, and with plain and fancy decoration. Travelers should call ahead and inquire about the availability and rates of the many different types of rooms.

BOTSFORD INN
Farmington Hills, Michigan

It was a late, lovely summer afternoon in Farmington and after taking one of the crossing roads from the Detroit Airport, I was on Grand Avenue headed toward Farmington and turned into the

parking lot of the Botsford Inn to see a number of people enjoying the tennis courts. A welcome breeze had come up, breaking the hot weather in Detroit, but I was still glad to know that my room at the Botsford would have air conditioning if I needed it.

I go back with the Botsford Inn—not way back to 1836 when it was first built or when the famous Innkeeper Botsford had it—but for quite a few of the more recent years. I can remember when I first heard of it, my reaction was, "Who would expect to find a country inn in Detroit." Well, the Botsford Inn isn't exactly a New England country inn, however, some of the 19th-century atmosphere has been preserved; first in the 1930s, with the help of Henry Ford, and continued by the present owner and innkeeper, John Anhut, who has a penchant for country inns.

"The late Henry Ford became interested in the preservation of the inn in 1924," John informed me. "He placed a great many of his own 19th-century antiques and treasures in it. Among them are furnishings from his country home, including a beautiful little inlaid spinet, a handsome horsehair sofa, his music boxes, a Simon Willard clock, an exquisitely inlaid mahogány table, and an attractive oil painting of the Botsford Inn showing people in the costumes of the late 19th century."

This historic inn, the oldest in Michigan, is still providing food and lodging. In 1841 it was converted into a tavern, and was a stagecoach stop on the Grand River plank road which followed the Indian trail that went to Lake Michigan. Milton C. Botsford acquired the inn in 1860 and it became a popular meeting place for drovers, farmers, and travelers.

John joined me for dinner in the main dining room with its oaken beams and broad picture window. We talked for a moment about the menu at the Botsford Inn and he had this to say, "We believe in serving predominantly American food; we aren't a French restaurant and have never tried to be one. Consequently, we have a lot of things on the menu that people come to associate with country living here in the Midwest." This idea of country food was certainly reflected in the salad bowl of crisp lettuce, pea beans, a sprinkling of carrots and celery and tomato sections. The dressing reminded me of my grandmother's, back in central New York State, a little on the vinegary side with bits of bacon in it. The short ribs that night were delicious. Each came in its own casserole and the sauce was excellent. I poured it over both the meat and potatoes; it was exactly what I wanted.

In 1836, Farmington was a day's journey from the banks of the river where Detroit was a burgeoning city. Today it is just a short drive from the hustle and bustle of the Motor City. At the Botsford Inn, everything possible has been preserved, particularly in the main building where there are many reminders of other times in Michigan.

Many of the bedrooms, furnished with reproductions, have the conveniences that American travelers often find not only helpful but necessary. Best of all, the spirit of country innkeeping and community service is very much alive.

BOTSFORD INN, 28000 Grand River Avenue, Farmington Hills, Mich. 40824; 313-474-4800. A 62-room village inn on the city line of Detroit. European plan. Dinner served daily except Monday. Breakfast and lunch Tuesday thru Saturday. Sunday brunch. Closed Christmas and New Year's Day. Tennis on grounds. Greenfield Village, skiing, and state parks nearby. John Anhut, Innkeeper.

Directions: Located in Farmington Hills on I-96 which is easily accessible from major highways in Michigan.

THE NATIONAL HOUSE INN
Marshall, Michigan

Michael McCarthy, the innkeeper at the National House Inn, was helping me to assimilate the experience of this unusual town. "Mr. Brooks was the most important factor," he said. "He was the man who had the vision of Marshall. But everybody in town has joined in. We are proud of the homes and the museums and we all work together. I am sure that we could not have restored the National House if it hadn't been a community effort. People helped out in so many ways.

"This is probably the oldest remaining hotel building in Michigan," he pointed out. "We learned that it was open in 1835 and undoubtedly was the first brick building of any kind in our county.

"At one time it was a windmill and wagon factory and more recently an apartment building," Michael continued. "Restoring it was hard work, but underneath the dirt and grime of dozens of years there was the solid, beautiful structure of the original brick as well as the irreplaceable woodwork. I'm particularly interested in that field because I am a restoration carpenter as well as an innkeeper. The apartments from the old building were converted into sixteen bedrooms and baths.

"As you can see, Marshall is very much a Victorian restoration. We searched everywhere—culled all the antique shops and removed furniture from our own homes. Many of our friends contributed some of their beloved pieces in order to help us recreate the atmosphere of Marshall before the turn of the century."

One of the most striking features of the National House is the passionate attention to detail. For example, each bedroom has its own ambience and there are colorful comforters, old trunks, marble top tables, bureaus, dried flower arrangements, electric lamps that are reproductions of gas lamps, candle sconces with reflectors, little corner sofas, special care with door knobs, and special attention is given to the linens. The bedroom windows overlook either the residential part of town, or a beautiful fountain in the town center park.

Breakfast is the only meal served, and is offered every morning in the dining room which has a most fetching collection of chairs and tables from great-grandfather's day. The color tones are warm brown and beige. The breakfast offerings include homebaked coffee cakes and muffins, nut breads, and the like. I spent an hour and a half at breakfast talking with many different people.

In the years since I have been visiting Marshall, which contains the finest examples of 19th-century architecture in the Midwest, a great many of the buildings and homes of the town have been added to the State of Michigan Historic Sites and to the National Register. The Marshall Historical Society sponsors a historic home tour during September of every year, certainly the most exciting yearly

event in the town. However, the tour of the town, which includes at least forty historic and beautiful buildings, can be experienced at any time.

One of the most impressive of these buildings is the National House Inn.

THE NATIONAL HOUSE INN, 102 South Parkview, Marshall, Mi. 49068; 616-781-7374. An elegantly restored 16-room Victorian-period village inn. Marshall is the finest example of 19th-century architecture in the Midwest. It has 15 State Historic Sites and 6 National Register Sites. European plan includes continental breakfast. No other meals served. Open year-round. Closed Christmas Eve and Christmas Day. Tennis, golf, swimming, boating, xc skiing nearby. Michael and Beth McCarthy, Innkeepers.

Directions: From I-69 exit at Michigan Ave. in Marshall and go straight 1½ mi. to inn. From I-94 use exit 110, follow old 27 south 1½ mi. to inn.

MICHILLINDA BEACH LODGE
Whitehall, Michigan

Whatever else there may be at Michillinda, the most exciting, pervasive, and inspiring feature is the presence of Lake Michigan. Everything at this American plan resort-inn centers around the lake and its thrilling moods. Throughout my visit with Don and Sue Eilers and their really attractive children, Kristin, eleven, and Kent, six, my attention was never far from the sound and the sight of this gorgeous body of water.

The scope of a Michillinda vacation with all of the recreational activities, both on the grounds and in the nearby town and country-side, is succinctly woven together in a very colorful brochure where the photographs show happy sun-tanned holiday-seekers of all ages sitting in the sun overlooking the lake, walking through the unusually expansive flower gardens, playing tennis, swimming in the pool, playing miniature golf or tetherball, riding the tandem bicycle among the chalets at lakeside, or relaxing in the pine-paneled library and living room. I have seven pages of typewritten notes about my visit.

Don and Sue are ideal people to be involved in a family-oriented resort-inn. They are young and enthusiastic and have growing children of their own. As Don says, "Basically we don't run organized activities, we have all of the recreation any young person could enjoy, and yet we don't have a social director encouraging guests to 'sign-up' for this or that, and putting them into a series of time slots. We have enough grounds here and enough indoor

recreation at the Surfside building so that kids can have their own fun and their parents don't have to worry about them."

Sue joined in, "I think we've always had an ideal mix of senior citizens and young children. Many of the older people don't see children as much anymore and they become 'vacation grandparents.'"

It takes a good-sized staff to keep all of the activities at Michillinda under control. Don and Sue told me that among other things they hire young people who have some theatrical and musical talent, because the staff puts on a variety show every Friday night. Sometimes the show will include a number or two by some of the guests.

Accommodations are in lakeview bedrooms with resort-furniture in both the main house and a series of small cottages and chalets on the grounds.

"With all of this outdoor activity, we serve three full meals a day," said Don, as we walked through the dining room and the kitchen. "We have a choice of three entrées every night and always have an eye towards what kids would like to eat, because kids are part of what this whole place is about."

I did something which I'm sure almost every Michillinda guest does just before departing: I walked out to the edge of the grassy bluff overlooking the beach and took one last look at the blue waters and indefinable horizon of Lake Michigan. I was caught up by the sound of the wind and waves and the warmth of the sunshine. I felt the tug of a small hand at my trousers, and there beside me was a little boy who asked me if I could help him tie his shoes.

MICHILLINDA BEACH LODGE, 5207 Scenic Dr., Box C, Whitehall, Mi. 49461; 616-893-1895. A 51-room American plan resort-inn 15 mi. north of Muskegon. Located on the shore of Lake Michigan. Blue Lake Fine Arts Camp nearby. Open June 19 to September 14. Tennis, swimming, mini-golf, shuffleboard on grounds; 6 golf corses, charter fishing nearby. No pets. No credit cards. personal checks accepted. Don and Sue Eilers, Innkeepers.

Directions: Follow U.S. 31 north from Muskegon, exit at White Lake Drive, drive west to South Shore Drive (4 mi.), left (5 mi.) on South Shore Drive. Follow signs to Scenic Drive, turn left (1 mi.) to lodge.

STAFFORD'S BAY VIEW INN
Petoskey, Michigan

Once again, Janice Smith and I were seated on the porch of Stafford's Bay View Inn looking out over Little Traverse Bay. I remember there had been a sailboat race in progress the last time we sat there.

"Do you remember," she asked, "when you and I took a little backroading tour and saw some of the Lake Michigan shoreline a few years ago?" I remember the day very well. Along with her son Reginald and her daughter Mary Kathryn, we had set out from the inn and I had gained a marvelous overview of that entire section of Michigan.

Reg has completed his second year at the Cornell Hotel School, and during the summer he works in the inn as a waiter and a cook. He wants to know more about all that good food he enjoys so he is assisting with cooking Sunday brunch at the Cornell Statler as well.

Mary Kathryn is finishing her last year at Wayland and I understand she's a gifted young actress. She'll be working at the Pier Restaurant as a salad girl this summer.

Thirteen-year-old Dean spends a lot of time trying to be like his dad. You'll see the two of them together at the buffet table for Sunday brunch. Dean cooks the waffles while Stafford carves the meat.

"I do wish you could be with us at Christmastime," Janice exclaimed. "The inn looks prettier than ever. "There are over 400 white lights decorating the outside of the inn and the Victorian cupola looks like a giant Christmas tree. As you enter the front door you are greeted by Kathy Hart's beautiful gingerbread village which actually takes about two months of loving care to prepare. We have families stopping all the time to show the children the trees and the village.

The inn is on the edge of the Bay View section of Petoskey, a summer resort community which has grown up around a program of music, drama, art, and religious lectures and services. The community began in the late 1800s when people rode on the Grand Rapids Indiana railroad or on lake steamers to reach Petoskey. The early residents built Victorian homes which are scattered throughout Bay View today.

One of the factors that contributes greatly to the inn's popularity is its capacity to make senior citizens feel most welcome. I found it to be a comfortable place for *all* ages; there are a lot of children around in the summer and some of the older guests take naturally to entertaining them—I think the best term is "surrogate grandparents."

"After Stafford went to the regional meeting of *CIBR* inn-

keepers, he came back with all kinds of wonderful ideas and conceived an idea called 'Stafford's Country Inn Cuisine.' The entrees include Lake Michigan whitefish, chicken Marengo, and a rack of lamb. We also offer veal Parmesan, herbed stuffed chicken and bay scallops. One of the innovations has been a mid-course refresher in the form of a lemon sorbet which Stafford says, 'cleanses the palate before the entree.' We've also eliminated our salad bar and guests are served a house salad of bibb lettuce with walnuts, raisins, and a raspberry vinaigrette dressing."

Things are really humming at Stafford's Bay View Inn.

STAFFORD'S BAY VIEW INN, Box 3, Petoskey, Michigan 49770; 616-347-2771. A 23-room resort-inn on Little Traverse Bay in the Bay View section of Petoskey. Modified American Plan omits lunch. Bed-and-breakfast plan also available. Breakfast, lunch, and dinner served daily to travelers. Open daily mid-May thru November 1; Thanksgiving weekend; Christmas week and long weekends during the winter sports season. Lake swimming and xc skiing on grounds. Bay View cultural programs in July and August. Golfing, boating, tennis, fishing, hiking, scenic and historic drives and Alpine ski trails and excellent shopping nearby. Pick-up service provided from Pellston Airport on request. Stafford and Janice Smith; Kathy Hart and Judy Honor, Innkeepers.

Directions: From Detroit: take Gaylord Exit from I-75 and follow Mich. Rte. 32 to Rte. 131, north to Petoskey. From Chicago: use US 131 north to Petoskey.

One of our most striking back roads is the delightful, winding, sixteen-foot-wide blacktop roadway that threads its way along the bluff for 21 miles from Harbor Springs to Cross Village. There is a steady succession of tunnels, shaded bowers and bosky dells, as well as historic touches. This is historic Indian country, graced with lingering softwood greens, tinged with hardwood red and purple and gold.

You start at the main intersection in Harbor Springs, head north up the high hill above the town, past Bluff Gardens, and continue on past the well-manicured links of the Harbor Springs Golf Club. This is followed by a solid mile of tree cover that leaps the road overhead; mostly maple, beech, oak, and cedar, with summer homes tucked away, barely in sight.

Continuing through West Traverse, the road passes an old country school and about five miles from Harbor Springs crosses Five-Mile Creek where there is an old mill. Next to it is a tiny "mom and pop" general store, typical of those to be found in Michigan's lumbering communities. Soon, one comes to a unique barnyard golf course where there are no green fees. Its sporting, rolling, cobby terrain has plenty of hazards and gorse-type rough.

After three miles of winding, woodsy road, you arrive at a scenic turnout high above the rocky beach of Lake Michigan. On the far shore of Little Traverse Bay, the huge greenish globe of the Big Rock Nuclear Plant looks like a marble perched on the beach.

The road continues past the old Indian mission church and on into Good Hart, which has a combination general store-antique

shop-post office. About fifteen miles from Harbor Springs, there's a century-old cemetery nicely kept in its setting of leafy dignity, and then a two-mile stretch of very old, very high, wind-blown sand dunes.

Now the road has taken you to Cross Village where you can continue along Emmett County Scenic Route 1—twenty miles to Mackinaw City by way of a magnificent array of sand dunes and open beach—or return the way you came, but nearer the lake by taking a couple of optional turns.

Stafford Smith
Stafford's Bay View Inn
Petoskey, Michigan

WHAT IS INNKEEPING REALLY LIKE?

"Reflecting over six years now, I think the nicest thing about innkeeping is the friendships we've made with our guests. I feel much a part of some of these peoples' lives now. I know their jobs, their children, and how they feel about certain issues. I look forward to seeing them open the front door and hearing of the new things that have happened to them. And it's not just Tom and me. There's little turnover with our staff so that they, too, have come to know our guests. It must be just as comforting for them to see our familiar faces as it is for us to see them come back again and again. But, perhaps, I'm just defining what a friend is."—Vermont

"Our winter season began well but the February rain succeeded in ending the season early. Even so, we had some interesting things occur in that short space of time. One night our power went out at 7 p.m. and we had 75 for dinner. We served by candle and little cautious steps. As we cook by gas the food stayed hot. The power came back at 2 a.m. and my son and I did dishes until 3:30 a.m. When the temperature went to 35° below and remained there 24 hours our gas line froze so we ended up doing breakfast for sixty on our newly installed wood stove."—New York

"I must say that it is very satisfying to find our inn guests gathered in the TV-sitting room getting acquainted over a ball game. So many people from all over the country come to visit here and they have so much to offer. It just amazes me how a house full of people can become one big happy family. I guess that is what innkeeping is all about. What fun it is!!"—New Hampshire

467

LOWELL INN
Stillwater, Minnesota

We were enjoying dinner in the Matterhorn Room of the Lowell Inn at a small regional meeting of inns in *Country Inns and Back Roads*. It had been a full afternoon starting with lunch in the Garden Room with its tinkling fountain. We were served at the large Lazy Susan tables.

Afterwards there was a tour of the many rooms at the Lowell Inn where we "oohed and aahed" at the French-style telephones, the exquisite French clocks, the mirror, comb, and brush sets, the tiny flacons of eau de cologne, the wonderful, elegant, and unusual showers in several rooms, the individual bedding in each room with specially chosen, coordinated quilts, pillowcases, and sheets. One of them was from a design created by actress Mary Martin. There are dimmers on the light switches and the bedrooms are larger than usual, because two rooms have been made into one. There were some very pleasant watercolors and prints and, of course, the ubiquitous ceramic cats which are found on each bed.

Now we were deeply immersed, both literally and figuratively in the fondue dinner which had opened with escargots and salad, followed by shiny fondue pots into which we dipped shrimp or cubes of beef on long-handled forks. Incidentally, this is the regular dinner at the Matterhorn Room every evening.

If all of this sounds rather innovative, indeed it is, because there is a tradition of enthusiastic innkeeping at the Lowell Inn that began with Arthur's mother and dad who spent a great deal of their youth and adulthood "on the road." As Arthur explained, "Mother was an actress and Dad was a pianist. They met and were married and when they were playing Stillwater, the opportunity to manage the hotel arose, so they stayed on and eventually became owners in 1945.

"I grew up here at this inn. I've held every job. I'm delighted to say Maureen, my wife, shares my enthusiasm for it as do a great many of our children." There are several photographs of Palmer family gatherings which over the years have been growing as sons- and daughters-in-law are being added.

In addition to the Garden Room and the Matterhorn Room, a third dining room reflecting the appreciation and love for antiques in the Williamsburg Colonial period, is also enjoyed by the inn

patrons. This room called the George Washington Room has Capo Di Monte porcelain, heirlooms descended from the artisans commissioned in 1743 by the King of Naples, Charles III. There is Sheffield silver service and a Dresden china collection. On the tables, the glassware, dishes, and ashtrays as well the hand-crested Irish linen, complement the authentic Williamsburg ladder-back chairs. There are portraits of George and Martha Washington that recall our nation's early beginnings. Diners may choose from conventional menu offerings in both the George Washington Room and the Garden Room.

The latest among the more recent innovations are the power-boat trips along the alluring St. Croix River aboard the inn's new fleet of express cruisers. Arthur refers to these as the "River Run." It's even possible to stay on board overnight.

Once again, I had the thought as I sat among these innkeepers from *CIBR* "talking shop" and exchanging ideas that Arthur's mother Nelle would have looked on with enthusiastic approval.

THE LOWELL INN, 102 N. Second St., Stillwater, Minn. 55082; 612-439-1100. A 22-room village inn 18 mi. from St. Paul, near all the cultural attractions of the Twin Cities. European plan. Lunch and dinner served daily except Christmas Eve and Christmas Day. Open year-round. No pets. Canoeing, tennis, hiking, skiing, and swimming nearby, including 4 ski resorts within 15 mi. Arthur and Maureen Palmer, Innkeepers.

Directions: Stillwater is on the St. Croix River at the junction of Minn. 95 (north and south) and Minn. 36 (east and west). It is 7 mi. north of I-94 on Hwy. 95.

THE ST. JAMES HOTEL
Red Wing, Minnesota

The original St. James Hotel was built in the mid-1870s and according to the history of the hotel, was a very impressively designed and decorated building with various reception rooms, parlors, and a large ballroom, and was well-known for its excellent food and service.

However, even at the top of its form it could not begin to approach today's *restored* St. James Hotel.

The entire project is a tribute to the fact that American ingenuity, capital, and know-how are able to reproduce successfully almost every type of furniture, ornamentation, decoration, and design of a hundred years ago, and still maintain the very best quality.

Almost all the furnishings in the St. James are copies of lamps, bureaus, tables, chairs, beds, and carpets originally manufactured during the Victorian era. All of this furniture is solid, well-made, and sturdy, and doesn't have the rickety feeling that sometimes occurs. Even the small details have been considered, including brass soap holders, towel racks, door knobs, hinges, and the like.

The hotel is a modern accommodation of today, but serves as a reminder of opulent days gone by. In addition to excellent reproductions, the photographs and prints taken in a bygone era, are further reminders of the past. Many of the walls are hung with pictures of Red Wing taken over a hundred years ago, both of the town and of the river steamers that made the town a regular stop.

What excites me most is that this small hotel in the heart of America *could* have been torn down and gone the way of so many others, but instead, it is making a contribution that bids fair to endure for at least another hundred years.

Turn-down bed service and the morning newspaper at the door are a couple of the niceties that add to the pleasure of a visit to the St. James. Bed linens and towels are of first-rate quality and the quilts for each bed were especially designed and made to harmonize with the furnishings and colors of the room. Many of the rooms look out upon the Mississippi River where the unending flow of barges provides constant entertainment. An excursion boat is available for guests who would like a closer look at the river.

Another interesting oddity is that the lobby of the old original hotel has been restored, but it is not used as the lobby of today's St. James. Instead, it has been set aside for parties, banquets, and special occasions. Photographs of the original 1870s investors, who put up all of $60,000, look down upon today's travelers with a certain undisguised smugness.

This entire restoration project took a great deal of courage and a great deal of money. In a day when so many restorations of old buildings fall considerably short of expectations, the *new* St. James Hotel is certainly a model for all such undertakings.

Since my original visit some interesting things have happened at the St. James Hotel, including the opening of nineteen additional bedrooms with a commanding view of the majestic Mississippi. In addition, the hotel's original historic main dining room, now known as the Victorian Dining Room, is open five nights each week. The Sunday brunch is now served on the fifth floor where there is another impressive view of the Mississippi.

No wonder those original founding father investors are looking so pleased.

ST. JAMES HOTEL, 460 Main St., Red Wing, Minnesota 55066; 612-388-2846. A 60-room restored country town hotel on the Mississippi River, 50 mi. from Minneapolis. Open all year. Breakfast, lunch, and dinner served to travelers. This is an in-town hotel with no sports or recreation on the grounds, but swimming, tennis, hiking, golf, bicycling, backroading, and river sightseeing trips are all very convenient. No pets. Gene Foster, General Manager.

Directions: From Minneapolis/St. Paul Airport take Hwy. 5 east, exit on Hwy. 55 to cross Mendota Bridge. Follow Hwy. 55 to Hastings where it joins Hwy. 61. Follow Hwy. 61, 22 mi. south into Red Wing. Accessible by Amtrak.

SCHUMACHER'S NEW PRAGUE HOTEL
New Prague, Minnesota

John Schumacher and I were talking about one of the original recipes he prepares at Schumacher's New Prague Hotel. "We call it quail Helenka," he said. "It is named for my mother."

"First," he said, with a mischievous look in his eye, "you catch two quail. Actually, the thing that's different is the fact that each quail is stuffed with a plum and then wrapped in two strips of bacon and baked for forty minutes at 350°; when they are done I spoon some brown sauce over them. They're particularly good served with red cabbage and hash-brown potatoes topped with melted swiss cheese."

John is a very innovative chef, having graduated first in his class from the Culinary Institute of America. His extensive dinner menu includes rabbit, pike, veal, pork, chicken, and homemade sausage, and all of the orders are cooked by him except when he takes an occasional day off.

A good example of a new breed of young innkeepers who gain great satisfaction and personal fulfillment in running a country inn, John declares, "It's been a wonderful experience since 1974 when I discovered New Prague and this hotel. Right from the start there were many things that had to be done, but it's been a highly satisfactory arrangement. Fortunately, I am the chef and I feel that a great deal of our reputation centers around the fact that the food is something I can control.

"The building was built in 1898 and originally was called the Broz Hotel. It was designed by the same man who designed the George Washington Bridge, the Supreme Court building in Washington, and the state capitol in St. Paul. His name was Cass Gilbert.

Abovestairs each of the inn's twelve bedrooms is named for a different month and has an atmosphere and personality all of its own. One has a large semicircular bed with a white eyelet canopy, an antique couch, and a genuine Bavarian wall bouquet.

"I've been in central Europe several times," John commented, "and I believe the decorations and the cuisine here reflect my identification with Germany and Czechoslovakia. We have imported cotton-covered goosedown comforters and pillows and there are many, many central-European decorative touches. We have hand-painted Bavarian folk scenes and patterns by Pipka, a native Czech who lives in Minneapolis.

"We don't have any television or telephones in the rooms, but our guests will find fresh arrangements of flowers and live plants, complimentary local newspapers, lots of books and magazines, and we even put candy under the pillows."

One of the things I found most intriguing about Schumacher's is that it has rapidly gained a reputation for being a place that honeymooners and anniversary couples enjoy. They often request a room that corresponds with their wedding month.

New Prague is just 35 miles south of the Minneapolis-St. Paul metropolitan area, and besides the fun of staying at Schumacher's there is a surprising number of things to do nearby, including golf on an 18-hole course, tennis, and cross-country skiing in the winter. The Minnesota River is just nine miles away and is ideal for canoeing. It is a good place for ten-speed biking as well.

SCHUMACHER'S NEW PRAGUE HOTEL, 212 West Main St., New Prague, Mn. 56071; 612-758-2133. (Metro line: 612-455-7285.) A 12-room Czechoslovakian and German inn located in a small country town approximately 35 mi. south of Minneapolis and St. Paul. European plan. Breakfast, lunch, and dinner served to travelers all year except three days at Christmas. Good bicycling and backroading nearby; also xc skiing, tennis, and golf. No entertainment available to amuse children. No pets. No credit cards. John Schumacher, Innkeeper.

Directions: From Minneapolis, take Rte. 494 west to Rte. 169 south to Jordan exit. Turn south on Rte. 21 for 9 mi. to New Prague. Turn left to Main St. at the stop sign, and the hotel is in the second block on the right.

ST. GEMME BEAUVAIS
Ste. Genevieve, Missouri

I was on Interstate 55 coming south from St. Louis. In a few minutes I would be turning off onto Highway 32 and paying another visit to Ste. Genevieve.

In 1974 I visited this historic Missouri community for the first time and met Frankye and Boats Donze and enjoyed staying in their little inn, St. Gemme Beauvais. At that time I also had a tour of the old part of the town and visited many of the carefully restored houses, including the Amoureaux House and the Beauvais House, both of which are personal projects of the Donzes.

I turned down the village street and soon found myself in front of the red brick inn with its two-story white pillars. As I approached, Frankye opened the door and said, "I'm so glad that you could come again." Boats joined us, we had a pleasant reunion, and they told me all the news.

They were very enthusiastic about the number of people who have visited the inn from reading about it in *CIBR*. "There are people from all over the country and our telephone is ringing constantly," exclaimed Frankye. "Travelers with "the book" just seem to love the inn and the town and I have taken quite a few of them on a tour. Sometimes we are terribly busy. A lot of people who saw the picture of you and the articles in the St. Louis papers have been here."

I looked around the dining room where we were having a cup of tea. Of course, nothing has really changed. Why should it? The beautiful walnut ladderback chairs, the Belgian lace curtains, the marble fireplace, the fine china, and the graceful stemware had the elegant look of a century ago. Because they were anxious to preserve the heritage of the town, Frankye said that they put great emphasis on French dishes for both breakfast and lunch. "We have crepes, French mushroom omelettes, quiche Lorraine, French toast with ginger fruit sauce, and other specialties," she explained.

The bedrooms are done in what I call "19th-century Missouri" which means that they have a collection of many different kinds of Victorian antiques including marble top bureaus, high-back beds, and old-fashioned flowered wallpaper. Incidentally, there are eight different suites in the inn, and each has at least two rooms. In a few instances there are two double beds. The bridal suite has an elegant crystal chandelier and big windows overlooking the main street.

During my earlier visit, I had only visited a few of the old, restored buildings, so I asked Frankye to show me more of historic Ste. Genevieve that afternoon. Any home built after 1860 is considered modern.

It was great fun to see the Donzes again. They are two of the most sincerely involved innkeepers that I have ever met. Just before leaving, I spotted once again the little sign that expresses the philosophy of this homey inn: "There are no strangers here, just friends we haven't met."

ST. GEMME BEAUVAIS, 78 N. Main St., Ste. Genevieve, Mo. 63670; 314-883-5744. An 8-room village inn about 1½ hrs. from St. Louis. Modified American plan includes breakfast only. Breakfast served daily. Lunch served Mon. thru Sat. Open year-round. Closed Thanksgiving and Christmas Day. Golf, hunting, and fishing nearby. No pets. Frankye and Boats Donze, Innkeepers.

Directions: From St. Louis, south on I-55 to Hwy. 32. Exit east on 32 to Hwy. 61 to the Ste. Genevieve exit.

Ste. Genevieve has a most unusual collection of well-preserved houses, many dating before 1800. The work in restoring and preserving is exemplary and, fortunately, many of them are open to the public.

These houses, museums, and churches uniquely preserve an era in the development of the Midwest which, I believe, is unequaled in any other location.

OLD RITTENHOUSE INN
Bayfield, Wisconsin

I came in on Route 13 and easily identified an impressive Victorian mansion as the Old Rittenhouse Inn. It is located on a tree-shaded street on a high bank considerably above the road. It has four stories with a white porch around the front and side.

I waited a few moments for the deluge to abate, and then, dodging raindrops, hurried through the front door into a world of delicate Victoriana. The first person I saw was Jerry Phillips, a

handsome bearded gentleman wearing a white, turn-of-the-century suit with a double-breasted vest, a red shirt with ruffles at the cuff, and a black, oversized butterfly tie.

"Welcome to the Old Rittenhouse Inn," he said. "We've tried to turn out for you in real style."

"Style" was exactly what I found in great abundance during that visit with innkeepers Jerry and Mary Phillips. Jerry showed me to my table and explained that he and Mary, who does all the cooking (with the exception of the desserts, which are Jerry's province), would join me for a long after-dinner talk.

I was served at a round oak table with a single candle. The cream and sugar and salt and pepper were a silver set. There was a green napkin on my plate in the middle of which was placed a small red blossom. Jerry presented the spoken menu, explaining very carefully the details concerning every individual course and the delicate content of each recipe. That evening, my first course was a mushroom Burgundy soup. The second course was a fruit salad made with fresh wild blackberries, raspberries, blueberries, peaches, and apples.

The six main courses included Lake Superior whitefish baked in wine, garnished with almonds, and served in a champagne butter sauce; ham baked in a spiced orange glaze and garnished with fresh fruits; ocean scallops sautéed in a very delicate curried drawn butter; leg of lamb roasted with fresh rosemary, garlic, and lemon served in its own sauce. There were four freshly baked breads available that evening, as well.

After dinner, when Jerry and Mary joined me, they explained that the house had been built in 1890 as a summer home. When they bought it, much restoring and redecorating were needed. "Furnishing it with Victorian furniture was fun," said Mary. "We've met every antique dealer between Duluth and Milwaukee getting the right furniture for five bedrooms and three dining rooms."

In 1980 a garden room and solarium were added, and special stained glass based on Chinese symbolism and art was put into four windows.

Both Jerry and Mary are active in the community and were among the prime movers in getting the entire district of Bayfield listed on the National Register of Historic Places.

Yes, the word for the Old Rittenhouse Inn is *style,* to which I must inevitably add the word *grace.*

OLD RITTENHOUSE INN, 301 Rittenhouse Ave., Bayfield, Wis. 54814; 715-779-5765. A 5-room Victorian inn in an area of historic and natural beauty, 70 mi. east of Duluth, Minn., on the shores of Lake Superior. European plan. Breakfast and dinner served to travelers. Open May 1 to Nov. 1. Advance reservations most desirable. Extensive recreational activity of all kinds available throughout the year, including tours, hiking, and cycling on the nearby Apostle and Madeline Islands. Not comfortable for small children. No pets. Jerry and Mary Phillips, Innkeepers.

Directions: From the Duluth Airport, follow Rte. 53-S through the city of Duluth over the bridge to Superior, Wisconsin. Turn east on Rte. 2 near Ashland (1½ hrs.), turn north on 13-N to Bayfield.

THE WHITE GULL INN
Fish Creek, Wisconsin

I have a T-shirt with the legend "Where the hell is Door County?" Well, I can assure you that once you've been to Door County you'll never forget where it is or what is there.

For me, the most important things in Door County are the village of Fish Creek and the White Gull Inn. Fish Creek is an unspoiled village which was settled about a century ago. It's on the shore of Lake Michigan and the best way I can describe it is to say that the main street looks very much like main streets in Vermont and New York State, except for the dominating presence of the lake.

The White Gull Inn was built as a part of a large resort area more than 75 years ago, during the days when hundreds of tourists would arrive in Fish Creek from Chicago and Milwaukee aboard such steamships as the *Georgia, Carolina,* and *Alabama.* They would be escorted from the dock to the inn, which in those days was known as Henrietta's Cottage. Nowadays guests drive and even fly to Fish Creek, but the main street, the beautiful waterfront, and the sparkling atmosphere here remained unchanged.

The inn is a white clapboard three-story building that doesn't put on airs at all with a definite open informality among the innkeepers, staff, and the guests. The rooms are tidy and neat and some of them in the main house share a bath. There are also spacious cottages in the rear.

Our Midwestern readers are probably very familiar with the term "Fish Boil," which is, as far as I know, a tradition limited to Wisconsin. The Fish Boil at The White Gull features freshly caught lake fish, boiled potatoes, homemade cole slaw, fresh-baked bread, and cherry pie. Russ, the master boiler, prepares a roaring fire and the fish are boiled in two huge iron cauldrons. This wood-smoke fire combined with the aroma of Lake Michigan fish creates truly gargantuan appetites. Russ also plays the accordion and leads everybody in lots of singing and clapping of hands. The White Gull has a Fish Boil every Wednesday, Friday, Saturday, and Sunday evening, and let me warn all of our readers that reservations during the height of the season are sometimes necessary weeks in advance, so don't hesitate to call. The recipe for this famous dish can be found in our *Country Inns & Back Roads Cookbook.*

According to a recent letter from Jan and Andy Coulson, the proprietors of the White Gull, the major project in 1982 was the renovation of the Beachcomber Cottage. "It has been completely redone on the inside, including the addition of a stone fireplace, refinished and antique furnishings, and now is winterized. This means we will have it as well as the nine-room lodge for the winter season. As you know, Door County has excellent cross-country skiing as well as snowshoeing, snowmobiling, ice fishing, and ice boating. During the winter we serve the Fish Boil on Saturday nights only."

The White Gull Inn in Fish Creek . . . . . . a Door County country inn for summer and winter.

THE WHITE GULL INN, Fish Creek, Wis. 54212; 414-868-3517. A 9-room inn in a most scenic area in Door County, 23 mi. north of Sturgeon Bay. Considerable outdoor and cultural attractions nearby. Rooms with and without private baths. Open year-round. European plan. Breakfast daily throughout the season. Lunches from mid-June thru Oct. and weekends thru winter. Fish Boils: Wednesday, Friday, Saturday, Sunday nights throughout the season. Early American buffet: Monday and Thursday. Dining room closed Tuesday nights. All meals open to travelers. Reservations requested for evening meals. Golf, tennis, swimming, fishing, biking, sailing, and other summer and winter sports nearby. Excellent for children of all ages. Pets allowed in cottages but not in main lodge. Andy and Jan Coulson, Proprietors; Joan Holiday, Innkeeper.

Directions: From Chicago: take I-94 to Milwaukee. Follow Rte. I-43 (141) from Milwaukee to Manitowoc; Rte. 42 from Manitowoc to Fish Creek. Turn left at stop sign at the bottom of the hill, go 2½ blocks to inn. From Green Bay: take Rte. 57 to Sturgeon Bay; Rte. 42 to Fish Creek.

JAMIESON HOUSE
Poynette, Wisconsin

Innkeeper Jeff Smith was explaining some of the many facets of his philosophy concerning innkeeping. "We are providing what is almost an escape for our guests," he said. "We feel they need a respite from the travails of life. We offer our guests a personal touch in a setting that is unique. They can escape from certain things that we associate with modernization, such as tv's and telephones. If the guest is on call he knows that the phone might ring and it is difficult to sit down and relax. When they come here they know the phone won't ring."

The occasion was a regional seminar of *CIBR* innkeepers from Wisconsin, Michigan, Minnesota, and Iowa, and we were all enjoying the unusual ambience of the Jamieson House, as well as the painstakingly prepared meals. These conferences are held several times every year in various parts of North America and provide *CIBR* innkeepers with the opportunity to exchange ideas and solutions to problems as well as to enjoy a little rest and relaxation.

The original building of the Jamieson was built in the late 1870s by Hugh Jamieson, who came to this section of the country from Scotland at the age of nineteen and soon established himself as a man of purpose.

Although the building had fallen upon evil days before Jeff saw its possibilities, its dismembered condition did not at all dismay him. In the process of restoration he found a number of surprises in many of the rooms in the form of carved mantel pieces, arched doorways, lovely woodwork, and the like.

The restoration of the main building and the elegant building across the street, which has been converted into a guest house, is now complete. Both have been furnished and decorated as authentically as possible, with 1890 as a pivotal date. All of the innkeepers toured the bedrooms and were most impressed with the carved headboards, marble-top dressers, horsehair sofas, molded ceilings, and wall hangings and paintings. Furnishings are a combination of Empire and Victorian.

One of the bedrooms has a handsome, black sunken bathtub surrounded by mirrors, and I'm told it is a favorite of honeymooners of all ages. Incidentally, guests are asked not to smoke in the bedrooms.

There are two dining areas; one on the first floor is available by reservation only. There are two sittings on busy nights. The menu is a carefully orchestrated five-course, fixed-price meal, and one of the entrée choices is always filet of beef served with Bearnaise sauce. There is also fresh salmon flown in from Seattle and cooked in Rhine wine. The desserts are a specialty of Jeff's associate, Tysh Wallesverd who has even gone into the business of supplying her exotic desserts to other restaurants in the area. This dining room is decorated in Victorian period furniture which is appropriate for the dark mahogany wood and tones of red in the wallpaper.

The menu in the downstairs dining room is a la carte and the mood runs the gamut from Victorian to Art Nouveau and Art Deco; the decorations remind me of the twenties and thirties.

"To us this has been an exciting labor of love," continued Jeff. "Our fulfillment is in watching the faces of the skeptics as they see now what we first saw—a spacious, elegant Victorian home that has been made into an inn. I'll bet Hugh Jamieson would love it."

JAMIESON HOUSE, 407 North Franklin St., Poynette, Wis. 53955; 608-635-4100. An elegant Victorian restoration 20 mi. from Madison with a restaurant and 7 lodging rooms. Breakfast included with room. European plan. Open 365 days. Dinner served to travelers. No recreational facilities at the inn, but tennis, swimming, state parks, the Wisconsin Dells, skiing, are within a short distance. Limited facilities for young children. No credit cards. Personal checks accepted. Jeffrey L. Smith, Innkeeper.

Directions: From Madison take I-90-94 north to County CS. Follow signs into Poynette (3 mi.). Angle left onto Main St., and go north. The Jamieson House is 3 blocks north of the business district on the right side. The Jamieson House is on the entire block.

One of our favorite back roads is a trek through the countryside between Seven Pines Lodge and Alpha, Wisconsin, to Crex Meadows. After meandering through our driveway, a simple left and right turn puts the traveler on a rural road that winds through pine-studded lakeshores, over one-lane bridges, past green pastures, red barns, and country schools to Alpha, a well-known cheese factory in the area. After spending much time trying to decide between the Provalone, string cheese, baby Swiss, or sharp or mild cheddar, one can wander over to the old general store, buy a couple of juicy apples and head for Crex Meadows a few miles away to enjoy his or her picnic lunch.

Crex Meadows is a wildlife sanctuary for rare birds and various and assorted forms of wildlife. If the traveler is lucky, he or she may find a wild strawberry or raspberry to nibble on as well. Crex Meadows covers thousands of acres of waterways, marshes, and dry land to provide this haven for man and God's little creatures—IT'S BEAUTIFUL! Then back to the Lodge for a sunset supper—what a grand day!

Joan and David Simpson
Seven Pines Lodge
Lewis, Wisconsin

Looking to the business at hand, let me tell you about one of my favorite back roads! I send people home via this route as they oftentimes like to pick up fresh-caught lake fish for their freezers at home and it routes them past the fish market where we buy our whitefish for our fish boils.

Travelers take Highway 42 out of Fish Creek to Egg Harbor, the first village south. At the Thimbleberry Inn, take County Trunk G, which winds along the Green Bay shoreline and provides beautiful glimpses of the bay. County G runs into County B, which should be taken the remainder of the way to Sturgeon Bay. Once in Sturgeon Bay, County B intersects Business 42 and just south of the "old" bridge is Andy's Fish Market. This route also takes the traveler past the shipyards in Sturgeon Bay which are very interesting.

Andy and Jan Coulson
The White Gull Inn
Fish Creek, Wisconsin

The portion of the Mississippi River from LaCrosse, Wisconsin, to St. Paul/Minneapolis is known as the Hiawatha Valley. The drive northward on U.S. 61 from LaCrosse to Winona is as scenic as any river road in the country. At Winona one should cross on Minnesota 43 to Wisconsin 35 on the east side of the river, and follow its ups,

downs, and turns along Lake Pepin to Red Wing—really superb
scenery and good roads, regardless of the season.

Gene Foster
St. James Hotel
Red Wing, Minnesota

SEVEN PINES LODGE
Lewis, Wisconsin

I set my alarm clock for two a.m. —not in order to get an early start on the trout fishing, or to follow the stream to its source to see the beaver and wild turkeys, or even to stalk the Canada geese. I set my clock for two a.m. so I could change from one single bed to the other and thereby know that I had slept in a bed that once had been occupied by President Calvin Coolidge!

Joan and David Simpson, along with their son John-David, and daughter Tina, are the innkeepers of this rustic hideaway in the Wisconsin forest. It was built in 1903 by Charles Lewis, a grain broker and financier from Minneapolis. Constructed of handhewn logs, the lodge had retained its original appeal and surprising elegance, including an array of interesting antiques which are an integral part of the decor. Ninety percent of the furniture and decorations have been here since Mr. Lewis's time.

Immediately upon my arrival I took a pleasant stroll with Joan and we passed through a grove of original pine trees, some of which are 115 feet high, scuffing through the dried leaves to the trout stream. Passing over a rustic bridge beside a melodious waterfall, we entered an almost pagoda-like, two-story log building with a full screened porch around four sides of the second floor. This is a summer sleeping porch, and I can just imagine the good times enjoyed by families in this woodland setting.

We followed the stream a short distance and came to a stone statue of a young Indian boy in the middle of a sylvan pool. As we were drinking in the quiet loveliness of the scene, Joan pointed to a finny denizen and said, "There goes a dinner."

She explained that many of the guests enjoyed fishing for brownies, rainbows, and brook trout, all of which are raised on the property.

Accommodations at Seven Pines Lodge are in the main building where there are five year-round bedrooms, and also in log outbuildings which can be used only during temperate temperatures. These have a real "woodsy" feeling.

That evening I joined the other guests around the dinner table and then we all adjourned to the friendly confines of the living room, which has a big oval table with an overhead lamp that provides convenient lighting by which to enjoy the many albums of fascinating photographs of the lodge as it was in earlier times.

Joan does all the cooking, and David and John-David take care of the tables. Guests frequently sit at the kitchen table while she prepares the Scandinavian bread, desserts, trout dinners, and the hearty meals that are welcomed by guests who usually have spent most of the day outdoors, whether it be summer or winter. There are miles of cross-country ski trails.

I wakened the next morning to the aroma of one of Joan's breakfasts and realized that I had slept through the two a.m. alarm, so I'm still not sure whether I've slept in a bed once occupied by Calvin Coolidge.

SEVEN PINES LODGE, Lewis, Wis. 54851; 715-653-2323. A 10-room rustic resort inn (most rooms have shared baths) in the Wisconsin woods about 1½ hrs. from Minneapolis. St. Croix Falls, Taylors Falls, National Wild River Scenic Waterway nearby. Open year-round. Closed Thanksgiving and Christmas Day. Trout fishing on grounds. Tennis, swimming, golf, woodswalking, xc, downhill skiing, backroading nearby. Very attractive for children of all ages since the innkeepers also have children. No pets. No credit cards. Joan and David Simpson, Innkeepers.

Directions: From Minneapolis / St. Paul: follow I35W or I35E north to US 8 at Forest Lake, Minn. East on US 8 through Taylors Falls, Minn. / St. Croix Falls, Wisc., to Wisc. 35 north to Lewis. Turn right at Shell station to "T," right 1 mi. to fork in road and turn left ½ mi. to 7 Pines Lodge entrance.

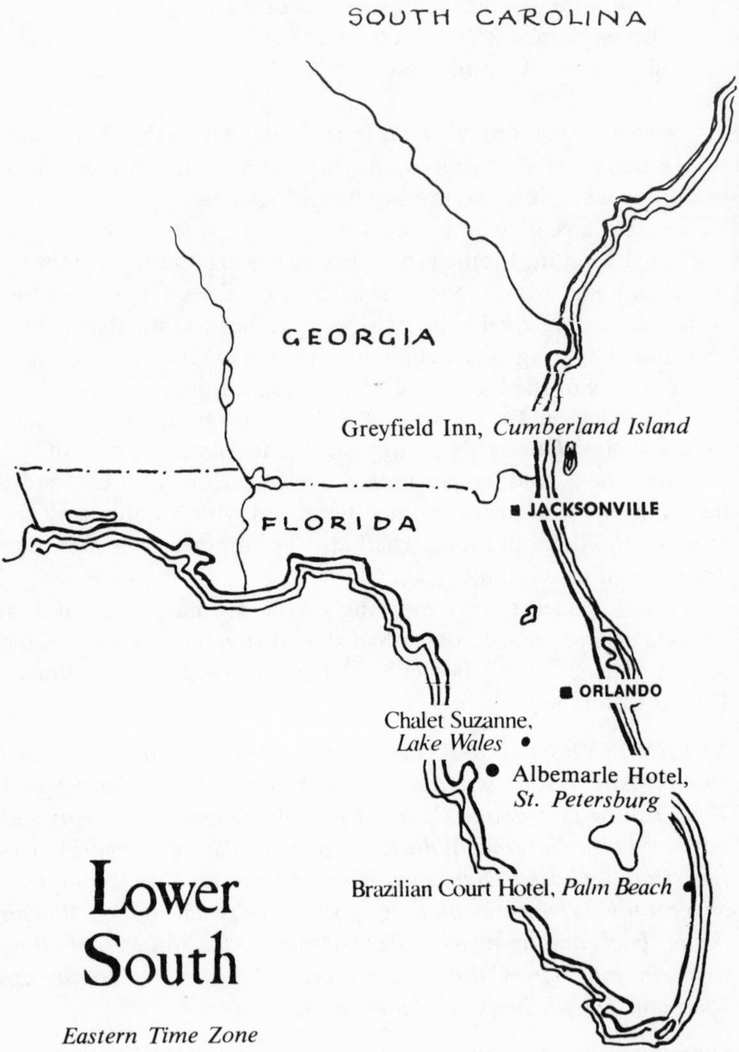

SOUTH CAROLINA

GEORGIA

Greyfield Inn, *Cumberland Island*

FLORIDA

■ JACKSONVILLE

■ ORLANDO

Chalet Suzanne, *Lake Wales* •

● Albemarle Hotel, *St. Petersburg*

Brazilian Court Hotel, *Palm Beach* ●

Lower South

Eastern Time Zone

CUMBERLAND ISLAND

Cumberland Island is the southernmost and largest of a chain of barrier islands that starts at Cape Hatteras and extends to the Florida-Georgia border. It is eighteen miles long and three miles wide at its widest point. There are 26 varieties of wild animals and 323 species of birds identified. The island has one road, Grand Avenue, a dirt and shell affair, which traverses the length of the island through the live oak.

In recent years the National Park Service acquired a great portion of the island and has taken the necessary action to forever maintain it as a nature preserve.

Marshland fringes much of Cumberland's shores protecting them from the current and the tide. Its principal inhabitants are the ubiquitous fiddler crabs and long-legged wading birds. The live oak avenues create an atmosphere akin to a cathedral.

The eighteen-mile beach is the most striking feature of the island and one can walk for hours in delicious solitude except for the sanderlings that scurry out of the clutching fingers of the waves, and the pelicans skimming the water. Shells abound and it's impossible to come back empty-handed.

The dunes, which are carefully protected, provide still another intriguing atmosphere. At the edge of the forest there is a group of lakes, which have their own particular wildlife. Egrets and herons fish these waters as well as ducks who stop off as they travel north and south.

Besides the wildlife there is a rich history of the island that covers pre-Columbian times as well as occupation by the Spaniards, the British, and later on some enterprising men from the new American republic. In the early 1800s there were a few plantations on the island, but after the War Between the States the island was dominated by the presence of the Carnegie family who raised an impressive mansion of brick and stone at Dungeness with formal gardens, swimming pool and stables. Unfortunately, it burned in 1959.

GREYFIELD INN
Cumberland Island, Georgia

This is the story of Lucy Ferguson and her great-grandmother who was once married to Thomas Carnegie (brother of Andrew). It's also the story of Janet Ferguson (known henceforth as Go-Go) and her brothers Andy and Mitty, as well as of the flora and fauna of one of the last remaining impressive nature preserves on the East Coast. It's a true story of Greyfield Inn, located on Cumberland Island off the southern coast of Georgia.

I paid my first visit to this gorgeous, haunting part of the world in 1975. I had the pleasure of spending part of a day with Lucy Ferguson, who was known as "Grandma" to everybody. It was Grandma who first introduced me to Cumberland Island with its seventeen-mile stretch of beach, fascinating dunes and secret ponds. She also showed me the ruins of Dungeness which was built by her great-grandparents and which unfortunately burned in 1959.

Once again, as on my first visit, I was on the ferry boat, *R.W. Ferguson,* and Captain Mitty Ferguson was up-dating me on Greyfield Inn. We left Fernandina Beach at 3 p.m. and were making the hour-and-a-quarter run up the passage between the island and the mainland to the Greyfield dock.

"Of course everything is much the same as it was when you were here the first time," he said, keeping a guiding hand on the wheel. "The big difference is that my sister Go-Go has joined Andy and me so that we're a family team dividing the chores among the three of us. We also have some excellent staff. One of them is our cook, Louise Millette, who's been cooking in a restaurant near you in Lenox.

By this time the ferry was within sight of the Greyfield dock and I could once again see the gleaming, three-story mansion through the mysterious grove of live oaks. Andy and Go-Go waved to us and soon, with the other guests, I was bundled into the jeep and driven to the impressive front entrance of the inn with its majestic steps and broad veranda. As soon as I stepped inside it all returned to me. The paintings, the oriental rugs, the mahogany furniture, the silver on the sideboard, the great fireplaces, and the great collection of books. Go-Go showed me to my corner room and then joined me for a cup of late afternoon tea in front of the fire as we renewed our acquaintance. We had played a lot of tennis in Stockbridge about two years earlier.

I joined the other guests at dinner in the candlelit dining room and the conversation dealt with the wonders of the unspoiled beach, which is usually deserted except for the shore birds and marine life, deer, wild horses, wild turkeys and the dense live oak forest. As one guest put it, "It takes a day just to find out what is here, and then at least two days to explore it."

The conversation continued after dinner in the drawing room around the fire and some of us made plans to do things together the next day.

It was wonderful to be back at the Greyfield once again.

Do not plan visiting the Greyfield Inn if you have only one night, and be certain to check with the inn about the ferry schedules. Incidentally, the 1735 House in Fernandina Beach is an excellent overnight stop before taking the afternoon boat to the island. The Greyfield Inn is the only public overnight accommodation on Cumberland Island.

GREYFIELD INN, Cumberland Island, Georgia (mailing address: Fernandina Beach, Fla. 32034); 904-261-6408. An 8-bedroom mansion on an island off the coast of southern Georgia. Accessible from Fernandina Beach, Florida, or on a National Park Service ferry from St. Mary's, Georgia. Check with inn on ferry times. Rates include full breakfast and dinner, as well as either box lunch or informal noon meal. Open every day in the year by reservation only. Beachcombing, swimming, fishing, clam digging, photography, birdwatching, bicycles, walking and driving tours, natural history tour. Island also accessible by small plane or helicopter. No pets. The Ferguson Family, Innkeepers.

Directions: The R.W. Ferguson leaves from the public dock at Fernandina Beach, Fla., at either 3 or 5 p.m., depending upon the day of the week (check with inn). Also check with inn on National Park Service ferry schedule from St. Mary's, Ga. Autos are left on the mainland.

ALBEMARLE HOTEL
St. Petersburg, Florida

"I've been vacationing in Florida for the last ten years, and I'm here to tell you that there's no place like the Albemarle!" It was March in St. Petersburg, and I was seated in the long, graceful lobby of the Albemarle Hotel having a conversation with a well-tanned gentleman. We were looking at a calendar of the month's activities at the hotel. "I'm one of those individuals who took an early retirement, and have never worked so hard in my life," he said. "About the middle of March I like to get away from our home in southwest Virginia and come down here to St. Pete because that's where the action is. Just look at what is going on here in the hotel this month:

There are travel movies, a craft and hobby show, English taxi rides, a cruise on Tampa Bay, a trip to Cypress Gardens, a book review by Jeanne Tucker, several party nights, and a St. Patrick's Day wine-and-cheese party. When I come here I want to *do* things . . . I just don't want to sit around and vegetate and watch TV!"

That statement, I believe, is the essence of the Albemarle and St. Petersburg—it's the opportunity to *do* things. When I mentioned this to Jeanne Tucker, she said, "That's absolutely right! The key to the Albemarle is planned entertainment and we have something going almost every day. It's not that our guests *have* to do it, but if they want to, they're certainly welcome . . . and they seem to want to.

"They enjoy going to Disney World, Busch Gardens, and we have dinner music, organ concerts, Bingo twice a week, and something for everyone. They can walk to the beach or the pier where there's usually an appearance by a show business personality.

They can play shuffleboard, or go lawn bowling, take a sail, or a speedboat ride, watch the major league baseball teams in training, and dozens of other things. Let's just say that no one can be bored at the Albemarle!"

This attractive in-town hotel has exactly the kind of atmosphere for which I was searching in Florida. In the first place, it has been owned by the same family, all of whom have been very active in management and staffing. Mrs. Grace Tucker raised her family right here in the hotel. "Yes, we've done everything there is to do at the Albemarle," said Tom.

The average tenure of staff members is fifteen years, but Sylvester Norton, the hall porter, has been here for thirty-five years! The lodging rooms are bright and comfortable and there's an elevator, a swimming pool, a shuffleboard court, and a sunbathing area.

The menu features dishes like Yankee pot roast, roast loin of pork, and lamb shanks — "The kind of dishes that people don't often serve themselves at home," added Tom.

Friends of George Stiles, who was for many years manager of the Asticou Inn in Northeast Harbor, Maine, will be delighted to know that he and his wife Esther are both at the Albemarle now and George is serving as manager.

Early in December, 1981, it was my pleasure to join several other CIBR innkeepers for a three-day annual meeting which was held at the Albemarle. Thanks to a great deal of organization and planning by Jeanne Tucker, who is married to Tom, and the Albemarle staff which was wonderfully cooperative, our meetings, a combination of work and play, were really a huge success. As we were making our goodbyes, one of the innkeepers took me aside and said, "Let's try and come back here again, very soon!"

THE ALBEMARLE HOTEL, 145 Third Ave., N.E., St. Petersburg, Fla. 33731; 813-822-4097. A 140-room hotel in a quiet section of St. Petersburg just a short walk from Tampa Bay, the sand beach, the Shuffleboard Center, the replica of the HMS Bounty, and many of the city's cultural and recreational activities. Mod. American and European plan. Open Nov. 1 to April 15. Breakfast, lunch, dinner served to non-residents. Swimming pool, shuffleboard on grounds. Golf, fishing, tennis, sailing nearby. A planned entertainment program for all guests. George Stiles, Manager; Jean Tucker, Innkeeper.

Directions: Leave I-275 at North Bay Dr. Exit and follow Fourth Ave. North to Beach Dr. N.E. Turn right 1 block to Third Ave. N.E., and right ½ block to hotel.

CHALET SUZANNE
Lake Wales, Florida

After my first visit to Chalet Suzanne a number of years ago, I began to wonder did it really happen, or was it like *Brigadoon,* the fictional village that returns for one day every 100 years. This is a reaction that I frequently get from guests who visit this unusual country inn in central Florida. Sometimes they can hardly believe it.

However, there is no doubt that Chalet Suzanne is a real place and not the result of an overactive imagination. The bridges, houses, steeples, cupolas, minarets, peaked roofs, flat roofs, castles, domes, treasures, junk, antiques, and pagodas are all there. It's Bavarian, Swiss, Oriental, French, English, Turkish, Chinese, and anything else you can think of.

It is also a 2450-foot airstrip and the home of the Chalet Suzanne Soup Factory.

In the past I have written about how Carl Hinshaw's mother, Bertha, started Chalet Suzanne in the early 1930s and how Carl and his wife, Vita, are continuing with their own touches. I have also written extensively about all of the crazy, wonderful accommodations which are available in the sugarplum rooms and fairyland castles. I also was happy to report the marriage of Tina Hinshaw and Bob Farewell.

This time I thought it would be fun to write about the dining room and the food. The restaurant overlooking the lake has been enlarged over the years. It contains all types and varieties of Victorian furniture, clocks, statues, lamps, stained glass, an old piano, wrought iron tables with tile tops, and a plentiful collection of goblets and stemware. At the far end there is a little table for two set in the front window.

"That's for honeymooners," explained Vita.

Almost everyone visiting Chalet Suzanne for the first time orders the well-known chicken Suzanne, beautifully browned and glazed. It is prepared by Carl who, in addition to being the "chief pilot" of the airfield and "principal stirrer" in the soup factory, is also the chef.

Of the famous Chalet Suzanne soups, which, I'm happy to say, have a permanent place on my kitchen shelf, the most popular is cream of romaine, but the New England clam chowder, vichyssoise, gazpacho, and seafood Newburg are not far behind. They are all concocted right there on the inn grounds and guests can visit the soup factory.

Dinner also includes the original baked grapefruit centered with a sautéed chicken liver, the famed Chalet Suzanne romaine soup, hearts of artichoke salad, petite peas in cream and butter, a grilled tomato slice, deliciously hot homemade rolls, a mint ice, and tiny crêpes Suzanne. The chocolate cream pie for dessert is magnificent.

A gentleman from Charlotte, North Carolina, wrote me recently: "We stayed one night at the Chalet Suzanne. Without any question we agreed that dinner there was the single best meal either of us has ever had."

Over the years many travel and food writers have raved over Chalet Suzanne, and it has caused writers to dig into their dictionaries for new and expressive adjectives.

If all of this sounds like a Disney movie, let me assure you that Chalet Suzanne is very serious about the business of hospitality. Accommodations, food and recreation facilities are all continually

praised. It is not far from the real Disney World and the beautiful Cypress Gardens with waterskiing shows. It has all of the Florida resort features that encourage guests to stay on and on.

And it is real.

CHALET SUZANNE, P.O. Box AC, Lake Wales, Fla. 33853; 813-676-1477. A 30-room phantasmagoric country inn and gourmet restaurant, 4 mi. north of Lake Wales, between Cypress Gardens and the Bok Singing Tower near Disney World. European plan. Dining room open from 8 a.m. to 9:30 p.m. daily. Closed Mondays June through October. Pool on grounds. Golf, tennis, riding nearby. Not inexpensive. The Hinshaw Family, Innkeepers.

Directions: From Interstate 4 turn south on U.S. 27 toward Lake Wales. From Sunshine State Pkwy. exit at Yeehaw Junction and head west on Rte. 60 to U.S. 27 (60 mi.). Proceed north on U.S. 27 at Lake Wales. Inn is 4 mi. north of Lake Wales on Country Road 17A.

BRAZILIAN COURT HOTEL
Palm Beach, Florida

I had found the *other* side of Palm Beach—not the glittering social facade, but the side with more genuine people. Furthermore, I was amazed to find a Palm Beach hotel with the simplicity and good taste that appealed to such people. It is called the Brazilian Court, although almost everyone refers to it as the "BC."

It was built back in the 1920s, and the Palm Beach residential area with sedate homes and beautifully landscaped gardens grew up around it. The building is a two-story Palm Beach Mission design with two completely enclosed patios. One patio, with several varieties of palm trees, begonias, and poinsettias, is a marvelous place to catch the morning sun.

The other patio really sets the tone for this discreet hotel. Dispersed among the royal palms, orange, banana, and African tulip trees are dining tables, many with umbrellas. Weather permitting, all three meals are served here, and each time of day has its own captivating mood.

In the evening, small lights twinkle on the inside of each umbrella and indirect colored lighting dramatically underscores the trees and exotic tropical plants. As night falls the lights become more brilliant against the dark blue sky. Now add a three-piece orchestra playing softly in the background and you have the complete picture.

The BC is reminiscent of the Black Point in Maine, and the climate brings to mind The Inn at Rancho Santa Fe, California.

Because there are many long-staying guests, the selections on the menu are numerous and varied. The broiled pompano amandine is delicious. The red snapper and Florida lobster Newburg are very appetizing also. There are several dishes prepared with Florida fresh fruit offered at each meal.

A beautiful new third court has been added, at the center of which is a swimming pool and a pool patio. Several of the lodging rooms looking over that scene now have sliding glass doors and private terraces. This means that BC guests can now enjoy not only the ocean bathing a few blocks away, but also the advantages of a new pool.

The lodging rooms and suites are furnished with quiet elegance. They overlook the residential area of town or the attractive inner patios.

The BC is basically a conservative resort-inn with quite a few of the amenities that guests find enjoyable. Great emphasis is placed on both the food and the service. The famous Worth Avenue shops of Palm Beach are just a few minutes away.

The Brazilian Court is part of my select group of inns and small hotels in larger cities including the Algonquin in New York, the Botsford on the Detroit city line, and the Albemarle in St. Petersburg. I think they meet a need for personal hospitality in urban areas.

BRAZILIAN COURT HOTEL, 300 Brazilian Ave., Palm Beach, Fla. 33480; 305-655-7740. A 125-room hotel in the heart of Palm Beach. A secluded patioed garden spot just a short walk from the ocean and Worth Avenue shops. European plan (includes breakfast) and Mod. American plan available to houseguests. Breakfast, lunch, and dinner served daily. Open from December to April. Swimming pool on grounds. Ocean swimming, boating, fishing, tennis, golf, and bicycles nearby. No pets. Dennis B. Heffernan, Owner; Geoffrey K. Temple, General Manager.

Directions: From Sunshine State Pkwy., take Exit 40 to Okeechobee Blvd. Turn left and proceed 6 mi. to Royal Palmway Bridge. Cross bridge and take first right, then turn left after 1 block on to Brazilian Ave. Hotel is two blocks east on Brazilian Ave.

*As one is heading down the main road to St. Michaels
(Route 33) there is, about a half-mile from the starting point at the
traffic light, a road that veers off to the right marked "to Tunis Mills,
Route 370." You'll know it because at the turn on the right is a small
country store where you can buy fresh vegetables and sodas.*

*As you head down that road you will pass some old wooden
homes with rickety rocking chairs on the porches that I would just
love to buy and refurbish sometime. The best things about this road
are the two bridges and the water scenes. The first bridge is a very old
drawbridge that crosses a part of the Miles River, and there is a
little man in the small cabin on the bridge ready to stop traffic and
let the boats through. Once you pass that bridge you will see the
very old ruins of a church on the right, covered partly in vines. We
have stopped there often with our boys, exploring and looking for
witches and ghosts. As you continue into the village of Tunis Mills
you will cross a truly storybook bridge that crosses Leeds Creek.
On the occasions when we were there local children were diving
into the water and there was a family of swans cruising around,
watching the goings-on. There are equally lovely simple homes on
either side of the bridge. It is a very quiet spot and for the moment
you might think you are actually Alice-in-Wonderland.*

Kenneth and Wendy Gibson
Robert Morris Inn
Oxford, Maryland

*My favorite back road in this area would be Goshen Pass, a
lovely twenty-minute drive up through Rockbridge Baths from here.
The pass through the mountains is beautiful any time of year. In the
fall the foliage is spectacular. In June, a drive out there is a must
for those who love to see the laurel and rhododendron in bloom, and*

in the summer, a swim in the Maury River is refreshing; or perhaps a canoe ride or a picnic would be fun. At any rate, from the Alexander-Withrow House, an outing through Goshen Pass, perhaps on to Grist Mill Square for lunch, dinner, or as a part of an "inn vacation" would surely be a pleasant way to spend some time.

Beth Thompson
Alexander-Withrow House
Lexington, Virginia

There are many back-road possibilities near Carmel. One of my favorite times is in the spring when there is a profusion of wild flowers and everything is so green. One of the closest valleys is Robinson Canyon, and another rewarding trip is a visit to the huge Oppenheimer ranch just over the hill from Carmel valley.

There's a most unique walk by the sea to watch the migrating grey whales. They are up to twenty feet long and pass quite close to the shore in their migration from the Arctic, south to the Gulf of Baja in Mexico, where they give birth to their calves. They are an endangered species, weigh several tons, and it is estimated there are about 72,000 of them. The peak of the southward migration is from mid-December to the end of January when they cluster in schools. It's an awesome sight to see so many leviathans strung out together. You can see them from Point Lobos State Reserve, which juts out into the Pacific Ocean and is one of my favorite beauty spots.

Graeme Mac Kenzie
Sandpiper Inn
Carmel, California

One of the more interesting side trips from the Black Point Inn would be a ride to Route 77, located approximately one mile from the inn. Going down Route 77 one will enjoy a stop at Higgins Beach, which is a small year-round community with its own beautiful community beach overlooking Richmond Island. Richmond Island sits about two miles from the beach, and is the location where Snow's Clam chowder grew their potatoes for their famous clam chowder. Continuing down Route 77, there are several vegetable and flower stands. A "must" stop would be Len Libby's homemade candy and ice cream shop. The shop is guaranteed to have an inventory of one million calories on hand. Continuing on Route 77, on the left is a beautiful village church, called the Spurwink Church, on the corner of Spurwink Avenue and Route 77. This church is used exclusively for weddings and funerals. On a typical Saturday, one can expect to see more than six weddings taking place, and looking at the church you can see why.

Still on Route 77, one will pass the land belonging to Ram Island Farm, which goes for two or three miles on the right. This farm is owned by the Sprague Oil Trust and is an actual working farm. As a matter of fact, the Ram Island Farm Market is open during the months of May through November. Beyond the farm one should be alert for the Crescent Beach State Park—a lovely place for picnics. Farther down the road is Two Lights State Park, another picnic location, and where there is cliff-climbing for the nimble-footed, overlooking the ocean. As one continues on 77, you will be in the heart of Cape Elizabeth on Shore Road. Traveling approximately three miles, you will find Fort Williams Park, which is owned by Fort Williams, and the location of the world-famous Portland Headlight. (You may recall that Portland Headlight appeared on the short-lived eighteen-cent stamp.) Total duration of this driving trip would be about two and a half to three hours, depending on stops and length of time spent at each stop.

Normand Dugas
Black Point Inn
Prouts Neck, Maine

The Waterford Inne is truly an inn in the country, and thus there are many back roads to travel. Our favorite is the journey that takes us from here to Lovell, Maine. As we leave the inn we go down the hill and turn right onto Route 37. The delights will vary according to the season. About a mile and a half down the road lies Lake Keoka, a rather small but clear lake—a haven for swimming, fishing, and canoeing. The village of Waterford overlooks this lake and a truly New England village it is, complete with many antique white

clapboard homes and buildings and the ubiquitous general store. The entire town has recently been listed by the National Register of Historic Places. Two small roads lead from the town to apple orchards where, during the fall, one may "pick your own" or purchase the same from a stand while watching cider actually being pressed. As we travel past the lake and approach South Waterford, we watch for a fork in the road and take the one to the right—the Sweden Hill Road. About a mile along the road we pass an old cemetery—gravestone rubbers take note—and about a mile farther there is Merritt M. Kimball's Hides and Furs, where one may sell his coyote or deer skins, or perhaps purchase some leather goods for family and friends back home. So now it's up and over the mountain, passing yet another orchard and pausing to gaze upon or photograph Mount Washington and the White Mountains in the now-near distance.

Barbara and Rosalie Vanderzanden
The Waterford Inne
East Waterford, Maine

INDEX

ALBEMARLE HOTEL
St. Petersburg, Florida, 490

ALEXANDER-WITHROW HOUSE
Lexington, Virginia, 371

ALGONQUIN HOTEL
New York, New York, 22

ASA RANSOM HOUSE
Clarence, New York, 20

ASPEN LODGE
Estes Park, Colorado, 350

AUBERGE HANDFIELD
St-Marc-sur-le-Richelieu,
Quebec, Canada, 426

BARLEY SHEAF FARM
Holicong, Pennsylvania, 74

BARROWS HOUSE
Dorset, Vermont, 176

BEAUMONT INN
Harrodsburg, Kentucky, 392

BED AND BREAKFAST INN
San Francisco, California, 288

BEEKMAN ARMS
Rhinebeck, New York, 24

BENBOW INN
Garberville, California, 296

BENN CONGER INN
Groton, New York, 26

BIRCH HILL INN
Manchester, Vermont, 180

BIRD AND BOTTLE
Garrison, New York, 28

BLACK POINT INN
Prouts Neck, Maine, 248

BLOMIDON INN
Wolfville, Nova Scotia,
Canada, 412

BLUEBERRY HILL
Goshen, Vermont, 182

BOONE TAVERN HOTEL
Berea, Kentucky, 388

BOTSFORD INN
Farmington Hills, Michigan, 458

BOULDERS INN
New Preston, Connecticut, 108

BRADLEY INN
New Harbor, Maine, 246

BRAMBLE INN
Brewster, Massachusetts, 126

BRAZILIAN COURT
Palm Beach, Florida, 494

BRIAR ROSE
Boulder, Colorado, 348

BRIARS, THE
Jackson's Point,
Ontario, Canada, 440

BRITT HOUSE
San Diego, California, 298

BUXTON INN
Granville, Ohio, 454

CAMERON ESTATE INN
Mount Joy, Pennsylvania, 70

CAPTAIN LORD MANSION
Kennebunkport, Maine, 242

CAPTAIN WHIDBEY INN
Coupeville, Washington, 328

CASA MADRONA INN
Sausalito, California, 302

CENTURY INN
Scenery Hill, Pennsylvania, 72

CHALET SUZANNE
Lake Wales, Florida, 492

CHARLOTTE INN
Edgartown, Massachusetts, 124

CHARMWOODS INN
Naples, Maine, 254

CHESTER INN
Chester, Vermont, 184

CLAREMONT INN
Southwest Harbor, Maine, 250

CLARKSON HOUSE RESTAURANT
Lewiston, New York, 32

COBB'S COVE
Barnstable, Massachusetts, 122

COLBY HILL INN
Henniker, New Hampshire, 216

COLLIGAN'S STOCKTON INN
Stockton, New Jersey, 62

COLONEL EBENEZER CRAFTS
INN
Sturbridge, Massachusetts, 128

CONWAY'S FARMHOUSE
Port Townsend, Washington, 332

COUNTRY CLUB INN
Rangeley, Maine, 250

COUNTRY INN, THE
Berkeley Springs,
West Virginia, 364

COUNTRY INN AT PRINCETON,
Princeton, Massachusetts, 132
CURTIS HOUSE
Woodbury, Connecticut, 106
CUTTLE'S TREMBLANT CLUB
Mont Tremblant,
Quebec, Canada, 432
DANA PLACE INN
Jackson, New Hampshire, 218
DARBY FIELD INN
Conway, New Hampshire, 222
DEXTER'S INN
Sunapee, New Hampshire, 226
DOCKSIDE GUEST QUARTERS
York, Maine, 258
DOE RUN INN
Brandenburg, Kentucky, 390
EAGLES MERE INN
Eagles Mere, Pennsylvania, 76
EILER'S INN
Laguna Beach, California, 284
EVERMAY-ON-THE-DELAWARE
Erwinna, Pennsylvania, 78
FAIRFIELD INN
Fairfield, Pennsylvania, 82
GARNET HILL LODGE
North River, New York, 36
GATEWAY LODGE
Cooksburg, Pennsylvania, 80
GENERAL LEWIS INN
Lewisburg, West Virginia, 366
GLEN IRIS INN
Castile, New York, 34
GOLDEN LAMB
Lebanon, Ohio, 452
GOOSE COVE LODGE
Deer Isle, Maine, 260
GRANDVIEW FARM
Huntsville,
Ontario, Canada, 434
GRAVES MOUNTAIN LODGE
Syria, Virginia, 386
GREENVILLE ARMS
Greenville, New York, 40
GREY ROCK INN
Northeast Harbor, Maine, 264
GREY WHALE INN
Fort Bragg, California, 306
GREYFIELD INN
Cumberland Island, Georgia, 488

GRISTMILL SQUARE
Warm Springs, Virginia, 378
GRISWOLD INN
Essex, Connecticut, 114
HANDFIELD INN
St-Marc-Sur-Le-Richelieu,
Quebec, Canada, 426
HARBOR HOUSE
Elk, California, 292
HARTWELL HOUSE
Ogunquit, Maine, 262
HAWTHORNE INN
Concord, Massachusetts, 138
HEARTHSTONE INN
Colorado Springs, Colorado, 352
HEMLOCK INN
Bryson City, North Carolina, 398
HERITAGE HOUSE
Little River, California, 294
HICKORY BRIDGE FARM
Orrtanna, Pennsylvania, 86
HICKORY STICK FARM
Laconia, New Hampshire, 230
HOLLOWAY HOUSE
RESTAURANT
East Bloomfield, New York, 38
HOMESTEAD INN
Greenwich, Connecticut, 118
HOMEWOOD INN
Yarmouth, Maine, 266
HOUND EARS LODGE
Blowing Rock, North Carolina, 396
HOVEY MANOR
North Hatley, Quebec, Canada, 428
INN, THE
Rancho Santa Fe, California, 318
INN AT CASTLE HILL
Newport, Rhode Island, 166
INN AT CROTCHED MT., THE
Francestown, New Hampshire, 220
INN AT PLEASANT HILL
Shakertown, Kentucky, 394
INN AT SAWMILL FARM
West Dover, Vermont, 186
INN AT STARLIGHT LAKE
Starlight, Pennsylvania, 90
INN AT STONE CITY
Anamosa, Iowa, 448
INN AT WEATHERSFIELD
Weathersfield, Vermont, 192

INN OF THE WHITE SALMON
White Salmon, Washington, 336
INN ON THE COMMON
Craftsbury Common, Vermont, 196
INNTOWNE, THE
Newport, Rhode Island, 170
INVERARY INN
Baddeck,
Nova Scotia, Canada, 410
JAMIESON HOUSE
Poynette, Wisconsin, 480
JARED COFFIN HOUSE
Nantucket Island,
Massachusetts, 142
JOHN HANCOCK INN
Hancock, New Hampshire, 210
KEDRON VALLEY INN
South Woodstock, Vermont, 178
KILMUIR PLACE
Northeast Margaree,
Nova Scotia, Canada, 414

LAKE QUINAULT LODGE
Quinault, Washington, 330
LARCHWOOD INN
Wakefield, Rhode Island, 168
LINCKLAEN HOUSE
Cazenovia, New York, 42
LODGE ON THE DESERT
Tucson, Arizona, 340
LONGFELLOW'S WAYSIDE INN
South Sudbury, Massachusetts, 130
LOVETT'S
BY LAFAYETTE BROOK
Franconia, New Hampshire, 232
LOWELL INN
Stillwater, Minnesota, 468
LYME INN
Lyme, New Hampshire, 228
MAINSTAY INN
Cape May, New Jersey, 64
MARATHON HOTEL
Grand Manan Island,
New Brunswick, Canada, 424
MARSHLANDS INN
Sackville,
New Brunswick, Canada, 422
MARYLAND INN
Annapolis, Maryland, 360
MEADOW LANE LODGE
Warm Springs, Virginia, 384

MICHILLINDA BEACH LODGE
Whitehall, Michigan, 462
MIDDLETOWN SPRINGS INN
Middletown Springs, Vermont, 188
MILFORD HOUSE
South Milford,
Nova Scotia, Canada, 416
MILLHOF INN
Stephentown, New York, 44
MORRILL PLACE
Newburyport, Massachusetts, 134
NATIONAL HOUSE INN
Marshall, Michigan, 460
NORTH HERO HOUSE
North Hero, Vermont, 198
NORTHFIELD COUNTRY HOUSE
Northfield, Massachusetts, 146
NU-WRAY INN
Burnsville, North Carolina, 402
OAK BAY BEACH HOTEL
Victoria, B.C., Canada, 338
OBAN INN
Niagara-on-the-Lake,
Ontario, Canada, 436
OJAI VALLEY INN
Ojai, California, 300
OLD CLUB RESTAURANT
Alexandria, Virginia, 370
OLD DROVERS INN
Dover Plains, New York, 46
OLD FORT INN
Kennebunkport, Maine, 244
OLD MILANO HOTEL
Gualala, California, 304
OLD NEWFANE INN
Newfane, Vermont, 200
OLD RITTENHOUSE INN
Bayfield, Wisconsin, 476
OLD SEAL BEACH INN
Seal Beach, California, 308
OPINICON, THE
Elgin, Ontario, Canada, 438
OUTLOOK LODGE
Green Mountain Falls,
Colorado, 354
OVERLOOK INN
Canadensis, Pennsylvania, 96

PARADISE GUEST RANCH
Grants Pass, Oregon, 326

PARTRIDGE INN
Underwood, Washington, 334

PATCHWORK QUILT
Middlebury, Indiana, 446

PEIRSON PLACE
Richmond, Massachusetts, 140

PELICAN INN, THE
Muir Beach, California, 312

PENTAGOET INN
Castine, Maine, 270

PHILBROOK FARM INN
Shelburne, New Hampshire, 236

PILGRIM'S INN
Deer Isle, Maine, 272

PINE BARN INN
Danville, Pennsylvania, 100

PINE CREST INN
Tryon, North Carolina, 404

PROSPECT HILL
Trevilians, Virginia, 382

PUMP HOUSE
Canadensis, Pennsylvania, 88

QUECHEE INN
Quechee, Vermont, 204

QUEEN ANNE INN
Chatham, Massachusetts, 144

RABBIT HILL INN
Lower Waterford, Vermont, 194

RALPH WALDO EMERSON
Rockport, Massachusetts, 148

RANCHO DE LOS CABALLEROS
Wickenburg, Arizona, 342

RATHFON INN
Port Colborne,
Ontario, Canada, 442

RED CASTLE
Nevada City, California, 310

RED FOX TAVERN
Middleburg, Virginia, 372

RED INN RESTAURANT
Provincetown, Massachusetts, 150

RED LION INN
Stockbridge, Massachusetts, 154

REDCOAT'S RETURN
Tannersville, New York, 48

RIVERSIDE INN
Pence Springs, West Virginia, 362

ROBERT MORRIS INN
Oxford, Maryland, 358

ROCKHOUSE MOUNTAIN FARM
Eaton Center, New Hampshire, 240

ST. GEMME BEAUVAIS INN
Ste. Genevieve, Missouri, 474

ST. JAMES HOTEL
Red Wing, Minnesota, 470

SANDPIPER INN
Carmel-by-the-Sea, California, 316

SCHUMACHER'S NEW PRAGUE
HOTEL
New Prague, Minnesota, 472

SEVEN PINES LODGE
Lewis, Winconsin, 484

1740 HOUSE
Lumberville, Pennsylvania, 84

1770 HOUSE
East Hampton, New York, 54

SHAW'S HOTEL
Brackley Beach,
Prince Edward Island, Canada, 420

SIGN OF THE SORREL HORSE
Quakertown, Pennsylvania, 94

SHERWOOD INN
Skaneateles, New York, 52

SILVERMINE TAVERN
Norwalk, Connecticut, 112

1661 INN
Block Island, Rhode Island, 172

SNOWBIRD MOUNTAIN LODGE
Robbinsville, North Carolina, 406

SPALDING INN CLUB
Whitefield, New Hampshire, 234

SPRINGSIDE INN
Auburn, New York, 56

SQUIRE TARBOX HOUSE
Westport Island, Maine, 276

STAFFORD'S BAY VIEW INN
Petoskey, Michigan, 464

STAFFORD'S IN THE FIELD
Chocorua, New Hampshire, 238

STAGECOACH HILL INN
Sheffield, Massachusetts, 152

STERLING INN
South Sterling, Pennsylvania, 98

SUTTER CREEK INN
Sutter Creek, California, 314

SWISS HUTTE
Hillsdale, New York, 60

TANQUE VERDE
Tucson, Arizona, 346

TAVERN, THE
New Wilmington,
Pennsylvania, 102

THREE MOUNTAIN INN
Jamaica, Vermont, 208

THREE VILLAGE INN
Stony Brook, New York, 58

TOWN FARMS INN
RESTAURANT
Middletown, Connecticut, 120

UNION STREET INN
San Francisco, California, 286

VAGABOND HOUSE
Carmel, California, 322

VICTORIAN INN
Whitinsville, Massachusetts, 156

VILLAGE INN
Landgrove, Vermont, 206

VILLAGE INN
Lenox, Massachusetts, 160

WATERFORD INNE
E. Waterford, Maine, 278

WAYSIDE INN
Middletown, Virginia, 380

WELSHFIELD INN
Burton, Ohio, 456

WEST LANE INN
Ridgefield, Connecticut, 116

WHISTLING OYSTER
RESTAURANT
Ogunquit, Maine, 274

WHITE GULL
Fish Creek, Wisconsin, 478

WHITEHALL INN
Camden, Maine, 280

WINDSOR HOUSE
Newburyport, Massachusetts, 162

WINE COUNTRY INN
St. Helena, California, 324

WOODBOUND INN
Jaffrey, New Hampshire, 212

WOOLVERTON INN
Stockton, New Jersey, 66

YANKEE CLIPPER
Rockport, Massachusetts, 164

WHAT THE REVIEWERS SAY ABOUT COUNTRY INNS AND BACK ROADS

"The best up-to-date guidebook remains the oldest: 'Country Inns and Back Roads' by Norman T. Simpson . . . "—*New York Times*

"Norman T. Simpson, often simply called 'Mr. Country Inn' . . . has probably been to more country inns in the United States, Britain, Ireland, and Europe than any man alive . . . "
—*Christian Science Monitor*

"The recognized authority on today's country inns . . . "
— *Yankee Magazine*

"'Country Inns and Back Roads' . . . the most personal . . . and probably the most fun to read . . . "—*New York Times*

" . . . the bible of country inns . . . "—*Philadelphia Inquirer*

"America turns inn-ward and Norman Simpson is showing the way . . . "—*Christian Science Monitor*